Communication Criticism

Communication

Criticism

Approaches and Genres

—————

KARYN RYBACKI
Northern Michigan University

DONALD RYBACKI
Northern Michigan University

Wadsworth Publishing Company
Belmont, California
A Division of Wadsworth, Inc.

Speech Editor: Peggy Randall
Editorial Assistant: Sharon Yablon
Production Editor: Carol Carreon
Managing Designer: James Chadwick
Print Buyer: Karen Hunt
Text Design: Peter Martin/Design Office
Cover Design: Peter Martin/Design Office
Copy Editor: Yvonne Howell
Compositor: TCSystems, Inc.
Cover Illustration: Dick Cole

Printed in the United States of America   85

1 2 3 4 5 6 7 8 9 10—95 94 93 92 91

Library of Congress Cataloging in Publication Data
Rybacki, Karyn C. (Karyn Charles), 1947–
    Communication criticism: approaches and genres/
Karyn Rybacki, Donald Rybacki.
       p.   cm.
    Includes bibliographical references and index.
    ISBN 0-534-14118-8
    1. Rhetorical criticism. I. Rybacki, Donald J. (Donald
Jay), 1945–   . II. Title.
    PN4061.R87   1991   90-38551
    808–dc20   CIP

Acknowledgments appear on page 366

Brief Contents

CHAPTER 1   The Purposes of Criticism   1

CHAPTER 2   The Process of Criticism   15

CHAPTER 3   The Traditional Approach   38

CHAPTER 4   The Dramatistic Approach   67

CHAPTER 5   The Fantasy Theme Approach   85

CHAPTER 6   The Narrative Approach   106

CHAPTER 7   The Cultural Approaches   130

CHAPTER 8   The Rhetoric of Public Speaking   159

CHAPTER 9   The Rhetoric of Film   205

CHAPTER 10   The Rhetoric of Television   236

CHAPTER 11   The Rhetoric of Song   275

CHAPTER 12   The Rhetoric of Humor   308

BOXES

Six Common Patterns of Organization 18

Devices of Adornment 21

The Five Canons of Classical Rhetoric 40

The Classical Canons in Contemporary Usage 41

Questions to Ask About the Rhetor's Background 42

Questions to Ask About Situational Constraints on the Rhetor 43

Questions to Ask About Situational Constraints of the Occasion 46

Questions to Ask About the Rhetor's Purpose 51

Questions to Ask About the Rhetor's Use of Invention 51

Common Types of Evidence 58

Common Patterns of Reasoning 59

A Pentadic Analysis of the Symbol *War* 77

Questions to Use in Analyzing Fantasy Themes 91

Questions to Use in Analyzing Fantasy Types 93

Questions to Use in Analyzing Rhetorical Visions 98

Premises About Human Behavior Underlying the Narrative Approach 109

Questions Used to Test Narrative Rationality 119

Common American Value Patterns 135

Questions to Use in Social Values Analysis of Rhetorical Acts 138

Questions to Use in Feminist Analysis of Rhetorical Acts 144

Questions to Use in Marxist Analysis of Rhetorical Acts 147

Rhetorical Tactics of Social Movements 153

Questions to Use in Social-Movement Analysis of Rhetorical Acts 155

Basic Film Concepts 216

The Persuasive Functions of Songs 277

Contents

Preface   xiii

CHAPTER 1

The Purposes of Criticism   1

The Nature of Rhetoric   1
Rhetorical Communication and   2
   Criticism
   Characteristics of Rhetorical Acts   2
   Doing Rhetorical Criticism   8
The Critical Impulse   8
Criticism as a Rhetorical Act   12
Suggested Readings   13

CHAPTER 2

The Process of Criticism   15

The Critical Process Model   16
The Obligation to Describe the   16
   Rhetorical Act
   Purpose   16
   Structure   17
   Argument and Idea Development   19
   Use of Symbols   20
   Concept of Audience   22
The Responsibility to Characterize the   23
   Rhetorical Situation
   The Exigence   24

The Rhetorical Audience   25
The Constraints on the Rhetor   27
Evaluating the Rhetorical Act   30
Judging Ethics   32
Judging Results   32
Judging Truth   33
Judging Aesthetics   34
Suggested Readings   36

CHAPTER 3

The Traditional Approach   38

The Rhetor   40
The Audience   45
Knowledge   48
Group Identification   48
Receptivity   49
The Message   50
Invention   50
Organization   60
Style   61
Delivery   62
The Traditional Approach and Critical   62
Evaluation
The Results Standard   62
The Truth Standard   63
The Ethical Standard   63
The Aesthetic Standard   63
Uses and Limitations   64
Summary   64
Suggested Readings   65

CHAPTER 4

The Dramatistic Approach   67

Rhetoric as Symbolic Action   68
The Function of Rhetoric   69
Motive   69
Society Is Dramatistic   70
Hierarchy   71
Acceptance and Rejection   71
Guilt, Purification, and Redemption   72
Identification   74
Rhetorical Strategies   75
The Pentad   76
Ratios   77
The Dramatistic Approach and Critical   79
Evaluation

The Ethical Standard 79
The Truth Standard 80
The Aesthetic Standard 81
The Results Standard 81
Uses and Limitations 81
Summary 82
Suggested Readings 82

CHAPTER 5

The Fantasy Theme Approach 85

The Nature of Fantasy 86
Fantasy and the Creation of Reality 87
Going Public with the Fantasy 88
The Technique of Fantasy Theme 90
  Analysis
  Fantasy Themes 90
  Fantasy Type 92
  Rhetorical Vision 96
Fantasy Theme Analysis and Critical 98
  Evaluation
  The Truth Standard 99
  The Results Standard 100
  The Aesthetic Standard 101
  The Ethical Standard 101
  Uses and Limitations 102
Comparative Concepts of Dramatism 102
Summary 103
Suggested Readings 104

CHAPTER 6

The Narrative Approach 106

Narrative as a Critical Approach 108
Narrative Structure 110
  Narrative Discourse: The Telling 111
  Narrative Story: The Tale 113
Narrative Rationality 118
The Narrative Approach and Critical 121
  Evaluation
  The Truth Standard 121
  The Aesthetic Standard 122
  The Results Standard 123
  The Ethical Standard 123
  Uses and Limitations 124
Dramatism, Fantasy Theme, and 126
  Narrative
Summary 127
Suggested Readings 128

CHAPTER 7

The Cultural Approaches 130

Social-Values Model	134
The Social-Values Model and Critical Evaluation	138
Jungian Psychological Model	139
The Jungian Model and Critical Evaluation	141
Ideological Models	141
Feminism	142
The Feminist Ideological Model and Critical Evaluation	145
Marxism	145
The Marxist Ideological Model and Critical Evaluation	148
Ideological Models and Critical Evaluation	148
Social-Movement Model	149
The Nature of Social Movements	150
Functions of Rhetorical Activity	152
Use of Rhetorical Tactics	153
The Social-Movement Model and Critical Evaluation	155
Summary	156
Suggested Readings	157

CHAPTER 8

The Rhetoric of Public Speaking 159

Public Persona Speeches	164
Apologia	165
Enterprise Speaking	168
Point-in-Time Speeches	173
Commemorative Speaking	174
Eulogy	175
Political Campaign Speaking	178
Initiation Speaking	182
Social Forces Speeches	185
Justificatory Speaking	185
Legislative Speaking	187
Dissent	192
Public Theology	196
Doing Rhetorical Criticism of Speeches	198
Suggested Readings	201

CHAPTER 9

The Rhetoric of Film 205

Message-Movie Criticism	211
Auteur Criticism	217

Genre Criticism   221
  The Western   221
  Crime Dramas   222
  The Comedy   224
  Science Fiction and Horror Films   225
  War   226
  Antiwar   231
Doing Rhetorical Criticism of Film   231
Suggested Readings   233

CHAPTER 10

The Rhetoric of Television   236

Television and Other Genres of   237
  Communication
Television's Technical Properties   244
  Lighting   244
  Camera Work   244
  Editing   245
News, Sports, and Documentary   246
  Programming
  News Coverage   247
  Sports Coverage   250
  Documentary   252
Fictional Entertainment   255
  Rhetorical Format   255
  Rhetorical Vision   261
Narrow-Casting   263
  Music Television (MTV)   264
Doing Rhetorical Criticism of   267
  Television
Suggested Readings   271

CHAPTER 11

The Rhetoric of Song   275

Historical American Message Music   278
Folk-Protest Music   290
Antiwar Songs   296
Rock and Roll   300
Doing Rhetorical Criticism of Music   302
Suggested Readings   305

CHAPTER 12

The Rhetoric of Humor   308

The Structure of Humor   311
Comic Devices   314

Wordplay   314
Invective   315
Irony   316
Parody   317
Satire   319
Audience Use of Humor   321
Superiority   321
Incongruity   323
Relief   323
Forms of Humorous Discourse   326
Stand-up Comedy   326
Cartooning   331
Electronic and Print Humor   341
Public Sloganeering   344
Doing Rhetorical Criticism of Humor   346
Suggested Readings   348

References   351

Acknowledgments   366

Name Index   368

Subject Index   372

Preface

Because we view every act of communication as having rhetorical potential, our purpose in writing *Communication Criticism* is to introduce our readers to the practice of rhetorical criticism and also to share with them our fascination with the variety of rhetorical acts and events in our nation's history.

Communication Criticism is designed to give the beginning communication critic the necessary skills and theories to become a fully functioning critic. To this end, we surveyed the most frequently employed methods of rhetorical criticism and have presented each of them as a separate approach to doing criticism. To make our readers sensitive to the variety of forms that persuasive messages take and to stimulate critical thought about the different genres of rhetorical activity, we surveyed the history of communication in America to determine what generic forms rhetorical acts seemed to have most frequently taken.

Organization

The first two chapters introduce the reader to the nature of rhetorical activity and the process of doing criticism. Chapter 1 defines rhetorical criticism, explains the common characteristics of rhetorical acts, and answers the question: Why do criticism? The process model for doing criticism in Chapter 2 represents the approach we have found to be most successful in helping beginning critics resolve the anxiety of: What do I do first? We have cast the process of doing criticism into three parts: describing the rhetorical act, considering the situation in which the act occurred, and choosing a critical approach to making an evaluation of the rhetorical act. This process provides information about content, context, and judgmental criteria that enables the beginning critic to do an indepth analysis and to make an effective evaluation.

Five Critical Approaches

Theories of rhetoric and approaches to doing rhetorical criticism have expanded widely in the past two decades. After surveying works of criticism published in communication journals, presented at conventions, and collected in anthologies, we determined that five critical approaches were most frequently used and should be made available for beginning critics: traditional concepts from public speaking, dramatism, fantasy theme analysis, narrative theory, and culturally oriented approaches.

Systematic Method for Beginning Critics

Our purpose in writing about the theoretical approaches to criticism has not been to generate new theory but to pull together existing concepts, describe the philosophy of communication behind each of them, and help the beginning critic in the use of each approach. A guiding principle in creating this book has been to put the approaches to rhetorical criticism into the kind of language and orderly system that the first-time critic can master and use. Each chapter that deals with a theoretical approach opens with an example of a rhetorical act and critical questions about it taken from a published work of rhetorical criticism. Each theoretical chapter also uses one running example to demonstrate how the approach is used to do criticism. Our presentation of each theoretical approach also offers a series of critical questions that can be used in doing criticism by that approach. Rather than including an anthology-style series of reprints of articles, each chapter on an approach concludes with a list of suggested readings that offer models of criticism using that approach and resources on the specific theory. These models of criticism were chosen to provide examples of using the approach that should be clear to the beginning critic.

Chapter 3 presents the traditional approach to doing criticism, drawn from theories of public speaking. Although it opens with a review of the neo-Aristotelian concepts of criticism, we elected to take a more contemporary approach to organizing material and have cast this approach in terms of analyzing a rhetorical act relative to the rhetor-message-audience relationship. We also chose to highlight concepts of argument under the heading of traditional criticism, developing detailed contemporary argumentative theory on reasoning, proof, and structure from the perspective of Stephen Toulmin. Also included in the discussion of argument are the concepts of enthymeme and metaphor as argument.

Chapter 4 presents Kenneth Burke's concept of dramatism. Our treatment of this approach focuses on Burke's view of society as a dramatistic process. The beginning critic is introduced to Burke's ideas on the nature of action, the view that rhetoric should be considered as seeking identification, and the view that human society is a dramatistic process. The critical techniques of this approach include using the concept of rhetorical strategies to achieve identification and use of the pentad as an analytical device.

Chapter 5 presents Ernest Bormann's fantasy theme analysis, an alternative view of dramatic critical concepts. To make this approach more accessible to the beginning critic, we have clarified the distinctions between fantasy theme and fantasy type and have explained the larger concept of a rhetorical vision. In particular, we have created a series of questions to use in distinguishing various fantasy types and rhetorical visions. The chapter concludes with a comparison of Burke's and Bormann's perspectives of dramatism.

Chapter 6 presents our discussion of narrative criticism. Our treatment of this approach draws on the work of Walter R. Fisher for its philosophical base and adds Seymour Chatman's theory of narrative structure for its analytical base. This treatment has the effect of placing some restrictions on narrative, but we believe they are reasonable ones for the beginning critic, who may need more structure than Fisher's view provides alone. This chapter concludes with a comparison of the approaches of dramatism, fantasy theme, and narrative because they have many similarities. We believe that each of these approaches offers the critic enough different options for doing criticism to warrant treating each in a separate chapter.

Chapter 7 presents a synoptical discussion of several cultural approaches to doing criticism. These approaches represent the newest trends in criticism and are still evolving. Because these various approaches derive from cultural values and ideologies, we begin the chapter with a discussion of how a critical approach or model is created. Included in this chapter are the social values approach, Jungian analysis, Marxist and feminist ideological models, and the social-movement model for doing criticism.

Genres of Communication

Our secondary purpose in writing this book was to open the minds of our readers to the history of American communication and the range of possibilities it affords for doing criticism. We are confirmed media junkies and have come to appreciate that Americans have always turned to a variety of communication forms in seeking information, inspiration, and understanding. We believe that the study of public discourse includes the study of public speaking, films, television, music, and humor. To prime the pump for doing criticism, Chapters 8 through 12 introduce our readers to the rhetorical features of these genres of communication.

The five genre chapters are this book's unique contribution to the study of rhetorical criticism. Our purpose in creating these chapters was to describe the rhetorical features that are unique to each generic type. Although our readers may have some appreciation for what makes a public speech rhetorical, understanding how a film, a television program, a song, or a humorous message is rhetorical is not always obvious. Our own life experiences and our study of communication history have suggested that guiding beginning critics into the possibilities offered by the rhetoric of film, television, song, and humor, along with the public speech is a worthy pursuit.

In each of these genre chapters, we chose to describe the rhetorical properties or uses of a particular form of communication, to provide a history of the form, and to suggest how to do criticism using the various critical approaches. Each genre chapter ends with suggestions for further reading, which were selected to provide examples of rhetorical criticism of the genre and useful resources for the further study of the history and rhetorical properties of the genre.

Chapter 8 describes the genre of public speaking. This genre has been the most widely investigated area of rhetorical activity. Because our presentation of the traditional approach to doing criticism focuses on the rhetorical properties of a public speech, we chose to survey subgenres of American public speaking. We cast these subgenres in terms of the differences in the rhetorical situations that have confronted speakers and the influence of the Puritan and colonial traditions of public speaking on all subsequent American speaking.

Chapter 9 describes film. Since the beginning of the twentieth century, Americans have turned to movies not only for escapism but also as sources of history, motivation, and role models. Our primary emphasis is on the "Hollywood" film, but we also discuss the documentary as a form of rhetorical activity. The rhetorical features of the genre are described in terms of message-oriented films, auteur theory, and the various subgenres of film, including the Western, crime drama, comedy, horror-science fiction, war, and antiwar movies.

Chapter 10 describes television. Television has become such an all-encompassing feature of contemporary life that its variety, format, and influence on the viewer are central to its ability to function rhetorically. Our focus on the rhetoric of television distinguishes television from film, so we consider what makes television a unique rhetorical genre. The rhetorical properties of television news, sports, and documentaries are considered as well as entertainment programming. We also present an alternative view developed by James Chesebro to the genre approach offered relative to film, which suggests analyzing entertainment programming in terms of its rhetorical vision.

Chapter 11 describes song. Because songs have played an important persuasive role in America, we chose to focus on the rhetorical properties of song lyrics. The ability of a song to rally people and to present their perceptions of society's problems are its important rhetorical features. An overview of the persuasive use of songs in the American Revolution and Civil War is provided, along with a discussion of protest songs.

Chapter 12 describes the rhetoric of humor. How humor can function rhetorically is discussed in terms of the nature of humor and its devices, how an audience uses humor, and the enthymematic structure of jokes. Humorous messages found in stand-up comedy, cartoons, electronic and print media, and public sloganeering are described.

Acknowledgments

Many people have influenced our involvement with rhetorical criticism, our fascination with media, and the production of this book. We especially thank our editors, Kristine Clerkin and Peggy Randall, for being exceptionally patient with us as the pages of the calendar turned past our original target date for completing this project. We would like to thank the members of the Wadsworth production team: Hal Humphrey, Yvonne Howell, Peggy Meehan, and Carol Carreon. We also owe thanks to our reviewers whose advice and encouragement have made significant contributions to the quality of the finished product: E. Neal Claussen, Bradley University; Celeste M. Condit, University of Georgia; Thomas Hollihan, University of Southern California; John Lyne, University of Iowa; Suzanne Osborn, Memphis State University; and Beth Waggenspack, Virginia Polytechnic Institute and State University.

We thank Dr. James F. Klumpp for helping us understand the full potential of Kenneth Burke's dramatism, Dr. Bruce E. Gronbeck for inspiring us to see the possibilities for rhetorical activity in many areas and for suggesting the conceptual system for Chapter 8, and Dr. Orville Hitchcock for teaching us the breadth and depth of American public address.

A special thank you to George Marolla, a former student who inspired us to include a chapter on the rhetoric of song. We thank all of the students who have studied communication criticism and history with us. This book was really their idea. They used and commented on much of the material as it was being developed. It is dedicated to them.

The

1

Purposes

of Criticism

Why did the keynote speaker at a political convention use metaphor to frame the arguments in his speech? How does a ritual sacrifice, firing a public official, address the national problem of racism? Why do some women turn to romance novels by a particular author to discover what leads to "true love"? How does a self-help support group provide a sense of empowerment to parents with problem children? How did newspaper coverage of a professional baseball team reaffirm cultural values about honesty and fairness?

These are some of the questions that have been answered by the rhetorical criticism of communication. Ordinarily, being critical reveals the extent to which we like or dislike something, or whether we agree or disagree with an idea or opinion. We are exposed to many acts of communication daily. Informal communication criticism is a matter of stating what appeals to us and what does not, what messages we accept and reject in these daily encounters. Criticism can also involve the application of formal standards. Formal communication criticism, the subject of this book, is also called *rhetorical criticism,* and our purpose is to help you develop the skills necessary for this form of criticism.

The Nature of Rhetoric

The term *rhetoric* has various meanings in our society. In popular usage, which is influenced by the mass media, the term almost always has negative connotations. When someone is described as using rhetoric, he or she is usually being accused of engaging in empty sloganeering, using bombastic language, or evading an issue. It is not difficult to find examples of communication that critics have labeled "rhetorical" or "mere rhetoric" in the most pejorative sense of the term.

However, *rhetoric* also means the process of making messages and the message produced by that process. Textbooks on rhetorical theory offer criteria and standards indicating what is possible and desirable in communication. In a public-speaking or composition class, you may have been concerned with how best to design a speech and present it to your audience, or how to structure an essay. Your speeches and compositions were graded according to the standards of what constitutes an effective speech or a good composition. Learning the principles of how to do communication, doing it, and being evaluated on the basis of how well you did it are all part of the process of rhetoric.

Another meaning of the term *rhetoric* relates to exploring "the rhetoric of" something. In this sense, the term usually refers to how a particular communication medium or form, such as a film, uses rhetorical properties. Rhetoric used in this way also enables us to refer to communication in a particular field or discipline by terms such as "the rhetoric of economics." This aspect of the word *rhetoric* is often used in explaining a particular type of communication, something we shall do in the last five chapters of this book.

Rhetorical Communication and Criticism

The central theme that runs through all of these aspects of the term *rhetoric* is that certain kinds of communication are rhetorical. *Communication* is the message-making activity that humans engage in to express attitudes and feelings and to seek solutions to problems. *Rhetorical communication* makes a message with verbal and often visual symbols that are deliberately chosen to influence an audience whose members have the ability to change their beliefs or behaviors as a consequence of experiencing the message. Rhetorical communication differs from some other communication because it is a deliberate attempt to influence the choices an audience makes.

Those who create rhetorical communication are called *rhetors,* and the messages they create are *rhetorical acts*. A rhetor makes choices about the verbal and visual symbols that she thinks will most strongly influence her audience to believe or behave in a particular way. Her rhetorical act may be a speech, a song, a cartoon, or some other form. Whatever choices she makes, her rhetorical act will contain the six characteristics found in all rhetorical acts.

Characteristics of Rhetorical Acts

Instrumental

We say that rhetorical acts are primarily instrumental because they are intended to do something. They have a purpose. They are concerned with addressing a society's problems and rely on using persuasion to cope with these problems. Rhetorical acts examine and evaluate what a society is and what it does and then suggest the most acceptable course of action from the rhetor's point of view. Therefore, almost any rhetorical act can be reduced to a proposition regarding the change in belief or behavior that the rhetor seeks from the audience.

Episodes from series television can function instrumentally as rhetorical acts. Alcoholism is a contemporary social problem that affects many people in every age group and socioeconomic category. Rhetors have used many forms of communication to address this problem, its consequences, and ways of dealing with it. The Columbia Broadcasting System's (CBS) popular television series, *Cagney and Lacey,* frequently focused on pressing social problems. In an instrumental use of a medium of entertainment, the program's 1986–87 season ended with a two-part episode on alcoholism.

The theme of alcoholism and its effects on the individual alcoholic, her friends, and family had been an ongoing part of the story line during the 1986–87 season. Christine Cagney's father was portrayed as unable to admit his alcoholism, which led to his death in the final episode. Christine's own drinking habits became more of a problem as she tried to cope with her father's alcoholism. In the final episode, she was able to admit her problem and seek help. *Cagney and Lacey* illustrates the use of communication to achieve a purpose: to warn the audience about the dangers of alcoholism and let them know that support groups, such as Alcoholics Anonymous, can help.

Social

Because its purpose is instrumental, a rhetorical act requires an audience of people who are capable of choosing to make the change in belief or behavior the rhetor seeks. It is this social quality of rhetorical activity that makes it susceptible to influence by cultural norms. Rhetoric is culture bound precisely because it grows out of and must be adapted to the society in which it is produced.

Speeches function socially to elicit a response from an audience. Richard Nixon is one of the most controversial political figures in recent history. The 1952 Republican convention nominated him to be Dwight Eisenhower's running mate as a concession to the conservative elements of the Republican party. Their campaign was run on the themes of peace, prosperity, and public morality.

> On September 17 [1952], morning editions broke a story claiming that Nixon had a "slush fund" for personal expenses. *The New York Post* headlines blared, "Secret Nixon Fund: Secret Rich Men's Trust Fund Kept Nixon in High Style Far Beyond His Salary." The Republicans cautiously awaited further developments. . . . On September 20 Eisenhower told reporters "off the record" that although he thought Nixon was honest, the vice presidential candidate would have to prove himself. (CULBERT, 1983, p. 206)

Most Republican leaders thought Nixon should remove himself from the ticket, but he chose to accept an offer from the National Broadcasting Company

(NBC) of free radio and television time to make his case to the nation. He told his audience that the funds had been legitimate contributions, used to cover the expense of running for legislative office. His rhetorical act was social. He took his case to the people and asked them to make the decision:

> I am submitting to the Republican National Committee
> tonight, through this television broadcast, the decision
> which it is theirs to make. Let them decide whether my
> position on the ticket will help or hurt. And I'm going to
> ask you to help them decide. Wire and write the
> Republican National Committee whether you think I
> should stay on or whether I should get off. And whatever
> their decision is, I will abide by it. (REIN, 1981, p. 215)

The audience response was overwhelmingly favorable. Millions of letters and telegrams, running 350 to 1 in his favor, kept Nixon's name on the ticket.

Verbal

Language is the verbal symbol system used to share experiences and promote mutual understanding. Symbols enable people to create meaning based on perceptions of their environment and to share perceptions with others who have a similar symbol system. The emotional properties of the words chosen reveal the rhetor's feelings. Even visual and aural symbols are discussed and interpreted by using language. It is impossible to discuss the meaning of a color or sound in precise ways without turning to language. Language is also the characteristic of rhetorical activity that gives it grace and artistry through the elements of style.

Rhetorical acts use language in a way that has symbolic value. In May 1961, the National Association of Broadcasters invited the new head of the Federal Communications Commission, Newton Minow, to address their annual convention. His speech, "Television: The Vast Wasteland," has become a lasting metaphor in television criticism. He told the assembled broadcasters:

> I invite you to sit down in front of your television set
> when your station goes on the air and stay there without a
> book, magazine, newspaper, profit-and-loss sheet or rating
> book to distract you—and keep your eyes glued to that
> set until the station signs off. I can assure you that you
> will observe a vast wasteland. You will see a procession of
> game shows, violence, audience participation shows,
> formula comedies about totally unbelievable families,
> blood and thunder, mayhem, violence, sadism, murder,
> Western badmen, Western goodmen, private eyes,
> gangsters, more violence and cartoons. And, endlessly,
> commercials—many screaming, cajoling and offending.
> And most of all, boredom. (MATSON, 1967, p. 253)

Not only did he coin the phrase "vast wasteland," Minow conveyed a sense of that wasteland in his description of the viewing experience.

Structural

Communication that has the expression of feelings as its primary purpose may seem to be nothing more than a random outpouring of symbols. However, rhetorical activity always follows some identifiable pattern of organization that facilitates its instrumental purpose, so we can study the structure and logic of rhetorical acts.

The political cartoon is a good example of both visual and verbal structure in a rhetorical act. Cartoonists are limited by space and (usually) the monochromatic nature of their medium. Part of their structure often involves exaggerating some feature of their subject as a way of focusing the reader's attention on a theme or person.

A cartoon by Jules Feiffer illustrates the visual and verbal elements of structure in a rhetorical act (Figure 1.1). To depict presidents Eisenhower, Kennedy, Johnson, Nixon, and Ford, and presidential adviser Henry Kissinger, Feiffer selected visual elements of hair and hairline, eyes, nose, mouth, and chin, to make each figure distinct and recognizable to the reader. Gerald Ford also wears an empty can on his head, Feiffer's device for symbolizing Ford as an appointed rather than elected president. A further structural element is the position of each figure. The presidents are seated in profile at a desk and gesturing, whereas Kissinger faces and points his finger at the reader.

The verbal content of cartoons must be brief, making the point efficiently yet humorously. The Feiffer cartoon is about who to blame for "losing" the Vietnam War. Each president makes the parallel claim, "not I." The verbal barb that gives the cartoon its humor is the contradiction of Kissinger's claim. It was the public's fault because they did not trust leaders who lead by ducking responsibility. The parallelism of "who is responsible" and the use of contradiction to make a point humorously are the elements of verbal structure in this cartoon.

Artistic

Rhetorical acts are artistic. Rhetorical acts have psychological impact because rhetors use symbols to capture attention, to produce a certain mood, and to stimulate the members of the audience to action. Therefore, the descriptors *poetic* and *aesthetic* are frequently applied to rhetorical acts. We can study the use of symbols in rhetorical acts on the basis of its poetic quality, its ability to be aesthetically pleasing.

Before Americans turned to electronic media for entertainment, lectures were popular and a few speakers who traveled the lecture circuit became nationally known. William Jennings Bryan, a four-time presidential candidate, probably spoke to more Americans face-to-face than anyone else in our history because of his involvement with the traveling lecture programs of the late nineteenth and early twentieth centuries. He used language masterfully.

One of his most famous speeches, the "Cross of Gold," delivered at the Democratic convention of 1896, actually reprised one of his popular lecture themes, that the free coinage of silver could relieve the economic pressure on the nation's farmers. Bryan's style favored simplistic moral and religious principles over more complicated arguments filled with facts and figures.

Figure 1.1

From *Feiffer: Jules Feiffer's America From Eisenhower To Reagan*, edited by Steven Heller. Copyright © 1982 by Jules Feiffer. Reprinted by permission of Alfred A. Knopf, Inc.

> There are two ideas of government. There are those who
> believe that, if you will only legislate to make the
> well-to-do prosperous, their prosperity will leak through
> on those below. The Democratic idea is, however, that if
> you legislate to make the masses prosperous, their
> prosperity will find its way up through every class which
> rests upon them. You come to us and tell us that the great
> cities are in favor of the gold standard; we reply that the
> great cities rest upon our broad and fertile prairies. Burn
> down your cities and leave our farms and your cities will
> spring up again as if by magic; but destroy our farms and
> the grass will grow in the streets of every city in the
> country. . . . Having behind us the producing masses of
> this nation and the world, supported by the commercial
> interests, the laboring interests, and the toilers
> everywhere, we will answer their demand for a gold
> standard by saying to them: You shall not press down
> upon the brow of labor this crown of thorns, you shall
> not crucify mankind upon a cross of gold. (BRANDT AND
> SHAFTER, 1960, pp. 188–189)

The hallmark of great artistry in communication is that it continues to have meaning from one age to the next. Even though some of the details have changed, there are striking similarities between Bryan's characterization of the problems facing the American farmer and those discussed today.

Ethical

Because rhetorical activity has as its purpose the shaping of attitude and action, influencing belief or behavior, it has the potential to be used for purposes ranging from those that promote great good to those that advocate great evil. Karl Wallace claimed that the substance of moral rhetoric is good reasons (Golden, Berquist, and Coleman, 1989), meaning that rhetoric ought to be used to persuade people on the basis of values and morés to do the "right" thing.

Musicians are often accused of having no purpose other than selling records or maintaining their image. Stevie Wonder stands out as a songwriter and recording artist who has always embodied the highest ethical standards in his work. He is popular among people of diverse age groups and all races because the messages contained in his music reach a national audience.

> Wonder's music promotes a dialog among cultures. As it
> transcends stylistic barriers, it breaks down barriers
> between people. . . . Stevie Wonder—the man and his
> music—fosters pluralism, peace, and universal oneness.
> His lyrical corpus encompasses the Platonic spectrum of
> love, and his music is cross cultural in its appeal. Wonder
> is a good man singing well. (WEISMAN, 1985, p. 149)

Our preceding six examples suggest that rhetorical acts can take a variety of forms including speeches, essays, television programs, news stories, and works of literature, drama, music, and art. In Chapters 8 through 12, we explore in detail five genres of rhetorical activity: speeches, films, television programs, songs, and humor. Knowing the six characteristics common to all rhetorical acts helps you move beyond reacting to such acts on the basis of what you like or dislike. You can ask and answer questions like the ones at the beginning of this chapter only by analyzing and evaluating rhetorical acts through criticism.

Doing Rhetorical Criticism

Rhetorical criticism is the analysis and evaluation of a rhetorical act. Analyzing a rhetorical act means systematically accounting for who created it, what was created, when it was created, and where it was presented. Analysis also means interpreting the rhetorical act by inquiring into how its verbal and visual symbols functioned. This inquiry is guided by the approach you choose to doing criticism: the frame of reference with which you analyze how a rhetor developed symbols, how they functioned in the message, and how an audience used them. A number of critical approaches exist and each suggests specific questions to ask and answer in analyzing rhetorical acts. In Chapters 3 through 7, we introduce you to five of these approaches to criticism.

The critical approach also guides your evaluation of rhetorical acts. To evaluate a rhetorical act is to make judgments about its consequences. Evaluating a rhetorical act moves the critic from asking how its symbols functioned as rhetoric to asking how well they functioned and why. Rhetorical acts are commonly evaluated on the basis of their success or failure in gaining results, conveying probable truth, representing ethical behavior, and being aesthetically pleasing. The approach selected for doing criticism affects the focus of evaluation because each approach emphasizes making a judgment in a different way.

This is a general explanation of what doing rhetorical criticism involves. In Chapter 2, we set up a model for the process of doing rhetorical criticism that explains how you begin analysis of rhetorical acts and what is involved in choosing an approach for doing criticism; we also discuss four standards for judging rhetorical acts.

The Critical Impulse

Doing rhetorical criticism is a complex undertaking, and you might wonder why anyone bothers. People engage in criticism so that they can better understand and appreciate rhetorical activity. The critic's desire for greater understanding and appreciation emerges from a fascination with human communication, born of the impulse to react to it and the curiosity to know more about how it works. There are several reasons why you might undertake criticism.

The Issue or Subject Matter

You are fascinated by the subject of the rhetorical act. If you are interested in the environment and feel strongly about preserving it, you may be drawn to those rhetors who address environmental issues. Your interest might stem from a desire to simply know more about the subject, what has been said about it, and by whom. Alternatively, your interest might stem from strongly held beliefs about acid rain, oil spills, or the destruction of the rain forests.

Criticism done as a result of a fascination with issues and subject matter represents a quest for meaning. You can attain greater understanding through criticism because formal rhetorical criticism aids the search for meaning. As individuals and as a culture, we attend to the communication of others to understand what they are urging us to accept or reject. We look for political meaning in the speeches of presidents, members of congress and political candidates. We look for religious meaning in the sermons, writings, and the television programs of various clergy and religious leaders. Formal criticism helps us understand our own reactions and those of others, on an intellectual basis as well as an emotional one.

Part of this search for meaning includes increasing our understanding of persuasion and how it operates in a society. As a social force, persuasion seems to have ominous power (Campbell, 1972). Recent rhetorical activities of groups have made a difference in the way our society perceives reality and enacts policy. Antinuclear groups and environmentalists have successfully waged persuasive campaigns to halt construction of nuclear power plants. Our concept of male and female roles has been influenced by groups such as the National Organization for Women. "Watchdog" groups, such as Action for Children's Television, have made us more aware of programming aimed at the child.

Rhetorical acts are like time capsules. Much can be discovered about a society or cultural era by studying its communication artifacts. Rhetorical acts past and present can reveal who the power brokers were and are, because a significant amount of rhetorical activity is devoted to gaining control of the issues (Andrews, 1983). By studying rhetorical activity, we learn what issues were significant to a society, who was important enough to have discussed and debated them, and what forces shaped the society. By discovering who controlled the issues, we learn who had the ability to affect social change and perceived reality. We can also ascertain what the society perceived to be "truth."

Fascination with an issue or subject may result from your strongly held personal views. Criticism can be undertaken as a way of becoming involved in social argument. Your criticism can interpret and evaluate a rhetorical act on the basis that it includes or excludes a social, moral, or political view and that, by doing so, it has a significant impact on society. You can take a stand supporting or rejecting the viewpoint of the rhetor as you judge the rhetorical act. When you do criticism for this reason, you are working for social change by sharing your understanding as a critic with others so that they will either appreciate the rhetorical act as you do or see its invalidity or the danger it poses as you do (Foss, 1989; Klumpp and Hollihan, 1989).

The Phenomenological Properties

You are fascinated by phenomena found in the rhetorical act. This impulse to do criticism does not initially stem from the issue or subject matter discussed in the rhetorical act. Instead you are drawn to a rhetorical act because it is interesting for reasons unrelated to its fundamental issues. Criticism is undertaken to explain and interpret the different phenomenological properties of rhetorical acts. Phenomenological properties include the six characteristics of rhetorical acts described previously; the rhetor, the audience, and the historical setting. Phenomenological criticism begins with an encounter of the rhetorical act. You may become interested in the music of the Beatles because something about it attracts you, perhaps nostalgia for an experience in your past, a fascination with the Beatles' part in the sixties counterculture, or the significance of their influence on rock and roll. You may be curious about the Beatles' *White Album* because of its effect on mass-murderer Charles Manson. Whatever the reason for your impulse to do criticism of the Beatles' music, it leads you to describe and interpret the phenomena of their music.

Phenomenological studies lead to examination of different forms and genres of communication to discover their unique rhetorical properties. Although the extent of rhetorical theory is substantial, it fails to account for all historical trends in rhetorical activity. For most of the history of the development of rhetorical theory and criticism, popular song lyrics were not regarded as rhetorical acts worthy of study. Today, music is recognized as playing an important persuasive role. Songs that were popular during the American Revolution reveal much about the colonial rebellion against the mother country. Rhetorical theory does not suggest a set of standards for what makes a "good" protest song, but works of criticism that examine the phenomena of protest music enable critics to devise such standards.

Verbal and visual symbols are important phenomena in rhetorical activity. What attracts you to a rhetorical act may be its use of language or the creation of a powerful nonverbal symbol. Some words are termed "fighting words," others are "conciliatory language." Visual symbols, particularly those such as a flag that already have potency, are phenomena capable of exerting great force. The desire to probe the creation of these symbols and their effect is a goal of phenomenological criticism.

A rhetorical act reaches an audience through a communication medium. You may have been impelled to do criticism because you are interested in the properties of a particular medium. Studying a rhetorical act includes studying the medium of its transmission and its properties. Rhetorical criticism can provide information about the communication technology or the favored media of a given period. Oral communication—public oratory and theatre—was the dominant communication form in ancient Greece. Greek speeches and plays tell us much about the people's style of communication and use of language, and about the kinds of persuasive appeals that were popular. Today, the electronic media play a major role in determining what communication artifacts become part of our common experience. Although we share an oral tradition with the Greeks, its style, language, and forms of appeal are mediated by our technology.

The Approach

You are fascinated by a particular approach to doing criticism. Each approach to doing rhetorical criticism grows out of a pragmatic or philosophical view of communication. As you learn how each approach can be used to ask and answer questions, you may find yourself drawn to one particular approach. It is not unusual for a critic to use the same approach to study many different kinds of rhetorical acts. This fascination with an approach leads to testing its limits.

Rhetorical theory has developed over centuries as writers examined the communication problems and practices of their times. Many theories grew out of practice as teachers put their methods for training students in oratory and composition into "treatise" form. Rhetorical theory ranges from these pragmatic efforts to highly speculative works that probe how the mind acquires and uses information in the process of making decisions. These theories of rhetoric provide the basis for critical approaches. Criticism plays an important role in the evolution of rhetorical theory. The search for appropriate criteria to use in judging rhetorical acts may involve consideration of several theories. On a personal level, this increases your knowledge of rhetorical theory.

Rhetorical criticism explores the limits of present knowledge and leads to the creation of new theories. Although the traditional approach to rhetorical criticism is derived from centuries-old classical and European theories of rhetoric, many useful approaches for studying rhetorical acts are relatively new. Many of these new ideas are still evolving, and their utility must still be tested. Each application of a critical method gives us more information about its usefulness.

A theory describes the ideal in communication, but it has a built-in time lag because it often follows, or responds to, practice. Criticism aids in discovering what constitutes effective practice. It also reveals what were once perceived to be standards of effective practice. At one time it was customary for speakers to use ornate language, extensive biblical references, and extravagant introductions and conclusions. Today, those practices seem phony, and the speaker might be criticized for using "rhetoric" in the pejorative sense of the term.

The fascination with an approach that leads critics to continue testing it helps us understand and appreciate temporal and cultural differences in communication practice. Keeping track of the changes in standards of excellence is important to rhetor and critic alike. The rhetor needs to know what is considered effective, appropriate, and ethical communication in society. Criticism that reflects these standards helps discover what is prized in communication practice. Standards of excellence embrace many elements of rhetorical activity, ranging from the kinds of evidence a rhetor uses to the length of time a rhetor speaks.

Human Behavior

You are fascinated by what studying rhetorical activity can tell you about the nature of being human. Rhetorical activity is part of human behavior, and studying it tells us a great deal about ourselves, our society, and what we value. Criticism is concerned with how rhetors have adapted language to solve practical problems (Thonssen, Baird, and Braden, 1970). Criticism is always an attempt to determine whether or not a rhetor has accomplished his purpose. By accumulating information about rhetorical purposes, and about successes and failures in attaining them, we understand more about human behavior in a variety of circumstances.

Fascination with rhetorical activity as human behavior leads to a discovery of the different kinds of messages rhetors create and how all the characteristics of a rhetorical act are present in that message. As a critic, you have the ability to call attention to certain rhetorical acts. Because humans are communicative beings, the number of rhetorical acts produced each day is staggering. Selecting a speech, essay, or film for criticism implicitly labels it as worthy of scrutiny because it possesses something of interest to a critic. This gives the act additional meaning, the stature of something of social importance. Part of your task as a critic is to choose objects for criticism that will actually increase understanding of contemporary or historical society. When you are drawn to a rhetorical act, consider how your criticism can increase understanding of the meaning of being human.

Being drawn to a rhetorical act because of an interest in human behavior can lead you to look at it from the audience's perspective, how it provided them with knowledge. A part of human experience involves interpreting reality based on the communication of others, and an audience may find a different reality from that which the rhetor intended. Doing criticism is a way of understanding the reason for this difference. You will learn more about the process of human communication and how our sense of reality is influenced by rhetorical activity.

Rhetorical criticism causes you to look at problems and their proposed solutions, issues and answers, and the kinds of appeals that seem to move people. As you study rhetorical acts that have achieved their purpose, you will gain greater appreciation for how the process of persuasion works, how core values are expressed, and how the importance of these values are demonstrated. Criticism enables you to explore the values of society in comparison with what you value and to gain greater appreciation of what it means to be human.

Criticism as a Rhetorical Act

Doing rhetorical criticism is not like solving a mathematical problem: There is no single right answer or correct conclusion. Several critics using the same approach to analyzing and evaluating the same rhetorical act may come to different conclusions about it, and because rhetorical criticism is subjective, all of them could be "right" if they have carefully thought through and argued the reasons for their judgments. The only standard of correctness that exists relative to rhetorical criticism is that the critic makes a sound case for any judgments rendered about the rhetorical act.

The mathematician engaged in problem solving operates from objectivity, the rhetorical critic proceeds on the basis of his or her *stance*. Political preferences, media-consumption habits, and other biases do not influence a mathematician's ability to determine the correct answer to a problem. Rhetorical criticism is different. First, the four impulses for undertaking rhetorical criticism are primarily subjective rather than objective; that is, the rhetorical critic's reason for approaching a problem is deeply personal. Second, the possibility of rendering many right though different, critical judgments about the same rhetorical act reflects the subjectivity of the outcome of the process of criticism. This can be perplexing because we are normally encouraged to be objective.

As our definition of rhetorical criticism suggests, making judgments about a rhetorical act is more than stating what you like or dislike about it. Criticism is argumentation and thus is a rhetorical act in its own right. You make a sound case for your opinions about a rhetorical act by stating your judgments and explaining your reasons for making them. A thorough analysis of the rhetorical act, using a critical approach as a method of inquiry to guide your analysis and help you form judgments, helps you make a sound case.

You can overcome the problems posed by subjectivity by using it as part of your stance in criticism. First, admitting the fascination that impelled you to do criticism and incorporating it into your criticism acknowledges your stance. If you were drawn to study the Beatles' music because you cannot understand why your parents think it is so wonderful, your stance includes the desire to explain the appeal of Beatles' music to "baby boomers."

Second, acknowledge that you need to marshal resources beyond those you presently possess. You can never know quite as much as you would like to know about a rhetorical act, its rhetor, and context. Because you have the responsibility for building a sound case for your judgments, you must discover as much as you can about the rhetorical act. By being able to support your judgments on the basis of your analysis and research you render them rational if not objective.

Because criticism is the unique product of your experiences, beliefs, and values applied to the rhetorical act of another, it provides a means to develop your skills and increase your knowledge. Criticism of contemporary rhetoric makes you better informed about what is going on in the world and increases your understanding of how communication produces change. You increase your understanding of how symbols are used and manipulated to provoke emotional and intellectual responses. Practicing rhetorical criticism gives you a greater understanding of rhetorical theory and makes you more aware of the common threads that exist across diverse views on rhetorical theory. The purpose of this book is to introduce you, as a beginning critic, to the formal process of criticism and some of the more common genres of rhetorical activity.

Suggested Readings

GOLDEN, J.L., BERQUIST, G.F., AND COLEMAN, W.E. (1989). *The rhetoric of western thought* (4th ed.). Dubuque, IA: Kendall/Hunt.
>   The authors survey rhetorical theory from classical Greek and Roman works to the present. The introduction provides a general understanding of what rhetoric is, with subsequent chapters devoted to specific theories. This is a particularly useful resource for the new critic because it summarizes major trends in rhetorical theory.

HAUSER, G.A. (1986). *Introduction to rhetorical theory*. New York: Harper & Row.
This book offers a systematic guide to principles of rhetorical theory drawn from both ancient and contemporary sources. In contrast to Golden et al., Hauser provides an expository treatment of rhetorical theory in an easy-to-read form. Especially useful are his discussions of rhetorical activity as risky business for the rhetor and his thorough discussion, from a contemporary perspective, of the basics of rhetorical theory: modes of argument, topical analysis and invention, ethos, and emotion. If you have not had a course in rhetorical theory, this book will give you a good understanding of its substance.

MEDHURST, M.J., AND BENSON, T.W. (1989). *Rhetorical dimensions in media: A critical casebook* (revised printing). Dubuque, IA: Kendall/Hunt.
This anthology examines many of the nontraditional genres of rhetorical activity through a series of original articles and materials reprinted from other sources. It contains examples of the rhetorical criticism of television, film, radio, graphic arts, music, magazines, public letters, literature, political action, and architecture. The methods of criticism are as varied as the genres criticized, ranging from fantasy theme analysis of television situation comedy to semiotic comparison of the mythic narratives of Disneyland and Marriott's Great America. An extensive bibliography on theory, method, and applications to various genres of rhetorical activity is also included.

2

The

Process

of Criticism

Because we view the world through the perceptual filters imposed by our experiences and apply our own interpretations to rhetorical acts, criticism is an individual undertaking. Any rhetorical act can have several equally valid but different criticisms performed on it. Critics do not necessarily agree on the merits or quality of an act of communication. You may have read movie reviews or watched television review programs in which one critic claimed a film was very good whereas his colleague found the same film a disappointment. Each had his own criteria for a "good" film. Like these film critics, you will make your own interpretation and apply your own standards for judging rhetorical activity.

Another feature that makes criticism challenging, and at the same time frustrating, is that you cannot know everything you might like to know about a rhetorical act. You may not be able to discover the rhetor's motives or the audience's receptiveness to the rhetorical act. The critic must make judgments about people and their social environment that are based on available information (Arnold, 1974). The limitation imposed by working with available information means that criticism takes the form of an argument in which you offer hypotheses about a rhetorical act and back them with available information. The process of rhetorical criticism described in this chapter is meant to provide a system for both thinking about criticism and completing a finished product of criticism.

The Critical Process Model

Our three-step model will guide you on your way to preparing a rhetorical criticism. Whether you want to analyze a speech, a film, a work of fiction or nonfiction, or any other rhetorical act, this model can help organize your thinking. Step 1 focuses on the *rhetorical act* and the critic's obligation to describe its significant or unique qualities. Step 2 shifts attention to the *rhetorical situation* and the critic's responsibility to characterize the elements of the context or setting that influenced the form of the rhetorical act. This step involves interpretation and analysis, answering questions such as whether or not the rhetorical act was appropriate for its setting and what choices the rhetor was required to make in creating the act. Step 3 involves *rhetorical evaluation* and the critic's task to render a judgment about the quality and consequences of the rhetorical act.

The Obligation to Describe the Rhetorical Act

Getting started is always the hardest part of any endeavor, so to ease your entry into the critical process, we shall follow conventional wisdom and suggest that you begin with the rhetorical act itself. Your choice of a rhetorical act for criticism may be based on your interest in its historical period, the rhetor who produced it, or the form of the act itself. However, communication is a process. Most models of communication suggest that all facets of the rhetor-message-audience relationship are interrelated and interdependent, mutually influencing each other in any rhetorical act. As a result, description of the rhetorical act cannot ignore the effects of the interplay of the context, the audience, and the individuality of the rhetor on the act itself.

Beginning with a description of the rhetorical act is useful because it can indicate how the rhetor perceived the audience and help you identify an appropriate critical approach, the methodology you will use in judging the act. Regardless of the circumstances that led to the production of the act and the methodology you eventually choose, you first need to describe the intrinsic elements of the rhetorical act: purpose, structure, arguments and ideas, use of symbols, and concept of audience.

Purpose

The purpose of a rhetorical act is found in its thesis statement, central idea, or argumentative conclusion. The rhetor's purpose in communicating was to achieve a response. Describing the rhetor's purpose reveals her intention: to solve a problem, to gain support, to arouse emotion, to generate interest or heighten awareness, to call to action, or to respond to a social problem. In many rhetorical acts, the purpose is spelled out in an introduction. Notice the purpose statement in this speech by Anne Rawley Saldich:

> Last December when TV's coverage of the mideast crisis
> was at full flood an Iranian was quoted as saying: "We've
> got America right by the networks." What he meant was
> that our hearts and minds soon would follow. That idea
> just about sums up two centuries of journalism's growth
> in the United States: our once-penney sheets are now
> powerful institutions. Perhaps because it is accepted
> political practice in his country, the Iranian seems to have
> understood better than we that television does govern.
> That is the pivot around which I will develop three
> problems in electronic democracy: how TV governs, why
> the First Amendment should apply differently to television
> than to print, and the need for public accountability. (O.
> PETERSON, 1981, p. 111)

Purpose statements are not always so easily identified. A rhetorical act may have multiple purposes aimed at different audiences. Presidential speeches delivered to a national audience via television may include messages for different political interest groups. Look for indications of multiple-purpose statements intended for different audience segments.

The purpose may not be explicitly stated, and you may have to verbalize it. Some rhetorical forms such as films and song lyrics have implicit purpose statements. *Country,* a 1985 film, had the rhetorical purpose of heightening viewer awareness of the plight of the nation's farmers. The viewer come to realize this purpose as the story unfolds, not because it is given in a purpose statement. If you outline the rhetorical act, you will be able to identify not only its purpose but also its structure and the development of arguments.

Structure

The structure of a rhetorical act is the rhetor's pattern of organization, his arguments and ideas. Structure is a matter of choice on the part of the rhetor, who decided what arrangement of main ideas, supporting materials, transitions, internal summaries, images, and appeals was most likely to accomplish his purpose. Describing structure reveals how the rhetor viewed the topic and how he wanted the audience to experience it. Making an outline of the rhetorical act helps you describe how the rhetor connected ideas and incorporated persuasive devices into a unified whole. Several common patterns of organization are used for structuring rhetorical acts: chronological, narrative, topical, problem-solution, cause-effect (effect-cause), and climax (See box on next page).

The structure of a rhetorical act may not always be apparent. Some messages use a combination of organizational patterns, especially if the message is segmented to address multiple audiences or to treat multiple subjects. Within a message that is *topical* in its overall structure, individual topics may be structured in different ways. In addition, some rhetors are more organized than others, and some forms of rhetorical activity are less obvious in their pattern of organization.

The *chronological* pattern of organization is used for presenting historical development or events that have a natural sequence. Rhetorical acts have a partial chronology when a rhetor provides background information as a form of support for his ideas.

The *narrative* is similar to chronology in that its story follows a fixed sequence of events. The narrative pattern of organization is used when the rhetor incorporates a story to arouse interest. If you choose to criticize a fictive work, such as a film, television series, or dramatic work, the narrative is usually the structure you identify as your outline describes the plot line or story elements.

The *topical* pattern of organization is used by a rhetor who discusses ideas that are related to each other only by her perspective on the subject matter. Three elements appeared in the purpose statement of the Saldich speech: how television acts as a governing agent, why the First Amendment should be applied differently to television than to print, and the need for public accountability. These are different topics that are related by the rhetor's perspective on the unique properties of television as a news source.

The *problem-solution* pattern of organization is easily recognized because it generally identifies the nature of a problem, offers a solution, and discusses the feasibility of the solution. Because rhetorical activity seeks change, this is a very common pattern of organization. A variation on this pattern is used when the rhetor's purpose is simply to heighten audience awareness of the existence of a problem for which the solution is implied or unstated.

In a *cause-effect* or *effect-cause* pattern of organization, a relationship between actions and outcomes or outcomes and the actions that preceded them is expressed. Using this organization, a rhetor identifies the temporal connection between behavior and its consequences.

The *climax* pattern of organization is used when the rhetor wants to build to some point. It is done by structuring the elements in a rhetorical act from simple to complex, from weakest to strongest argument, or from the known to the unknown.

To describe a rhetorical act effectively, it is very important to outline what you see happening in it. The length and detail of this outline will vary with the complexity of the rhetorical act being studied. For rhetorical acts that primarily employ visual forms of communication, such as films or political cartoons, you must be inventive in constructing an outline.

Argument and Idea Development

Rhetorical acts communicate reality from the rhetor's point of view, responding to issues and perceptions of the situation in which she has found herself. She is asking the audience to share this view of reality. To achieve her purpose, the rhetor chooses strategies that she believes will best enable the audience to accept her point of view. Because the rhetor's goal is change, she has to reason with the audience to achieve it. Strategies of reasoning include the order in which arguments are presented, the amount of evidence provided in each unit of argument, and the kind of reasoning used to link conclusions and evidence.

Her argument could take the form of a joke, a cartoon, a film, a speech, or some other form of communication, but the development of her purpose into a rhetorical act can be described in terms of an argument. In describing the rhetorical act, you must identify each unit of argument used. Each approach to criticism has techniques for analyzing argument that you might use, but in describing the rhetorical act you can identify units of argument using the following concept.

An *argument* includes a claim, the evidence that supports it, and the rational process that links the evidence to the conclusion. *Claims* are conclusions, opinions, and assertions: thinking that the rhetor wanted the audience to accept as true. Claims are proven to accurately portray reality by supplying *evidence* that the audience is likely to accept as credible. The *reasoning process* explains why, given the evidence, the claim should be accepted as probably true.

The evidence used to support a claim's probable truth is an important part of the argument. Many rhetorical acts such as speeches, editorials, and essays rely heavily on carefully documented and reasoned arguments for their persuasive impact. As you outline a rhetorical act, pay special attention to the use of claims and evidence.

Many kinds of materials are used to support claims. Testimony from eye witnesses, the opinions of respected authorities, scientific research, examples, illustrations, statistics, and analogies are all potential forms of support. As you outline the rhetorical act, identify and describe these materials and the claims they support. Also identify the purpose served by each use of evidence according to your understanding of the rhetorical act.

Not all forms of communication lend themselves to the development of argument to the same degree. Primarily visual forms such as commercials, films, and political cartoons offer arguments, but the supporting materials derive mostly from visual impressions or the depiction of ideas or images that the audience "knows." Although on the surface it may be difficult to describe some films as rhetorical, the arguments in films such as *The Day After, Salvador,* and *Country* are very apparent, with proof drawn from dramatizing current events with which the audience is already familiar. What the characters of the film experience becomes a kind of eyewitness testimony that supports the film's premise.

Use of Symbols

A *symbol* reflects a rhetor's verbal or visual interpretation of an idea, object, place, event, or person. Symbols stand in place of the rhetor's own experience or knowledge of people, places, objects, and concepts. A rhetor's creation or choice of a symbol is based on his perception of the world, and his choice of symbol may differ from that which another rhetor might choose to represent a similar experience. The concept of language symbols reflects principles of general semantics: The word is not the thing, and the meanings assigned to a symbol may vary. Understanding the variability of symbols is important to being able to describe how they are used in rhetorical acts.

A rhetor chooses symbols he believes will best communicate his view of reality to the audience so that they will virtually "see things as the rhetor does." *Virtual experience* is a goal in choosing symbols for a rhetorical act so that the rhetor's experience is in some way re-created by the audience (Campbell, 1982). Because a symbol is not the thing but a representation of it, there is no guarantee the audience will interpret it in the same way the rhetor does. In fulfilling your obligation to describe the rhetorical act, determine which symbols serve as a declaration of the rhetor's view of reality.

Verbal symbols (that is, language) not only declare issues and identify cause-effect relationships but also create mood and tone. As you describe the rhetor's creation of arguments, consider how language functions in arguing. The grammar and syntax of the language used helps you isolate the rhetor's purpose and the claims and reasoning used to achieve that purpose.

Language also plays an important part in the rhetor's efforts to create virtual experience for the audience, creating word pictures and conveying the rhetor's feeling about issues and the subject matter. Words have an emotive, connotative dimension. The words a rhetor chose expressed his attitudes, the degree of formality he perceived to be appropriate to the circumstances in which he communicated, and the emotion he wanted the audience to experience.

Language used to create mood and tone contributes to the style of the rhetorical act, and the devices of language are known as *adornment*. Look for devices of adornment (see box on next page) as you describe a rhetorical act.

Adornment, especially the creation of metaphor, was a hallmark of the speaking style of Dr. Martin Luther King, Jr. His speech, "I Have a Dream," is regarded as great literature. Dr. King's argument, simply stated, is that the government has made promises to all citizens but has not fulfilled them for black citizens, and he hopes they will be fulfilled. Expressed in Dr. King's unique style, this argument has far greater emotive impact:

Devices of

Adornment

An *allegory* is a series of metaphors.

An *allusion* refers to shared cultural heritage. The most common forms of allusion reference legends, myths, or literature known to most people.

Alliteration is the repetition of first consonants. A related device, *assonance,* involves repetition of vowel sounds.

Antithesis contrasts opposing ideas. When stated in inverted parallel phrases, "Ask not what your country can do for you, but what you can do for your country," the figure is called a *chiasmus.*

Climax can be an overall pattern of organization or a figure of style. As a stylistic device, climax builds to a point.

Hyperbole is the use of great exaggeration.

Metaphor uses a word or phrase in a way that differs from standard usage.

Metonomy substitutes a name, such as a person's given name, for the official title of something.

An *oxymoron* uses a combination of contradictory terms that is in reality an accurate characterization.

Repetition, also called *epanaphora,* repeats words or phrases.

A *rhetorical question* expects no direct response from the audience, being used instead to focus thought.

Synecdoche substitutes part of something for the whole or the whole for a part.

In a sense we have come to the nation's capital to cash a check. When the architects of our republic wrote the magnificent words of the Constitution and the Declaration of Independence, they were signing a promissory note to which every American was to fall heir. This note was a promise that all men, yes black men as well as white men, would be guaranteed the unalienable rights of life, liberty, and the pursuit of happiness.

It is obvious today that America has defaulted on this promissory note insofar as her citizens of color are concerned. Instead of honoring this sacred obligation, America has given the Negro people a bad check; a check which has come back marked "insufficient funds."

> But we refuse to believe that the bank of justice is
> bankrupt. We refuse to believe that there are insufficient
> funds in the great vaults of opportunity of this nation. So
> we have come to cash this check—a check that will give
> us upon demand the riches of freedom and the security of
> justice. (REID, 1988, pp. 723–724)

Although all words in a rhetorical act may have strong emotive content, it is unnecessary to identify each and every word in your description. Instead, determine the emotions the rhetor wanted to arouse and what devices of adornment he used to arouse them. In some rhetorical acts, the use of technical terms and complex sentences may be an important part of style and language use. You may also want to note the rhetor's style and form of address when it is apparent. Is the style personal or impersonal? Is the form of address direct or indirect?

A rhetor's choice of visual symbols can include everything from the way a speaker is dressed to the creation of an imaginary world in a science fiction film. Visual symbols are commonly found in the use of color, graphics, props, costume, camera techniques, and set design. Visual symbols may be discussed in terms of the devices of adornment. A visual symbol may create an allegory, an oxymoron, or synecdoche. Visual symbols have their own grammar and syntax, which may vary with the medium of communication. We shall discuss some of these visual symbol codes in the chapters devoted to different rhetorical genres. Your description of a rhetorical act should include accounts of the verbal and visual symbols used.

Concept of Audience

A defining characteristic of rhetorical communication is that it is public: It is aimed at an audience. In some rhetorical acts, the rhetor has identified the audience or made reference to them. In a speech, the introduction often acknowledges the listeners' presence in some way. As you describe a rhetorical act, note how the message identifies its audience. What does the rhetor acknowledge about the audience, occasion, and setting? Ceremonial speeches sometimes do more than just commemorate an occasion. A speaker might address the audience present but aim his message at a broader audience, as George Marshall did in using commencement exercises at Harvard on 5 June 1947 to reveal the major tenets of the Marshall Plan to the nation.

As you look for evidence of the rhetor's concept of audience in the text of a rhetorical act, keep two things in mind. First, the actual rhetorical audience exposed to the act may be different from the one the rhetor conceptualized in formulating it. You will concern yourself with this actual audience in step 2 of the critical process model. Second, the rhetor may have conceptualized the audience in as many as four ways: the ideal audience, the empirical audience, the agents-of-change audience, and the created audience (Campbell, 1982).

The *ideal audience* is the one the rhetor would like to address, the one that shares her experience, is responsive to her point of view, and is open to change.

The converted or open-minded audience makes the rhetor's task easier, but it is not always available. The *empirical audience* is the one that is actually likely to be exposed to the rhetorical act and may or may not be made up of individuals who comprise the ideal audience. For example, suppose an editorial writer wants to argue against arms reductions, which are a product of improving U.S.-Soviet relations. Her ideal audience would be comprised of people informed about the history of U.S.-Soviet relations and skeptical about Soviet trustworthiness on the basis of that knowledge. Her empirical audience would be determined by the reader demographics of the publication in which her editorials appear.

The *agents-of-change audience* is composed of those capable not only of changing their own belief or behavior but also of influencing others to change. Agents of change have political, social, or economic power. As a result, they play an important role in public acceptance of the rhetor's point of view. Agents of change would typically be included in the rhetor's ideal audience unless the rhetor's point of view is so different from theirs that they would be unlikely to be persuaded by the rhetorical act. If our hypothetical editorialist's rhetorical purpose is at odds with the views of agents of change in our society, she will have to look to others who may not think of themselves as agents of change.

When people do not perceive themselves as having the power to influence the course of events, they are unlikely to do anything. They will only act if the rhetor can create in them a sense of empowerment through their participation in the rhetorical act. The *created audience* is one that feels this sense of empowerment. Our hypothetical editorialist might attempt to create among her readers the sense that they are the majority and that if they will only raise their voices in protest, the political power brokers will accede to their wishes. The content of the rhetor's act would reveal not only her interpretation of reality but also her concept of these various audiences.

The first step in the critical process is only complete after you have made a thorough description of the rhetorical act. Why is it important to make such a detailed description of the rhetorical act? It provides data useful in shaping your thinking about the quality of the act. You need this information to interpret and analyze the act and ultimately render an informed judgment about it. The information you discover by describing the act will be helpful to you in steps 2 and 3 of the critical process. As various methodological approaches are discussed in this text, we shall provide more detail about the description of some of these elements of the rhetorical act.

The Responsibility to Characterize the Rhetorical Situation

Rhetorical acts do not happen on a whim. They occur for specific reasons, usually in response to some previously or simultaneously occurring event, with a specific group of receivers in mind. The *rhetorical situation*, conceptualized by Lloyd Bitzer (1968), identifies the components of the context of rhetorical activity.

A rhetorical situation is a mix of people, events, objects, relationships, and perceptions that produce the event or *exigence* addressed by a rhetor. Rhetorical action occurs because we believe that we can solve problems, meet crises, or overcome obstacles by reasoning together about them. The rhetorical act is offered as an explanation of how to deal with the exigence.

When a momentous event occurs, such as the terrorist hijacking of a TWA flight in the summer of 1985, people become concerned, fearful, and wonder what can be done. It becomes a situation that demands a fitting response. We expect political leaders, such as the president, to solve the problem and reassure us that our political system is viable and able to protect us. An exigence may also be the product of a series of events; the federal budget deficit is such a problem. Because terrorist acts, economic problems, and other events are societal problems, we expect appropriate ways of dealing with them to be found and explained to us.

Recall the characteristics of rhetorical acts. Rhetorical activity is pragmatic; it functions to produce action that results in change. It uses techniques of communication to change the audience's perception of reality. Rhetorical action is persuasive because it addresses the audience, creating in them the sense that they are the mediators of change. A rhetorical situation exists when a serious and compelling need exists that calls forth a rhetorical act. The rhetor creates a message that offers the audience a way to cope with the exigence directly or indirectly if they feel empowered by it.

In step 1 of the critical process model, you described the rhetorical act. Now, in step 2, you examine the rhetorical situation that called forth the act. Because rhetors attempt to provide an appropriate response to a situation, as a critic you must be able to determine whether or not a rhetorical act was appropriate. The rhetorical situation controls the rhetorical act, making demands on the communicator and creating boundaries within which the act must function to be identified as appropriate. Rhetorical acts are influenced by their historical and social setting, occasion, audience, and the personality of the rhetor. As a critic, you must be able to characterize the rhetorical situation in terms of the exigence, the rhetorical audience, and the constraints on the rhetor.

The Exigence

The exigence is the first element in the rhetorical situation: an urgent problem, obstacle, something that is not as it should be. We label an act *rhetorical* when it addresses those exigences that can be remedied through persuasive communication. The need to deal with terrorist attacks on American citizens and to solve the federal budget deficit have been identified as exigences. You will encounter many other examples of exigences, of an immediate or ongoing nature, in your study of rhetorical activity.

Each rhetorical situation contains one *controlling exigence*. As a critic, discovering the controlling exigence requires you to play the role of historian. It is necessary to learn about the culture and the social climate because rhetoric is a product of both. Social, political, economic, and cultural forces create a climate in which a rhetorical act is set. Whether the rhetorical act you select for criticism is contemporary or took place in the remote past, you must examine what was occurring at the time the act was produced.

Rhetorical acts seldom occur in isolation. There is usually an ongoing dialogue about an issue, so you must examine events that preceded and followed the rhetorical act. The two examples cited, terrorism and the budget deficit, have been the subject of much rhetorical activity. Interpreting and analyzing an individual rhetorical act is a matter of viewing it in the context of this ongoing dialogue. Every rhetorical act competes for the audience's attention and acceptance with the messages of other rhetors, some of whom represent other points of view on the issue. As you investigate the rhetorical situation, be sure to look at competing rhetorical activity because the act you are criticizing may have been a response to it.

Also consider the social pressures or forces that surround the dialogue as part of the circumstances producing the exigence. To interpret and analyze a rhetorical act, you need to know how society viewed the exigence. What persons, events, objects, relationships, or cultural values made the exigence important. Although general concern about acts of terrorism had existed for some time, the hijacking of an airliner with American citizens on board in June 1985 made terrorism an immediate concern.

As a critic you are interested in how the exigence was perceived by the audience of the rhetorical act. This is determined by reconstructing the public consciousness (Andrews, 1983) in terms of the norms and values prevailing at the time. Perceptions of an exigence always have a basis in what society thinks is ethical or right behavior. According to our norms, hijacking an aircraft, taking people hostage, and threatening the safety of those traveling abroad are not ethical forms of political expression. In criticizing rhetorical acts flowing from this exigence, you would need to discover American "reality" during the summer of 1985 relative to beliefs about terrorism and the ability of our government to deal with it.

An exigence is a problem perceived as important because it threatens society, compelling the search for a solution. For an exigence to exist, people must perceive it. Their perceived reality is based on a society's beliefs about what is happening and its norms or values about appropriate and inappropriate behavior. The exigence is the central element in the rhetorical situation because it motivates response. Rhetorical acts responding to an exigence are controlled by the audience and their perception of what is necessary to deal with the exigence.

The Rhetorical Audience

From the small, intimate audience of the public-speaking context to the large audience, mass-mediated by the technology of films and television, rhetorical audiences vary in size and in how their perception of the message is influenced by the medium of its transmission. The mass media have changed the concept of a rhetorical audience. Technology, which makes possible the wide and rapid dissemination of messages, affords the rhetor the opportunity to address multiple audiences simultaneously. The tendency of national news media to select parts of messages, "sound bites," for rebroadcast changes our concept of the message itself. These factors make identifying the audience, and analyzing how a message has been adapted to it, a challenge for the rhetorical critic.

Discovering accurate information about the audience may be the most difficult aspect of criticism. In the absence of precise information, you need to draw inferences about the nature of the audience (Hillbruner, 1966). In most cases these inferences can be derived from a reconstruction of history. For contemporary rhetorical acts, mass media have the potential to make the nation the audience for a rhetorical act. Even in the days before communications technology influenced the composition of the audience, many messages were aimed at a national audience. Those not on hand to hear a speech in person would read its text in a newspaper or periodical. Therefore, a thorough description of the relevant history of a rhetorical act provides information about the audience.

Rhetorical activity is always aimed at an audience, the ultimate change agent, even though it may be neither large nor multiple. In the summer of 1985 a second exigence emerged, less dreadful than terrorism but nevertheless rhetorically interesting. As a marketing strategy, Coca-Cola announced that they were changing the Coke formula, something which had not happened in most people's memory. For many self-styled "old Coke" drinkers, this created an exigence. Their favorite beverage was about to be lost forever. Their rhetorical activity took the form of letters, phone calls, editorials in newspapers and magazines, direct contact with dealers, and the formation of a protest organization, "Old Coke Drinkers of America." The audience for this activity was narrow and specific, the Coca-Cola Company, because only the company had the old formula and the ability to act as change agent.

If you are studying rhetorical activity that is directed toward a less-specific audience than that in the campaign to bring back old Coke, it can be characterized in terms of who is acknowledged to be the change agent. The rhetorical audience includes those who can be influenced by the persuasive message and bring about change. It can be determined in a number of ways. Searching the content of the message for evidence about the audience has already been suggested because the message itself may include references to its intended audience.

Demographic variables, such as sex, age, marital status, education, economic status, cultural heritage, religion, occupation, and political beliefs, have traditionally been used to characterize audiences. Demographics can be used to make inferences about audiences based on knowledge of who watches a television program or attends a film. Such variables may lead to the discovery of information about the attitudes, beliefs, values, and norms held in common by people in a demographic group.

Rhetorical audiences may also be characterized in terms of their disposition toward the purpose of the rhetorical act. Three broad classifications of audience disposition exist: favorable, unfavorable, and uncommitted. Determining the audience's disposition involves making inferences about their social and psychological state. If most audience members are members of a single demographic group, subscribe to the same periodical, or are members of the same profession, this information may yield clues to their social and psychological predisposition toward a message. It is also important to determine their degree of involvement (Campbell, 1972) because a highly committed audience is less likely to remain inactive when encouraged to act as a change agent.

We can safely assume that the management of Coca-Cola was favorably predisposed and strongly committed to making profits. Therefore, when a substantial number of rhetors communicated the message that for them "Coke was no longer it," the company responded by resurrecting the old formula under the "classic Coke" label. Knowing the audience's probable predisposition and degree of commitment is important to making intelligent judgments about the results of rhetorical activity.

Social-psychological characterization of an audience derives from an examination of the attitudes, values, and emotional state of its members. Not all of an individual's attitudes are equally important. You need to determine which attitudes were strongly held and actively engaged relative to the purpose of rhetorical activity (Arnold, 1974). Value conflicts or conflicting standards of ethical behavior can also influence the audience's predisposition for or against a message.

The sources of information used in the message may trigger an emotional response. Some people respond positively to the use of biblical references in a message whose purpose is secular, others automatically reject them and the message that contains them. Other competing exigences may induce an emotional state in the audience that nullifies or magnifies the perceived importance of the exigence addressed by the rhetor. For example, reducing the federal budget deficit by eliminating aid to colleges and universities is not a message that plays well with a campus audience. Identifying the social-psychological characteristics of an audience provides information indicating their possible predispositions.

By definition, a rhetorical audience is subject to influence and is capable of change. Use this principle to characterize the audience by discovering what group is subject to influence and capable of change in the rhetorical situation. Characterizing the nature of the rhetorical audience may be difficult, but it is an important part of the critical process. Understanding the rhetor-message-audience relationship is very important if you are to render an intelligent judgment about the merits of a rhetorical act.

The Constraints on the Rhetor

A *constraint* is something that confines, restricts, forces, or compels. In a rhetorical sense, a constraint influences or shapes the rhetorical act. The elements in the environment of the rhetorical act that can influence it are beliefs, attitudes, culturally important documents, scientific research, acknowledged fact, traditions, images, and interests. The constraints in a rhetorical situation are imposed by the audience, circumstance, and personality characteristics of the rhetor. As you determine what constrained the content of a rhetorical act, you move beyond information gathering to interpreting the rhetorical act in terms of the constraints imposed on it by the rhetorical situation.

The two sets of constraints are those controlled by the rhetor, which she may choose to employ, and those beyond her control to which she must adapt. No universal list of constraints exists. Constraints are uniquely determined by each rhetorical situation. Characterizing the constraints on rhetorical activity assists you in interpreting the content of a rhetorical act. As you examine a rhetorical act, you must decide what constraints were controlled by the rhetor and what constraints were beyond her control.

As you determine what constrains a rhetorical act, first consider the sources of the rhetor's beliefs about society. Why did she express the ideas in the rhetorical act? What inferences can be made about the influence of the rhetor's background on the character of her ideas? Because we all act on the basis of our past experience, a rhetor's personal history is a valuable source of information about the origin of her ideas. Being born male or female, black or white, rich or poor is certainly beyond the rhetor's control, but the experiences associated with growing up as a part of one of these groups as opposed to another clearly impose constraints on the rhetor.

There are many sources of information about prominent individuals, past and present, including biographical dictionaries, histories, memoirs, diaries, letters, and biographies. One thing to remember about biographies, particularly those authorized by the individual or her family, is that they tend to be favorable and may suffer from distortion (Hillbruner, 1966). The opposite can occur in unauthorized biographies, in which the biographer's purpose was to write a sensational or highly negative exposé.

Traditionally, the rhetor's background was used to develop *ethos*. The classical concept of ethos dictated that, in good oratory, speakers must demonstrate character, intelligence, and goodwill toward their listeners. The Roman rhetorician Quintilian taught that only a "good man" could be a truly effective persuader because he would emphasize social well-being. Contemporary concepts of "speaker credibility," though less sexist, are based on this tradition. The credible communicator is one who upholds our laws and traditions, respects cultural values, and concerns herself with the audience's welfare.

The rhetor, classical or contemporary, is constrained by the demands of image. The classical rhetor had to show himself to be a good man speaking well. His modern counterpart is further constrained by the fact that the audience, exposed to mass-media information, may already have formed impressions about his character. In either case, the content of the rhetorical act is constrained in a manner not of the rhetor's choosing.

In addition to the rhetor's background and character, anything that exists at the time of the rhetorical act might constrain it. Events contingent upon or in competition with the rhetorical act may have constrained it. The occasion that called forth rhetorical activity may have dictated its formality or informality, the extent to which dialogue and debate were permitted, and the time allotted for the performance of the act. The physical features of the setting in which the act took place may also have constrained it. For example, a speech to be delivered on television, as opposed to a live audience, must be adapted to that medium.

Although the decision to accept the constraints imposed by presenting the speech on television is the rhetor's, once that decision is made, the constraints imposed are beyond her control. The impact of the constraints upon the rhetorical act are interpreted by juxtaposing an understanding of the nature of the constraints imposed by the medium with a close inspection of the content of the act for signs of its influence.

The symbols chosen by a rhetor to express her beliefs, attitudes, and values are, to a great extent, under her control. The rhetor has the ability to manage meaning by deciding what to say and in what order to say it. In this regard also, it is important to know something about the rhetor. Biographical material provides information that helps you interpret the symbol choices she made in constructing the message. Who was she? What resources were available to her? What experience and training did she have? Experience, knowledge, education, previous rhetorical acts, and social status are all potential constraints on the message and its reception by the audience.

Even though the rhetor was the product of an environment over which she exercised little control, the way in which she chose to capitalize on the benefits and cope with the limitations inherent in her experience were under her control. This control can be exercised primarily through the use of language. As education became more universal, rhetors were afforded greater ability to transcend social status linguistically. The rhetor had the option of conforming to or violating the linguistic expectations surrounding the rhetorical situation.

Pennsylvania Senator Edward Everett was invited to be the featured speaker at the dedication of a cemetery on 19 November 1863. He was to be introduced by another politician of lesser oratorical prowess. Rather than merely introducing Senator Everett or making reference to the occasion, this individual's brief speech identified the resolve that was required for the Union to see the Civil War through to the end. His remarks were not well received at the time.

The man's name was Abraham Lincoln, and his "Address at the Dedication of the Gettysburg National Cemetery," more commonly known as "The Gettysburg Address," violated expectations. Although it was nominally a Union victory, the Battle of Gettysburg had been extremely costly to both sides. Lincoln recognized this. That his remarks represented a more fitting response to the situation is proven by the fact that most people can recite passages from the Gettysburg Address from memory, and practically no one remembers who Edward Everett was.

The concept of constraints is global. It requires you to interpret the rhetorical act in terms of what the rhetor had to work around and what was done to accomplish the act's purpose. Anything, from the rhetor's public reputation to the form the message took, may have constrained the rhetorical act. Constraints are determined by examining the rhetor's background, the audience, the social-historical setting, and the message itself.

The rhetorical situation functions as a vehicle for interpreting the rhetorical act in terms of the circumstances surrounding it. Characterizing the rhetorical situation is step 2 in the critical process model. This step requires you to interpret the rhetorical act by drawing inferences about the exigence to which the rhetorical act responded, the audience subject to influence and capable of responding to the exigence, and the constraints the rhetor faced in constructing the message. Use these concepts as a guide to thinking as you collect information. Next, in step 3 of the critical process model, you will select a more specific set of principles on which to base your final judgment about the rhetorical act.

Evaluating the Rhetorical Act

A critical approach is a system for evaluating rhetorical acts. Critical essays in speech communication journals and anthologies are all based on some approach, frequently referred to as a *methodology*. An approach, or methodology, is a set of standards or norms derived from a particular theory or philosophy of communication. The third step in the critical process model begins with the selection of an approach.

Why do you need a critical approach to evaluate a rhetorical act? Have you not already completed your criticism by describing the rhetorical act and characterizing the situation? Describing the rhetorical act provides you with information about its content, and characterizing the rhetorical situation yields information about the context. This is not criticism. It neither analyzes nor evaluates. Up to this point, you have just been collecting "evidence" to build your case.

Your evaluation of a rhetorical act is an original contribution to the process and, as such, is rhetorical action in its own right. Like any other rhetor, you have certain obligations. Your opinions must be demonstrated to have validity, to be based on a foundation of fact. The evidence collected in the first two steps of the process of doing criticism provides those facts. You make your case in the third step. An approach for criticism gives you a rational system for analyzing and evaluating.

Like any other arguer, you risk having your judgments misunderstood or rejected. To minimize this risk, thorough preparation for rendering a judgment is necessary. It is also important to consider your audience's expectations regarding good criticism. Your goal is to increase the reader's understanding and appreciation of a rhetorical act by making judgments about its quality, value, and consequences (Campbell, 1972). You are obliged to clearly identify the criteria used to make those judgments. Good criticism offers the reader insight into how persuasion is used in society. It deals with the morality of individual rhetorical acts (Brockreide, 1974; Campbell, 1972). Being able to apply these critical standards is a matter of knowing the theoretical approaches to doing criticism.

Each of the five critical approaches to be discussed is based on a different philosophy of how communication works in a culture. Learning various critical approaches is worthwhile because many of the functions of criticism described in

Chapter 1 result from learning and applying appropriate criteria. Each approach represents a frame of reference for how you should think about communication and how you should judge a rhetorical act. Think of an approach as a template for effective communication that you use to determine the validity of your judgment about the rhetorical act you are studying.

Simply matching an approach against a rhetorical act and stating that you find examples of the principles of the approach in the act is not criticism; it is categorizing (Brockreide, 1974). If you are using an approach that says, "rhetors use metaphors to arouse emotion," discovering a metaphor in the act does not explain *why* the rhetor used that particular metaphor, *what* emotion it attempted to arouse, or *whether* it was appropriate. Furthermore, using a critical approach in this way can become an exercise in frustration because you cannot always fit all the elements of a rhetorical act neatly into the confines of the template. Critical approaches should be thought of as having flexible boundaries that serve your purposes as a critic.

There are two ways to apply critical approaches flexibly. The first is referred to as *formulary criticism,* the second as *organic criticism.* In doing formulary criticism, you choose a critical approach and decide which of its concepts about effective communication you want to use in evaluating a rhetorical act. Formulary criticism usually means applying most of the concepts of an approach to the rhetorical act to analyze and evaluate it. How much of the "formula" you decide to use depends on what you discovered in describing the rhetorical act and characterizing the rhetorical situation. When the rhetorical act you are studying seems to fall within the bounds of a particular approach, it makes sense to stay within its confines by doing formulary criticism. However, just as the rhetorical situation constrains the rhetor, choosing to be bound by a single critical approach constrains the critic.

You make a decision about which critical approach to use as you investigate the content and context of the rhetorical act. Your knowledge of different critical approaches, what to look for in describing the rhetorical act, and characterizing the rhetorical situation all contribute to your decision about how to approach analyzing and evaluating the rhetorical act. What may happen is that you begin to see that combining a concept from one approach with a concept from another best enables you to analyze and evaluate the rhetorical act. This is an organic approach to criticism.

Organic criticism can also involve creating an approach that is new, choosing theories of communication from established approaches, and posing new questions to apply to rhetorical acts. No single critical approach establishes the optimal criteria for evaluating every example of rhetorical activity. Rhetors have numerous options in creating a message. As a critic, you must consider the properties of each rhetorical act.

Regardless of whether you opt for formulary or organic criticism, your selection of a critical approach should serve the following purposes: (1) It should allow you to make a fair judgment; do not stack the methodological deck to produce an inappropriately positive or negative result. (2) It should be compatible with the form of the rhetorical act, be it film, political cartoon, speech, or song lyric; your choice must enable you to analyze and judge it. (3) It should enable you to judge the quality or social utility of the rhetorical act.

Armed with your knowledge of the rhetorical act, the rhetorical situation, and a critical approach on which to base your evaluation, you are ready to determine the quality, value, and consequences of the rhetorical act. Rhetorical judgment centers on four issues regarding the act: Did it pursue ethically desirable ends for society, did it achieve the desired results, did it present a truthful account, and was it aesthetically satisfying (Andrews, 1983; Campbell, 1982, 1972; Cathcart, 1966; C.R. Smith, 1976).

Judging Ethics

The ethical standard of rhetorical judgment examines the worthiness of the rhetor's purpose. The focus is on the rhetor, his personality, and how his act may be viewed to have promoted social well-being. Ethics has long been a standard of rhetorical judgment.

Greek rhetoricians taught that establishing ethos was an important part of speech development, and the Roman rhetoricians refined the concept. The Roman rhetorician Quintilian taught his students that the ideal orator was a man of good character who espoused public morality and service to the state, "a good man, speaking well" (Golden et al., 1989). In contemporary terms, we view the rhetor as an advocate for a pattern of belief or behavior. We judge a rhetor's ethics on the basis of whether or not his advocacy promoted the best interests of society.

A rhetor's credibility, how he is regarded by society, is based on his public image as constructed in the minds of his audience. What contributes to credibility? Perceptions of the rhetor's trustworthiness, character, intelligence, knowledge or experience, goodwill or identification with the listener, and power or charisma are all potential elements of a rhetor's credibility (Golden et al., 1989). The ethical rhetor shares values with an audience, either by identifying existing common values or by creating a new shared value, through the rhetorical act. The ethical rhetor avoids undermining the social or political system while attacking it, by offering constructive criticism that addresses its weaknesses (C.R. Smith, 1976).

To judge the rhetor's ethics you must examine the values of both rhetor and audience. As a criterion for rhetorical judgment, the ethical standard includes examination of the rhetor's motives, evidence of his concern for social welfare, and the values expressed in the rhetorical act. It also includes a determination of the audience's prior perception of the rhetor's reputation and any indications of changes in perception in the aftermath of rhetorical activity.

Judging Results

Rhetorical acts are judged effective when the rhetor's purpose is achieved. The purpose sought by the rhetor, changing minds or persuading people to act, is the result of rhetorical action. Determining results is often difficult because it is not always possible to establish a cause-and-effect relationship between a rhetorical act and what subsequently transpired. A change in belief or behavior may have resulted for a number of reasons other than the rhetorical act. The rhetorical act under study may represent one voice among many requesting the same change. If change occurred, was it the product of the single rhetorical act being studied or of the campaign for change in toto? Could change have occurred as a part of the normal course of events and not as a result of any of the rhetorical activity surrounding it?

Judging a rhetorical act on the basis of whether or not it accomplished its purpose must also take its historical impact into account. When you judge only on the basis of results, you are examining the pragmatic aspects of rhetorical activity: Did it do anything? The problem facing the critic is what to conclude if nothing happened immediately. Is the act to be judged a failure?

There is always the question of long-range purpose to consider. Some rhetors do not expect their purpose to be achieved instantly. Dr. Martin Luther King, Jr.'s "I Have a Dream" speech would be judged a failure using a short-term results standard because it did not produce racial equality. However, because its dream metaphor suggested a long-range purpose, any judgment regarding its results must take its historical impact into account.

The other problem facing the critic who is using only the results standard is that a lie can be very effective in changing beliefs and behaviors. In the 1970s, some state legislatures refused to ratify the Equal Rights Amendment (ERA) because of a campaign based on such claims as the "fact" that the ERA would mandate unisex public restrooms. History provides other examples of successful lies. Using the results standard alone might produce a distorted critical effort. The third standard of judgment, "truth," can be employed to reduce such distortion.

Judging Truth

In judging whether or not a rhetorical act represents the truth of a matter or a true portrayal of the rhetorical situation, we are concerned with the *probable truth*. In human affairs, it is usually impossible to talk about things that are absolutely true or absolutely false. This does not mean that rhetors or audiences do not believe they know the truth of the matter. It does mean that in rhetorical activity, truth is subjective; so when you evaluate a rhetorical act by the truth standard, you must consider how truth is intersubjectively created by the rhetor and the audience.

Truth is intersubjectively determined, time bound, and probabilistic. This means that in matters that are uncertain, people decide what is true or false. The truth about some things is what people choose to believe about them. People once believed in an earth-centered universe in which the sun went around the earth. That was their truth, the truth they agreed on, the only one that existed for them.

Nicolaus Copernicus changed that truth in the sixteenth century, illustrating its time-bound quality. His theory that the planets revolve around the sun and that the rotation of the earth on its axis accounts for the apparent rising and setting of the sun was based on new information. Actually, the facts were as old as the solar system. What was new was that someone interpreted them correctly. Truth is intersubjectively determined from current information. As information is expanded and reinterpreted with the passage of time, what was true becomes time bound, captured like a fly in the amber of its age.

Finally, truth is probabilistic, existing and possibly moving along a continuum ranging from the absolutely probable, or true, to the absolutely improbable, or false. Copernican theory was an idea that was termed absolutely improbable at the time it was proposed. It moved to the opposite end of the true-false continuum as a result of scientific inquiry, a form of rhetorical action. Not all rhetorical action is able to determine absolute truth because it remains intersubjective and time bound, even if it involves scientific inquiry. To some, a fetus is an insentient bit of protoplasm; to others it is a living human being.

The problem the critic faces in using truth as a standard of rhetorical judgment is that much rhetorical activity addresses controversial issues and attempts to establish what is probably true in circumstances in which absolute truth cannot be determined. The concept that truth is only probable implies that the rhetor, given the information available to her, advised her audience regarding what seemed likely to be the best course of belief or behavior, not what was without question the best course. In this way, rhetorical activity becomes a means of adjusting ideas to people and people to ideas (D.C. Bryant, 1973). A rhetor attempts to present her ideas in such a way that her audience perceives them to be probably true.

Truth is compromised as a standard of rhetorical judgment if you allow your own concept of the truth to interfere. If you are studying rhetorical activity that took place in the distant past, you probably have the benefit of access to information that was unknown to the rhetor and her audience, time bound as they were. You probably bring different values and attitudes to bear than they would have brought in intersubjectively deciding what is true because religion, economic status, political affiliation, group memberships, and a host of other demographic and psychological variables influence perceptions of reality and truth. It is not your personal standard of truth that is at issue but truth as it was intersubjectively determined by the rhetor and her audience.

This does not mean you must uncritically accept the rhetorical activity of a person or group that you find objectionable. Some approaches to criticism are ideological, more concerned with the content than the form of rhetorical activity. If your stance as a critic warrants selection of one of these approaches, it will provide a competing standard of truth against which you can legitimately question those ideas that you find objectionable.

Judging Aesthetics

One of the properties of a rhetorical act is its poetic dimension. The fourth standard of rhetorical judgment evaluates how successfully the rhetor used the aesthetic principles of the form: speech, song lyric, political cartoon, film, and so on. The focus of aesthetic judgment is on how a set of rhetorical principles concerning its form facilitated the act's ability to achieve its purpose. Your judgment concerns how well the rhetorical act embodied the best qualities of a particular form. When applied in this manner, the aesthetic standard is limited to a consideration of the stylistic properties of the rhetorical act. Judgments are made about the qualities of symbols selected by the rhetor and the use of devices of adornment or the special grammar and syntax of the communication genre or message medium.

Because aesthetic principles of rhetoric identify how an "ideal" performance is enacted, aesthetics can become a much broader standard that includes aspects of results, truth, and ethics (Cathcart, 1966), because an aesthetic standard can be derived from any other rhetorical principle. For example, it is possible to judge a rhetor's development of argument and use of evidence under the heading of aesthetics, based on how well it represents theories of good argumentation or realistic presentation of the subject.

Notice how describing the rhetorical act and characterizing the rhetorical situation facilitates your ability to make critical judgments by providing evidence to support conclusions about ethics, results, truth, and aesthetics. Also notice that although the four standards are not mutually exclusive, you can elect to focus your criticism. Many of the examples of rhetorical criticism published in journals and anthologies touch on all four standards, but their primary focus may be on only one or two of them.

How do you determine which standard or standards of rhetorical judgment to feature in your criticism? The choice of critical approach makes a difference. Some critical approaches suggest use of all four criteria, others focus on one. The genre of the rhetorical act may also influence your decision. For example, if you were criticizing congressional debate on sanctions against South Africa, the locus of the rhetorical act in the political arena may suggest a focus on truth and ethics as the most appropriate standards for evaluation whereas criticism of a film depicting apartheid might focus on the aesthetic standard.

This chapter has presented a model of the critical process to help you successfully evaluate a rhetorical act. The three elements of criticism include describing the rhetorical act, characterizing the rhetorical situation, and rendering a rhetorical judgment. The critical process model may be thought of as a series of guidelines to research and thinking prior to preparing written criticism.

In thinking through the process of rhetorical criticism, it is important to remember that not all of these guidelines are equally useful across a variety of approaches to criticism. Also, the nature of the rhetorical act, whether it is a speech, editorial, television program, or cartoon, requires some flexibility in how you use this system.

It is a good idea to read critical studies in speech communication journals and anthologies to gain a sense of the variety of techniques of criticism. You will find references to examples of criticism in the suggested reading lists at the end of each chapter. These readings were selected because we believe they are exemplary models of using critical approaches, either in formulary or organic criticism. The suggested reading lists also provide resources for doing criticism that offer information on the critical approaches, genres of communication, or reference material we believe you will find useful.

The importance of selecting an approach for rhetorical criticism has been discussed in this chapter without detailed reference to the specifics of various approaches. Later chapters examine five critical approaches. Read about these methodologies with an eye toward how each might provide an appropriate frame of reference for evaluating the kind of rhetorical activity you are most interested in studying.

Suggested Readings

Examples of Criticism

CHALY, I. (1977). John Adams and the Boston massacre: A rhetorical reassessment. *Central States Journal, 28,* 36–46.

> The purpose of this critical essay was to examine the courtroom techniques of John Adams in defending British soldiers in the Boston massacre trials of 1770. Chaly does this in the context of constraints unique to colonial courtroom procedures. The focus of criticism is on Adams' choices as a defense lawyer. This is a very readable example of historical criticism that deals with an interesting incident.

Resources for Doing Criticism

BITZER, L.F. (1968). The rhetorical situation. *Philosophy and Rhetoric, 1,* 1–15.

> In this article, Bitzer first conceptualized the rhetorical situation. It includes his justification for studying rhetorical acts from the perspective of situations. It provides an extensive discussion of exigences and constraints. Bitzer develops several good examples, especially regarding presidential speaking, to illustrate his ideas about rhetorical situations. This article exemplifies how a critic creates concepts for doing criticism.

CATHCART, R.S., (1966). *Post communication.* Indianapolis, IN: Bobbs-Merrill Co.

> This text, intended for the novice critic, is a step-by-step treatment of "how to do" criticism. It contains a good discussion of the critic's responsibilities and strong emphasis on the aesthetic standard of judgment, which Cathcart claims embodies all other aspects of judgment. It has a public-speaking orientation, an excellent view of what were long regarded to be the limits of rhetorical criticism.

HILLBRUNER, A. (1966). *Critical dimensions: The art of public address criticism.* New York: Random House.

> This text was also written for the beginning critic and is another example of the "way we were." The process of criticism is illustrated with examples of criticism of public speeches. The strength of this text is its discussion of the context of rhetorical activity. You may also find Hillbruner's division of the process of criticism into intrinsic and extrinsic factors useful.

RUBIN, R.B., RUBIN, A.M., AND PIELE, L.J. (1990). *Communication research: Strategies and sources.* (2nd ed.). Belmont, CA: Wadsworth.

This text surveys research techniques used in the communication field and describes every type of published material. It is a valuable resource, providing helpful information about using the library, electronic literature searches, and American Psychological Association style. The sections on how to do reviews of literature and how to get started on a research project are particularly relevant to doing criticism.

The

Traditional

Approach

3

Why does the keynote speaker at a political convention face a difficult task? What constraints must be managed? Can a rhetor use a device of adornment, metaphor, as an argument? New York Governor Mario Cuomo was selected as the keynote speaker for the 1984 Democratic convention. He chose the theme "Tale of Two Cities" to frame his response to President Ronald Reagan's vision of America as a "shining city on a hill." Governor Cuomo wrote his own speech, drawing on the values and traditions common to all Americans and his own family experience. His speech was structured by the controlling metaphor of two cities, one shining with wealth and prosperity and the other dimmed by poverty and despair. He did not attack President Reagan but claimed that the president's vision failed to take in this other city.

The keynote speech is a convention ritual in which praise is heaped upon the speaker's party and blame upon the opposition, making most keynote speeches rather predictable. One of the constraints a keynote speaker faces is the multiple audiences for the speech: conventioneers and a television audience made up of members of both parties and those potential voters who identify strongly with neither party. In 1984, Cuomo faced an added constraint: Many middle-class voters who usually voted Democratic had shifted their allegiance to Ronald Reagan in 1980. He wanted his keynote speech to appeal not only to hard core party members but also to those who liked Ronald Reagan (Henry, 1988).

Did Mario Cuomo succeed in reaching both of his target audiences? Was metaphoric structure an effective argument? Why did Republicans Ronald Reagan and Barry Goldwater praise the speech? For an analysis and evaluation of the speech using concepts from the traditional approach to criticism, see David Henry's "The Rhetorical Dynamics of Mario Cuomo's 1984 Keynote Address: Situation, Speaker, Metaphor" listed in the suggested readings at the end of this chapter.

The forces that cause scholars to philosophize about communication give rise to theories of communication. Rhetorical theory is an organized, consistent, understandable way of teaching people what is needed to create and present a functional message (Ehninger, 1968). Any rhetorical act, such as Governor Cuomo's keynote address, is a product of the communication practices and theories of a society, and it is judged to be good or bad, relevant or irrelevant, depending on the extent to which it effectively addresses an issue. As a critic, you consider the relationship between a theory of communication and rhetorical activity.

We begin discussion of critical approaches with the oldest one, the traditional approach, which is rooted in classical rhetorical theory. This approach is based on the philosophy that we are rational beings who can be persuaded by compelling arguments. As you consider the approaches discussed in subsequent chapters, you will find the influence of the traditional approach in the ways that other approaches conceptualize and suggest we evaluate the products of human communication.

The traditional approach is sometimes referred to as *neo-Aristotelian criticism* because Aristotle's *Rhetoric* had a significant influence on theories of communication. A theory attempts to explain relationships among phenomena that produce particular results. In classical Greece and Rome, public speaking was extremely important, and it was noted that some speakers were more successful than others in getting laws passed and judgments in their favor. The recognition they received and the techniques they used were observed, critiqued, and codified by classical theorists such as Plato, Isocrates, Aristotle, Cicero, and Quintilian. Rhetoric became a philosophy, the basis for a system of education, and the formulas for successful public speaking. Classical rhetoric viewed the process of persuasion as a consequence of the skillful manipulation of five elements, or *canons,* of rhetoric (see box on next page).

Rhetorical activity occurs when there is an exigence and the rhetorical situation requires someone to explain probable truth in the situation. By manipulating the five canons, the rhetor exercised control over the situation and managed the constraints imposed by it. For centuries, these five elements were the basis for communication theory and practice.

Although customs, tastes, and technology may have changed, the five canons still form the core of contemporary public-speaking pedagogy and practice. The Greeks and Romans recognized, as we do today, that although each canon had distinct properties, they were also interrelated. Nancy L. Harper (1979) has recast the canons in terms of their contemporary functions: (see box on page 41).

> **The Five Canons**
>
> **of Classical**
>
> **Rhetoric**
>
> *Invention,* the process of the speaker's choosing an appropriate topic and discovering the ideas and proof to use
>
> *Arrangement,* the final selection of ideas and proof that would best fit the speaker's purpose, audience, and occasion; the decision about how to sequence these ideas and proof and the amount of time to be devoted to each in the speech
>
> *Style,* the speaker's grammatical usage, choice of language, and the expressive devices used to present ideas
>
> *Delivery,* the speaker's use of voice and body movement in the oral presentation
>
> *Memory,* the codes and mnemonic devices the speaker relied on to recall lengthy speeches

Contemporary textbooks discussing successful rhetorical activity are not always organized around the five canons as were most classical texts, but you will find that these concepts still form the core of how we teach speaking and writing.

The traditional approach is based on the assumption that a rhetorical act is *reasoned discourse.* This means that the nature of argument, reasoning, and proof are at the heart of the traditional approach. Rhetors have purposes; they try to establish facts, make value judgments, and/or urge pursuit of courses of action. Audiences are believed to be open to persuasion by virtue of their predisposition to rationality. The function of rhetoric is to make truth knowable through the application of logic.

The five canons of classical rhetoric have been used as a critical approach to analyze numerous rhetorical acts. Because rhetorical theory was an outgrowth of observations of the practice of public speaking in classical cultures, the canons are particularly appropriate to the analysis of speeches. Rather than structuring our discussion of the traditional approach around the five canons, we follow the more contemporary organizational scheme of rhetor, audience, and message. Our discussion of the elements of the traditional approach incorporates contemporary views of the nature of argument.

The Rhetor

A rhetorical act is produced by a rhetor, who may be an individual or a team. Because it is based on theories about public speaking, criticism using the traditional approach focuses mainly on individual rhetors and often features a discus-

The Classical

Canons in

Contemporary

Usage

Conceptualization (invention) is the rhetor's acquisition and interpretation of information. The rhetor looks into a present concern to discover the information available about it. Conceptualization involves interpreting social reality. To address an audience, the rhetor must know and interpret their beliefs, attitudes, and values, their culture, and the kinds of arguments and evidence that are most likely to be acceptable to them.

Organization (arrangement) is the rhetor's adaptation of units of argument to the situation. An audience is more likely to respond positively to a message that conforms to its expectations about message structure. Organization patterns may vary depending on who is involved, on the speaker's purpose, and on where and how the message is delivered. Organization consists of both message structure and the relationships among rhetor, audience, and context.

Symbolization (style) is the use of symbols, words, actions, and contexts that cue recall in the minds of the audience. A symbol may be a specific term, a march or demonstration, an article of clothing, decoration, or furnishing—anything deliberately chosen to help accomplish the rhetor's goal.

Operationalization (delivery) is the physical form of the message's presentation. The medium of presentation —live speech, printed essay, or music video— influences all other elements of the rhetorical act. Operationalizing a message is a matter of analyzing various media to determine the effect of the manner of presentation on message meaning and choosing the most appropriate form of presentation.

Categorization (memory) is the perception, storage, and recall of information. Everyone learns through sensory perception. Personal experience and formal education indicate what information is important and what can be ignored by what is stored and is capable of being recalled. This accumulated information influences the symbols called up in a given situation, the meaning assigned to them, and the degree of importance attached to them by rhetors and their audiences. (HARPER, 1979)

Questions to Ask

About

the Rhetor's

Background

1. What biographical information can be found about the rhetor?

2. Did the audience perceive the rhetor in some particular way, such as a national hero, expert, leader, liberal, conservative, demagogue, or traitor?

3. What qualities made this rhetor an effective or ineffective communicator?

sion of delivery techniques. Our discussion of the rhetor also focuses on the individual, but you should realize that a team that crafts a message may also be considered, in terms of their collective characteristics, as rhetor. It is helpful to learn about the rhetor in terms of biographical information and the rhetor's role in the situation. How an audience regards a rhetor is due to a combination of the rhetor's prior reputation and how he or she responds to the rhetorical situation.

In classical rhetoric, the rhetor was evaluated in the context of the invention process because it was expected that the speaker would use appeals to create *ethos,* a certain impression of self, in the course of the speech. Today, we term ethos *credibility* and consider it in terms of the rhetor's prior reputation and what the rhetor does in the rhetorical situation. What the audience believes about the personal qualities of the rhetor is viewed as a major factor in how they respond to the message.

Studies reveal four components of a rhetor's credibility: *character,* the degree to which a rhetor is perceived as trustworthy; *intelligence,* the amount of knowledge or expertise a rhetor is thought to have; *goodwill,* the extent to which a rhetor is identified with the audience and their concerns; and *power,* the charisma and influence, real or inferred, that a rhetor is thought to possess (Golden et al., 1989). The extent to which character, intelligence, goodwill, and power are attributed to the rhetor is determined by his or her reputation with the audience and the audience's subsequent perception as a result of their exposure to the rhetorical act.

Your evaluation of a rhetor's reputation should start with a description of his or her qualifications, experience, training, formal education, social status, family background, and visibility in society. Because the traditional approach emphasizes the use of argument, you should consider the rhetor's background as it relates to the ability to argue effectively (see box above).

In addition to the rhetor's reputation apart from the rhetorical situation, elements of the situation potentially play a part in how the audience perceives the rhetor. These elements of a rhetor's credibility can be found by considering questions about situational constraints (see box on next page).

Questions to Ask

About Situational

Constraints on

the Rhetor

1. What was the exigence and what was the rhetor's position in relationship to it?

2. What was the rhetor's position in the social-political environment; what issues, causes, groups, or individuals might have shaped the rhetor's position on the exigence?

3. What attitudes did the rhetor project toward the audience and the subject matter?

4. Did the rhetor adapt to the audience and acknowledge their experiences, views, and feelings?

5. Was the rhetor sincere, honest, and open about his or her motives?

6. Was the rhetor's message consistent, free from contradictions and misrepresentations?

One of the most masterful speakers in American history, in terms of his management of ethos in the rhetorical situation, was Theodore Roosevelt, 26th president of the United States. He had the advantage of a strong, positive reputation with the American public. He was known as a colorful speaker, and he exuded personal vitality. He called himself a preacher, referred to his speeches as "lay sermons," and described the presidency as a "bully pulpit" (Braden, 1987). His personal history and the office of president combined to make him a very charismatic speaker (Behl, 1947).

Perceptions of Theodore Roosevelt's character, intelligence, goodwill, and charisma derived from his reputation as a speaker and the experiences he brought to political life. He was nationally known as an author, lecturer, naturalist, and adventurer before becoming president. One of his most famous speeches, regarded as a hallmark of his style, was "The Man with the Muckrake," delivered on 14 April 1906 on the occasion of laying the cornerstone for the new House of Representatives office building (Beltz, 1969; Murphy, 1955).

At the beginning of the twentieth century, America was growing, booming, a prosperous nation. It was also burdened by social problems which popular authors and journalists brought to the nation's attention. Upton Sinclair's *The Jungle* chronicled the abuse of laborers and the unsanitary conditions in the Chicago meatpacking industry in grisly detail. Lincoln Steffens' *The Shame of the Cities* portrayed metropolitan America as a hot bed of graft and corruption. Steffens, along with Ida Tarbell and Ray Standard Baker, took on Standard Oil and other industrial giants in the pages of *McClure's* magazine. William Randolph Hearst built a fortune on newspapers featuring "yellow journalism."

As president, Roosevelt condoned neither the greed of wealthy industrialists and the powers of political bosses nor the revolutionary fervor of these authors and journalists. The event that precipitated "The Man with the Muckrake" was a series of articles by David Graham Phillips in *Cosmopolitan* entitled "The Treason of the Senate." In it he accused some of Roosevelt's friends and political allies of impropriety in their relationship with big business (Behl, 1947; Beltz, 1969; Downie, 1976; Reid, 1988).

An evaluation of Theodore Roosevelt's management of ethos in "The Man with the Muckrake" would consider both the credibility he brought to the situation and that which he developed in the speech itself. Perception of his reputation was influenced by his role as a trust buster, proponent of the Pure Food and Drug Act, and his support of the 17th amendment to the Constitution, which allowed the popular election of senators (Behl, 1947; Beltz, 1969; Downie, 1976). Roosevelt was a reformer in his own right who, by 1906, had achieved a national reputation for personal courage, fairness, trustworthiness, and sincerity. He was publicly perceived as a good man (Behl, 1947).

Intriguing evidence of Roosevelt's management of ethos is found in the speech itself. The introduction to "The Man with the Muckrake" acknowledged public concern with what was wrong in the country and demonstrated the president's goodwill.

> There are, in the body politic, economic and social, many and grave evils, and there is urgent necessity for the sternist war upon them. There should be relentless exposure of and attack upon every evil man whether politician or business man, every evil practice, whether in politics, in business, or in social life. (T. ROOSEVELT, 1926, p. 416)

Roosevelt did not condemn journalists who wrote about abuses by saying there was nothing for the muckrakers to criticize. Early in the speech he specifically recognized the value of public scrutiny but suggested it must be done responsibly.

> I hail as a benefactor every writer or speaker, every man who on the platform, or in book, magazine, or newspaper, with merciless severity makes such attack, provided always that he in his turn remembers that the attack is of use only if it is absolutely truthful. The liar is no whit better than the thief, and if his mendacity takes the form of slander, he may be worse than most thieves. It puts a premium upon knavery untruthfully to attack an honest man, or even with hysterical exaggeration to assail a bad man with an untruth. An epidemic of indiscriminate

> assault upon character does not good, but very great
> harm. The soul of every scoundrel is gladdened whenever
> an honest man is assailed, or even when a scoundrel is
> untruthfully assailed. (T. ROOSEVELT, 1926, p. 416)

This is the purpose statement of "The Man with the Muckrake" and was intended to cast Roosevelt as truth seeker. The honesty he projected was to be viewed as uncompromising, the attitude he projected was that of a man of integrity. He wanted the American people to know his position on personal and presidential honesty: No matter how worthy the goal, it was never acceptable to lie to achieve it.

Audience perceptions of a rhetor and the rhetorical situation are always relative to what the audience believes is important or necessary. The rhetor who strikes the right chord will be perceived as credible. To our ears, Theodore Roosevelt's speeches may sound stilted, but this was not the case in 1906. "The Man with the Muckrake" was so publicly important that the term *muckraking* instantly caught on and was applied to what we call "investigative journalism" today (Reid, 1988). Your criticism of a rhetor's management of ethos must consider it in terms of its cultural era and situational context.

A rhetor's credibility is not constant. It can vary over time, particularly as it pertains to his or her prior reputation. President Richard Nixon resigned under the cloud of the Watergate scandal, and President Jimmy Carter was not reelected partly because of his failure to free American hostages in Iran. Both men eventually outlived their negative images and are now regarded as senior statesmen by their respective political parties. A rhetor's credibility may also vary from audience to audience, simultaneously being seen as possessing character, intelligence, goodwill, and power by one audience while being reviled as an incompetent, a charlatan, and a demagogue by another.

A rhetor's ability to manage ethos in a rhetorical situation is directly related to the audience, the occasion, and the exigence. Much contemporary speaking, particularly politcal speaking, is addressed to multiple audiences. The rhetor who seeks to avoid offending any segment of such an audience may create a bland, indecisive rhetorical act, which can decrease his or her credibility and would constitute mismanagement of whatever resources of ethos the rhetor had with various segments of the audience.

The Audience

Consideration of audience in the traditional approach involves analysis of the occasion for the rhetorical act and of the people who made up the audience. Occasion and audience constrain message form and content. The extent to which a rhetorical act succeeds or fails is almost always determined by the rhetor's ability to adapt it to the occasion and the audience.

The occasion for a rhetorical act may be the specific event as well as the social-cultural context of the rhetorical setting. A speech takes place at a specific time, and the reason for the speaker and audience coming together constrains the message. Speech introductions often acknowledge the occasion and the immediate audience, as "The Man with the Muckrake" presented at a ceremonial occasion, acknowledged in its opening:

> Over a century ago Washington laid the cornerstone of
> the Capitol in what was then little more than a tract of
> wooded wilderness here beside the Potomac. We now find
> it necessary to provide by great additional buildings for
> the business of government. (T. ROOSEVELT, 1926, p. 415)

Because a rhetorical act responds to an exigence in the rhetorical situation, occasion frequently extends beyond the immediate setting. Occasions of various kinds, such as commencement exercises, holidays, lecture series, and convocations, all provide opportunities to address the issues of the day. Historical, social, political, and economic forces all contribute to the exigence of the rhetorical situation and should be considered in your analysis of the occasion. Concepts about the rhetorical situation presented in Chapter 2 are particularly appropriate to analyzing the interplay of rhetor and audience in terms of the traditional approach. The details of the occasion are situational constraints that are revealed by considering several questions (see box below).

Questions to Ask

About Situational

Constraints of

the Occasion

1. What were the immediate circumstances of the occasion in terms of time, date, location, and the nature of the occasion (ceremony, special event, etc.) and the media of communication?

2. What other events immediately preceded or followed the rhetorical act?

3. What expectations did the occasion create in the audience?

4. What was the historical, social, political, and economic setting of the rhetorical situation, and how did these forces create expectations for the audience?

5. How did the exigence addressed by the rhetorical act relate to the immediate circumstances of the rhetor addressing an audience?

"The Man with the Muckrake" was really a response to what President Roosevelt saw as journalistic abuse and a reform agenda that "everyone" was talking about. Phillips' articles on the Senate in *Cosmopolitan* triggered Roosevelt's recognition of the exigence, the ceremony of laying the cornerstone was merely a convenient event to use to make a speech on the larger issue of muckraking. Even though laying the cornerstone was important enough in its own right to attract press coverage, the White House leaked word to the press that the president would make an important statement to ensure national attention (Reid, 1988). After acknowledging the occasion of laying the cornerstone, Roosevelt got to the point of his speech:

> This growth in the need for the housing of government is but a proof and example of the way in which the nation has grown and the sphere of action of the National Government has grown. We now administer affairs of a nation in which the extraordinary growth of population has been out stripped by the growth of wealth and the growth in complex interests. The material problems that face us today are not such as they were in Washington's time, but the underlying facts of human nature are the same now as they were then. Under altered external form we war with the same tendencies toward evil that were evident in Washington's time, and are helped by the same tendencies for good. It is about some of these that I wish to say a word today. (T. ROOSEVELT, 1926, p. 415)

Roosevelt's introduction signaled the audience that he was going to address problems caused by both the constants of human nature and the variables of social and economic conditions in America in 1906.

How many audiences was Roosevelt addressing? Presidential rhetoric—inaugurals, state-of-the-union messages, press conferences, and policy statements—usually have multiple audiences. As part of your analysis of a rhetorical situation, you need to determine audience composition. An audience may consist of only those present for the speech, or it may include a larger national audience who experience the message as mediated by print and electronic journalism. "The Man with the Muckrake" addressed three audiences: those government dignitaries and members of the press attending the ceremony, those writers and journalists who wrote muckraking stories, and a national audience who read the muckraking stories and who would read about the speech.

Your analysis of the audiences for a rheteroical act should rely on contemporaneous news reports, commentaries, reviews, and histories for information about the nature of the audience. There are three important variables to use in describing and analyzing the audience: *knowledge, group identification,* and *receptivity to the topic and purpose* (Andrews, 1983).

Knowledge

An audience can be described in terms of what it knows or thinks it knows about the subject, and the message can be analyzed in terms of what it reveals about the rhetor's perception of audience knowledge. As a critic, you want to learn what you can about the relationship between the audience and the subject of the message. Although an audience may have special knowledge of the subject addressed by the rhetorical act, all audiences have general knowledge as a result of education, experience, and the general availability of information.

Audience knowledge is an important variable because rhetors create messages based on what they believe the audience already knows. If a rhetor perceives the audience as already knowledgeable, argument and proof in the rhetorical act can be abbreviated. The same rhetor, in addressing a less-knowledgeable audience, may use more detailed arguments and more elaborate proof.

In "The Man with the Muckrake," Theodore Roosevelt addressed the members of his multiple audiences in ways that suggest he believed they were already familiar with various examples of muckraking. He referred to the practice of muckraking in only the most general terms:

> In "Pilgrim's Progress" the Man with the Muckrake is set forth as the example of him whose vision is fixed on carnal instead of spiritual things. Yet he also typifies the man who in this life consistently refuses to see aught that is lofty, and fixes his eyes with solemn intentness only on that which is vile and debasing. Now it is very necessary that we should not flinch from seeing what is vile and debasing. There is filth on the floor, and it must be scraped up with the muckrake; and there are times and places where this service is the most needed of all the services that can be performed. But the man who never does anything else, who never thinks, or speaks, or writes, save of his feats with the muckrake, speedily becomes, not a help to society, not an incitment to good, but one of the most potent forces for evil. (T. ROOSEVELT, 1926, pp. 415–416)

Roosevelt did not identify specific authors or journalists. He did not mention any of the books and articles by name. He used the allegory of Bunyan's story to cue audience recall of examples.

Group Identification

The second variable used to describe and analyze an audience is the identification of the groups to which they belong. Group identification includes demographics, which classify an audience by age, sex, race, ethnic origin, occupation, and income. Working women between the ages of 18 and 45 may perceive child-care issues differently than senior citizens. Knowing the groups with which an audience may be identified provides a way of analyzing how the rhetor adapted the message to the audience. Search the text of the message for evidence of adaptation.

Group identification can also reveal sets of values, beliefs, attitudes, and ideologies held by an audience composed of individuals who share an organizational membership. Members of teachers' unions such as the National Education Association and the American Federation of Teachers may be predisposed to support issues tied to their special interests such as property-tax increases, school bonds, or state lotteries earmarked to support education. Your analysis of audience and message should consider how the rhetor attempted to adapt to, or recognize, the special interests of the audience on the basis of their group identification.

Receptivity

How much knowledge audiences possess and what groups they belong to influence the extent to which they are receptive to the topic of a message and the rhetor's purpose. An audience's receptivity to topic and purpose is a matter of saliency (Andrews, 1983). *Saliency* relates to perceptions of the exigence in the rhetorical situation. Is the topic important? To the extent that an audience perceives a problem, they may find the rhetor's topic and purpose salient. Since perceived salience is not automatic for every audience, rhetors sometimes must manage meaning in the rhetorical situation to make the subject salient in order to secure an audience's attention. Your analysis of the audience should consider perceived salience of the exigence in the rhetorical situation.

Theodore Roosevelt did not have to create salience, he drew on a subject that was important and much discussed in 1906. His primary purpose in "The Man with the Muckrake" was to create doubt about the muckrakers' motives in the minds of their readers (Downie, 1976). His secondary purpose was to signal the muckrakers that relying on sensationalism and exaggeration to sell newspapers and magazines was harmful to the reformers' cause (Beltz, 1969). The reading public responded very favorably to Roosevelt's speech. The term "muckraking" caught on and became part of the national vocabulary. Encouraged by the speech, other speakers and writers began to criticize journalistic excess.

One segment of the audience took "The Man with the Muckrake" very personally. Some authors and journalists believed that, even though the president had not named names, he had singled them out as individuals. Tarbell, Steffens, Sinclair, and others felt betrayed because the president had seemed to support the reform movement earlier, meeting with leading reform writers and supporting reform legislation (Beltz, 1969). Roosevelt chose a middle-of-the-road approach in developing the speech, praising objective journalism and castigating sensationalism. From our historical vantage point, we know that he was trying to be objective while calling public attention to the abuses of muckraking and trying to rein in the excesses of William Randolph Hearst's newspapers.

The constraints an audience imposes on the rhetorical situation are the ones a rhetor has the least control over. Even the most favorably disposed audience may fail to embrace the rhetor's topic and purpose. Your analysis of the audience should consider who the members of the audience were, what they were likely to have believed, and how the message was adapted to meet the constraints they imposed on the rhetorical situation.

The Message

The emphasis of criticism using the traditional approach is on how well the arguments and proof functioned in a rhetorical act. The rhetorical act is viewed as a set of individual units of argument. Even though each unit may have a different emphasis or present a different interpretation of the facts in the situation, all must fit together in a way that facilitates achievement of the rhetor's purpose.

The message is the element in a rhetorical situation over which the rhetor exercises the most control. The five canons of classical rhetoric explain how a speaker crafts a speech, classical rhetoric's system for managing the message. Aristotle said that rhetoric is concerned with finding all of the available means of persuasion in a situation and then choosing which to use. The text of a rhetorical act reflects the choices the rhetor made in response to the situational constraints.

In Chapter 2 we said that you should begin the process of criticism by describing the rhetorical act—in terms of its purpose, structure, arguments and ideas, use of symbols, and concept of audience—to discover the choices a rhetor has made. Analyzing and evaluating these choices is the essence of criticism using the traditional approach and is done in terms of the rhetor's use of invention, organization, style, and delivery.

Invention

From its origin in classical rhetoric, invention focused on the use of three types of proof: ethos, logos, and pathos. *Ethos,* already discussed under "The Rhetor," is addressed by the rhetor's attempts to build credibility in the rhetorical situation. In a speech, ethos is usually part of the argument. In other forms of communication, ethos may be used more subtly, suggested, for example, by the sense of professionalism that accompanies a well-made documentary. *Logos,* the logical development of arguments, focuses on the use of information and techniques of reasoning to appeal to an audience's rationality. *Pathos,* arousing the emotions, relies on both information and style to achieve the effect of engaging the audience's humanity.

Appeals to ethos, logos, and pathos are not mutually exclusive. In fact, a single passage from a rhetorical act may contain elements of all three of these

Questions to Ask **About the** **Rhetor's Purpose**	1. What was the rhetor's persuasive goal? 2. What change in belief or behavior or what commitment did the rhetor seek from the audience? 3. What was the rhetor's point of view about the exigence?

forms of proof. Although the rhetorical situation and the medium of communication may constrain the form of proof a rhetor chooses to emphasize, rhetors use ethos, logos, and pathos in adapting their messages to the audience and the occasion.

The traditional approach views rhetorical acts as arguments because they constitute the rhetor's response to the exigence and offer the rhetor's interpretation of reality. Your analysis of the rhetor's use of invention should start by identifying his or her purpose statement from which the arguments in the rhetorical act flow (see box above).

A rhetor's purpose is usually stated in the introduction and is often repeated in the conclusion. After you identify the rhetorical act's purpose, you can determine what responsibilities for developing arguments and using proof the rhetor consequently had to assume. As a critic, your examination of invention must assess the validity of the rhetor's arguments (see box below).

Questions to Ask **About** **the Rhetor's** **Use of Invention**	1. Did the rhetor's arguments in toto, the persuasive case, constitute an appropriate response to the rhetorical situation? 2. Were the arguments adapted to the audience? 3. Did the rhetor understand or correctly interpret issues as they were generally understood at the time? 4. If the rhetor offered a new interpretation, was a persuasive case built to support it? 5. Did the rhetor use information accurately and consistently?

Three models of argument, one classical and two contemporary, afford you maximum flexibility in analyzing and evaluating a rhetor's use of invention. We shall describe the Toulmin model, the enthymeme, and metaphor. The Toulmin model identifies the elements of a valid argument and the relationships among them. The validity of arguments in a rhetorical act must often be assessed by reconstructing the rhetor's units of argument. *Reconstruction* becomes necessary when, for reasons of style, audience adaptation, or media choice, all elements of the argument, as described by Toulmin, may not have been presented in the rhetorical act. Identifying each unit of argument is something you do in describing the rhetorical act. The concepts of enthymeme and metaphor can also be used to reconstruct arguments.

The Toulmin Model of Argument

A contemporary model of argumentative structure is based on the work of Stephen Toulmin (1958) and Toulmin, Rieke, and Janik (1984). We begin our discussion of inventional argument with the Toulmin model because it offers the most complete view of how arguments can be structured.

The *Toulmin model* affords the critic a way to describe the parts of an argument, diagram how the parts fit together, and assess the argument's validity by analyzing the relationship among its parts. An argument has three basic parts:

> *Grounds,* the information or evidence, consisting of fact and opinion statements, interpreted by the rhetor as supporting the claim
>
> *Claim,* the conclusion the rhetor draws from the available information or evidence
>
> *Warrant,* the reasoning, stated or implied, that justifies the inferential leap from grounds to claim

An argument is strengthened and its limitations specified by three additional parts of the Toulmin model:

> *Backing,* additional information or evidence that provides support that is specific to the warrant, legitimizing it as a "good" reason for making the inference
>
> *Qualifier,* a statement of the amount or degree of certainty a rhetor attaches to the strength of the claim
>
> *Rebuttal,* a statement of any limitations on the claim, offered in anticipation of objections to it or stating circumstances under which it is invalid

A particular unit of argument in a rhetorical act may not contain all six parts or even the three primary parts. An argument in television producer Norman Lear's keynote address at a 1984 conference on television ethics, sponsored by the Academy of Television Arts and Sciences and Emerson College, contained four parts. See if you can reconstruct it using the Toulmin model.

TV coverage of the 1984 presidential campaign was a triumph of images over substance. It was the horse race and hoopla of the campaign, not the ideas and merits of the issues, which received the most attention. From the primaries through to November 6th, the big story most evenings was the result of the latest poll. Again and again, the candidates were seen on the evening news, responding to the same tired questions: "The polls show you so many points behind, Mr. Mondale. How are you going to catch up?" "The polls show you slipping a little among this or that constituency, Mr. President. What are you going to do about it?

And talk about being *weaned* by the media: convention delegates no longer complain if their view is obstructed by TV cameras and crews. The real floor manager at political conventions is the man who points the camera. "Spontaneous" demonstrations are schedluled to last twelve minutes, *precisely,* to satisfy the needs of the convention floor, Olympus-like, and senators of great renown scurry like beggars from booth to booth hoping that Dan Rather or Tom Brokaw will think them worthy of an interview.

I had the privilege of travelling with a presidential candidate in the 1980 primary campaign, and I was fascinated to observe the minuet for news coverage that was danced by the politician and the TV journalist. It took place each afternoon, when everyone paused, the TV lights were on, the cameras pointed, and every Sam Donaldson on the tour sought to ask the provocative fifteen-second question which would elicit a sharp twenty-second response that would assure *him* a place on the evening news along with the candidate. (O. PETERSON, 1985, p. 203)

Rhetors do not always include all the parts of an argument as described by Toulmin for reasons of style and audience adaptation. The Toulmin model enables you to diagram units of argument in step-by-step fashion so that you can judge their validity, something you need to do as a critic to be able to judge whether or not the argument worked and why it failed or succeeded. Examine arguments you diagram using the Toulmin model to see what they present and what they seem to assume about the audience that read or heard them. Norman Lear's argument relies on personal observations to prove his claim and was probably appropriate because he was addressing members of the television industry. He could rely on their knowledge and experience to fill in some of the detail. This is our reconstruction of Lear's argument, which was offered without any qualifiers or rebuttals.

Claim: Television coverage of the 1984 presidential campaign was a triumph of images over substance.

Grounds 1: In 1980 I observed how television journalists controlled candidates. The network reporters asked provocative fifteen-second questions in hopes of getting candidates to give sharp twenty-second answers. From the reporter's perspective it is important that the reporter himself gets the television coverage, the candidate is only secondary to them.

Grounds 2: Evening news programs focus on the same question about how the candidate is doing in the polls. The "horse race" of candidates is more important to the news than the issues.

Warrant: The interests of television networks determine what story is most newsworthy and will receive coverage. Because decisions about what to cover are made by the networks, the real floor manager at a political convention is the person who points the camera.

Backing: Convention delegates no longer complain if television cameras and crews obstruct their line-of-sight to the convention; "spontaneous" demonstrations are timed to last twelve minutes to accommodate television; and politically powerful and respected politicians hope the television anchors will think them worthy of an interview.

As a critic, you want to know how an argument functioned, what purpose it served in the rhetorical act. To determine function, you want to identify the kinds of information the rhetor used and what reasoning techniques linked that information to the rhetor's claim in an argument.

The Enthymeme

The *enthymeme* was the standard unit of argument in classical rhetoric. Today, we regard the enthymeme more as a device for building an argument that draws heavily on audience knowledge. An enthymeme is an argument the rhetor creates by drawing on beliefs, attitudes, and values the audience possesses, making rhetoric a transaction between the rhetor and the audience (Campbell, 1982). Because success or failure of an enthymeme depends on whether or not the audience supplies what the rhetor expects them to, it is imperative for you as a critic to discover as much as you can about an audience in order to analyze and evaluate the effectiveness of enthymemes in the rhetorical act.

Two-thirds of "The Man with the Muckrake" was devoted to developing the argument that the man with a muckrake can do evil that outweighs any good he might do. Using anecdotes, stylistic devices, and historical references, Roosevelt made this argument in several ways, one of which stated the following:

> The men who with stern sobriety and truth assail the
> many evils of our time, whether in the public press, or in
> magazines, or in books, are the leaders and allies of all
> engaged in the work for social and political betterment.
> But if they give good reason for distrust of what they say,
> if they chill the ardor of those who demand truth as a
> primary virtue, they thereby betray the good cause,
> and play into the hands of the very men against whom
> they are nominally at war. (T. ROOSEVELT, 1926,
> p. 419)

Theodore Roosevelt provided the conclusion he wanted his audience to reach but did not name the muckrakers, good or bad, or make reference to a single example of muckraking. He relied on the audience to fill in the details from their own experiences and to provide the warrant that these excesses were typical. This had an interesting effect on the muckrakers in his audience. Upon learning of the president's theme in advance of the speech, Upton Sinclair was convinced that Roosevelt was attacking his work, *The Jungle,* and wrote a note and sent a telegram to the president objecting to his purpose (Beltz, 1969).

What was Theodore Roosevelt trying to accomplish with the muckrakers in his audience? Fearing that the ideas of socialism and class warfare were gaining popularity in Europe at that time, he wanted to invoke American values of justice and fair play. He also wanted the audience as a whole to reject the reform movement of the muckrakers and support his more moderate campaign for social change (Beltz, 1969). The validity of Roosevelt's enthymeme can be assessed by judging the appropriateness of his use of "the man with the muckrake" allegory from *Pilgrim's Progress* and his deliberate vagueness about who the bad muckrakers were.

Because the enthymeme is jointly constructed by the rhetor and the audience, it is necessary to reconstruct arguments in a rhetorical act that does not contain much evidence or that seems incomplete in some way. Reconstruction requires that you find out as much as possible about the audience the rhetor wanted to reach and their knowledge of the subject. Press coverage of Theodore Roosevelt's speech, his personal papers, historical accounts of the era, and investigative journalism provide abundant information on Roosevelt's perception of his audience. In assessing the validity of an enthymeme, your task is to discover the extent to which the audience participated, that is, filled in the missing parts to complete the argument, and then to judge the strength of the argument they had joined the rhetor in constructing.

Metaphor as Argument

The second contemporary concept of how arguments are structured is *metaphor,* which resembles the concept of the enthymeme in some ways. Like enthymeme, metaphor depends on having rhetor and audience share knowledge in some key area if it is to function properly as an argument. Theodore Roosevelt's speech was built around the metaphor of muckraking, and it could be analyzed in terms of how the metaphor served as an argument for Roosevelt's progressive reforms.

Metaphor has typically been considered as adornment, but argumentation theory has begun to recognize that metaphors function as arguments. An argument interprets the rhetorical situation, offering reasons why the audience should interpret reality as the rhetor does. Metaphors also offer reasons for believing something; but instead of supplying the audience with claims, grounds, evidence, warrants, and backing, the rhetor uses metaphor to simplify the message, relying exclusively on the communal knowledge shared by rhetor and audience.

The structure of a metaphor has two parts: tenor and vehicle. *Tenor* is the principal subject, the focus of the metaphor; *vehicle* is the secondary subject, the metaphor's frame of reference. The vehicle frames the principal subject, which the metaphor's argument addresses (Leff, 1983). By definition, a metaphor applies a word or phrase to something it does not literally fit.

Consider metaphor in a speech by AFL-CIO President Lane Kirkland marking the 100th anniversary of the American labor movement.

> He was the original interior decorator of this economic house of ill repute. Now that the sirens are sounding and the bust is due, he has his story ready. He was only the piano player in the parlor. He never knew what was going on upstairs. (O. PETERSON, 1982, pp. 157–158)

The tenor of the metaphor refers to David Stockman, President Ronald Reagan's chief economic adviser during the first year of his presidency, and the metaphor is an argument about Stockman's stewardship of the economy. The vehicle frames Stockman's performance in the context of activities in a house of prostitution, something not typically associated with presidential decision making.

How did Lane Kirkland's metaphor function as an argument? He did not think very highly of David Stockman's ideas and how those ideas had become part of the Reagan administration's economic policy. The speech was given after Stockman had resigned and was disclaiming the extent of his influence on economic policy. The argument said in essence: Do not believe what David Stockman says. The frame of reference created by a metaphor's vehicle creates a terministic screen for understanding something about its subject, conveying the rhetor's attitudes, values, and stand on issues in the rhetorical situation. Lane Kirkland might have chosen any of a number of vehicles to frame his metaphor, but he chose a house of prostitution to encourage his listeners to think of David Stockman's input and the resulting economic policy in terms of illicit acts, immorality, and facile excuses.

A metaphor joins tenor and vehicle to produce a meaning that neither has on its own, an argument that narrows the possible interpretations of the rhetorical situation to the one the rhetor wants the audience to accept. A rhetor's use of metaphor as argument must be analyzed on three levels: tenor, vehicle, and audience participation. First, examine the choice of tenor. Who or what was the focus of the metaphor? A metaphoric argument draws a conclusion about the principal subject that is the focus of the argument. Second, examine the vehicle the rhetor chose to frame the argument about the focus. In what kind of unusual context does the vehicle place the tenor? How did the vehicle serve as a terministic screen, revealing the rhetor's attitudes, values, and stand on issues? Finally, an argument created as a metaphor depends upon the audience's ability to supply key information about tenor or vehicle, or both. Did the audience have enough knowledge or the right knowledge to be able to appreciate the metaphor as an argument? Would anything have restrained the audience from supplying the information they possessed, preventing the metaphor from functioning as an argument?

Reconstructing the argument begins with finding the metaphor. In describing the rhetorical act, look for metaphors and decide whether or not they function as arguments. Not every metaphor is an argument; typical language use is filled with metaphors. A rhetor may also use a group of related metaphors, a *metaphor cluster,* to serve as an argument. Identify what serves as tenor and what serves as vehicle. Because the vehicle serves as the frame of reference and the rhetor's terministic screen, it is usually articulated in detail whereas the tenor may be unstated or only briefly mentioned. Reconstruct the metaphor and identify the kind of communal knowledge required from the audience. Describe the conclusion the metaphor points to, the rhetor's terministic screen, and the communal knowledge the audience must supply to make the metaphor function as an argument. As with the enthymeme, you judge the strength of the argument as it was jointly created by rhetor and audience.

Judging a rhetor's invention of arguments from the perspective of the traditional approach to criticism, regardless of whether they were fully articulated, enthymematic, or metaphoric, is ultimately a matter of determining how effectively they were crafted. Were the arguments capable of influencing the audience? Because an argument is reasoning to a conclusion on the basis of information, your reconstruction of a rhetor's arguments should examine the kind of information used, the technique of reasoning, and what was required of the audience. To facilitate this analysis, the following classification of types of information and reasoning is helpful.

In contemporary usage, we generally label the information used in an argument as *evidence*. Evidence has both logical and psychological properties. It has logical force because it is the basis for reasoning, the concept of grounding one's claims in the Toulmin model. Evidence also has psychological force because it creates or evokes experience and makes the argument real for the audience. In enthymeme and metaphor, it is often the audience that supplies part or all of the evidence to prove an argument. You must infer both psychological force and the amount and kind of evidence an audience supplied from its own resources.

A rhetor may supply evidence in abundance or simply cue the audience to call up their own experiences as evidence to ground claims. Your task in criticism is to identify the kinds of evidence the rhetor used or expected the audience to supply (see box on next page) and to evaluate its usefulness.

Common Types

of Evidence

Examples and *illustrations* describe events and phenomena. Examples are brief accounts and illustrations are more detailed.

Statistics present numerical information about people, events, and phenomena. Statistics have no meaning until interpreted in the context of the argument.

Scientific evidence is a report of laboratory or field experiments, usually stated as the results or findings of the effect of one variable on another.

Artifacts are exhibits, objects, audio- and videotapes, and other visual representations of things.

Premises are facts everyone acknowledges as true because they reflect uniform patterns of human experience.

Opinions are statements of an expert in a field, sometimes the rhetor, evaluating or interpreting relevant factual information in that field.

Beyond classifying the kinds of evidence used in the rhetorical act, you also must evaluate the reliability, quality, and consistency of that evidence. The *reliability* of evidence is determined by its accuracy and recency. The *quality* of evidence is assessed in terms of whether or not it is sufficient, representative, relevant, and clear. Evidence should be *internally consistent* so that it does not contradict itself and *externally consistent* so that it is not contradicted by the preponderance of other reliable, high-quality evidence on the subject. To evaluate use of evidence in an argument, you need to consider it in the historical context of the rhetorical situation, the adaptations the rhetor made in choosing evidence to use, and the degree of audience knowledge the rhetor's choices suggest.

Arguments use the reasoning process, the inferential leap that links evidence to the conclusion it supports. Whether you are using the Toulmin model, enthymeme, or metaphor to reconstruct a rhetor's arguments, it is this inferential leap that is most frequently implied rather than stated. Some rhetorical acts fail or are misunderstood because an audience was either unwilling to make that inferential leap or made some leap other than that expected by the rhetor. As you reconstruct the rhetor's arguments, identify the type of reasoning used or implied (see box on next page).

By analyzing a rhetorical act as a series of arguments made up of evidence, reasoning, and the conclusion they suggest, you can evaluate the choices the rhetor made in adapting to the audience and designing a fitting response to the

Common Patterns

of Reasoning

Cause-effect reasoning seeks a temporal connection between events and shows that one event produced another. Reasoning may link an effect to its cause or a cause to an effect. Causal reasoning explains how or why something happened.

Sign reasoning infers that some symptom, condition, or indicator points to the existence of a certain state of affairs. Sign reasoning describes a situation.

Generalization is an inference that what is true of a series of sample cases is true of the whole class or group from which those cases were drawn.

Parallel case reasoning infers that because a known case is similar to an unknown case in certain critical ways, it is possible to speculate reliably about other properties of the unknown case. This is a common reasoning pattern in arguments about the future or a proposed course of action.

Analogy attempts to show resemblances between events that are otherwise entirely dissimilar. Such "apples and oranges" comparisons commonly use figurative language for stylistic and psychological effect. Metaphoric arguments frequently rely on this form of reasoning.

Definition attempts to classify or categorize.

Dilemma shows that in an either-or situation a choice must be made between equally unacceptable alternatives.

exigence in the rhetorical situation. These arguments are probably more than logic alone because each can contribute to the creation of an emotional climate.

As part of adapting the message to the audience, the process of invention includes the rhetor's use of psychological proof, pathos. Psychological appeals either create a state of mind in the audience or appeal to an already existing one. These appeals attempt to induce an audience to respond by arousing emotions such as fear, satisfaction, pride, or suspicion.

In analyzing and evaluating a rhetor's use of psychological appeals, you want to consider how the rhetor drew on the audience's beliefs, motives, desires, and values. An example of how a rhetor builds a psychological climate is found in a speech by Chancellor Dr. Joseph S. Murphy, University of New York, to members of the American Association of University Professors on 14 November 1985.

In recent days we have seen this Administration announce its plans to use federal funds—Star Wars funds—to lure faculty into personally lucrative research efforts. They promise that technology developed with public sector defense grants can then be peddled for individual gain in private sector markets. Coercion can come in many forms, and we may soon have evidence on this issue that grants can be as inimical to free thought as is out and out censorship.

The drive to turn universities into tools of economic productivity, with the encouragement of more contractual linkages between the campus and the corporation, poses another set of threats; how many institutions will jeopardize big dollars for the sake of a few faculty members lingering loudly outside the dominant consensus and criticizing capitalism in general and the affiliated corporations in particular? As colleges compete for more private sector dollars, how many will be immune from the fear that a negative press created by dissident professors will alienate potential clients, as it might alienate potential students and potential donors? (O. PETERSON, 1986, p. 104)

Dr. Murphy's questions were designed to instill fear of how economic and political pressure might restrict academic freedom. He provided no specific details, relying instead on the audience of university professors to supply their own examples.

Psychological appeals do not exist in a vacuum. They frequently emerge from the rhetorical situation and are deeply rooted in the values and experiences of rhetor and audience. The medium used to present a message influences the rhetor's options for creating psychological appeals. For example, a speaker often uses stylistic devices, such as the rhetorical questions in Dr. Murphy's speech, to produce the desired psychological effect.

Organization

All rhetorical acts have a pattern, the sequence in which units of argument and other materials are presented. A pattern of organization helps the listener, reader, or viewer follow and recall the message. As a critic, you want to determine how the pattern of organization helped or hindered the audience's understanding of the message. The best way to determine the pattern of a rhetorical act is to make an outline of it.

In Chapter 2, we discussed the common patterns of organization used to sequence rhetorical acts: chronological, narrative, topical, problem-solution, cause-effect, and climax. Messages typically follow the form: introduction, purpose statement, discussion or body, and conclusion. How a rhetor organized a message may have been constrained by style, choices about units of argument, the media chosen to convey the message, or some aspect of the rhetorical situation.

Besides providing a framework for arguments, the organizational pattern of a rhetorical act establishes emphasis. An idea the rhetor wants to highlight usually receives the most time and development. Theodore Roosevelt had three main points in "The Man with the Muckrake," but his discussion of the evils of muckraking received more attention than his other points on the need for a progressive tax and the need to supervise corporations engaged in interstate commerce. Today, few people associate the last two points with the speech.

Style

The overriding purpose in evaluating style is to determine how it contributed to achieving the rhetor's purpose and ability to manage the rhetorical situation. Style is artistic, a conglomeration of language use, sentence structure, vocabulary, formality of tone, the denotative and connotative properties of language, and the devices of figurative language. What constitutes good or effective style is a matter of both personal taste and cultural norms.

Style is influenced by media choice and the rhetorical situation. Oral style tends to be less formal, with more repetition and colloquial language. It emphasizes the use of personal pronouns and direct questions to the audience. Written style is more formal, demands correct grammar and sentence structure, and relies less on repetition. Other media such as film and videotape can bring visual elements to style, taking the critic into nonverbal concepts of style.

The traditional approach to criticism pays special attention to public speaking and oral style. The hallmarks of good speech style today are clarity, vividness, and appropriateness (DeVito, 1987). The main objective of style in speaking is to achieve clarity through economical use of language, specific terminology, and the use of transitions, summaries, and enumeration. Vividness is achieved by using active verbs, strong verbs, figures of speech, and imagery. Appropriateness of style is achieved if a message is adapted to an audience through the use of familiar terms, if the language is socially acceptable and if the style matches the degree of formality suggested by the rhetorical situation.

The greatest cultural variation in what constitutes good style probably lies in the use of figurative language. The poetic dimension of rhetorical acts lies in the use of such embellishments. From the colonial era to the beginning of the twentieth century, American oratory tended to be ornate, using complex sentence structure, literary references, and elaborate figures of speech. Even though a less ornate style is preferred in contemporary speaking and writing, the devices of adornment identified in Chapter 2 are common to language use today. You can analyze and evaluate a rhetor's style by means of these devices of language.

Stylistic devices are an inherent part of a rhetor's language. They add the artistic element to rhetorical activity and are particularly important in assessing how a rhetor created a psychological climate for his or her message. In criticizing a rhetor's style or use of stylistic devices, remember that you must go beyond identifying examples of particular devices in the message to interpreting and judging the impact, quality, and appropriateness of the rhetor's management of style.

Delivery

Criticism of the delivery of a message requires thorough knowledge of the medium of its presentation. Were camera techniques, color, special print faces, or layout design used? Were costumes and sets involved? In criticizing delivery, you want to consider the quality, effectiveness, and appropriateness of the medium of transmission.

In public speaking, which is the emphasis of the traditional approach, delivery has come to mean those nonverbal aspects of a speaker's presentation of the speech. Ineffective or poor delivery detracts from a message. Delivery is related to the rhetor's ethos; poor delivery can create a negative image whereas powerful delivery can enhance a rhetor's reputation.

Delivery is judged in terms of how well speakers use voice, gesture, body movement, and space to convey emotions and attitudes. The speaker's ability to project confidence, enthusiasm, sincerity, irony, and fear is more often a matter of delivery than the words and phrases used in the speech. Delivery creates the persona the speaker is trying to project. A speaker may wish to be thought of as a teacher, judge, parent, preacher, or hero. The persona should fit the rhetorical situation and be appropriate to the rhetor, message, and audience.

The Traditional Approach and Critical Evaluation

Because its philosophy of human communication is both pragmatic and rational, the traditional approach places the most importance on the judgmental standards of results and truth. As a critic, you want to know the consequences of the rhetorical act. Was the rhetor's persuasive purpose accomplished because the audience accepted the truthfulness of the rhetor's view of reality?

The Results Standard

The results standard of judgment is the cornerstone of the traditional approach. Because the assumption behind the traditional approach is that rhetorical activity is reasoned discourse, evaluating whether the rhetorical act accomplished anything is the most important standard to apply. The worth of a rhetorical act is measured in terms of how well the rhetor's management of credibility with the audience, the occasion, and the elements of message design were able to elicit a response from the audience.

In using the traditional approach, you should judge how all aspects of the rhetor-audience-message relationship contribute to the rhetor's ability to achieve his purpose. Results should be considered on the short-term basis of the immediate response to the rhetor's message and its long-term effects.

Judging the results of a rhetorical act by using concepts from the traditional approach, you should examine what happened to the rhetor, the audience, and society at large as a result of the rhetorical act. Was the act part of an ongoing debate? How did this particular act fit into that debate? To determine results, you should examine news reports, polls, commentaries, reviews, editorials, and historical accounts of the era to determine what happened as a result of the rhetorical act.

The Truth Standard

The traditional approach's rational philosophy of communication requires that if you adopt it as a critic, you are committed to judging the nature and quality of the rhetor's reasoning. You want to determine the extent to which the rhetor's use of argument created probable truth. To make judgments about truthfulness, you must evaluate the logical adequacy of a rhetor's arguments and test the quality and sufficiency of the evidence and reasoning techniques. Compare the rhetor's analysis of the issues with how others in the rhetorical environment analyzed them, and consider the adaptations the rhetor made in tailoring arguments to the needs of the audience.

The Ethical Standard

Because the traditional approach focuses on the rhetor, the ethical standard of judgment is also important in criticism using this approach. Discussion of the rhetor's prior reputation and management of ethos in the rhetorical situation is part of your application of the ethical standard. As you examine the rhetor's background and what he or she did to create credibility in the rhetorical act, you will be concerned with the rhetor's ethics. Because they have the ability to create tone and climate, elements of style and delivery can be part of the ethical dimension of a rhetorical situation. Did the rhetor honestly represent the views of the society, him- or herself, and the situation?

The Aesthetic Standard

Finally, your consideration of rhetor, message, and audience might focus on the artistic elements of the rhetorical act. The creation of logically cogent arguments, the flow of a well-organized message, the enhancement of language through devices of adornment, and the nonverbal properties of delivery can all be considered under the aesthetic standard of judgment.

Uses and Limitations

Traditional rhetorical criticism has always concerned itself with public speaking and is most applicable to communication forms that closely resemble public speeches. Because its treatment of all parts of the act of speaking is so thorough, it is still one of the most useful approaches for analyzing and critiquing speeches. The critic may focus on a single speech or speaker, a series of speeches or a debate on a single issue, or the use of speaking by a social movement identified with a particular issue. This is the greatest advantage of using the traditional approach, and also its greatest limitation.

The chief limitation of the traditional approach is that it is best suited to criticizing speeches. In the past two decades, sensitivity has increased to the fact that rhetorical acts occur in forms other than public speaking and that electronic media have altered our concept of the public speech. In 1965, Edwin Black's *Rhetorical Criticism: A Study in Method* attacked the traditional approach because it limits criticism to oral discourse and relies too much on the results standard of judgment. However, he neither advocated abandoning the traditional approach nor claimed that studying public speaking was a pointless endeavor. Black's goal was to force critics to think about adapting and expanding the traditional approach to fit changes in our culture.

The study of public speeches has experienced a renaissance as we near the end of this century (Lucas, 1988), and the traditional approach is still a respected technique for criticism (Andrews, 1983; Mohrmann and Leff, 1974). The traditional approach focuses directly on the process of rhetorical activity and the relationship between rhetor and audience. It provides a complete set of principles that facilitate full consideration of a rhetorical act.

Summary

For much of its history, speech education and rhetorical criticism meant applying principles of rhetorical theory derived from classical sources to public speaking. Most criticism in the traditional mode has focused on "great" speakers and speeches as social history, the source of ideas that stimulated campaigns, social movements, and influenced attitudes and values.

Because it rests on a philosophy of humans as rational beings, capable of making choices and desiring the truth, the traditional approach emphasizes techniques of arguing. In tradional criticism, critics focus on the relationship between rhetor, message, and audience, asking what problems or constraints the rhetor overcame, what choices the rhetor made, and how these choices helped accomplish the rhetor's purpose.

The traditional approach has had a lasting influence on subsequent theory development. Traditional concepts of rhetoric serve as the starting point for developing new theories or for providing contrast when cultural differences dictate a shift in thought. Perhaps the most enduring contribution of the traditional approach is that subsequent theory development has consistently addressed the rhetor-message-audience model of communication.

Suggested Readings

Examples of Criticism

BEHL, W.A. (1947).   Theodore Roosevelt's principles of invention. *Speech Monographs, 14,* 93–110.

> This is one of the better examples of the way rhetorical criticism was done in the past using concepts from classical rhetoric. Behl uses Aristotle's theory of invention to study Theodore Roosevelt's speaking, going into great depth on the sources and applications of his ethos, logos, and pathos. This article is well-written, an excellent resource if you are studying Roosevelt and a good example of in-depth criticism of the rhetorical activity of an individual rhetor.

FULKERSON, R.R. (1979).   The public letter as a rhetorical form: Structure, logic, and style in King's "Letter from Birmingham Jail." *Quarterly Journal of Speech, 65,* 121–136.

> Some modes of written communication, such as a letter to the editor, resemble speeches in structure, logic, and style. Fulkerson looks at the use of argument and the personal tone that Dr. Martin Luther King, Jr. achieved in his use of the public letter as part of the civil rights campaign. This is an excellent adaptation of the traditional approach to the study of a social movement and a significant rhetorical event from it.

HENRY, D. (1988).   The rhetorical dynamics of Mario Cuomo's 1984 keynote address: Situation, speaker, metaphor. *Southern Speech Communication Journal, 53,* 105–120.

> This critical essay examines the unique constraints on a political convention keynote address. Henry explains how Cuomo's speech was a fitting response to multiple audiences and how Cuomo's use of invention made the speech memorable. The use of metaphor as argument rather than as a stylistic device is the focus of criticism in this essay. This well-written article is a good model of criticism of metaphor as argument.

MEDHURST, M.J. (1987).   Eisenhower's "Atoms for Peace" speech: A case study in the use of language. *Communication Monographs, 54,* 204–220.

> This Eisenhower speech is analyzed as operating on several levels, a rhetorical maneuver to gain a psychological victory over the Soviets in the cold war. Medhurst reconstructs the explicit and implicit arguments of the speech and examines the rough drafts of the speech to demonstrate how Eisenhower's speech writers influenced the development of his position. This article is an excellent example of how to analyze the rhetorical situation, how to judge the role speech writers play in rhetorical activity, and how to use concepts of argument in the traditional approach to criticism.

ZAREFSKY, D. (1986).   The Lincoln-Douglas debates revisited: The evolution of public argument. *Quarterly Journal of Speech, 72,* 162–184.

This article examines the debates between Abraham Lincoln and Stephen Douglas in 1858 from the perspective of how both men managed invention. Zarefsky employs concepts of logic to analyze how each candidate approached the issues. The debates are viewed in the context of the rhetorical situation created by the Dred Scott case and the proposal to admit Kansas to the Union as a slave state. This is an excellent example of historical criticism that focuses on issue development and the role of debates in political campaigns.

Resources for Doing Criticism

RYBACKI, K.C. AND RYBACKI, D.J. (1991). *Advocacy and opposition: An introduction to argumentation* (2nd ed.). Englewood Cliffs, NJ: Prentice-Hall.

> This basic text on argumentation offers a more complete discussion of the Toulmin model, uses and tests of evidence, kinds of reasoning, and fallacies in logic than we have provided in this chapter. You may also find the chapters on propositions of fact, value, and policy useful if you are doing an in-depth analysis of the logic of argument.

THONSSEN, L., BAIRD, A.C., AND BRADEN, W.W. (1970). *Speech criticism* (2nd ed.). New York: Ronald.

> This is the most complete treatment of the traditional approach written in this century. It follows the five canons and offers a detailed discussion of the history of rhetoric. The most comprehensive list of devices of style you will ever need is contained in this book.

4

The

Dramatistic

Approach

What happens when a racist remark by a public official creates a rhetorical situation? At the height of the 1976 presidential campaign, Secretary of Argriculture Earl Butz was on his way to Arizona to dedicate a screwworm facility. He decided to share a joke with his first-class cabin mates Pat Boone, Sonny Bono, and John Dean. Dean recalled the joke in a *Rolling Stone* article; other journalists repeated it in print, subsequently connecting it to Butz; and the racist tone of his humor became a front-page story. The secretary of agriculture became a public embarrassment to Republican candidate Gerald Ford and a threat to the success of his presidential campaign. President Ford fired Earl Butz, a ritual form of public sacrifice, in an attempt to cleanse the Republican party and his candidacy of any stains of Butz's sin (Klumpp and Hollihan, 1979).

Racism, public and private, has been a frequent, often violent, problem in America. For too much of our history, race has determined one's place in the social hierarchy. Media coverage of Butz's racist joke caused millions of Americans to discuss the incident and confront the continuing existence of racism. How is a ritual sacrifice rhetorical? What exigences were created by the racial overtones of the joke? Was the sacrifice of Butz's public persona an adequate response to the problem of racism in society? How can we increase public awareness of lingering racism in private life? These questions are addressed from the perspective of the dramatistic approach in the article by James F. Klumpp and Thomas A. Hollihan, "Debunking the Resignation of Earl Butz: Sacrificing an Official Racist," listed in the suggested readings at the end of this chapter.

The dramatistic approach is based on a philosophy that embodies William Shakespeare's claim that "all the world's a stage." In dramatism, human behavior is seen as a series of social dramas in which humans are *actors* performing *scripts* on the public stage of their lives. When a rhetor makes a speech, writes a book, draws a cartoon, or makes a film, he is acting an episode in a social drama, living in and responding to society. Dramatism is more than a metaphor connecting rhetorical activity to theatrical performance. The creation of a rhetorical act is a choice or series of choices for which the rhetor must take reponsibility. There is a strong ethical dimension to the way the dramatistic approach to criticism examines these choices.

The philosophy that life can best be understood as a social drama is not the sole province of rhetorical criticism. Related disciplines such as sociology, psychology, law, political science, and history use the concept of dramatism to study the relationship between the use of symbols in social structures and the ability of leaders to gain and/or maintain power. In rhetorical theory, two critical approaches have developed from the concept of life as a social drama. In this chapter, we examine the approach developed by Kenneth Burke. A second critical approach, fantasy theme analysis, will be discussed in the next chapter.

Rhetoric as Symbolic Action

The first major concept in Burke's theory of rhetoric is that when people use language—that is, verbal symbols—they are acting in response to some situation. Humans are symbol-using creatures; they make symbols, use and misuse them, and say what they are not. We human beings invented the negative (Burke, 1969a), which enables us to moralize. Symbols enable us to say what is permitted and what is prohibited behavior (Golden et al., 1989).

In Kenneth Burke's dramatistic philosophy, the ability to symbolize verbally is the defining characteristic of humanity. As symbol users, humans are also actors. Verbal symbols enable us to perform many kinds of acts: to define, to accept, to reject, and to pursue the ultimate good. Communication explains what being human is, what problems humans face, how humans should act, and how the ideas and concepts of other humans are to be used (V.L. Holland, 1955). In dramatism, the essence of being human is being caught up in the tension between motion and action.

Motion occurs in the natural realm of the physical world: birth, death, the change of seasons, and the physical drives to maintain life. Nature does not use symbols to change the face of the world (Burke, 1966). Erosion, fall color changes, and the birth of a child are physical, not symbolic, processes. *Action* is the counterforce to motion in the substance of humanity: Nature moves; people act. People are still part of nature, but they use action to overcome nature and to respond to situations in the natural realm. For a demonstration of this, examine the rhetorical activity that occurs after a natural disaster causes a massive loss of life or property.

Action and the sense of morality that comes from acting differentiate humans from the rest of the creatures in the natural world. Instead of just letting things happen, people give elaborate reasons for why they eat, defend territory, take mates, and so on. We create, we act through rituals, ceremonies, procedures, and ideologies—all made up of symbols—to separate ourselves from merely existing in nature. Actions are the dramatic processes we use to separate ourselves from nature (Combs and Mansfield, 1976).

Why is the motion-action dichotomy important to the rhetorical critic? The view of people as symbol using means that our behavior is primarily rhetorical. Action is language using. Whatever we try to *do,* we use language as the mechanism for doing it. This is why Burke equates language and action. When a rhetor perceives something to be wrong, unjust, or immoral, he uses language to address his grievance. Famine in Africa, acquired immune deficiency syndrome, and the homeless in America are examples of wrong that individuals, and even groups, are powerless to overcome. Solving these problems takes massive cooperative effort. Symbols in the form of speeches, songs, demonstrations, documentary and commercial films, editorials, and fund-raising events are used in an attempt to forge a cooperative consensus. These are all actions. As a philosophy of human communication, dramatism broadens the concept of rhetorical activity. Burke's dramatism sees all of literature and speech as a response to human situations in which each verbal expression has rhetorical potential.

The Function of Rhetoric

The traditional concept of the function of rhetoric, handed down from classical works, was *persuasion,* the rhetor's deliberate use of language designed to accomplish a speaker's purpose. Burke offers a new way to view the function of rhetoric: *identification.* In our "natural" state, each person is unique, separated from all others because each possesses unique values, opinions, and meanings based on individual experience. Misunderstandings come about because of this uniqueness. Humans had to become symbol users precisely because the symbol is the only way to overcome uniqueness. Symbols represent a common core of interest, need, and experience. For any common action to take place, common interests must be publicly proclaimed. Rhetoric, then, is the use of language in symbolic form to unite people, to induce cooperation.

Notice what this means to you as a critic. Rhetorical criticism focuses on language. In any rhetorical act, the symbols used by the rhetor reveal his attitudes. Because part of the critic's task is to discover as much as possible concerning the rhetor's motives for creating a rhetorical act, the more that is known about symbol making in a rhetorical act, the more informed the evaluation of it will be.

Motive

Rhetors use symbols to respond to both human and natural events (action and motion). What can be learned from studying this use of symbols? First, reality is constructed through symbol use. Symbols have meaning in terms of situations. A rhetor's act reflects his perception of reality, even that part of nature he and the audience are experiencing directly is perceived through symbol use. Second, symbols are used to name or label things, to characterize relationships and functions among things as friendly or unfriendly (Burke, 1961). This naming and labeling reveal the rhetor's attitudes or motives.

Knowing about symbols is important for the functioning critic. Rhetorical acts concern society's problems. Symbols used in verbal acts are strategies for overcoming or coping with social problems. In a hostage crisis, we may not be able to free our hostages, but tying yellow ribbons to trees symbolizes our concern for them, our desire that they return, and our determination to persevere in our efforts to free them until they are safely home. Due to uniqueness, each rhetor has her own symbols for reality. One rhetor may label something "friendly" while a competing rhetor labels it "unfriendly." Part of the critic's task is to understand a symbol of reality and determine its sources.

A motive is the combination of language use and action in a given situation. A critic determines the rhetor's attitudes by examining the language symbols chosen for the rhetorical act. Rhetors do not respond to situations in the ways they do without cause. The critic must determine what constraints operated in the situation, and the concept of motive helps her discover them.

Rhetors have strategies for responding to social circumstances. One symbol or group of symbols is chosen over others as a result of the rhetor's characterizations of things into friendly or unfriendly categories. If a rhetor labels an event as friendly, he has been constrained to do so by something in the situation. Yellow is usually associated with cowardice in western culture, but a popular song made the act of tying a yellow ribbon to a tree symbolically friendly.

This may seem like a very complex way of saying that rhetorical activity is not arbitrary. The point of Burke's division of life into action and motion is that both can be present in a rhetorical situation, but it is action that humans use to change situations. Even though communication has "natural" properties, it is not critiqued in terms of the neurological activity of the brain in processing symbols or explained in terms of the production of sound by the vocal mechanism. Rhetorical critics want to discover how and why symbols become meaningful in a situation and what impels a rhetor to choose one symbol over another.

Society Is Dramatistic

The second major concept of Burke's dramatistic approach is that society is created and maintained through symbols, which are used to control behavior (Burke, 1966). All social interaction is based on appeals to others to respond in a specified manner, to satisfy some need, be it social, physical, personal, or metaphysical (Duncan, 1968). Human action involves using symbols, and social drama is the form this action takes (Burke, 1966). A *drama* implies the presence of conflict in the social order. Society represents a dramatistic process of hierarchy, acceptance and rejection, guilt, purification, and redemption.

Hierarchy

Social relationships have structures ranging from informal with loose structure (a group of friends who attend a football game together) to formal with rigid structure (the U.S. Air Force). Hierarchies in the social order are structures that divide people into categories that are based on the power—social, economic, or political—that they possess. Power is never evenly distributed in a society. Some people always have authority over others, and power determines this authority. When the power structure changes, shifts in authority usually follow.

Hierarchy is an ordering principle characteristic of all societies regardless of their political ideology. A hierarchy is a complex of relationships. In her various relationships in the hierarchy, an individual is superior, subordinate, or equal, with passage from one position to another determined by birth, aging, and death (Duncan, 1968). Occupancy of some positions in a hierarchy are fixed, but even these can be filled by other people when their passage is sanctioned by appropriate symbolization. When the president dies in office, the vice president is constitutionally sanctioned to move up in the hierarchy after taking the oath of office. If you join a social organization, an initiation ceremony, which in some instances may be as simple as paying a membership fee, transforms you from a nonmember into a member.

Hierarchies are not as inflexible as they might seem. Because change is inherent in both action and motion, hierarchies always try to provide for orderly change. "Passage always involves desanctifying the old, providing bridges from the old to the new, and entering—or, more rarely creating—a new role" (Duncan, 1968, p. 34). Hierarchies operate according to rules, which are often codified into constitutions or laws in political, corporate, and religious hierarchies.

One's role in a hierarchy is played through symbol manipulation. Leaders dramatize symbols of power to induce members lower in the hierarchy to follow. Symbols of loyalty and acceptance are invoked to persuade superiors to accept followers. Symbols of agreement create equal relationships. All of this is done in accordance with the established rules of the hierarchy (Duncan, 1968). A leader, the Bank of America, solicits you as a follower; you receive an invitation to apply for their credit card. You provide symbols of loyalty, your credit rating, in order to be accepted as a card holder. Symbols of agreement include the issuance of monthly statements and equal treatment for all card holders with respect to interest rates, payment schedules, errors in billing, and the procedure to follow if the card is lost or stolen.

Acceptance and Rejection

A drama implies conflict, and hierarchies provide the stimulus of dramatic action. Because symbol use can be positive or negative, friendly or unfriendly, people have the ability to accept or reject the social order and their position in its hierarchy. Acceptance is a positive or friendly reaction to the hierarchy; rejection is a negative or unfriendly reaction. Rejection results in alienation or disorder.

To the extent that you accept the rule that you must pay interest on the unpaid balance of your credit card account, you do not perceive interest charges as unfriendly. Many persons, however, have rejected the banking hierarchy's rules, not about interest but about the rate of interest charged on credit cards. They have begun to characterize their relationship as unfriendly, questioning the right of the hierarchy to put that rule into effect at the present level of interest.

Guilt, Purification, and Redemption

As a social critic, Kenneth Burke tended to see all hierarchies and social orders as continually engaged in dramas. Action occurs because people object to the functions and relationships imposed by hierarchical structure. Burke (1965) suggested that this objection is similar to objections to the Christian doctrine of original sin; rejection of some part of a hierarchy always occurs because people find it impossible to comply with all the demands it makes on them. Furthermore, the individual has to cope with multiple hierarchies. We are all members of the political hierarchy of the nation and of social groups, each with its own hierarchy, including family, career, church, school, interest groups—and more. When the demands imposed by one hierarchy conflict with those of another, rejection of one must necessarily occur.

In rhetorical criticism, the object of criticism frequently involves a rhetor's advocacy of the supremacy of one hierarchy over another. As more women with young children have entered the labor force and professions, the hierarchy of family versus the hierarchy of career has become the subject of rhetorical activity. The birth of a child may be a motion, but deciding how best to raise that child is a matter of action, as the debate over child care has shown.

According to Burke (1965), rejecting a hierarchy, such as a woman's rejection of the traditional role of mother in the family hierarchy, produces a feeling of guilt. Because society is continually engaged dramatically, it also exists in a state of perpetual guilt, an original sin caused by the very nature of the hierarchy. The working mother is continually made to feel guilty by a hierarchy that dictates "A woman's place is in the home." As a psychological state, guilt is uncomfortable because it leads to fear, stress, and potential loss of order (Duncan, 1968). Guilt causes relationships to be challenged, power to change hands, and concepts of appropriate behavior to change. The working mother demands that her role in the family hierarchy be changed from that of sole caregiver to co-provider. The working mother may transfer her guilt to the government, her employer, or her spouse. Such challenges and demands disrupt the social order; so, from time to time, public action is needed to remove the guilt. Public dramas purify the guilty by purging, in symbolic form, that which has made them feel guilty.

To resolve the guilt, two forms of *ritual purification* are common in the social drama, mortification and victimage. *Mortification* involves personal sacrifice by the guilty. The individual or group experiencing guilt makes a symbolic offering to appease society and thus restore balance to the social order. A person accused of wrongdoing acknowledges it publicly and may offer an explanation or perform some other act of contrition. Recognizing the loss of public confidence because of his role in the Watergate cover-up, Richard Nixon resigned from office. Vanessa

Williams gave up her crown as Miss America when it became known that she had once posed nude for photographs.

Dramas are more often based on the principle of *victimage,* in which a scapegoat is publicly saddled with the guilt (Duncan, 1968). A presidential adviser rather than the president is made the scapegoat for a failed policy. The commander of the U.S.S. *Stark* was blamed for the loss of life when his ship was attacked in the Persian Gulf and the crewmen who were monitoring the Aegis weapons system on the U.S.S. *Vincennes* were blamed for shooting down an Iranian airliner, rather than blaming the president for the policy that placed those ships in the area.

The act of purification must be appropriate to the sin of the guilty for the drama to succeed as an act of redemption. The extent of self-sacrifice or scapegoating must equal the degree of guilt caused by the rejection of the social order (Scott and Brock, 1972), otherwise redemption is not achieved. Removal from office or loss of position in the hierarchy may be either insufficient or excessive punishment relative to the disruption suffered by the social order.

The relationships among rejection, guilt, purification, and redemption are very much a part of our social and literary history. In colonial America, British rule was viewed as unfair by the colonists. The guilt resulting from disrupting ties to the mother country was removed by blaming the Parliament for its failure to understand the needs of the American colonies. Redemption was achieved through blood sacrifice, the complete rejection of the social order, and its replacement by a new one, the United States of America. Three-quarters of a century later, Harriet Beecher Stowe's *Uncle Tom's Cabin* rejected the hierarchy created by slavery. The popularity of the novel helped spread the message of abolition, contributing to the secession of southern states and the Civil War.

You may recognize religious overtones in dramatism and its similarity to concepts of sin, confession, and absolution achieved through the mystery of priesthood. The dramatistic process is based on the notion that we are imperfect creatures who appeal to an authority higher than ourselves for absolution from our own weaknesses (Rueckert, 1963). The religious metaphor of dramatism helps to explain why a society is in a continuous state of enacting dramas. Because they are created by imperfect humans, social hierarchies always have flaws that lead to their rejection. Sometimes the muddle of rejection and guilt is so great that only an event *deus ex machina,* an artificial or unexplainable intervention, can perform the purification ritual. This is the explanation of the U.S. failure to heed signs the Japanese might attack Pearl Harbor offered by the revisionist historians, who suggest a "sneak" attack was the only way President Franklin Roosevelt could overcome the opposition of isolationist senators such as Burton K. Wheeler to U.S. involvement in World War II.

Kenneth Burke's concepts of humans as symbol-using creatures and society as a dramatistic process are descriptive and analytical tools for rhetorical criticism that enable you as a critic to view communication from the frame of reference of a social drama. These concepts give us a way of talking about individuals and groups as they respond to their environment. In the outline of the critical process in Chapter 2, one of your tasks was said to be to characterize the rhetorical situation. Describing the rhetorical situation as a social drama involving the rejection of a hierarchy followed by the redemptive process of purification is one way to explain why a rhetorical act occurred and what constrained it. The dramatistic approach has even more to offer, however. Burke discussed two additional concepts that help the critic to structure criticism. *Identification* is the concept used to find attitudes or motives that reveal what the drama is about; the *pentad* offers a system for describing these attitudes as they are articulated in the drama.

Identification

People became symbol users to compensate for those factors of individuality that divide us from one another. Burke's theory of rhetoric is based on how people communicate in pluralistic societies: Rhetoric must be viewed as identification rather than persuasion because its function is to proclaim unity (Burke, 1969a). "A is not identical with his colleague B. But insofar as their interests are joined, A is *identified* with B. Or he may *identify himself* with B even when their interests are not joined, if he assumes that they are, or is persuaded to believe so" (Burke, 1969a, p. 20). Thus, in Burke's dramatistic approach, rhetoric is a symbolic means of creating cooperation.

People use language symbolically in forming attitudes and altering the attitudes of others. One of the ways rhetors alter attitudes is by creating new patterns of identification, causing audiences to see their interests as joined with those of the rhetor. The great paradox of humanity is that we exist in a state of being simultaneously divided and unified. Each person and group has an identity that makes them unique and distinguishes them from all other persons and groups. Burke (1969a) called this uniqueness *substance*. Identification is necessary to overcome substance so that the "acting together" that is necessary for societies and their attendant hierarchies to survive can occur. Unity is created through rhetorical activity in which "common sensations, concepts, images, ideas, [and] attitudes" are symbolically expressed (Burke, 1969a, p. 21). An individual rhetor's use of language will reveal the substance (identity) out of which he expects to achieve identification between himself and the receiver of the message. This substance is directly related to the motive and constrains the rhetorical situation. Remember that some rhetors will speak in defense of the hierarchy; not every rhetorical act is a rejection of the social order.

The usefulness of the dramatistic approach in criticism relies heavily on the interpretation of the rhetorical act in terms of the rhetorical situation. "Burke contends that the rhetorical critic must understand the substance of man, what he is, what his problems are, why he acts as he does, and how he molds the thoughts and concepts of others" (V.L. Holland, 1955, p. 352). It is out of substance, his uniqueness, that the rhetor creates strategies for achieving identification. Rhetors can attempt to create one of two states: unification, drawing people together in one great unified mass, or faction, making a select group aware of a common identity that separates them from all other groups in society.

A labor song written for striking freight handlers in New York City in 1882 demonstrates the use of substance:

> *There's Field, Jay Gould, and Vanderbilt, their millions they*
> *did save*
> *By paying starvation wages and working men like slaves;*
> *They hum around honest labor as the bee does the flower,*
> *And suck the sweetness of your toil for 17 cents an hour.*
>
> REFRAIN
> *We're on the strike and we won't go back,*
> *Our claims are just and right;*
> *Trade unions and the public press*
> *Will help us with all their might.*
> (FONER, 1975, pp. 238–239)

The song is a factionalizing message whose purpose is to reinforce the separate identity of union members striking against their employer. It names the "unfriendlies," the railroad barons, and reinforces one element of the substance of unionism, the right to strike for fair wages.

Identification is an important critical device, helping to structure insights into a rhetor's handling of the rhetorical situation. Rhetors use a series of strategies for unifying or factionalizing an audience. A rhetor has attitudes about ideas, people, and institutions, all the things that make up his society. The language—the rhetor's use of symbols—will reflect those attitudes. Likewise, an audience has attitudes, and how they interpret the rhetor's symbols reflects their attitudes. Identification occurs when the audience accepts and rejects the same things the rhetor does (Scott and Brock, 1972). As a critical device, identification is applied directly to a rhetor's language. The critic looks for *rhetorical strategies,* groupings of language that show the rhetor's attitude toward the hierarchy and how he viewed the process of guilt, purification, and redemption.

Rhetorical Strategies

A rhetorical strategy is any choice made by the rhetor that enables him to fulfill the need to respond to a specific constraint in the rhetorical situation. Rhetorical strategies are comprised of the entire stock of verbal behavior available to message makers: naming, argumentation, narration, definition, description, repetition, use of figurative language, patterns of organization, and any device of adornment. Strategies also include the role the rhetor plays relative to the audience: interpreter of meaning, exhorter for a cause, justifier of what was done, explainer of reality, and so on. Rhetorical strategies cannot be catalogued in a master list of all strategies. Each rhetor approaches a rhetorical situation from his own point of view.

Rhetorical acts, however, tend to fall into genres, categories of rhetorical acts having similar properties. There are, for example, rhetorical acts of eulogy, inauguration, self-defense, and justification. Genres of rhetoric exist because they fit recurring problems, issues, or situations. Individual rhetorical acts within a particular genre share features of style and philosophy, enabling critics to talk about them as a group (Campbell, 1972).

The concept of genres of rhetorical activity is not new, nor is it Burke's creation. Classical rhetoricians categorized three kinds of oratory: forensic, deliberative, and epideictic. When you view life as a social drama, you have the critical opportunity to consider the recurring patterns of action, unique strategies, that are found in particular types of dramas. The concept of rhetorical strategies, with certain strategies recurring in particular genres, is an idea that is widely used in rhetorical criticism.

The Pentad

In the dramatistic approach, discovery of a rhetor's development of identification uncovers the meaning of a message. The message communicates the rhetor's view of reality as she uses verbal symbols to express her attitudes toward the social hierarchy and the process of guilt, purification, and redemption. The critic looks for the rhetorical strategies used to represent the drama. How does the critic find these? Burke (1969b) said that the critic discovers what people are doing and why they are doing it through a *pentadic* process.

Situations are made up of five elements, a dramatistic pentad, that frame analysis of the rhetorical act:

> *Act* names what took place in thought or deed: what was done. Criticizing a rhetorical act is itself an act. Act is the central term of the pentad. Everything in the situation revolves around action. Doing criticism is an act.
>
> *Scene* is the background for the act, the context in which the act occurred: when or where the act was performed. The scene may be the actual physical setting in which the act took place, or it may be the social, political, or economic environment of the rhetor and audience. Completion of a college degree is the scene against which you as a critic are doing criticism.
>
> *Agent* is the person or kind of person performing the act: who did it. The agent can be an individual or group: friends or enemies, coagents or counteragents. When you do criticism, you are the agent in the critical act.
>
> *Agency* is the means, methods, or instruments used in performing the act: how the act was done. This is a

broad category that includes those elements that contribute to the accomplishment of an act. An agency can be a law, an institution, a machine, a device, an attitude that promotes an act, or a process that allows an act to take place. The pentad itself is an agency for analyzing messages, which you might elect to use as a critic.

Purpose is the reason the act was done: the end sought by the agent. We usually think of the purpose as the rationale or belief system that leads to action. Critics perform rhetorical criticism to enhance our knowledge of communication, acting on the belief that doing criticism expands what is known about rhetorical activity.

People are actors who have reasons for acting. Acts occur through both symbolic and physical action. Action takes place in some setting of time and place, physical or psychological. As a critic, you must carefully examine communication in terms of the pentad because rhetorical strategies are unique to their creators. Even when we group strategies into communication genres, there is still great latitude for the individual rhetor. Burke (1969b) provided an example of how the verbal-symbol *war* can have five strategic uses (see box below).

Ratios

The five terms of the pentad are the keys to human motives. They answer the critic's questions about how to discover what people are doing and how they are doing it. Although it may be possible to find rhetorical acts in which balanced

---

A Pentadic

Analysis of the

Symbol *War*

1. When war is a means to an end, it is an agency.

2. War is also a collective act made up of many individual acts.

3. For the draftee, war is the scene, the setting which caused him to undergo training to fight.

4. In myth and legend, war is some sort of superagent, as in the form of a god of war.

5. War may become purpose in a culture that worships aggression and uses the attitude of "our finest hour" as a reason for its actions. (BURKE, 1969b)

emphasis on the five elements occurs, the strategy of a rhetor will more likely focus the message on a combination or *ratio* between elements. For example, a rhetor wants to focus guilt on the agent. To develop this point, she emphasizes the scene-agent ratio (the federal government is responsible for the pollution of the Great Lakes) and the act-agent ratio (the federal government's failure to enforce environmental protection regulations, thereby allowing polluters to continue to dump toxic wastes into the Great Lakes).

Burke (1969b) called these ratios "principles of determination" that help the critic determine the relationship the rhetor used strategically in responding to the situation. The pentad provides ten ratios:

scene-act	act-purpose	agent-purpose	agency-purpose
scene-agent	act-agent	agent-agency	
scene-agency	act-agency		
scene-purpose			

In using these ratios as principles of determination, the critic looks at how the rhetor has related the two elements in a pair to each other. If description of the rhetorical act suggests that the rhetor used a scene-act ratio, it would be your job as the critic to decide whether or not the act "fit" the scene. That is, was the action appropriate under the circumstances? Isolating each element in the pentad as it occurs in a rhetorical act, and then determining which elements are emphasized in the rhetor's predominant strategy or strategies, enables you to understand the kind of identification the rhetor tried to create. The pentad is the device of the dramatistic approach for helping a critic interpret the message.

The example used to open Chapter 3, Governor Mario Cuomo's keynote speech at the 1984 Democratic convention, can also be viewed from the dramatistic perspective.

> Ten days ago, President Reagan admitted that although some people in this country seemed to be doing well nowadays, others were unhappy, and even worried about themselves, their families, and their futures. The President said he didn't understand that fear. He said, "Why, this country is a shining city on a hill." The President is right. In many ways we are a "shining city on a hill." But the hard truth is that not everyone is sharing in this city's splendor and glory.
>
> A shining city is perhaps all the President sees from the portico of the White House and the veranda of his ranch, where everyone seems to be doing well. But there's another part of the city, the part where some people can't pay their mortgages and most young people can't afford one, where students can't afford the education they need and middle class parents watch dreams they hold for their children evaporate.
>
> In this part of the city there are more poor than ever, more families in trouble. More and more people who need

help but can't find it. Even worse: there are elderly people
who tremble in the basements of houses there. There are
people who sleep in the city's streets, in the gutter, where
the glitter doesn't show. There are ghettos where
thousands of young people, without an education or a
job, give their lives away to drug dealers every day. There
is despair, Mr. President, in faces you never see, in places
you never visit in your shining city.

In fact, Mr. President, this nation is more a "Tale of
Two Cities" than it is a "Shining City on a Hill." Maybe if
you visited more places, Mr. President, you'd understand.
(O. PETERSON, 1985, p. 24)

Governor Cuomo uses "the shining city on the hill" metaphor and the literary
allusion to Charles Dickens' A Tale of Two Cities. Concepts from the dramatistic
approach explain how those devices function. This portion of the speech focuses
on the scene-agent ratio. The nation, through the city metaphor, is portrayed in
scenic terms as a place of rich and poor. The agent, President Reagan or the
Reagan administration and its policies, is portrayed as having a very narrow view,
a poor understanding of the scene. Governor Cuomo, acting as a representative of
the Democratic party, reinterprets the scene for the audience with his allusion to a
well-known Dickens novel.

Implicitly, the message is that the Democrats, as counteragent, have a broader
view of the scene whereas the agent sees only a limited portion of it. This
emphasis on scene-agent ratio is one of the strategies used in the speech to fix
guilt on a scapegoat, the Republican party and its incumbent, Ronald Reagan. In
such circumstances, redemption would be attainable only through an act of
victimage: voting the incumbent out of office.

Some things might be discovered about the genre of keynote addresses at
political conventions by using the dramatistic approach. If a critic examines
several examples of campaign rhetoric, he may discover that scapegoating the
incumbent is a common feature of the rhetorical acts of members of the party that
is out of power. A principle of keynote speaking might be inferred: The keynote
speaker at the convention of the nonincumbent party should cast the incumbent
in the role of scapegoat for the nation's ills.

The Dramatistic Approach
and Critical Evaluation

The Ethical Standard

The critic who chooses the dramatistic approach must have a strong commitment to the ethical standard of judgment because the underlying assumption of
Burke's theory of rhetoric is that cooperation through identification is rhetoric's
function (Campbell, 1972). Because identification can join people together while

separating them from some larger group (factionation), identification can be destructive as well as constructive. Because it focuses on what language is doing in a particular rhetorical act, the dramatistic approach draws the critic into judging the fitness or unfitness of the act. Does it harm or help the social order? Is its use of the dramatistic process—guilt, purification, and redemption—constructive?

The rhetoric of white supremacy enacted by the Ku Klux Klan and the American Nazi party represents a destructive kind of identification. Its purpose is separation of the races and subjugation of nonwhite races. Using the ethical standard, a critic judges a rhetorical act to determine whether the rhetor's use of symbols is constructive, promoting the social good, or destructive, disrupting social order.

However, not all destructive rhetoric automatically reduces the social good, nor does all constructive rhetoric automatically enhance the social good. The nonincumbent political party in a presidential election year always seeks rejection of the incumbent, as Mario Cuomo's 1984 keynote speech did. A rhetorical act that seeks to overturn the existing social order and reconstruct it with a new way may ultimately be judged ethical.

The rhetorical acts of John and Samuel Adams, Benjamin Franklin, Patrick Henry, Thomas Jefferson, and Thomas Paine were all destructive. Their speeches, articles, pamphlets, and demonstrations advocated disruption of British control of the American colonies. Whether your criticism judges something as ethical or unethical depends on your frame of reference, in addition to how you use the critical approach you have chosen.

We generally believe that an ethical or humane use of rhetoric encourages people to see themselves as capable of making choices, acting in ways that produce changes that benefit society rather than destroy it (Campbell, 1972). Ethical rhetors create rhetorical strategies aimed at mutual understanding rather than domination. Although a rhetor may emphasize the substance of a group of people, the ethical rhetor does not use substance to justify the subjugation of other groups.

The Truth Standard

The truth standard can also be used in evaluating rhetorical acts from the perspective of the dramatistic approach. Identification can be viewed as the process a rhetor uses to create social truth. The dramatistic approach can be used to judge the rhetor's creation of reality in terms of how it compares with competing views. Does the rhetor's use of the dramatistic process of guilt, purification, and redemption represent a legitimate way for society to cope with its problems? If the exigence is economic, such as a budget deficit, a rhetorical strategy emphasizing the act-agent ratio (Congress passes budget resolutions that are never in balance) may inaccurately portray economic or political reality. Is it accurate, or truthful, to blame Congress alone, seeking purification through victimage?

The dramatistic approach encounters the same problem in applying the truth standard that it encounters when using other approaches. Truth is, at best, difficult to discover, and social truths can be discovered only by comparing different versions of what people say is truth. The dramatistic approach does offer the critic who is searching for the rhetor's truth the advantage of being able to use communication genres and the dramatistic process. The critic can search for strategies commonly used in confronting similar situations. If a series of different rhetorical acts all point to the same scapegoat (rhetors commonly agree that Congress is responsible for deficit spending), it may be possible to determine the probable truth of the matter. One of the functions of criticism is to discover these commonalities and draw conclusions about human substance. If all rhetors isolate a workable strategy, given the subject (make Congress the scapegoat when anything goes wrong in Washington), a standard is created for judging future rhetorical action.

The Aesthetic Standard

The idea that symbolic action involves the use of rhetorical strategies also means that the aesthetic standard of judgment is available to the critic operating within the dramatistic approach. To view people as symbol users and misusers is to focus on how symbols are used in a linguistic sense as rhetors attempt to establish identification. The dramatistic approach gives the critic a vocabulary for studying the artistic uses of language. You are not limited merely to saying that a rhetor used metaphor, or any other form of adornment for that matter. As a critic you can go on to judge the function and effect of specific linguistic strategies by evaluating how the metaphor functions in the rhetor's attempt to create identification.

The Results Standard

Dramatism also enables you to assess results by determining whether or not the rhetor achieved identification. A union organizing drive is a series of rhetorical acts designed to create identification between the individual workers and the union that is trying to organize them. These rhetorical acts can be evaluated individually or collectively based on whether or not they achieved the desired results: getting sufficient votes in the certification election.

Uses and Limitations

One of the limitations of using the dramatistic approach in determining results is that a lie can form the centerpiece of an effective attempt to achieve identification. Religious cults, white supremacists, and other groups we may not consider socially responsible can be successful in establishing identification between themselves and those they are trying to recruit. This may not impose limitations on you as a critic if part of your purpose is to discover why people are attracted to such groups or how their message is antithetical to social order.

Summary

The dramatistic approach is based on a rhetorical theory of symbolic interaction in which people are viewed as actors in life's dramas, accepting or rejecting the human condition. Kenneth Burke's system for viewing and criticizing rhetorical activity encourages the critic to examine all relationships in a rhetorical act. The pentad provides a system for discovering these relationships.

Society is seen as a process of symbolic interaction in which people are constantly involved in rhetorical activity. Understanding the meaning of a message requires analyzing the joint efforts of rhetor and receiver in the drama. To make sense of a rhetor's use of symbols in pursuit of identification, the critic must examine the social order in which the rhetor operates and the strategies he creates to respond to the social order. The dramatistic approach enables you as a critic to describe, analyze, and evaluate rhetorical acts in terms of the following.

> *Motive.* Determining the rhetor's attitude in a given situation as she creates reality based on prior experience of both action and motion, knowledge of symbols that represent human behavior, and knowledge of symbols that represent nature.
>
> *Identification.* The rhetor's expression of the desire to unify self and audience for the purpose of action regarding the social order: defending or rejecting it. Identification is characterized in criticism by the dramatistic process of guilt, purification, and redemption.
>
> *Rhetorical strategies.* The rhetor's choices of symbols to achieve identification. Rhetorical strategies are patterns of symbols, language devices, and the rhetor's choices concerning which best reflects his motive. These strategies can be discussed in terms of their interrelatedness in achieving identification. The pentad of act, scene, agent, agency, and purpose is the structure for describing these relationships.

Because the dramatistic approach offers such a flexible method for criticism, it is not easily described in a step-by-step plan for doing criticism. Furthermore, it is not a single method but a family of methods because it is common for critics to choose one aspect of the approach as the focus for their criticism, to combine aspects of this approach with elements of other approaches in organic criticism, or to search Burke's writings for rhetorical concepts not yet included in the dramatistic approach.

Suggested Readings

Examples of Criticism

APPEL, E.C. (1987). The perfected drama of Reverend Jerry Falwell. *Communication Quarterly, 35,* 26–38.

Jerry Falwell's messages in his syndicated program "The Old Time Gospel Hour" are analyzed by using all of the concepts in the dramatistic approach. The author uses Burke's idea of human communication as straining after perfection as the starting point for studying Falwell's brand of Christian fundamentalism as a rhetoric of perfection. Appel offers his own interpretation, creating a "perfected" and "intensified" version of dramatism. This is a good example of how a critic uses this approach, but the author adds to it in the process of being a critic.

BRUMMET, B. (1981). Burkean scapegoating, mortification, and transcendence in presidential campaign rhetoric. *Central States Speech Journal, 32,* 254–264.

The author looks at the campaign rhetoric of the three major presidential candidates in the 1980 election: Jimmy Carter, John Anderson, and Ronald Reagan. This article offers a good synthesis of the dramatistic process and illustrates how a critic goes about describing the critical approach he is using. Brummet uses only a part of dramatism, the idea of scapegoating, as he looks at two speeches by each candidate. He focuses on what each candidate stood for in the social order as revealed by the selected campaign speeches.

CHAPEL, G.W. (1975). Television criticism: A rhetorical perspective. *Western Speech Communication, 39,* 81–91.

The author's purpose is to justify considering television programs as having rhetorical properties. He says that we should examine both entertainment and news programming to see how they communicate ideas, attitudes, and values. Three popular series of the 1970s are highlighted: *All in the Family, The Jeffersons,* and *The Mary Tyler Moore Show.* Chapel uses concepts from Burke's theory of rhetoric to argue that television in general is rhetorical and uses the pentad to explain how series and news programs are rhetorical. This is an example of how a part of an approach can be used and combined with ideas from mass communication theory in an organic approach to criticism.

KLUMPP, J.F. AND HOLLIHAN, T.A. (1979). Debunking the resignation of Earl Butz: Sacrificing an official racist. *Quarterly Journal of Speech, 65,* 1–11.

This article uses Burke's concepts of hierarchy, guilt, purification, and redemption to critique the rhetorical activity surrounding the forced resignation of Earl Butz in 1976 after a racist joke he had told in private was made public. This is an excellent application of Burke's concepts of motive and hierarchy to political communication and an extension of Burke's ideas of social criticism to problems of American racism.

PETERSON, T.R. (1986). The will to conservation: A Burkean analysis of dust bowl rhetoric and American farmers. *Southern Speech Communication Journal, 52,* 1–21.

The author critiques the messages of Franklin Roosevelt's administration on soil conservation and land management. The pentad and key ratios are used to explain the conflicting motives in Depression-era conservation rhetoric. This is a good example of how a critic uses the pentad as an analytical device and how certain critical ratios can be used to explain meaning in a message. Also, notice the conclusion in which Peterson extends her analysis of 1930s conservation messages to the environmental concerns of the present. She uses the pentad to make recommendations about how environmentally sound land use messages should be strategically structured for today's farmer.

SANBONMATSU, A. (1971). Darrow and Rorke's use of Burkean identification strategies in New York vs. Gitlow. *Speech Monographs, 38,* 36–48.

This is an application of part of the dramatistic approach to a legal case, the trial of Benjamin Gitlow, a self-proclaimed communist, charged with criminal anarchy. Clarence Darrow for the defense and New York assistant district attorney Alexander Rorke as prosecutor are the subjects of this critical essay. The trial occurred during one of the great "red scares" in 1920. The author provides a very good discussion of the exigence and constraints imposed by this rhetorical situation. The strength of the essay lies in its discussion of how both prosecution and defense attempted to achieve identification, not in its application of the pentad. Of particular interest are Darrow's rhetorical strategies in responding to the rhetorical situation, using the value system of 1920 to make particular American values fit Gitlow, whose communistic ideology was decidedly anti-American.

Resources for Doing Criticism

COMBS, J.E., AND MANSFIELD, M.W., EDS. (1976). *Drama in life*. New York: Hastings House.

> Burke's dramatistic theory is only one approach reflecting the philosophy that life is a series of social dramas. This text will give you a comprehensive view of dramatism, including Burke's version of it. The preface to this anthology provides an excellent discussion of the philosophy behind dramatism. We also recommend Part One, "The Variation of Perspectives," a collection of essays on different ways of understanding life as a social drama. The remaining parts offer essays on social interaction, mass communication, politics, organizations, and culture, all written from the dramatistic perspective.

GRONBECK, B.E. (1980). Dramaturgical theory and criticism: The state of the art (or science?). *Western Journal of Speech Communication, 44*, 315–330.

> This article looks at both the Burkean and fantasy theme versions of dramatism, summarizing how various critics have come to understand the concept. The section "All the World's a Stage" is particularly useful to understanding how and why communication is an enactment of our public lives. A good diagram of the dramatistic philosophy appears on p. 317. This article will give you an idea of how many different wrinkles critics had introduced into the two approaches by 1980.

RUECKERT, W.H. (1963). *Kenneth Burke and the drama of human relations*. Minneapolis: University of Minnesota Press.

> This text offers a thorough synopsis of Burke's works up to 1960. Although Rueckert's purpose was to focus on Burke as a literary critic, the social focus of Burke's concepts of dramatism is included. We recommend Chapter 4, "Dramatism: Language as the Ultimate Reduction." Rueckert faithfully renders dramatism as conceptualized by Burke. One of the problems with reading Burke's own works is that his style is rather free form, that is, his words follow wherever his mind wishes to roam. His writing is filled with literary references and can be difficult going if you have not read the same things he has. Rueckert's synopsis is much easier to manage and will give you the essence of Burke's thought.

The

5

Fantasy Theme

Approach

What is true love? Readers of best-selling romance writer Barbara Cartland think they know. True love is sanctioned by God as a reward for virtuous women and the men who choose them over temptresses. The heroine of a Cartland novel is always subservient to men; she is vulnerable, childlike in her physical fragility, naive, nurturing, self-sacrificing, and spiritual. The heroine's role in life is to stand behind her man and build his confidence. A Cartland hero is wealthy and powerful; he has been successful in business, war, society, and especially with "other" women. As a result of his success and experience, he now seeks spiritual fulfillment. The other woman, a temptress in Cartland's romantic world, is independent and assertive; she knows what she wants and goes after it, but she never gets the hero (Doyle, 1985).

How do the characters interact and seek true love in a Cartland romance? At the outset, the heroine is beset by some peril that threatens her life, reputation, or virtue. She is powerless to save herself. Enter the hero, who rescues her from other men who want to take advantage of her. The hero is tempted by a woman of easy virtue, but he rejects her in favor of the virtuous heroine. A Cartland heroine engages in some act of benevolence to a family member or an unfortunate, or she is caught up in some other situation that calls forth her spiritual qualities. The hero recognizes a good thing when he sees it and rejects the other woman, finding true love with the heroine (Doyle, 1985).

Is this rhetorical activity? How would you, as a critic, approach something like a Barbara Cartland novel? To discover more about the lives of her fictional characters and their adventures, which often serve as indirect stimuli for the reader, gradually changing beliefs and behaviors, read the article "The Rhetoric of Romance" by Marsha Doyle, described in the suggested readings at the end of this chapter. Fiction, as well as actual events, are often understood in terms of heroes and heroines, villains and evil forces, acting out an adventure and revealing motives for belief and behavior.

It is human nature to personalize the impersonal, to try to understand events in personal terms. When confronting complex social forces, we try to understand them in terms of characters of a certain type, with appropriate motives, who act in ways we expect (Bormann, 1983). With a little help from television, U.S.-Soviet relations were dramatized as a "Miracle on Ice" in 1980 when a young, truly amateur group of hockey players defeats an older, more experienced professional Soviet team to win the Olympic gold medal. Every contest between an American and a Soviet athlete becomes a drama of East-West confrontation. From our perspective the heroes are the Americans, who with limited resources and motivated by sheer desire to become champions are pitted against nationally financed foreign villains who have special training programs.

The Nature of Fantasy

In the previous chapter, we discussed dramatism from a sociological perspective as described by Kenneth Burke. In this chapter, we consider a critical approach that is still evolving. The fantasy theme approach analyzes public communication as a fantasy created by a group to answer the questions: What is really happening here and what is the nature of our reality?

Ordinary use of the term *fantasy* conjures up an imaginary world in which nothing is real. In the context of rhetorical criticism, the term *fantasy* is used to describe the "creative and imaginative interpretation of events that fulfills a psychological or rhetorical need" (Bormann, 1983, p. 434). In fantasy theme analysis, although a fantasy may concern purely fictional events, it usually involves things that actually happened: people, events documented by news reports, historical reports, or the oral history and folklore of a group. These events, however, are removed from the here-and-now of those who are fantasizing.

This approach to the interpretation of life as a social drama was first discussed in 1972 when Ernest Bormann began to notice similarities in studies of rhetorical criticism and small-group communication. He was looking for a theory that would explain the connection between message content and the role of spectator-actors in creating meaning for that message (Bormann, 1982a). The theory that was developed became popularly known as *fantasy theme analysis,* although Bormann now calls it *symbolic convergence theory.* It has developed in response to the variety of communication media available for study (Bormann, 1972, 1983, 1985).

Bormann and others who have used the concepts of fantasy theme analysis wanted to resolve the dilemma posed by culture-bound rhetorical theories and find those universal communication principles that could be used to guide the analysis of any act of communication. Is there a way to say meaningful things about all human communication? Is there some overriding principle? Bormann said yes, the human impetus to fantasize as a way of accounting for what happens.

Traditional views of rhetorical activity did not provide a means of accounting for why members of an audience became caught up in some rhetorical acts and not others:

> Aristotelian-based theoretical explanations of speaking phenomena did not provide a very satisfying explanation of why tens of thousands of people would cheer hysterically when Alabama Governor George Wallace said, "By God, if one of those long-haired hippies laid down in front of my car, it would be the last time"; or why many thousands of people still get teary eyed when they hear a recording of John F. Kennedy saying, "Ask not what your country can do for you, but ask what you can do for your country"; or Martin Luther King relating, "I had a dream last night." (CRAGAN AND SHIELDS, 1981, p. 45)

Fantasy theme analysis rests on two communication principles. First, people use communication to create reality. A fantasy is a means of communicating the probable truth about something in the rhetorical situation. People create symbols to explain what they perceive is really going on. Second, people can share the symbols they create. This means that their symbols converge in a joint creation of reality, a sense of reality that has exceptional salience and truthfulness for them.

Symbolic convergence theory takes a perspective on the rhetor-message-audience relationship that differs from the traditional approach to criticism. The role of the audience, particularly in the sense of an audience as a group of people who accept a message, takes on greater importance. Although message content is important, it is the sharing of the message as a salient, truthful explanation of reality that is most important. The critical focus of fantasy theme analysis is that the audience is absorbed by the message because they perceive it as truth. To have a better understanding of how fantasy theme analysis is used as a critical approach, it is useful to examine why people turn to fantasies to create reality and how these fantasies spread to other groups.

Fantasy and the Creation of Reality

Why do groups fantasize? Why are dramas created? Fantasizing is a human need and an activity that is common to individuals and groups. We know this from studies that range from medical psychology by Sigmund Freud to social psychology by Robert Freed Bales (Gronbeck, 1980). The need to establish a social reality, to determine the meaning of what has occurred, is occurring, or might occur in the future, leads groups to fantasize explanations.

Fantasizing is used by zero-history groups (people who come together for the first time) to create a common culture so that a frame of reference exists for further communication. Established groups need to review and reaffirm their attitudes and values, determine what is good, and make commitments to group values. Fantasizing is crucial to attitude formation and change. "Values and attitudes of many kinds are tested and legitimized as common to the group by the process of fantasy chains" (Bormann, 1972, p. 398).

Although the process of group fantasizing may go on at any time, a group's creation of fantasy chains is especially evident in times of trouble, as a way of interpreting or making sense of limited information. When a situation is chaotic and confusing, and no acceptable interpretation of events is provided, people tend to fantasize a way out of the situation or a way to explain it. In times of uncertainty or rapid change, fantasies are the explanatory system for events. Rumors are examples of such fantasizing (Bormann, 1972, 1982a).

Messages take the form of *fantasy chains,* systematic ways of explaining events. The system of fantasy theme analysis considers how communication articulates a drama. It consists of analyzing a message in terms of dramatis personae, the characters of heroes, villains, and supporting cast; scenarios, the plot lines that develop the story; and the setting of the drama, the scene for dramatic action. The content of fantasy chain "consists of characters, real or fictitious, playing out a dramatic situation in a setting removed in time and space from the here-and-now transactions of the group" (Bormann, 1972, p. 397). The complete drama offers a *rhetorical vision.*

What is the relationship between fantasies and reality? To understand the philosophy of fantasy theme analysis, you have to view reality from a new perspective. What is contained in the rhetorical act *is* reality for those people who either shared in creating the fantasy or elected to accept the fantasy of a single individual, such as Barbara Cartland. Reality is what the group's symbols have converged on; it is their rhetorical vision, regardless of whether they were responsible for producing the vision or simply chose to identify with it.

Going Public with the Fantasy

A fantasy may remain the rhetorical vision of the group that created it, or the group may decide to seek other audiences by going public with their vision of reality. Fantasies follow a three-stage life cycle when the group decides to share a fantasy by going public. The first stage is the original fantasy creation (and failure to accomplish the second or third stage indicates a lack of public viability). First, *consciousness-creating communication* is an innovative process. Fantasies are shared among individuals within a group, the fantasy is formed, and the original chaining of the dramatic elements of the fantasy takes place. Second, *consciousness-raising communication* is used to recruit and convert newcomers to the group's message. The original creators of the fantasy may redramatize it and apply pressure to newcomers to share the fantasy. Third, *consciousness-sustaining communication* reviews established fantasies and renews group commitment to them or modifies them to maintain the symbolic convergence (Bormann, 1983).

The fantasy theme approach suggests that what is true of small groups is also true of large groups. Much public or mass communication may have its genesis in small-group communication. Some dramas chain out from small groups to become part of public speeches or enter the mass media in other ways. Eventually, the drama may chain out to the larger publics, building a social reality populated by a particular set of heroes, villains, scenes, and plots, allowing the emotions and attitudes of the group to become part of the public consciousness (Bormann, 1972). A group of speech writers drafts a major presidential statement, the writers of a popular television series decide how to address the problem of racism, or a group of community activists state their concerns about a low-level nuclear waste dump. Each group is involved in fantasy creation and going public with the fantasy.

Much public communication comes to us via the mass media. Magazines, television programs, movies, music, popular fiction, and nonfiction books all offer their consumers the opportunity to participate in fantasies that have chained out and gone public. In this way, the audiences of mass-mediated fantasies can share the fantasy; experience common emotions, the acts of heroes and villains, and views of good and bad behavior; and share interpretations of what the drama means (Bormann, 1985). Going public via the mass media can make a rhetorical vision a nationally shared one. Although we can certainly criticize the mass media for their distortions, media act as a filtering system that takes the vast number of daily events and distills them into more manageable forms (Sharf, 1986). This filtration determines which fantasies have sufficient public exposure to succeed as salient explanations of reality.

In Chapter 1 we said that rhetorical acts were primarily instrumental in that their purpose is to influence belief or behavior. Additionally, rhetorical acts are social, use symbols, have structure, are artistic, and have ethical implications. A critical approach should cover all aspects of rhetorical activity but especially its instrumental and artistic aspects.

The instrumental properties of rhetorical acts, particularly the use of argument, its substance, and structure, are related to the sharing of fantasies. Fantasy sharing is a precondition for argumentation because a fantasy helps set the ground rules for what constitutes proof in an argument (Bormann, 1982b). For example, if a fantasy includes a view of science as heroic, then what science tells us may become important in determining our reality.

Fantasizing tests assumptions and values, which in turn determine what a particular group needs to prove in order to establish its reality as part of the public consciousness. A salient rhetorical vision cannot be achieved if these needs are not met. When a fantasy goes public, its message is shaped for public consumption. The originators of the fantasy test it by asking such questions as What is the nature of proof? How much proof is sufficient? Who are the publicly respected sources we turn to for proof?

The Technique of Fantasy Theme Analysis

Fantasy theme analysis involves three elements: discovering the communication patterns of fantasizing, considering the elements of the fantasy, and explaining how and why the fantasy works for a particular group of people. In the last element, you will want to consider the stages in the life cycle of a fantasy and whether what you are evaluating is a consciousness-creating, consciousness-raising, or consciousness-sustaining fantasy. As this approach has evolved, three terms have been used to identify the kind of information the critic needs to discover in order to do fantasy theme analysis: *fantasy theme, fantasy type,* and *rhetorical vision.*

Fantasy Themes

As you begin the process of criticism, examining the rhetorical acts you have chosen to study, you search for fantasy themes. This means looking for dramatic characters, heroes and villains and their supporting cast; scenarios, the plot lines that develop the fantasy; and setting, the scene in which action takes place. At this point, you are in the descriptive stage of the process of criticism, so you should collect all the evidence you can on the content of the fantasy. Because fantasy theme analysis frequently considers a series of rhetorical acts, such as the novels of Stephen King or the rhetorical activity of the civil rights movement, your task is to discover and describe the drama that has chained out.

Fantasy themes are developed as a group dramatizes an event by selecting heroes and villains, the central activity of fantasizing. Without good guys and bad guys and the inherent dramatic tension of good struggling against evil, there is no drama. Fantasy themes shape and organize experience, slanting it in a way that attributes motives to the central characters and makes the interpretation of events possible. Bormann (1972) cites several questions that can serve as guides in describing the fantasy theme (see box on the next page).

To see how fantasy themes are discovered and described, consider the following historical example. In the last decade of the nineteenth century, the United States began to think of itself as a world power because of its success in the Spanish-American War. Victory had given the United States dominion over Cuba and the Philippines, which led to heated debates over whether the Philippines should be free and what the American role should be in governing Hawaii, Cuba, and Puerto Rico. The American empire fantasy themes were created and made public during the congressional elections of 1898 and were refined in subsequent congressional debates.

One of the most famous speeches of the period was delivered at a Republican political rally in Indianapolis by Albert J. Beveridge in 1898. "The March of the Flag" was a political sermon on behalf of imperialism that combined with other rhetorical acts of speaking, cartooning, editorializing, and reporting in forming a

Who Are the Dramatis Personae?

1. Is some abstract entity such as "the people," "God," or "the young" personified to legitimize the drama?

2. Who are the heroes and villains, the supporting characters?

3. How much detail is given to characterization and are motives attributed to the behavior of characters?

4. What kinds of behavior are praised, condemned, requested, and what kinds of behavior are attributed to insiders, outsiders, friends, and enemies?

5. What values are attributed to each character type?

Where Are the Dramas Set?

1. Is the drama set in a city, wilderness, frontier, supernatural realm (heaven or hell), or fictional territory, or in a more specific scene such as the office, home, Oval Office, or an actual geographic place?

2. Is there some supernatural or official sanction of the setting such as "the land promised by God" or an act of government?

3. Are there important props that are part of the setting such as costumes, weapons, sacred texts, or secret documents?

What Are the Typical Plot Lines?

1. What action involves the heroes, villains, sanctioning agent, or supporting cast?

2. Are there neutral acts?

3. What are the lifestyles of heroes and villains?

4. What emotions are portrayed in the action?

5. What is the place of the drama in history; that is, is there some sense of the historic importance of the action? (BORMANN, 1972)

rhetorical vision. The heroic fantasy of an American empire, sanctioned by God to expand its sphere of influence, is found in the opening of Beveridge's speech.

> It is a noble land that God has given us; a land that can feed and clothe the world. . . . It is a mighty people that He has planted on this soil; a people sprung from the most masterful blood of history; a people perpetually revitalized by the virile, man-producing working folk of all the earth; a people imperial by virtue of their power, by right of their institutions, by authority of their Heaven-directed purposes—the propagandists and not the misers of liberty. (REID, 1988, p. 609).

Villains in the drama were the other world powers, particularly Germany, and the people of the nations to be "protected" by the American empire were seen as incapable of self-government.

> Shall we turn these people back to the reeking hands from which we have taken them? Shall we abandon them with Germany, England, Japan, hungering for them? Shall we save them from those nations to give them a self-rule of tragedy? (REID, 1988, p. 610)

Dramatic action in the imperial vision was a quest, the march of American tradition to other lands. Notice the litany of American heroes Beveridge offered as examples of those who had participated in similar marches in the past.

> And, now, obeying the same voice that Jefferson heard and obeyed, that Jackson heard and obeyed, that Monroe heard and obeyed, that Seward heard and obeyed, that Grant heard and obeyed, that Harrison heard and obeyed our President today plants the flag over the islands of the seas, outposts of commerce, citadels of national security, and the march of the flag goes on! (REID, 1988, p. 611)

Fantasy themes in a message establish the drama and include characters, scene, and action. Whether you discover a fantasy theme in a single rhetorical act or in a group of acts, it is considered a single case. That is, if in one speech you find evidence of three different fantasy themes, they constitute three cases; but if you find one fantasy theme repeated in several speeches by the same speaker, or in a variety of rhetorical acts on the same subject, then this theme constitutes a single case.

Fantasy Type

A fantasy type is a stock scenario that is repeated or shared over and over again. Although there may be slight variations in elements of a fantasy theme, the same characters or character types, the same settings, and the same plot lines are

Questions to Use	
in Analyzing	1. Are the same people or institutions cast as heroes and villains?
Fantasy Types	2. Is there a repetition of the same plot line or the same scene?
	3. Are some scenes considered sacred, profane, or neutral territory?

repeated. When a fantasy theme has been repeated often enough, it no longer has to be repeated in its entirety to have rhetorical impact. The members of the audience know the missing details. Such a fantasy type becomes a kind of shorthand, a symbolic cue or trigger, that recalls the drama for the audience without repeating all of its supporting details.

Deciding whether a fantasy theme has gone through enough repetitions to stand as a fantasy type is a matter of collecting a sufficient number of examples of the fantasy so that you can observe if, or when, its details are no longer provided. You look for the appearance of a dramatic trigger that acts as a summarizing reference in the message. A dramatic trigger may be "A code word, phrase, slogan, or nonverbal sign or gesture; it may be a geographical or imaginary place or the name of a persona; it may arouse tears or evoke anger, hatred, love and affection as well as laughter and humor" (Bormann, 1985, p. 132).

As a critic, you are free to cluster similar fantasy themes into fantasy types. Look for patterns that cut across several dramatic cases (see box above). On the basis of this collected evidence, you can then construct the representative fantasy type. This is similar to what film critics are doing when they refer to "biker pictures of the Sixties," "creature" films, or "slasher" movies.

Consider the political cartoon as an example. Political cartoons often represent a particular fantasy type, and the meaning of the cartoon derives from the symbolic cues contained in its visual and verbal elements. The cartoon has dramatis personae and some sense of dramatic action, and usually references a fantasy theme (Bormann, Koester, and Benett, 1978). The cartoons in Figures 5.1 and 5.2 appeared in *Harper's Weekly* almost exactly a year apart, on 24 March 1900 and 16 March 1901, respectively.

The fantasy of American empire was sufficiently well formed in the public's mind by the turn of the century so that cartoonists could have confidence in public understanding of their portrayal of competing world powers as predatory animals (wolves and crocodiles) that threatened innocent children (Puerto Rico and Cuba) who wanted our protection, symbolized by a substantial brick house and Uncle Sam. The fantasy as developed in the speeches, cartoons, news reports, and writings of the era (Barkan, 1966; Bloomfield, 1974; C.G. Bowers, 1932;

"LET ME IN."

Figure 5.1
W.A. Rogers, Harper's Weekly, 24 March 1900.

Brandt and Shafter, 1960; D. Holland, 1973) produced six fantasy themes and six fantasy types.

1. The *humanitarian* fantasy portrayed America as a nation of missionary zealots, bringing Christian virtue to those suffering in spiritual darkness and economic deprivation.
2. The *vanguard of republicanism* fantasy offered America as the custodian of good government and civil liberty.

"That wicked man is going to gobble you up, my child!"

Figure 5.2

W.A. Rogers, Harper's Weekly, 16 March 1901.

3. *Social Darwinism* was a popular fantasy that suggested that there was a struggle for the survival of the fittest among nations and that an isolationist foreign policy was a trait of a politically unfit nation.

4. The fantasy of *Anglo-Saxon supremacy,* partly an aggressive reaction to successful imperialism by other countries and partly a defensive reaction to industrial and commercial competition from Germany, asserted

the superiority of America's Anglo-Saxon culture and customs.

5. The fantasy of *strategy and security* grew out of a desire for new markets and arguments about the military advantages of the proposed Panama Canal and a strong navy.

6. The *end of the frontier* fantasy represented a realization that the only frontier left for America to conquer lay beyond our borders.

The usefulness of finding or creating fantasy types in doing criticism is that it enables you to make judgments about rhetorical activity. You can assess just how widespread a particular fantasy is by assessing the ability of its trigger to arouse similar responses from different audiences. "Star Wars," as a trigger for Ronald Reagan's fantasy of defense policy and nuclear deterrence, draws its dramatic elements from the films of George Lucas, a fantasy type that celebrates the triumph of good over evil and is recognizable to a great many Americans. In another case of politics imitating art, "Camelot" became the fantasy type ascribed to the Kennedy Administration. It is illustrative of the time-bound nature of fantasy types that Camelot has less meaning as a trigger for Americans in the 1990s than it did in the 1960s.

Fantasy types also provide a category system for describing a rhetorical situation that produces a number of different, possibly competing, dramas. It is much easier to talk about the tumultuous rhetorical situation of the late 1960s by referring to the fantasy types of "the Woodstock Nation," "hawks and doves," and "hippies and hard-hats." Categorizing by fantasy type also may make it easier to discuss the exigences, constraints, and responses to a rhetorical situation.

Rhetorical Vision

In using the fantasy theme approach to do criticism, you ultimately want to be able to evaluate a rhetorical act or set of acts in terms of the judgmental criteria of results, truth, ethics, or aesthetics. The goal of fantasy theme analysis is to explain how and why a fantasy became a shared reality for a group. A group's shared reality is found in its *rhetorical vision,* "a unified putting together of the various scripts that gives the participants a broader view of things" (Bormann, 1985, p. 133).

An individual fantasy theme offers one script of characters, setting, and plot. A fantasy type is the abbreviated statement of the fantasy theme and allows the fantasy theme to be referred to in a rhetorical act without supplying all the details. A rhetorical vision is the total of all the communication acts that, when taken together, comprise the index of the complete drama. All of Barbara Cartland's novels, viewed together, define the complete drama, her rhetorical vision of true love.

A rhetorical vision contains the complete articulation of a group's fantasy. Analogies such as the New Deal, the Cold War, the New Frontier, Black Power, the New Left, the Silent Majority, and the Moral Majority are examples of master analogies that index rhetorical visions in twentieth-century America with a key phrase or label. The master analogy pulls the elements of a fantasy together into a meaningful whole. Examining the fantasy themes and types subsumed in the master analogy enables the critic to evaluate how and why a rhetorical vision functions as a shared view of reality for a group.

All of the rhetorical acts advocating imperialism as U.S. foreign policy constituted the rhetorical vision of an American empire. By the truth standard, this vision was embraced by the public largely because the six fantasy themes had widespread appeal as a view of reality. By the results standard, the Philippines, Cuba, Puerto Rico, and the Virgin Islands were made subject states and the Hawaiian Islands were annexed, eventually gaining statehood. American empire as a rhetorical vision continued to be a salient fantasy well into the twentieth century.

The sharing of a rhetorical vision as a salient and meaningful view of reality is the most important feature of fantasy. Those who share the rhetorical vision make up a *rhetorical community*. Membership in the rhetorical community may be formal and involve swearing an oath of membership, paying dues, or adopting a certain lifestyle. Membership in the rhetorical community may also be informal and consist of simply sharing a view of reality. Not all groups are equal; neither are all rhetorical visions widely shared.

> Some of these visions may be shared by only a few people and the visions may last only for short periods of time. On the other hand, some rhetorical visions are so all-encompassing and impelling that they permeate an individual's social reality in all aspects of living. Such all encompassing symbolic systems can be considered *lifestyle rhetorical visions;* many of the religious and reform rhetorical visions in the United States fall into this category. A person who crosses the boundaries of the rhetorical community to become a convert to the rhetorical vision of the "agitators for abolition" or a "born-again Christian" finds his or her entire life changed. (BORMANN, 1985, p. 133)

The following box lists questions to help in evaluating the rhetorical vision.

As our discussion of the rhetorical vision of American empire illustrates, a rhetorical vision is usually found by searching for fantasy themes and types across several rhetorical acts. A rhetorical vision shapes social reality for a group, enabling it to function as a rhetorical community. A rhetorical community may be large or small, and it can converge around one or more rhetorical visions. Just remember that though a rhetorical vision is most frequently the product of the group process of chaining out, it can also represent the world view of a single person whose message is sufficiently attractive to cause others to coalesce into a kind of rhetorical community dedicated to that vision.

Questions to Use

in Analyzing

Rhetorical Visions

1. How encompassing was the rhetorical vision? Was the rhetorical community small or large?

2. What community life-cycle stage did the vision represent: consciousness creating, raising, or sustaining? Did the vision draw more members to the rhetorical community?

3. What was the relationship of this rhetorical vision to competing visions? Did it isolate the group because its fantasy was incompatible with other interpretations of reality?

4. How did the vision provide a coherent, comprehensible way for the members of the rhetorical community to cope with or adapt to a time of trouble or a chaotic and confusing situation?

5. What motivation to act did acceptance of the vision provide members of the rhetorical community? What standards of belief and behavior were advocated in the vision?

6. How compelling was the vision for participants? Did sharing the vision commit members of the rhetorical community to a life-style change, or was acceptance of the vision the only change community members experienced?

7. What were the aesthetic properties of the vision? Were the characters one-dimensional figures who enacted stereotypical melodramas, or were they fully developed as people who enacted a range of behaviors in a fully articulated setting? Was the drama logically complete?

Fantasy Theme Analysis and Critical Evaluation

The focus of the fantasy theme approach is on the message symbols contained in rhetorical acts and the sharing of fantasies to explain experience. Ultimately, fantasy chains cause rhetorical communities to form as members of a group converge on the same explanation of what is going on. As a critic, you are interested in the boundaries that defined membership in one of these rhetorical communities. One of the functions of fantasy theme criticism is to go beyond studying individual rhetorical acts to consider the rhetorical communities that produced them, their visions, and their place in history.

The Truth Standard

Because fantasy theme analysis focuses on people's sharing of symbols to interpret and explain events and create a vision of reality, criticism evaluates the extent to which a rhetorical vision functioned as truth. The truth standard is the most important criterion in the fantasy theme approach. Rhetorical visions reveal what constituted truth for those who shared the vision. Truth is intersubjectively determined, and when a fantasy becomes a compelling rhetorical vision, it does so because a rhetorical community has intersubjectively determined it to be true. The vision constitutes truth for a particular rhetorical community but does not necessarily constitute truth for other groups in society. A part of the rhetorical vision of American empire was the fantasy theme of Anglo-Saxon supremacy, which is the view that white people are intellectually and culturally superior. Today, there are white-supremacy groups such as the Ku Klux Klan and the Aryan Nation, but for most Americans the inherent falseness of white supremacy is recognized, and its rhetorical vision is not well received.

In using the truth standard of evaluation to judge a rhetorical act, you should also consider the extent to which reality as determined by a rhetorical community deviates from reality as conceived by other groups in society. If a group is attempting to go public with its rhetorical vision and fails to do so, the failure may be because the fantasy contradicts commonsense evidence of events.

Many Elvis Presley fans are unwilling to accept his death. In the spring of 1988, small groups of fans began to promulgate the fantasy that Elvis was still alive and had been seen recently in a fast-food restaurant in Kalamazoo, Michigan. The fantasy chained out as more details of the "Elvis lives" myth were made public. For most of us, this whole episode was probably so bizarre that we treated it as a joke, the kind of story that rates a headline only in those tabloids generally displayed in grocery store checkout lanes. For those who were not rabid or morbid Elvis fans, the fantasy had limited appeal.

Truth is also time bound: What was once a salient fantasy can lose its ability to depict reality in the future. In the early 1970s, *Dune* was an enormously popular science fiction novel by Frank Herbert. With the Arab oil embargo and gasoline shortages, the rhetorical vision of the novel symbolized the oil crisis and the danger of fanatical political leaders. It was consistent with the everyday evidence of news stories and the experiences of many Americans. The film version of *Dune,* released in 1983, was faithful to the novel but less salient. It did not become a popular rhetorical vision as the book had. Commonsense evidence and everyday life contradicted the fantasy of an energy-starved world in which resources were under the control of a fanatic political-religious figure.

In using the truth standard of rhetorical judgment, you should also consider how a fantasy theme may have changed over time, creating new interpretations of reality. What constitutes reality can shift, recasting the heroes and villains of a drama. This is particularly true in complex fantasies that have many elements in their scenarios.

The rhetorical vision of U.S.-Soviet relations has shifted several times since the end of the alliance of the two countries in World War II. The cold-war vision of the Soviet Union as a villain bent on enslaving the world, opposed by American heroes standing vigil at the Berlin wall or on the DEW line of the Strategic Air Command, explained and justified American foreign policy of the 1950s and 1960s (Cragan, 1981). In the 1970s, this vision lost salience as the Nixon administration established a policy of detente. Ronald Reagan revived the old cold-war vision in the early 1980s when he characterized the Soviet Union as an evil empire. But Soviet withdrawal from Afghanistan in 1988 and Mikhail Gorbachev's policies of glasnost and perestroika have softened this vision.

The recasting of a fantasy theme can turn a hero into a villain. Consider the various fantasies about the college athlete that have developed over time. From the 1930s through the 1960s, students, alumni, and fans of college sports believed that football and basketball players were students who went to classes, graduated with degrees in academic subjects, and played their sport in whatever time they had left. This rhetorical vision was articulated in movies that portrayed athletes as heroes, such as George Gipp in *Knute Rockne All-American*. In the 1980s, the fantasy of the student athlete was quite different. Athletes became villains and victims in a fantasy in which they were admitted to college because of physical prowess, despite a lack of academic aptitude; they did not take rigorous academic courses, seldom went to class, received special favors and money under the table, and seldom graduated. Incorporated into the fantasy were events such as the imposition of the "death penalty" by the National Collegiate Athletic Association (NCAA) on Southern Methodist University's football program, news coverage of allegations of recruiting improprieties, and films such as *One on One*, which chronicles a young man's initiation into the "realities" of big-time college basketball.

What is acknowledged to be the truth can be discovered only by comparing the various fantasies that people use to conceptualize reality. As a critic, you must examine competing rhetorical visions to determine if the same people or institutions are cast as heroes and villains, if similar plot lines are used, and, especially, if recurring patterns of symbolization are used in different visions. Or you may find that widespread convergence is not occurring and that several competing versions of the truth exist. The one "true" rhetorical vision for a particular time is the one that achieves convergence.

The Results Standard

The results standard of judgment is also important in evaluating how and why some fantasies are sufficiently compelling to attract large numbers of adherents. A shared fantasy, one that moves people to act on their belief in its reasonableness, is a successful fantasy. Using the results standard, the critic looks for cause-effect relationships between rhetorical visions and changes in belief and behavior. This means paying special attention to rhetorical acts as efforts to achieve consciousness-creating, as well as consciousness-raising and consciousness-sustaining behavior.

The Aesthetic Standard

The aesthetic standard of judgment becomes important at the level of determining how symbols, particularly fantasy types, are used to cue the rhetorical vision. Any symbol that serves as a trigger for the whole fantasy has great emotional and rational power. Applying the aesthetic standard to investigate the power of a fantasy type requires consideration of the use of language. In the excerpts from Albert J. Beveridge's "March of the Flag" speech, recall the use of repetition of the phrase "heard and obeyed," which suggested what was appropriate action for adherents to this fantasy.

The aesthetic standard is also employed when the fantasy itself suggests that other communication theories ought to be organically included in the methodology. If, for example, the fantasy emphasizes reasoning and the use of evidence, the rules of evidence and argumentation are appropriate methodologies to evaluate the fantasy. The aesthetic standard is particularly important in evaluating how a group goes public with its fantasy. The fantasy may have been adapted to different audiences by featuring different heroic qualities, shifts in scene, new villains, or changes in key symbols. The failure of a fantasy to create, raise, or sustain public consciousness may reflect an artistic failure. Furthermore, the act of going public requires the members of the group to employ some means of communication, even if it is only word of mouth. The selection of a medium for disseminating the fantasy carries with it the need to understand, if not conform to, the constraints imposed by that mode of communication.

Finally, the aesthetic standard can be used to judge a fantasy in terms of how the elements of its drama function. Theories of film and drama may be appropriate at this level of artistic judgment. How do the characterizations of the dramatis personae function? Are they believable characters? What metaphors or mythic figures are presented? Is the scene well crafted? Are all the scenic elements present? Is this a good drama in terms of its use of the stock elements of comedy or tragedy? Using appropriate theories in this way requires you to approach the fantasy in much the same way that a movie critic approaches a film: Does the fantasy work in a dramatic sense?

The Ethical Standard

Because the ethical standard of judgment focuses on the rhetor and the social worth of the rhetorical act, it may not always be applicable to the fantasy theme approach. Fantasy theme analysis is more concerned with the sharing of a message than with who produced it, regardless of whether the message was chained out by a group or a single individual such as Barbara Cartland. However, it may be possible to look at the ethical behavior of the group or individual that originally chained out the fantasy. Was the group perceived as credible? What motivated them to converge on this particular rhetorical vision and what was their purpose for going public with their fantasy? Judgments about the ethical dimension of fantasies can also be made when discussing the truth or results standards.

Uses and Limitations

The greatest value of the fantasy theme approach may lie in analyzing public communication in an age of mass media. Today, who it is that says something is frequently not as important as how and why people buy into the message, converging on its symbols and making them their own. The fantasy theme approach focuses on the sharing of a message rather than on the rhetor, enabling the critic to concentrate on what it is about a message that renders it salient to mass-mediated publics.

The fantasy theme approach encourages critics to dig deeply into the historical-social settings of rhetorical acts. In this approach, criticism is not an exercise in isolating a single speech, song, or movie to study. Instead, the critic is encouraged to look at an entire episode of the creation and dissemination of a public fantasy. Because fantasies appear in a dramatic form with heroes, villains, plots, and scenes, the approach is particularly useful for studying rhetorical acts with narrative structures (Gronbeck, 1980). The approach can also be useful in trying to analyze the very abstract notion of the "mind set" of a small group, a social movement, or even an entire society; as such, the fantasy theme approach is a useful technique for studying attitude formation.

The fantasy theme approach may be limited by being an incomplete theory still in the process of development. There are still unanswered questions about how symbolic convergence occurs and whether or not fantasizing is more a psychological process than a rhetorical process in human behavior (Mohrman, 1982). The concepts of fantasy theme, fantasy type, and rhetorical vision overlap somewhat and are therefore difficult to use (Gronbeck, 1980; Mohrman, 1982). The connection between fantasizing and acting still needs to be tested by research. Using the fantasy theme approach to do criticism gives you an opportunity to participate in testing the theory.

Comparative Concepts of Dramatism

Ernest Bormann's and Kenneth Burke's concepts of human communication share the same general belief that human behavior takes the form of a social drama in which actors perform scripts on the public stage. There are, however, some distinct differences between these two approaches to dramatism. Burke's concept of dramatism grew out of his background as a social critic, focusing on an act performed by an agent who is acting in a scene and employing an agency to achieve a purpose. Burke studied a range of social events, thus producing a more inclusive sociology of human communication. Bormann's symbolic convergence theory is based on the investigation and criticism of specific instances of communication. "Symbolic convergence differs from Burke's dramatism in that it relates only to the content of messages whereas Burke emphasizes the totality of unfolding human action" (Bormann, 1980, p. 190).

What does this mean to you as a critic? It changes the focus. Burkean dramatism has the critic study the structure of society, the efforts of rhetors to create patterns of identification with their audiences, and the interplay of all five elements of the pentad in a social drama to discover the rhetor's strategic choices in creating a particular rhetorical act. Bormann's notion of symbolic convergence turns the process around and begins with the content of the message.

Turning the process around does not mean that you ignore the rhetorical situation or the public presenter of the message if there is one. It means that you begin with the assumption that the message is a publicly expressed explanation or interpretation of social phenomena and events. Instead of searching for an explanation of why such phenomena and events produced the message, the critic focuses on the message, the rhetorical vision, as a statement about the meaning of these phenomena and events. Whereas Burke's dramatism has you examine society and its structures to critique rhetorical activity, Bormann's symbolic convergence theory has you examine the message as an explanation of what some group thought to be true.

Summary

Fantasy theme analysis views human communication as a process in which meaning is jointly created in situations. Groups create, and individuals buy into, fantasies that are salient for them. Critics who use fantasy theme analysis should focus on the message rather than its creators, because it is the message that reveals those elements of the fantasy that made it salient for its creators and those who adopted its rhetorical vision to explain reality. Fantasy theme analysis enables critics to describe, analyze, and evaluate rhetorical acts in terms of the following.

Fantasy themes: The elements of a fantasy, including the dramatic characters, scenarios, and plot lines and the setting of the fantasy. Events are dramatized through fantasy themes.

Fantasy types: When a particular theme has been repeated so many times that audiences are able to recite the details of its characters, scenario, and setting, a fantasy type has been created, which can serve as shorthand for the entire fantasy.

> *Rhetorical vision:* The interpretation of social reality
> consisting of fantasy theme and type. Rhetorical visions
> illustrate what is perceived as important, real, and valid
> for a group or individual.

Fantasy theme analysis focuses on how symbols are used to interpret events and experiences and helps explain how people form rhetorical communities that share a world view.

Suggested Readings

Examples of Criticism

BORMANN, E.G. (1982). A fantasy theme analysis of the hostage release and the Reagan inaugural. *Quarterly Journal of Speech, 68,* 133–145.

> One of the problems in using fantasy theme analysis has been that "breaking news stories" really have not had a chance to chain out in the way Bormann originally postulated. In this article, he considers how chaining out occurs in real time in the news-media coverage of the simultaneous events of the release of the American hostages by Iran and the inauguration of Ronald Reagan. Bormann explains how both events were interwoven by television journalism in a fantasy that reinforced and amplified the vision of Reagan's inaugural speech. Reagan and Carter as dramatis personae are compared and a fantasy type, "restoration," is presented as the key symbol of Reagan's inaugural. This demonstrates the approach in use and criticism focusing on fantasy type.

DOYLE, M.V. (1985). The rhetoric of romance: A fantasy theme analysis of Barbara Cartland novels. *Southern Speech Communication Journal, 51,* 24–48.

> This is an excellent example of how to use fantasy theme analysis to analyze multiple acts by a single source, which uses all four judgmental standards. The author demonstrates that popular fiction can have rhetorical properties; for example, Barbara Cartland's novels influence the male-female relationships of her readers. This article is well written, makes excellent use of research to describe the rhetorical situation that makes romance novels popular, and serves as a good model of how to use the approach.

GOODNIGHT, G.T., AND POULAKOS, J. (1981). Conspiracy rhetoric: From pragmatism to fantasy in public discourse. *Western Journal of Speech Communication, 45,* 299–318.

> This article offers an excellent synopsis of the conspiracy drama, which has been one of the most frequently discussed types of fantasy themes. The authors explain that for much of American history conspiracy dramas have been chained out by groups from the radical right and from others with extremist views. However, in more recent history, the conspiracy drama has been a feature of mainstream rhetorical activity. The Watergate scandal is analyzed at length as an example of conspiracy drama, though the authors provide several other examples of conspiracy dramas. This article provides a good discussion of fantasy in conspiracy rhetoric.

SHARF, B.F. (1986). Send in the clowns: The image of psychiatry during the Hinckley trial. *Journal of Communication, 36,* 80–93.

This is an excellent example of a multimedia analysis based on the fantasy theme approach. Using cartoons, print, and electronic media, the author analyzes the media's vision of psychiatrists that chained out during the trial of John Hinckley for the attempted assassination of President Reagan. Public perception of psychiatry became a comedy as the news media and editorial cartoonists dramatized the insanity defense, and Sharf speculates about the impact these comedic negative images have on people who have little first-hand experience with psychiatrists. This article is well written and a good example of how to use fantasy theme, type, and rhetorical vision in doing criticism.

Resources for Doing Criticism

BORMANN, E.G. (1972). Fantasy and rhetorical vision: The rhetorical criticism of social reality. *Quarterly Journal of Speech, 58,* 396–407.

This is the original article on fantasy theme analysis and reflects some of the problems with labeling various concepts of the approach. This article provides a good discussion of the basis of the theory in small-group research and rhetorical theory. The fantasy theme perspective is developed through an analysis of the rhetorical vision of the Massachusetts Bay Colony. The article is a good example of how an author argues for the usefulness of a "new" theory.

BORMANN, E.G. (1985). Symbolic convergence theory: A communication formulation. *Journal of Communication, 35,* 128–138.

Bormann presents symbolic convergence theory and relates it to narrative, one of the predominant ways people communicate with each other. He explains the use of general and special communication theories and defines the components of fantasy themes, types, and visions. This is the most complete synthesis of the approach to date. Although no extended examples of criticism are offered, the explanation is fairly clear.

CRAGAN, J.F., AND SHIELDS, D.C. (1981). *Applied communication research, a dramatistic approach.* Prospect Heights, IL: Waveland Press.

This anthology, devoted to fantasy theme analysis, goes beyond purely rhetorical applications. If you want to discover everything that can be done with fantasy theme analysis, this book will show you. Part I presents the theory, including Bormann's original 1972 piece. Elements of symbolic convergence theory appear here but are not as clearly explained as in Bormann's 1985 article. Part II offers several good examples of rhetorical criticism based on the approach, including the Cold War rhetorical vision, the conspiracy dramas of the American Indian movement, Malcom X and the black unity vision, and the dumping of Thomas Eagleton as the vice-presidential candidate by the 1972 McGovern campaign. The rest of the anthology illustrates how fantasy theme analysis can be used to analyze and suggest management techniques for political campaigns, can be applied to organizational communication, and can be used to do market research.

The

6

Narrative

Approach

How do the parents of children with severe behavioral problems, including substance abuse, violence, and disobedience, deal with the situation? By sharing their stories of life with a problem child with other parents, members of a Los Angeles area chapter of Toughlove are able to find hope. Tales of a return to discipline and the value of respect for their family are found to be superior to Dr. Spock's advice of tender loving care and the advice-giving stories of other child-care professionals who blame the parent. In the Toughlove narrative, the parent of a problem child is not always at fault. A corollary theme of Toughlove is that parents can help their children by establishing rules, the "bottom line," for what is appropriate behavior (Hollihan and Riley, 1987).

The Toughlove group is a self-help support system. It uses the narration of each member's experiences and a collective approach to dealing with problem children to orient new members and reinforce the commitment of old members to disciplining their children. The group's narratives provide comfort, involvement, continuity, and a sense of empowerment. The rhetorical acts of sharing and combining stories form the basis for finding solutions to the family exigence of problem children (Hollihan and Riley, 1987).

What stories capture the attention of parents with problem children? What risks do they take in accepting the Toughlove story lines? What can the rest of us learn from the Toughlove story? How do we judge it? These questions are answered in "The Rhetorical Power of a Compelling Story: A Critique of a

'Toughlove' Parental Support Group," by Thomas Hollihan and Patricia Riley, found in the suggested readings at the end of this chapter.

The use of narratives as a primary communication form predates human history. Before organized education systems, before written languages, the values and rules of tribal or communal life were transmitted to children and reinforced for adults through narratives. In some ancient societies such as that of the Celts, the position of storyteller, or bard, was revered and powerful in the social hierarchy. With tales of heroes and heroines overcoming great obstacles and winning fierce battles, the storyteller preserved history and interpreted experience. They were frequent travelers, moving from tribe to tribe or village to village, in an age when most people seldom ventured more than a few miles from where they were born. Storytellers were the news services of the ancient world, bringing with them not only the latest news but also a stock of myths and legends.

Like our ancestors, we also tell stories to instruct, explain, reinforce, influence, advocate, and entertain. The availability of mass media has expanded our options for storytelling. Experiencing the rhetorical acts of the speaker, priest, or traveler "live" has become less important in an age of regular newscasts, daily papers, and on-the-scene reports of breaking stories. Electronic recording and inexpensive printing allow us to transcend time and space, bringing us stories of life not only in our age and locale but also in others. Media afford us the opportunity to tell our tales and to be an audience for the narratives of others twenty-four hours a day.

Where are you likely to encounter a narrative? Discourse in narrative form occurs in live public speaking, messages transmitted or recorded electronically (television, radio, film, videotape, audiotape, and computers), and the print media (newspapers, magazines, books, and brochures). We also find narrative in the media traditionally associated with storytelling: novels, live and recorded music, play scripts, and live theatrical performances (M.J. Smith, 1988).

Each of us has a limited amount of direct experience, but that does not make us ignorant or out of touch; we do as our ancestors did, use stories for forming a world view. For every group of people, stories preserve their culture. Although our technology would astound our ancestors, we have much in common with them regarding the aesthetics of storytelling.

A Celtic bard was a one-person show who used his or her skills of voice, body, and symbolism through language to present a story. We share the preference of the bard's audience for communication in story form, though some of our most important sources of narrative discourse are films, videotapes, and television (M.J. Smith, 1988). We have learned about the Civil War from the film *Gone with the Wind,* the television miniseries *North and South,* and its sequel *Love and War.* We have learned about the experiences of the men and women who served in Vietnam from films such as *Apocalypse Now* and *Platoon* and from the television series *Tour of Duty* and *China Beach.*

Some of the earliest theories of communication dealt with the use of narrative. Greek concepts of poetics acknowledged the importance of using dramatic tales to guide belief and behavior. In the fifth century B.C., the comedies of

Aristophanes supported traditional values and poked fun at new trends in politics and education because part of the purpose of Greek theatre, part of artistic development by the playwright, was to provide wise counsel for the state (Fisher, 1985a).

Classical rhetoric interpreted narration as the persuasive case and the use of myth and anecdote. The Roman *narratio* involved telling the facts of a case in story form, as legal depositions do today. Quintilian's rhetoric claimed that putting the facts in story form made the litigant's case more persuasive to the judge because the *narratio* made the case appear more probable, more compelling (Lucaites and Condit, 1985).

Like dramatism and fantasy theme analysis, the narrative approach focuses on humans as symbol users who create dramas as a way of explaining and interpreting their world. The same ideas of characters, setting, and plot are part of the narrative approach. What distinguishes narrative from dramatism and fantasy theme analysis is the technique you employ as a critic and the focus of your evaluation, which results from using the narrative approach to analyze and critique rhetorical activity.

As you read this chapter, remember that the term *narrative* is equivocal and has different meanings in different critical contexts. In Chapter 2, we used the term to identify the organizational pattern of a rhetorical act that chronicles a sequence of events. Narrative theory is also used in studying literature, philosophy, and social sciences such as anthropology, as well as communication. Although these disciplines all use the term *narrative* to denote stories or storytelling, narrative can also be a structure, genre, or paradigm, and there is great variation among disciplines in what those three uses of the term mean.

In this chapter, narrative means both a system for doing rhetorical criticism and a message structure. We define narrative as rhetorical acts conceptualized in story form, that is, symbolic action in the words and deeds of characters that provide order and meaning for an audience, who then create, interpret, and live that action.

Narrative as a Critical Approach

Walter R. Fisher (1978, 1980, 1984, 1985a, 1985b, 1987a, 1987b, and 1989) takes the position that all forms and genres of human communication are fundamentally storytelling. Rather than considering narrative simply as a message told in story form, Fisher expands the concept of narrative to argue that narrative is a complete theory, a paradigm, of human communication. Fisher suggests that it is in our nature as humans to use stories to get at truth. If you see *Apocalypse Now* or read *Everything We Had* and say, "I understand, war is not only physically but also psychologically devastating," you have discovered a truth through narrative. Five premises about human behavior establish Fisher's narrative paradigm (see box on next page).

The truth of a narrative is a combination of what the rhetor intends and the audience interprets in any rhetorical act. A narrative can affirm new ideas and

Premises About

Human Behavior

Underlying the

Narrative

Approach

1. Humans are storytellers by nature; this is not a characteristic that has to be taught to a person.

2. Beliefs and behaviors are based on *good reasons;* good reasons are found in different forms which are determined by the situation and available media.

3. We determine what a good reason is from factors of history, biography, culture, character, and the structure of our native language.

4. The rationality of any story depends on whether or not it "rings true," whether it is consistent with other stories.

5. The world is full of stories, and we must choose among them to determine which ones offer us good reasons. (FISHER, 1984, 1987a)

images, seeking acceptance for them. Narratives can reaffirm existing ideas and images, revitalizing or reinforcing them. A narrative can purify ideas and images by healing or cleansing them. Narratives can subvert ideas and images by discrediting them. Finally, a narrative can eviscerate ideas and images, showing their impossibility or absurdity (Fisher, 1987a).

Narratives rely on a combination of intellect and emotion. They draw on the reasoning skills and the imagination of rhetors and audiences alike. Although a formal education improves reasoning skills, the standards used to determine the rationality of narrative—whether it affirms, reaffirms, purifies, subverts, or eviscerates—ask if the narrative's tale is complete and true. We acquire a sense of the completeness and truthfulness of storytelling through involvement in our culture. Family, church, town, state, and so on teach us how to test the rationality of a story, whether we have a formal education or not.

Fisher (1989) states that his writings on narrative constitute neither a rhetorical theory nor a methodology for rhetorical criticism. He calls his narrative paradigm a "foundation" for developing a structure to explain how and why symbolic messages are created, organized, adapted, and presented to audiences and are received by them. He suggests that though his paradigm can provide rhetorical critics with ideas about the interpretation and evaluation of rhetorical messages, critics must go beyond his concept of narrative to ask questions about the text of narratives, genres of communication, rhetors, the intended and actual audience, and how to reconstruct and deconstruct texts.

In constructing our approach to narrative criticism, we have taken two concepts from Fisher's narrative paradigm. First, that narrative can be used to interpret human communication as a rhetor's response to a rhetorical situation through the creation of symbols that tell a story of characters, their deeds, and the setting in which those deeds were performed. Second, that communication can be evaluated on the basis of narrative fidelity and rationality, judgmental standards that measure the truthfulness and completeness of a rhetorical act.

Fisher's concept of narrative as a message containing characters, actions, and setting is consistent with the drama-based philosophy of communication that says people perform messages on a public stage. It is different from Kenneth Burke's dramatism in that it focuses on individual storytellers and why their stories ring true for the audience, rather than on society as the locus of the dramatistic process. It is different from Ernest Bormann's fantasy theme analysis in that fantasy theme views the drama as removed from the here-and-now of the people who chain out fantasies about it. Fisher's concept of narrative allows for the telling of stories about the here-and-now of the rhetor and audience and those that are removed from it. We shall have more to say about what this means to you as a critic at the end of the chapter.

Because Fisher's concept of a narrative paradigm does not contain a methodology for analyzing the texts of messages, we have added concepts from the work of Seymour Chatman (1978) to provide analytical tools for doing criticism. Chatman's work has concentrated on the structural properties of individual units of discourse, expanding the boundaries of narrative theory in fiction and film. The narrative approach of this chapter combines analytical techniques from Chatman and evaluation criteria from Fisher to give you a system for doing rhetorical criticism.

The narrative approach provides a means for testing the rationality of a story. Consider as narrative *Apocalypse Now,* a story about war, one man's psychic and physical journey up a river that metaphorically corresponds to the psychic and physical devastation of the Vietnam War (Palmer, 1987). Words and visual images symbolizing the horror of war are offered to help the viewer interpret and understand the Vietnam War experience. After seeing the film, you might find yourself agreeing with film historian and critic William J. Palmer (1987), that *Apocalypse Now* provides good reasons to regard war as an invalid foreign policy option. How can you test the goodness of those reasons, the rational and aesthetic qualities of the film as a rhetorical act? You could analyze it in terms of its narrative rationality: What does an audience see as the truth of it?

Narrative Structure

Analyzing the rationality of a narrative depends on your knowledge of its structure. Therefore, you must begin the critical process in the framework of the narrative approach by describing the structure of the rhetorical act in narrative terms. Consider the narrative on two levels. The *discourse* level involves the means used in telling the tale, how the story is presented, the medium used to express its content. The *story* level is the tale being told, its content, the chain of events that are recounted, and what happens to the characters in the tale. This separation of the story from the medium in which it is presented (Chatman, 1978) is useful in describing the rhetorical act because it helps you see the logic of the story as well as the aesthetics of the discourse. You can more successfully evaluate both the reasoning of the tale and the artistic use of a medium to tell it if you consciously separate them first.

As a critic, you benefit from considering story content separate from the medium of discourse because storytelling does not always start at the chronological beginning of a chain of events. In addition, media choices constrain the telling of a story in a variety of ways. All narratives have wholeness, recounting a chain of events (Chatman, 1978), but sometimes you have to rearrange the story elements to discover the wholeness. Episodic television series with large casts of continuing characters and multiple story lines are good examples of why this is necessary (Deming, 1985). *Hill Street Blues, St. Elsewhere,* and *L.A. Law* may spin out a single tale over several episodes before its conclusion is reached. Separating the story line from the medium of its telling facilitates analyzing an individual tale.

Story lines are also transportable across media (Chatman, 1978). You may want to discuss the way different media constrain the telling of the story. *Inherit the Wind,* with its tale of reason versus emotion, science versus religion, has been told through its play script, theatrical production of a live stage play, a commercial film, and a made-for-television movie. Although the story did not change, as a critic you might be interested in the constraints imposed on its telling by different media, different audiences, and different cultural contexts. You might also compare the fictional tale of *Inherit the Wind* to the real-life story of the Scopes trial with its real-life cast of Tennessee high-school science teacher John Scopes as defendant, his lawyer, Clarence Darrow, representing reason and science, and the prosecutor, William Jennings Bryan, representing emotion and religion.

Narrative Discourse: The Telling

The discourse part of narrative is the telling, or *statement* of the story. Two kinds of statements are used to present stories: process statements and stasis statements. The story is enacted through *process statements* (Chatman, 1978). The most common process statements are the dialogue spoken by the characters to each other and the action they engage in. Process statements present characters speaking to one another, running, driving vehicles, riding horses, fighting, and so forth.

Because process statements constitute the saying and doing parts of the telling of the tale, focusing on them enables you to determine which character serves as "designated rhetor," putting into words and deeds the argument of the story. You may also discover that a group of characters serves this function, acting as a sort of Greek chorus. Finally, examining process statements helps you to discover instances in which a secondary character's words and deeds offer a crucial bit of proof for the overall point of the story. Process statements help you describe and analyze how dialogue and action contribute to the structure of a narrative.

One of the recurring process statements in *Apocalypse Now* is the intrusion of the past lives of the characters into the telling of their involvement in the war. Symbolically, this serves the narrative purpose of demonstrating the absurdity of expecting anyone to make sense of their present, the war, given their past lives back home. In one of these process statements, a sailor nicknamed Chef gets off a boat that is taking Captain Willard upriver. Chef wants to pick mangoes, imposing some of his past life as a New Orleans chef on the present of his life, helping the hero track down and kill a fellow army officer. Chef's search for a mango tree ends when a tiger leaps out of the jungle at him. The mangoes symbolize his past life, the tiger, his present life, the war. The process statement demonstrates that the two cannot be mixed. Although this is only one small scene in the over two and one-half hours of *Apocalypse Now,* it combines with other process statements in the film to symbolize the confusion over that war as experienced by those who fought it.

Stasis statements, the second kind of narrative discourse statements to look for, are elements that exist in the story over and above what the characters do and say. Stasis statements expose, identify, or qualify the story told through process statements (Chatman, 1978). Special effects, music, and narration are stasis statements. In *Apocalypse Now,* Captain Willard frequently serves as a narrator, making a series of stasis statements. For example, after Chef's experience with the tiger, Willard says to himself and to the audience, "Damn right! Never get off the fucking boat." In other words, if you want to survive Vietnam, do not allow yourself to be distracted by memories of your past life.

Narrative uses stasis statements to present complicated symbols through artistic effects. The opening of *Apocalypse Now* is a good example of this.

> Coppola chose the technique of superimposition as his means of initially defining the psychology of his grunt Everyman, Captain Willard. That technique introduces the symbolic conception of life in the Vietnam War as a layered phenomenon, a situation in which widely separate realities are constantly being overlaid, superimposed upon one another. . . . Over the image of a simultaneous napalm strike/helicopter assault is superimposed the looming inverted head of Willard. . . . What seemed to be the physical reality of the war is really the psychological reality of Willard's possessed mind. The ceiling fan symbolizes Willard's wounded psyche pulsing out the waves of nightmare. And over these superimposed visual images is superimposed yet another layer, the verbal images in the words of Jim Morrison's apocalyptic song "The End." (PALMER, 1987, pp. 220–221)

This layering was producer-director Francis Ford Coppola's technique for saying something about how the mind works and for describing the social and psychological complexities of the Vietnam War visually and verbally. Identifying stasis statements, the artistic elements in the narrative, enables you to describe and analyze how symbols are developed in the telling of the tale.

Narrative Story: The Tale

Earlier we classified *story* as the chain of events, the characters, and the setting. We now want to focus on the narrative elements of plot, characterization, and setting, which must be abstracted from the narrative text in your descriptive analysis. What you discover about these elements will help you to analyze the narrative rationality of the rhetorical act.

Plot

All narratives have plots; it is logically impossible for a narrative not to have one (Chatman, 1978). The plot may not be obvious, especially if stasis statements are used for artistic effect or if the telling of the tale seems to begin in the middle or at the end.

There are many variations in plot development. Plots may involve problems to be solved, relationships to be worked out, obstacles to be conquered: any situation in which change must occur. Sometimes events themselves are not important: Things will remain pretty much as they are. What is important, insofar as the plot is concerned, is that an existing state of affairs is revealed (Chatman, 1978). Even though all narratives do not conform to traditional plot structure—movement from a beginning state of stability through destabilizing complications of causes and their effects to a stable ending—all narratives seem to involve some degree of crisis and conflict (Martin, 1986).

One ongoing pursuit of narrative theorists is to develop a comprehensive list, or taxonomy, of plot types. Aristotle's *Poetics,* one of the earliest narrative theories to suggest plot types, discussed the successes and failures of heroes and villains and how such outcomes were supposed to be perceived by audiences. Literary theories of narrative have identified various plot types: romance, tragedy, and comedy.

We can make limited uses of plot typologies as a kind of shorthand to describe cultural preferences. Our common culture and individual life experiences are heavily influenced by television and film, so it is possible, even useful, to talk about the plot types of soap opera, situation comedy, western, cop show, kung fu movies, creature features, exposés, and so on. Critics create typologies and sometimes use existing ones because they establish a context in which competing narratives can be compared.

Used in this manner, typologies become formulas that describe certain typical details about plot, character, and setting. When a particular narrative fails to fit neatly into any existing type, the critic creates a new type or introduces variations on old ones. "Dramedy" is an example of this, a recently created category for narratives that blend comedy and tragedy.

Unfortunately, purely content-based plot typologies do not work very well because too many examples of narrative rhetoric do not neatly fit typologies. The best advice we can offer you is to treat each instance of narrative on its own and consider it in terms of the common culture and probable unique life experiences of the audience exposed to it (Chatman, 1978).

Another approach to the idea of a plot type may prove more useful because it is relatively content free: the monomyth. A *monomyth* is a universal story line and a way to explain plot development (Jewett and Lawrence, 1977; W. Martin, 1986). The monomyth theory of plot claims that there is a common plot structure in all narratives in popular culture that contains three elements (W. Martin, 1986):

1. A hero of royal birth or distinguished parentage (a god, king, or someone with great power or talent) is conceived or born under unusual circumstances.
2. The hero escapes death in early childhood, is raised by foster parents, and reaches adulthood to seek his destiny.
3. The hero goes on a journey, has many adventures, overcomes a great obstacle or wins a great battle, and marries a princess or is given great honor.

You may recognize these plot elements in the popular film *Star Wars* and, if you are old enough, the popular 1960s television series *The Fugitive*.

Analysis of several popular narratives, including the television series *Star Trek* and *Little House on the Prairie* and the film *Jaws,* concluded that there is an American version of the monomyth:

> A community in a harmonious paradise is threatened by evil: normal institutions fail to contend with this threat: a selfless superhero emerges to renounce temptations and carry out the redemptive task: aided by fate, his decisive victory restores the community to its paradisal condition: the superhero then recedes into obscurity. (JEWETT AND LAWRENCE, 1977, p. XX)

As with plot typologies, the usefulness of monomyth is that it offers a means of comparing and contrasting narratives. Viewing a narrative as reflecting a socially held monomyth is also useful in discussing how a rhetorical act was or was not a fitting response to a situation. The American monomyth is a redemption drama in which a savior aids society, usually in a nondemocratic way. The myth's message is soothing and satisfying because it says there is always a way to deal with problems that cannot be solved by ordinary human means (Jewett and Lawrence, 1977). If the rhetorical activity you are examining challenges existing institutions and offers a novel or heroic solution to a social exigence, the monomyth might be a useful analytic device.

Whatever approach you eventually use to describe and analyze plot, you must view it as a key element in the narrative story, the tale told in the rhetorical act. All plots have a pattern, and human interest determines how events fit together in a particular narrative (W. Martin, 1986). Human interest is a matter of good reasons, determining which sets of belief-attitude-value are important in a given rhetorical situation (Fisher, 1987a). Your analysis of the story should consider the plot in terms of whether or not its structure offers sufficient detail for it to be considered a good reason.

Not every plot element is of equal importance, and narrative plots always have a certain logic of connection and hierarchy. Major plot elements are the kernel and minor plot elements are satellites (Chatman, 1978). The *kernel* is the point in a narrative that brings events into focus, the moment at which a choice is made, usually by the protagonist, to move in one direction rather than another. In a sense, the kernel is the plot; remove it and you destroy or change the logic of the narrative.

A narrative may have more than one kernel. In *Apocalypse Now,* Captain Willard's decision to accept the mission, to terminate Colonel Kurtz's command, is the first kernel. A second kernel is his decision to kill a wounded Vietnamese woman rather take her to an aid station, which would have interrupted his journey upriver. The final kernel is Captain Willard's decision to kill Kurtz rather than join him. Because *Apocalypse Now* is the story of Everyman's journey into himself and the war (Palmer, 1987), all three events are pivotal to the plot. We do not know what would have happened if he had made other choices, but we know the outcome would have been different.

Satellites are minor plot events, not critical to the logic of the narrative, which embellish the story. A satellite may enhance the aesthetics of the narrative through character development and supporting detail. Satellites provide the details necessary for the rhetor and the audience to work out the logic of the choices made in the kernels.

In *Apocalypse Now,* Captain Willard is offered his mission over lunch. The details of the menu, table settings, and the sounds of helicopters outside obviously do not influence his choice but enhance the overall effect of the unreality and disorientation of the war by juxtaposing the elements of normal life with the abnormal circumstance of the military ordering the execution of one of its own officers.

Kernels and the satellites that develop them are not necessarily in sequence in the tale. When multiple plot lines are present in a single narrative text, your description of the rhetorical act may include rearranging elements of the narrative story into contiguous chronologies so that you can analyze them. Finding kernels and satellites helps you evaluate the consistency of the tale's plot and judge its narrative rationality.

Characterization

Along with a structurally coherent plot, a narrative must have memorable characters. Characterization is central to storytelling, and the extent to which a story is believable often depends on its characters, their motives and behavior. Characters are defined by their decisions and actions and the values reflected by their choices (Fisher, 1987a). Character is also a matter of audience perception of what constitutes heroic or villainous behavior. A narrative contains explicit or implicit evidence of a character's personal qualities, what kind of person he or she is: young or old, rich or poor, black or white, educated or uneducated, experienced or inexperienced, strong or weak, ad infinitum. To this evidence, the audience adds their own experience, real or imagined, of what constitutes acceptable and unacceptable behavior for this type of person, given the circumstances (Chatman, 1978).

Because character is determined by audience perception as well as by the narrative story told by the rhetor, a character who is too fantastic, too far removed from the boundaries of conceivable human experience, may fail to meet tests of rationality. We expect characters who are like us to behave predictably, within our understanding of the bounds of human behavior (Chatman, 1978; Fisher, 1987a; W. Martin, 1986). Monsters, creatures, extraterrestrials, and superbeings are, therefore, endowed with some human qualities to make them understandable to the audience. When a character behaves improbably, the behavior must be explained, some feature of plot or setting must legitimize the behavior. Usually this happens by revealing or implying a motive for the behavior (Chatman, 1978; Fisher, 1987a).

It is not improbable that a hero might engage in some inappropriate, possibly villainous, behavior if he has worthy motive for doing so. Killing is usually inappropriate, but in the context of a war it is legitimized by national policy. Even in war, however, killing people on your own side is inappropriate. Captain Willard's role as Colonel Kurtz's executioner is made to seem appropriate because it is alleged that Kurtz has gone insane and is himself acting inappropriately.

Characterization and narrative rationality regarding heroes boils down to a question of trust: Does the audience develop sufficient identification with the hero's humanity to trust him or her? Is it probable for a heroic character to think or act in the way portrayed, and is that behavior consistent with human nature? For villains, the questions are of distrust and consistency with our expectations of those who are evil. A narrative used for rhetorical purposes attempts to change the audience's belief or behavior by getting them to accept the message contained in the story being told. A character's motives for behaving in a certain way may symbolize the narrative's rhetorical purpose. Audience identification with that character is a matter of whether or not they accept the motivation.

In *Apocalypse Now,* Captain Willard is a symbolic figure, his motives and behaviors represent the often contradictory nature of American involvement in the Vietnam War. He experiences the confusion many people in this country experienced during that era concerning how the war was conducted. To the extent that members of the audience were able to identify with Captain Willard because they found his characterization to be a probable and rational explanation of the Vietnam experience, they would accept the film's message: The war was a physical and psychological hell for the men and women who served in Vietnam.

Setting

Because a narrative's story can take place in any number of temporal and physical settings, narrative theory does not offer as much detail about the setting, other than to advise that the mood, tone, and emotional content of a narrative are influenced by its setting (Chatman, 1978; W. Martin, 1986). Setting must conform to the same requirements of probability and fidelity as plot and characterization. Even if a tale is set "a long time ago, in a galaxy far, far away," its setting is constrained in some ways by human experience and, more significantly, imagination.

We suggest that for purposes of rhetorical analysis and criticism, it is useful to think of setting in terms of the rhetorical situation. For nonfiction narratives, the setting is the historical-social time and place in which the rhetorical act occurs. The case of Toughlove's narrative story, which opens this chapter, is an example of nonfiction narrative. Set in the present and focused on the problems of family life in America, Toughlove group members tell their stories about the here and now and their experiences with child rearing. For them to talk about the same topic as it pertained to life in Elizabethan England or in "a galaxy far, far away" would make no sense. Toughlove narratives respond to the rhetorical situation of parents with problem children.

The tales told in news stories, public speeches, documentaries, and other nonfiction narratives are constrained by audience expectations. Narratives about the nuclear accidents at Three Mile Island and Chernobyl are not fiction, nor can they be easily treated as such. Recasting any of these tales into a fictional setting is a creative choice open to the rhetor, but it may be a risky one if the audience cannot transcend the immediate setting of the rhetorical situation. *China Syndrome,* a fictional film that tells a similar tale of the dangers of nuclear power, can be dismissed as "only a movie."

However, in a situation in which the rhetor wants to talk about the future, there is no choice but to adopt a fictional, albeit probable, setting. Ratification of the U.S. Constitution in 1788 was opposed by many prominent men. Patrick Henry's speech against ratification in the Virginia convention was a narrative telling a tale cast in the future. His speech questioned the wisdom of ratification by offering a series of what-if scenarios. For example, he argued against the wisdom of making the president the commander in chief of the military, a situation that produced concern many years later in the last days of the Nixon presidency. In your examination of nonfiction narratives, consider the setting in terms of how its rendering by the rhetor corresponds to the historical-social setting of the rhetorical situation.

Setting in purely fictional narratives usually involves both the tale's fictional setting and the rhetorical situation posed by the historical-social context in which it is told. Sometimes the fictional setting is allegorical. Arthur Miller's play *The Crucible* is set in colonial Salem during the witch hunts. Its plot and characterization develop the theme of "guilt by association." Miller's play, written in 1952 and first performed on 22 January 1953, was an allegory for the "witch hunts" of Joseph McCarthy's pursuit of domestic communism. Although the setting was recast to the seventeenth century, the issue of guilt by association was very much a part of the rhetorical situation of the early 1950s.

The connection between the fictional setting and the rhetorical situation may be made by the audience, rather than intended by the rhetor. Arthur Miller deliberately chose to write a play about the Salem witch hunts to communicate his message about McCarthyism. The film *Gone with the Wind* was released in 1939, primarily to make money by entertaining its audience. Audiences made a connection between the Civil War and the rhetorical situation imposed by the beginning of World War II. Even though we were not in the war yet, the stage for our entry was being set through a series of lend-lease agreements and the pro-British sentiments of the Roosevelt administration. The link between *Gone with the Wind* and America circa 1939 was that the film was a story about change brought on by war. Theatre audiences identified with characters in the film whose lives were changed by that war in ways they did not foresee and worried because they saw that it could happen to them. If you consider works of fiction as rhetorical acts, look for the possible links an audience may have forged between the narrative's setting and the historical-social context of their own times.

Fictional worlds may be entirely the product of the rhetor's and the audience's collective imaginations. Much of science fiction is rhetorical, reflecting on human behavior or the impact of technology on humanity. Over the past two decades, James White has written a series of novels set at Sector General, a galactic center for healing, that promotes tolerance for differences. *Star Surgeon, Hospital Station, Major Operation, Ambulance Ship, Code Blue,* and other novels in the series feature the human hero-physician Conway and tales of his adventures as a healer. White's rhetorical purpose in telling these tales is to overcome xenophobia and prejudice and instill an appreciation for all intelligent life.

Not all fictional narratives are set in imaginary places. *Apocalypse Now,* set in Vietnam during the height of American involvement, was released four years after the American presence had ended with the fall of Saigon in 1975. The film was set relatively close to the experience, real or imagined, of its audience. In 1979, the rhetorical situation included the aftershock of defeat and the fact that after almost a decade of involvement in the war, Americans were still trying to sort out what it all meant. For audiences in 1979, the fictional setting for *Apocalypse Now* and the historical-social setting in which it was told were very similar. Fictional narratives take on some of the properties of nonfiction when they are set close to the audience's experience.

Describing and analyzing the narrative story in terms of plot, characterization, and setting enables you to evaluate the tale's rationality, the basis of its ability to influence belief and behavior. What you discover about plot, characterization, and setting, along with the details of how the tale was told, how process and stasis statements were used in the narrative discourse, will enable you to consider its rationality.

Narrative Rationality

The form a rhetorical act takes is not what determines whether or not it will influence belief or behavior. In the right circumstances, a song can be more persuasive than a speech, or an enormously influential film can be made from a novel few people read. The values embodied in a narrative, values that an audience accepts as good reasons to change belief or behavior, are what make that narrative persuasive. Basically, a narrative provides advice about how to think or what to do about something.

In the narrative approach, analysis of the elements of plot, character, setting, and presentation involves testing the probability and fidelity of the story. You examine the story in terms of whether or not it offers a complete and plausible depiction of reality. Ultimately, you must judge whether the narrative was a source of good reasons. A good reason is that which the audience finds in the narrative and uses to authorize, sanction, or justify a belief or behavior.

Fisher (1987a) describes the logic of good reasons used to test narrative rationality. The goodness of the reasons offered in any story can be measured in terms of several kinds of questions (see box below).

In determining the completeness of a narrative and its accuracy in making assertions about social reality, you should treat the narrative as an argument grounded and warranted by its plot, characters, setting, or manner of presentation. An audience initially responds to a narrative according to the aesthetic properties—Is it a good story told well?—but this aesthetic response can lead to

---

Questions Used

to Test Narrative

Rationality

Questions of Fact: What are implicit and explicit values in the rhetorical act?

Questions of Relevance: Are the values in the message appropriate to the kind of decision, change in belief or behavior, asked of the audience? Are values omitted, distorted, or misrepresented?

Questions of Consequence: What is the result of adhering to the values in the narrative? What happens to concepts of self, behavior, relationships, society, and the process of rhetorical action? How are values operationalized? What is the morality of the story?

Questions of Consistency: Are the values confirmed or validated in the personal experience of the audience and the life stories or statements of credible others? Does the narrative make its appeal to some ideal audience?

Questions of Transcendent Issue: Above and beyond a story's response to the rhetorical situation with a complete set of reasons or a fitting response, do the values reflected in the story constitute an ideal for human behavior? (FISHER, 1987a) reasoned belief. The characters, their words and deeds, and the consequences of their behavior become proof, created by the rhetor and interpreted by the audience. In testing narrative rationality, you are trying to determine why an audience accepts a story as true, a good reason for belief or behavior, judged on the basis of its completeness. It also must be judged on its competitiveness.

We have used *Apocalypse Now* as a running example to illustrate how a critic describes and analyzes narrative structure because it is immediately recognizable as a story. How can you use these concepts of structure to analyze a rhetorical act, a speech for example, that is not recognizable as a story? In the "telling" part of narrative analysis, process statements are those parts of the message that are the original thoughts of the rhetor. Stasis statements can be regarded as material the rhetor takes from other sources, such as quotations, anecdotes, and allegories.

Nonfiction rhetorical acts can also be analyzed using the concepts of the tale by thinking of plot in terms of the theme or central idea the rhetor wants to communicate. Kernels are the main ideas of the rhetorical act, and satellites are auxiliary elements which may include introductory and conclusionary material, asides, or departures from the central theme. Nonfiction works also offer characterization, even if it is just the projected persona of the rhetor.

Apocalypse Now is one example from among hundreds of works of fiction and nonfiction that rhetors and audiences have used to explain and understand the Vietnam War. Many are commercial endeavors that compete for economic success. At least a part of that success comes from telling a tale that strikes a responsive chord in the audience, providing a vision of a truth or what the audience wishes were a truth in the tale being told. Thus, narratives compete to offer the best explanation, consciously or unconsciously providing good reasons to believe in or to do something about the men and women who served in Vietnam and about America's role in the affairs of other nations. When you read, view, or participate in any other way in one of these Vietnam narratives, you test the logic of its advice.

Although narratives compete to offer the best set of good reasons, they can also be examined cumulatively. Taken in toto, the Vietnam narratives provide a series of reasons that lead to or reference values about life, patriotism, and security. Collectively, they may become self-validating, with each successive narrative adding to what the audience has already come to believe.

Using the logic of good reasons, we might evaluate the completeness and competitiveness of *Apocalypse Now* as an argument about American intervention in the affairs of other nations. Used singly or in combination, the five questions of fact, relevance, consequence, consistency, and transcendent issues would help determine what an audience finds in *Apocalypse Now* that would cause them to accept the premise that we must never again become involved in such a war.

Identifying the narrative's audience is important to your ability to test its rationality. Your evaluation establishes why the values expressed in a narrative were relevant and consistent, had consequence, and were tied to other values by referencing the rhetorical situation. You have to know the nature and function of values, which values took precedence over others and which values were in conflict specific to the rhetorical situation that existed at the time the tale was told.

Many narratives have a long life: Films are reproduced on videotape; novels and nonfiction are reprinted in paperback and are available from public libraries; and a popular television series may go on for years and then go into syndication. Therefore, identifying an audience and what it might value depends on your reason for doing the criticism. For example, if you want to evaluate *Apocalypse Now* as a source of good reasons, you might only consider 1979 and 1980, when the film was in theatrical release. However, if you consider the film as part of the larger Vietnam narrative that includes recent films such as *Gardens of Stone, Platoon,* and *Full Metal Jacket,* as well as oral histories from the mid-1980s such as *Everything We Had* and *Nam* and personal accounts of the Vietnam experience such as *Home Before Morning,* your concept of audience might focus only on the present or might include the period from 1979 up to the present.

Narrative rationality measures the extent to which a story functions as an argument to believe or do something. One or more values warrant or justify accepting the story. To determine if a value is relevant, you must consider it in terms of the rhetorical situation and the values of the time as expressed in other narratives or by credible sources. Testing the consistency, consequence, and transcendence of a value requires examination of the complete narrative structure as a statement of the value. Through this process, you will be able to draw conclusions about whether the narrative was regarded as true and thus influenced belief or behavior, as well as about its aesthetic and ethical properties.

The Narrative Approach
and Critical Evaluation

The narrative approach focuses criticism of a rhetorical act on its truth and aesthetic standards because a narrative combines reason and art. Emphasis on a logic of good reasons and tests of narrative rationality lead to application of the truth standard as you test the soundness of a story's values by looking for factualness, relevance, consequence, consistency, and transcendent issues.

The Truth Standard

Evaluating the rhetorical act for its narrative fidelity is the key to judgment using the truth standard. The story of a rhetorical act is judged against what the audience believes to be true; you ask how truth as represented in the rhetorical act jibes with what the audience has experienced. Audiences accept as truth those stories that resemble or represent their own experiences.

Even imaginary tales can be evaluated on the basis of narrative fidelity. Although commonsense tells us that the Galactic Federation of James White's science fiction stories exists only in his imagination, his stories identify what produces prejudice, xenophobia, and racism. His stories argue that by working at it, intelligent beings can overcome their differences, work together, and make life better. This argument can be separated from its imaginary setting and its fidelity tested. Evaluation of a narrative uncovers the truths reflected in its story elements.

Rhetorical evaluation using the narrative approach is concerned with audience response, how they were likely to interpret the truths contained in the tale and use them to make decisions about how to live. Although the rhetor can be allowed some poetic license in telling a fictional tale, the logic of good reasons suggests that an audience will reject an irrational story or a story based on a lie. Although we expect that nonfictional narratives such as biographies, histories, and news reports will refrain from exaggerating or interpreting facts in ways that render them invalid, the logic of good reasons can be used to uncover narrative lies in nonfiction as well.

The Aesthetic Standard

Because the narrative approach is concerned with the structural elements of a story, how it is told, the aesthetic standard is also important in evaluation. Fisher's (1987a) claim that audiences first react to the aesthetic properties of a narrative means that how a story is told is important to its success as a rhetorical act. A good tale poorly told is likely to fail.

Whereas print narratives are judged on the ability of words on a page to engage the reader's emotions and imagination, the aesthetic properties of narratives delivered through other media can be evaluated on a wider range of criteria. Film, video, and live performance depend on the aesthetics of sound, special effects, exotic settings, costumes, props, and music to tell a story.

The symbols used in the rhetorical act have aesthetic properties which are not ignored in the narrative approach. Symbols are key factors in how a narrative addresses the exigence in the rhetorical situation, and the way that a symbol engages the audience's emotions and logic depends on the medium used to communicate it. Therefore, judgments about the aesthetic properties of a narrative must take into account how process and stasis statements were adapted to the constraints imposed by the narrative's medium of communication and how the tale's message was influenced by the manner of its telling.

Because narratives have plots, typologies or monomyths can be useful in evaluating aesthetic properties. As in fantasy theme analysis, you should consider the story structurally. How do plot development, characterization, and setting contribute to a certain type of story development? Is that development believable or compelling, given the tale? For example, the conventions of science fiction, as a type of story development, may not be the best genre to use to argue for improved human relations.

The Results Standard

The results standard of judgment is useful in evaluating how one narrative competes with another. Why do some stories succeed when other stories offering the same argument fail? The results standard may combine with the truth standard so that stories perceived as true are more likely to gain public acceptance.

In some instances, the medium of communication separates the rhetor of the narrative from the audience. In such cases, it may be necessary to consider both an implied audience and a real audience. The *implied audience* is the one the rhetor had in mind as ideal, the sort of people most likely to respond favorably to the story (Chatman, 1978; Fisher, 1987a); this is the concept of an ideal audience discussed in Chapter 2. *Real audiences* are those who used the narrative in some way, interpreting it and seeing it as having some connection to their own lives; this is a composite of the empirical, change agent, and created audience discussed in Chapter 2. The real audience may or may not have much in common with the implied audience (Chatman, 1978). A narrative's success is judged in terms of the extent to which a real audience accepted its message.

Those narratives that are commercial endeavors are communicated through media in which results are measured statistically. You can find out how many copies of a book, recording, or video were sold. You can use television ratings and theatre ticket sales to determine how many people watched a program or attended a performance. What these measures cannot tell you is what the people experienced and how they were affected.

Qualitative rather than quantitative measures of the success of these narratives are found in reviews and commentaries. Monitor what critics say about a book, film, recording, play, or television program. This type of results assessment also has limitations. The box office success of the critically ridiculed "Rambo" films says something about the influence of professional film critics on public taste. Unless a critic influences the decision of potential members of the audience to buy, read, rent, or watch the narrative, and further influences their affective response, the critic's words are only one person's opinion.

The Ethical Standard

Novelists are linked to their work to the extent that we refer to novels as "the new Stephen King book" or "a Barbara Cartland romance." A speaker may be linked to a subject as Russell Conwell is linked to his "Acres of Diamonds." Directors are often linked to their films because they exert such a tremendous influence on the final product; thus we speak of Frank Capra or Alfred Hitchcock films as having the imprint of their style. When there is a clear link between the rhetor and the narrative, judging worthiness of narrative purpose—the ethical standard of judgment—is both important and possible.

Just as narratives have implied and real audiences, they can also have implied and real rhetors. The *real rhetor* is the person or group who constructed the narrative, arranged its elements, and adapted it to its medium (Chatman, 1978; Deming, 1985). Speeches are often written by teams of speech writers and consultants; films and television programs are the work of several layers of creative specialists.

The *implied rhetor* is created by the audience's interpretation of who is the teller of the narrative's tale (Chatman, 1978; Deming, 1985). Whether the message is overt, as is the antiwar message of the Vietnam documentary *Hearts and Minds,* or covert, as are the messages about relationships in *Cagney and Lacey,* the determination of implied rhetor is made by the audience as it experiences the narrative. Even an object can become the implied rhetor, as it often does in a film in which the audience experiences the scene of the narrative from the point of view of "the camera" through a series of shots from different angles (Deming, 1985). Evaluating the ethical behavior of such an implied rhetor involves deciding whether or not the audience was being deceived or manipulated by media tricks.

Another dimension of the ethical standard as it applies to narrative is the characterization of implied rhetors. Because characters serve as role models, characterization in narrative is how morality is demonstrated. Because characters confront situations that demand moral choices (Lewis, 1987), using the ethical standard to evaluate their behavior is appropriate. If you were using the narrative approach to evaluate *Cagney and Lacey,* you could apply the ethical standard to evaluate the behavior of the implied rhetors, usually Christine or Mary Beth, relative to honesty, dedication to duty, and other professional values.

Uses and Limitations

One of the advantages of the narrative approach is that it allows examination of media as a purveyor of social values. It also provides a way to account for what an audience does with a narrative. Audiences accept stories because they find a truth in them and then use those stories to validate belief and behavior. Fisher's adaptation of principles of reasoning and his logic of good reasons provide a way of evaluating narrative as argument so that you can discuss what makes it persuasive.

The narrative approach attempts to make the connections between emotion and logic. One problem in rhetorical criticism is how to judge something that engages both the audience's emotions and their reason at the same time. The narrative approach does not separate these aspects of human response, asking instead: Do stories provide new, recurring, and useful insights about society? (Bennett and Edelman, 1985). Because it is human nature to tell stories, the narrative approach gives you a way to examine how rhetors use the elements of plot, characterization, and the aesthetics of storytelling to make their messages appealing and compelling (Rowland, 1987).

Walter R. Fisher has advocated acceptance of a narrative paradigm as a universal communication theory that encompasses all rhetorical activity and offers the judgmental criteria for testing the fidelity and rationality of communication-as-story. Some communication scholars do not accept the narrative paradigm as Fisher has developed it. His critics cite two deficiencies: The theory loses its explanatory ability when all communication is seen as narrative, and the paradigm lacks critical structure (Lucaites and Condit, 1985; McGee and Nelson, 1985; Rowland, 1987 and 1989; Tompkins, 1988; Warnick, 1987).

Robert Rowland (1989) puts the limitations of Fisher's narrative paradigm in perspective, stating that conceptualizing all rhetorical activity as stories undervalues those rhetorical acts of fiction and nonfiction that very obviously use a story structure. Rowland claims that the narrative paradigm works very well when applied to works that are obviously stories but begins to break down when applied to many other communication forms. With many nonstory rhetorical acts, the critic must deconstruct the text to find elements of character, plot, and setting and then reconstruct it in story form to test narrative fidelity and rationality. In so doing, it is possible to lose sight of the significance of some rhetorical acts, and a different approach to criticism may be more appropriate.

We suggest that you consider narrative as the structural communication type: story. This emphasizes the dual nature of narrative as both a structure and a mode of communication. This reflects our philosophy of a narrative approach to criticism as presented in this chapter: A narrative methodology is apppropriate for analyzing rhetorical acts that take the form of stories. We also suggest that Fisher's evaluation system for testing stories on the basis of fidelity and rationality is a major contribution to the development of a rhetorical view of narrative.

We are not suggesting that you should use only the narrative approach to analyze and evaluate works of fiction. Although we do not concur with Fisher that all rhetorical activity is storytelling, we do believe that a significant amount of rhetorical activity is presented in story form. As you describe a rhetorical act and begin to consider your options for criticism, you should consider the structural form of the act. Does it have the structural properties of a narrative? If it does, the narrative approach may be the most appropriate choice of a critical method.

Also consider the connection between the audience and the rhetorical act. The narrative approach does not rely on the rhetor's intentions alone to determine whether something is or is not a rhetorical act. Stephen King may write "horror" fiction because he enjoys it or because he can make a living doing it. As such, we might not classify his novels and short stories as rhetorical acts. However, if King's readers use his narratives to understand and cope with things that cause fear, their use makes his narratives rhetorical.

You may also want to combine concepts from narrative with concepts from other approaches, an organic approach to criticism. For example, Fisher (1987a) suggests that principles of argumentation, from the traditional approach, be used in testing narrative rationality. Incorporate concepts from Chapter 3 on types of reasoning, tests of evidence, or the Toulmin model of argument in testing narrative fidelity and rationality. You might also incorporate concepts from fantasy theme analysis in place of the techniques of structural analysis described in this chapter.

Dramatism, Fantasy Theme, and Narrative

Burke's dramatism, Bormann's fantasy theme analysis, Fisher's narrative paradigm, and Chatman's theory of narrative structure all reference the dramatic conventions of plot lines, characterization, and scenes in which action takes place. The philosophy of "life as a social drama" makes these approaches similar. There are also distinct differences among these approaches in terms of the kind of criticism each produces.

Dramatism is an inclusive sociology of human communication. It says that overcoming division through a strategic combination of act, agent, agency, scene, and purpose to produce identification is the goal of rhetorical activity. Fantasy theme analysis is a theory of message making. It says that people create detailed fantasies through the process of chaining out in order to explain or interpret reality. Some fantasies succeed, become complete rhetorical visions, and reappear in many rhetorical acts as salient explanations of the world. Narrative theory says that storytelling is one of the most common forms of human communication. Through the vehicle of the story, the rhetor offers an argument that, if judged to be true, offers the audience good reasons to justify belief and behavior.

The narrative approach shares elements of dramatism and fantasy theme analysis in its emphasis on plot, characterization, and setting but puts a different emphasis on what you do with these elements in analyzing and evaluating rhetorical acts. Like dramatism, narrative uses a concept similar to identification in determining why an audience accepts a particular story as a source of good reasons because the act of accepting one story over another is an act of identification with it as the most reasonable explanation to justify belief and behavior.

The difference between dramatism and narrative lies in how you examine the rhetorical act. Using dramatism, you do criticism by thinking of people who act out roles prescribed by scene, agency, and purpose within a social hierarchy. Criticism focuses on the strategic choices the rhetor made in creating relationships. Because rhetorical strategies are designed to overcome divisions among people through identification, the ethical standard of evaluation focusing on a rhetor's strategies is crucial in dramatism.

Although narrative is also concerned with how symbols and dramatic action join people together or separate them from some larger group, it is less concerned with how the rhetor managed language to achieve identification. Instead, narrative is concerned with the rationality of an act, how a story functions as an argument about good reasons. Therefore, narrative criticism places greater emphasis on the truth standard of evaluation and on the degree of accuracy that a story is seen to have compared with others in a rhetorical situation.

Like fantasy theme analysis, narrative views humans as perceiving events in terms of the dramatic elements of heroes and villains, plots, settings, and props found in the structural properties of narratives. Like fantasy theme analysis, narrative focuses criticism on the story, but narrative evaluates the success of a story based on its rational properties. Although fantasy theme analysis is also concerned with the story's probable truth, it is more concerned with how a particular story catches on and attracts a rhetorical community of people who share its fantasy, a very narrow distinction.

The greater distinction is that narrative is slightly more flexible in allowing consideration of the rhetor-message-audience relationship, because fantasy theme analysis is more concerned with the audience's role of cocreating or sharing a fantasy. Fantasy theme analysis views all messages as concerning that which is removed from the here-and-now of those who create and share the fantasy. Narrative conceptualizes rhetors as storytellers who may set their tale in the here-and-now or in some other location. A further distinction is that though a fantasy often concerns real people and events, the creators of the fantasy are not the people who populate it. In narrative, the rhetor may be the central character, and the audience may play a part in the story.

Compared with narrative, the critical process in dramatism and fantasy theme analysis places less emphasis on separating the structure of the story from the medium of its transmission. The critical process in the narrative approach, as presented in this chapter, urges separation of the tale from the manner of its telling and consideration of how the choice of medium of communication affects what is communicated. In some instances in which the same story is told by different means, the narrative approach may help you discover how people use media and how media differ in what they contribute to a story's persuasiveness.

Summary

The narrative approach views human communication as combining the persuasive properties of argumentation and the aesthetic properties of literature. Critics using this approach are encouraged to examine the rhetorical act in terms of both the tale and its telling and to consider how the story serves an audience as a good reason for belief and behavior.

Storytelling is part of human nature and has been an important means of communication in every period and culture. Understanding how we use stories to influence belief and behavior involves looking at the structure of a story to determine what about it causes an audience to perceive it as a truth. The narrative approach enables critics to describe, analyze, and evaluate rhetorical acts in terms of

> *Narrative, the tale:* The content of the story found in the chain of events that happen to characters in the story's settings; the tale to be told.
>
> *Narrative discourse, the telling:* How the story is told through a particular medium and the constraints imposed on the narrative by media choice; the telling of the tale.
>
> *Narrative rationality:* The ability of the story to serve as a reliable and desirable guide for belief and behavior. The

accuracy of the story as a "truth" compared with competing narratives in the rhetorical situation depends on its probability and fidelity. Narrative probability is concerned with the tale's structural properties: is the story complete and free from contradictions? Narrative fidelity examines the truthfulness of the story by applying the logic of good reasons. Narrative rationality evaluates a story's ability to warrant accepting it as a good reason.

Used alone or in conjunction with other approaches, the narrative approach provides a framework for examining genres of rhetorical activity such as novels, films, biographies and histories, television programs, song lyrics, and plays as persuasive arguments.

Suggested Readings

Examples of Criticism

CARPENTER, R.H. (1986).   Admiral Mahan, "narrative fidelity," and the Japanese attack on Pearl Harbor. *Quarterly Journal of Speech, 72,* 290–305.

> The writings of American naval historian Alfred T. Mahan influenced Japanese military strategy and the decision to attack Pearl Harbor on 7 December 1941. This article critiques Mahan's work, *The Influence of Sea Power Upon History,* examining how its narrative was a warrant for Pacific expansion. Carpenter uses Japanese accounts of naval strategy to explain how and why they saw Mahan's book as a "truth" about naval power. This is an excellent example of narrative analysis and criticism of nonfiction applying Fisher's concepts.

HOLLIHAN, T.A. AND RILEY, P. (1987).   The rhetorical power of a compelling story: A critique of a "Toughlove" parental support group. *Communication Quarterly, 35,* 13–25.

> Concepts from Burke's dramatism and Fisher's narrative paradigm are used to examine the use of stories in a Los Angeles area Toughlove group to emphasize strict discipline for problem children and absolve the parent of blame for a child's misbehavior. This is an excellent, well-written example of narrative criticism. It demonstrates how critics can evaluate "live" nonfiction narratives from a rhetorical perspective.

LEWIS, W.F. (1987).   Telling America's story: Narrative form and the Reagan presidency. *Quarterly Journal of Speech, 73,* 280–302.

> Ronald Reagan's distinctive style has earned him the title, Great Communicator. As a storyteller, Reagan relies primarily on anecdotes, short stories, myths, and interpretations of American history. Lewis uses narrative concepts from Fisher to examine Reagan's reputation and style and the effects of his rhetoric. This article is a good example of how to analyze narrative rationality because Lewis offers an extensive discussion of truth as found in Reagan's presidential messages.

SMITH, L.D. (1988).   Narrative styles in network coverage of the 1984 nominating conventions. *Western Journal of Speech Communication, 52,* 63–74.

Using narrative concepts from Chatman and Fisher, this article analyzes the ABC, CBS, and NBC coverages of the 1984 Democratic and Republican conventions in terms of story content and manner of expression. Smith shows how a critic types story lines, and he discusses each network's coverage in terms of plot types: NBC's *Laugh-In,* CBS's *Father Knows Best,* and ABC's *Wide World of Sports.* His analysis includes a discussion of how podium statements, films, anchor commentary, floor commentary and events, and commercials were all interwoven into each plot type. This article provides an excellent demonstration of how concepts from Chatman and Fisher can enhance narrative criticism.

Resources for Doing Criticism

CHATMAN, S. (1978). *Story and discourse, narrative structure in fiction and film.* Ithaca, NY: Cornell University Press.

Chatman explains concepts of time and space, kinds of narrators, and characterization to develop his structural theory of narrative. We drew from Chatman in our development of a narrative approach, so if you would like to learn more about narrative structure, we strongly recommend this text. Many of the examples are drawn from film, and Chatman treats the technical aspects of filmmaking in some depth. He also provides excellent comparisons of the structural differences between the film and the novel as narrative forms.

DEMING, C.J. (1985). *Hill Street Blues* as narrative. *Critical Studies in Mass Communication,* 2, 1–22.

Deming focuses on how the narrative structure of *Hill Street Blues* contributes to the program's quality. Although this is not a rhetorical evaluation of the series, you will find that her discussion of how viewers responded to the program offers insight into its narrative rationality. Deming uses Chatman's theory of narrative, and her work is an excellent example of structural analysis. This article demonstrates why it is necessary to separate story from its manner of presentation to produce effective criticism.

FISHER, W.R. (1987). *Human communication narration: Toward a philosophy of reason, value, and action.* Columbia, SC: University of South Carolina Press.

Fisher's essays on narrative paradigm are reproduced in this book, which is a little difficult to read because concepts vary from chapter to chapter, and the reader has to piece everything together. Fisher challenges the "old rhetoric," what he calls the "rational paradigm" of science and logic, and suggests that all communication is narrative. He offers several extended examples in justifying his view of communication and the utility of narrative paradigm. The first two chapters provide a nice synopsis of rhetorical theory from classical times to the present as Fisher explains the turf battles over which theory best accounts for what communication is and does.

MARTIN, W. (1986). *Recent theories of narrative.* Ithaca, NY: Cornell University Press.

Literary theories of narrative can be confusing if you lack a strong background in literature. We find Martin's synoptic approach to literary theory to be the most useful and readable work for the neophyte on narrative in literature. He acknowledges that narrative analysis must be concerned with both the rhetorical and the structural properties of literature, incorporating both views in his text. If you want to learn more about narrative theory from a literary perspective, this is a good source.

The

7

Cultural

Approaches

What messages and media reaffirm American cultural values of honesty and fair play? Sport, amateur and professional competition, is one of our great social institutions, and baseball is our "national pastime." Baseball also has a long-standing relationship with American newspapers because its popularity paralleled the growth of daily newspapers in mid-nineteenth century America. The symbiotic relationship between baseball and the mass media continues today (Trujillo and Ekdom, 1985).

Soon after the 1984 baseball season opened, the Chicago Cubs were in last place in their division. Failure turned into fortune as they went on to dominate the National League Eastern Division. Sportswriting about the Cubs reflected American cultural value clusters, which provided an interpretive framework to explain the Cubs' success. Baseball coverage in the *Chicago Tribune* used six pairs of opposing values to describe failure and fortune: winning and losing, tradition and change, teamwork and individualism, work and play, youth and experience, and logic and luck. One-half of a pair explained the other. Losing, for example, was used to explain winning. Losing was merely a temporary setback because even the best teams occasionally lose a few. The failures and fortunes of a favorite team often serve as a metaphor for the human condition because even the best of us lose once in a while (Trujillo and Ekdom, 1985). Thus, sportswriting about the Cubs served as a metaphor for the human experience and as a way of knowing about the nature of humanity.

Did coverage of the Cubs play a part in affirming American values? Can we learn anything about American value conflicts by reading about our favorite teams in the newspaper? Is there a rhetorical thrust to the sports page? Nick Trujillo and Leah Ekdom (1985) identified elements of a rhetoric of sportswriting, which in addition to explaining the rags-to-riches rise of the Cubs also provided a synthesis of those values underlying American culture as reflected in our national pastime. To learn more about cultural analysis and the rhetoric of sportswriting, see "Sportswriting and American Cultural Values: The 1984 Chicago Cubs" by Trujillo and Ekdom, listed in the suggested readings at the end of this chapter.

In Chapter 1 we said that rhetoric is culture bound, influenced by what exists in the culture from which it emanates. This means that elements of the parent culture are, logically, a potential source of criteria to use in interpreting and evaluating rhetorical acts in that culture. Contemporary communication criticism does just that. Because our culture is dominated by mass-mediated communication, cultural criticism is frequently concerned with devising models to evaluate the rhetorical products of the mass media.

Culture is a complex of collectively determined sets of rules, values, ideologies, and habits that constrain rhetors and their acts (Gronbeck, 1983). It is also a political term, incorporating all the meanings found in the collective experience of a society. Meaning and the making of meaning are what constitute culture (Fiske, 1987a). Cultural approaches to criticism examine the creation and distribution of meaning in contemporary society.

Contemporary Western societies are complex networks of divergent groups engaged in a struggle for social power. Groups are divided by demographic and psychographic characteristics such as gender, race, ethnic origin, age, religious preference, occupation, education, and political affiliation. The politics of culture are dynamic; dominant groups strive to maintain their influence while subordinate groups attempt to gain control of cultural meanings.

Culturally based criticism can explain, analyze, and account for the rhetorical exigences and acts that gave rise to the civil-rights, feminist, antinuclear, and environmental movements in our history. Culturally based criticism also explains, analyzes, and accounts for the popularity of the products of mass culture, such as films, songs, television programs, books, and newspapers, because it is through these media that audiences learn or reaffirm cultural rules, values, ideologies, and habits, as was the case when sportswriting explained values for Cubs fans.

In the various forms that cultural approaches to criticism take, both the message of a rhetorical act and the medium of its transmission are potential objects of criticism. Culturally based criticism acknowledges Marshall McLuhan's celebrated thought that the "medium is the message," being concerned as it is with how a message is shaped by its medium. What does this mean to you as a critic? Social, political, and economic forces create the rules, values, ideologies, and habits that define a culture. Cultural critics consider these forces in rendering judgments about rhetorical acts and their media of transmission. Thus, cultural approaches to criticism may conclude that a television program reflects social, political, and economic forces in its message and that the medium of television has social, political, and economic consequences for the culture. When you use one of these approaches as your critical focus, you are trying to discover the impact, consequences, and morality of both the message and the media relative to the cultural milieu from which they emanated.

Cultural approaches to criticism focus on what communication does for a culture. Criticism is based on the assumption that rhetorical acts, particularly those conveyed by popular or mass media, are the social record of a culture. Culturally based criticism is concerned with how messages and media reflect the values of society and how the popular culture industry of mass media exploits those values (Wander, 1981). A cultural critic might conclude that a protest song such as Phil Ochs's "Draft Dodger Rag" represented antiestablishment values while the music industry advanced a different, possibly contradictory, set of values by popularizing the song through mass distribution and play.

In previous chapters, the concept of each approach was more focused, an approach constituted a single method for doing criticism. Cultural approaches to criticism are the most organic methods for communication criticism because they do not depend on a single theory base. Because there are so many possibilities for doing cultural criticism, no single approach can be identified as "the cultural approach."

Even though operating from a cultural perspective allows you a great deal of freedom in designing a formula for doing criticism, all studies representing a cultural approach follow a similar fundamental process. Cultural criticism always begins with the message itself, usually termed the *text,* and proceeds with the development of a methodology based on what is found in the message. This is the same basic idea as the "conventional wisdom" we told you to follow (in Chapter 2) relative to beginning the critical process. Look for what can be established as fact and negation in the rhetorical act and its medium of transmission.

Fact in cultural criticism is what is found through direct observation of the text and its medium (Wander, 1981). You might, for example, count the frequency of acts of violence against women as opposed to men in a horror film or the relative number of infidelities committed by men or women in a soap opera. You might also make observations about the medium, such as the number of wide-angle versus close-up shots of violence in the horror film or the use of mood music in the soap.

Negation, what is *not* found in the text and its medium, also has significance in cultural criticism (Wander, 1981). The absence of Hispanic, Asian, or older characters in prime-time series television is noticeable. Exterior shots may be absent in a television situation comedy, or a particular recognizable name-brand product may not be used as a prop.

Simply counting the number of instances of fact and negation is only the beginning. In addition to collecting this information, you must interpret it. This is the most subjective aspect of cultural criticism. Because critics are a part of their own cultures, how you interpret a fact is subjectively determined by your own beliefs, attitudes, and values. If you are Caucasian and of Belgian ethnic origin, the absence of Asian characters in heroic roles in television programs might not seem significant in your observation of negation. If you are Asian and of Korean ethnic origin, you might decide that the absence of Asian heroes tells you something about the social, political, and economic status of Asian-Americans in our culture. You might decide that what is or is not there reflects the influence of certain vested interests that cause the content of the rhetorical act to mask or reveal significant facts about the culture from which it emanated.

Cultural criticism and the development of a cultural methodology is an inferential process. You observe what is there and what is not there and try to explain your findings through generalizations about the culture. In the example that opens this chapter, Trujillo and Ekdom observed *Chicago Tribune* stories about the Chicago Cubs, found opposing values paired in the stories, and inductively generalized that these stories told us something about how Americans rely on value opposition to explain the human condition.

Cultural criticism is also done deductively when the critic begins with a generalization about the culture. For example, Marxist and feminist criticism begins deductively with ideological premises about the social structure, filters observations of fact and negation in specific rhetorical acts through these ideological generalizations, and offers conclusions about what the act demonstrates about its parent culture.

Whether you approach description of a rhetorical act inductively, as an account of what can be found or what is missing in the act, or deductively, through the generalizations imposed by an ideological filter, description leads to the organic creation of a cultural model for criticism. In this chapter we shall present several examples of cultural models created by contemporary communication critics. You should also feel free to create your own model, using cultural concepts of your own choosing.

A *model* is an individualized approach, a prototype that lays out the questions to ask and answer about a rhetorical act (Rosenfield, 1972). In the example that opens this chapter, the critics inductively examined sportswriting and created a value model that asked questions about what sportswriting revealed about American values and how value opposition could be used to explain human behavior and experience in our culture. All communication criticism employs models that were either created by individual critics or adapted from past practice. These models can be grouped into three categories: thematic models, symptomatic models, and didactic models.

Thematic models are based on rhetorical theories. They are either inductive or deductive, depending on whether the model is in the process of being created or is already an accepted and widely used methodology. The traditional, dramatistic, fantasy theme, and narrative approaches are deductive thematic models used by students and scholars practicing criticism today. These models are used to identify the rhetorical features of acts and media and to construct theories about the practice of rhetoric (Farrell, 1980). Because their development was relatively recent, the inductive development of the fantasy theme and narrative

approaches is reported in recent issues of scholarly journals and other communication criticism textbooks. These two approaches now function deductively
rather than inductively as critics concentrate on expanding their use instead of
attempting to establish their viability.

Symptomatic models are primarily inductive. They view rhetorical acts as
indexes or symptoms of larger social issues. Rhetorical acts, particularly those
embedded in popular or mass culture, are emblems of social consciousness and
provide evidence that certain values are important to that culture. The critic
constructs a model inductively from one or more rhetorical acts; the model may
later be used deductively when it is applied to other rhetorical acts (Farrell,
1980). Symptomatic criticism frequently creates social-values models such as the
one created by Trujillo and Ekdom and social-psychological models based on the
symptoms of psychological states revealed by rhetorical acts.

Didactic models are primarily deductive because they begin from an ideological point of view. These models view rhetorical acts as vehicles used to convey
ideas and philosophies in a culture. The critic may proceed inductively by
collecting examples of acts that convey these ideas and philosophies, as has been
the case in much of the rhetorical analysis and criticism of social movements.
Critics may also do a philosophical reading of a rhetorical act to determine its
fidelity or lack of fidelity to a particular ideology. Although any ideology may
serve as the basis for a didactic model, Marxism and feminism are the leading
didactic models in use today.

All of the approaches presented earlier in this book are, in a larger sense,
culturally based because they grew out of the practices and demands, the ideas
and philosophies, of various cultures. We distinguish cultural approaches to
criticism from other critical approaches on the basis either of the *value orientation
of the cultural model* or the *ideological nature of the approach*. All other approaches
discussed in this book differ from cultural approaches by their linkage to communication theory rather than to values or ideologies.

Culture is complex and always evolving in response to social, political, and
economic forces. This means you have a number of options for creating your own
critical models based on what you find in the general culture and its various
subcultures. In the remainder of this chapter, we present several culturally
derived models of criticism that you could employ deductively in doing cultural
criticism or that might serve as examples to guide you in inductively creating your
own cultural model.

Social-Values Model

One approach to cultural criticism is to create a model that generalizes about
the value systems of a culture. Social-values models begin with the assumption
that a culture represents the collective consciousness of basic values. Because a
number of incompatible values may compete with one another for preeminence,
rhetorical activity usually involves conflict, real value conflict or the potential for
value conflict (Rushing, 1983).

The social-values model recognizes that culture is dynamic and that social change is a regular occurrence. Moreover, social change is not capricious but follows a recognizable pattern. Janice Hocker Rushing and Thomas Frentz developed a five-part model to explain the process (Rushing and Frentz, 1978; Frentz and Rushing, 1978; Rushing, 1983).

Dialectical Opposition

A society's collective consciousness consists of broad value clusters, which are reflected in images, dreams, and myths. These values exist in a state of tension, dialectical opposition, so the potential for social change always exists. If one value has precedence over another, a reversal of the order of precedence would necessitate a corresponding social change.

Six values that are common in our culture (Rieke and Sillars, 1984) create dialectical opposition (see box below). As you read about them, think about how they complement or contradict one another and about their logical opposites. Consider the tension each is capable of producing in our society.

Common

American Value

Patterns

1. *Puritan Work Ethic:* The obligation to God and society to do one's best, to work hard. This value standard has a strong moral component.

2. *Progressive Value System:* The pragmatic view that society should always move forward, increase productivity, and pursue technological change.

3. *Enlightenment Value System:* System that emphasizes the individual's ability to reason and make decisions. It views government's purpose as the protection of the rights of the individual.

4. *Transcendental Value System:* System that holds that self-knowledge is best and that each indivdual should seek meaning within his or her own consciousness.

5. *Personal Success Value System:* The materialist view that one's accomplishments as an individual are what is most important in life and the primary measure of personal worth. The myth of the "rugged individual" is part of this value system.

6. *Collectivist Value System:* System that favors teamwork, law and order, and the regulation of the tendency toward excess or the exclusive pursuit of self-interest on the part of individuals. (RIEKE AND SILLARS, 1984)

Symbolic Conflict

Value change occurs whenever the predominant myth or value cluster no longer provides viable solutions to society's problems. An individual or a rhetorically active group may question prevailing values, but individuals and minority groups are incapable of producing value change until the collective consciousness of the culture begins to acknowledge the decline or inadequacy of predominant values in present circumstances. When this happens, the time is ripe for value change to occur. Social and artistic critics may herald the time for change by publicly proclaiming the decline or inadequacy of certain values.

Value conflicts are often enacted as verbal or physical battles between opposing individuals or groups. The presidential campaign is an example of this symbolic conflict. In the 1988 presidential campaign, George Bush affirmed the Reagan value of patriotism to which he added the hope for a "kinder, gentler America" in opposition to Michael Dukakis's emphasis of pragmatism. Apparently the time was not ripe for significant value change in 1988 because Bush won the election.

Patterns of Change

Symbolic conflict is the prelude to value reorientation. Value change takes one of two forms. Through *dialectical transformation,* value change occurs when one value standard replaces another, winning out over it. In *dialectical synthesis,* a new value standard is created by merging elements of the competing value standards. Cooperation rather than competition is characteristic of this synthesis. Dialectical transformation is the more common form of value change and the simplest because it does not require creating a new value standard. Dialectical synthesis is more complicated and less likely to occur because it necessitates the integration of the competing value standards in a way that preserves all parts of both standards.

Psychological Prerequisites

The change agent in a rhetorical act, speaker, candidate, or character in a fictional work is not free to suggest just any pattern of value change. The change agent has to have experienced the new values psychologically for them to be even considered as a potential replacement for the prevailing value standard. This explains why dialectical synthesis is the more difficult form of change. The change agent embodies the new value standard. For an individual or a group to be effective in this role, the synthesis of opposing values has to have been a part of their psychological experience. It is obviously difficult to experience being an individualist and a collectivist at the same time. Dialectical transformation is the norm because it is more likely that the change agent has a strong psychological experience with the desirability of one value over its opposite.

Audience Role

The audiences for rhetorical activity are spectators witnessing the symbolic conflict. The role of the audience varies from intensified awareness to active participant. Intensified awareness is characteristic of dialectical transformation. The audience is made to feel dissatisfaction with a value they perceive to be no longer viable for solving problems. The change agent takes the lead, promotes a new value standard, and the audience follows this lead and publicly acknowledges that change is necessary and good. Dialectical synthesis makes the audience active participants in creating the new value standard. The change agent serves as a facilitator, involving the audience in synthesizing the competing sets of values.

The five-part model (Figure 7.1) suggests the appropriate questions to ask when examining a rhetorical act. The critic analyzes the rhetorical act in terms of the dialectical opposition of values, the form the symbolic conflict takes, the psychological prerequisites demanded of the change agent, and the role of the audience. Questions are phrased to determine how the rhetorical act reflects social change relative to these five categories (see box on next page).

This model has been applied primarily to films, revealing that films are an effective vehicle for presenting value conflict and reflecting value change in America. Frentz and Rushing (1978) applied the model to the Academy Award winning film *Rocky* and concluded that the film represented the American synthesis of moralism and materialism reflected in the election of Jimmy Carter in 1976. Rushing has also examined value opposition in the American western myth as told through films, concluding that Ronald Reagan's election in 1980 was a pseudosynthesis of opposing values. Voters saw Mr. Reagan as a sort of *Urban Cowboy* who, like John Travolta's character in the film, synthesized the opposing value standards of the old-time westerns: individualism and community. The

1. Values exist in dialectical opposition.
2. Symbolic conflict is the necessary condition for value reorientation.
3. There are two patterns of symbolic conflict:
   — dialectical transformation;
   — dialectical synthesis.
4. Psychological prerequisites:
   — dialectical transformation necessitates non-integrated change agent;
   — dialectical synthesis requires integrated change agent.
5. Audience role:
   — participation in a generative process heightens experiential involvement in dialectical synthesis.

Figure 7.1 Social Value Model

From J.H. Rushing and T.S. Frentz, copyright 1978 by the Western Journal of Speech Communication. Reprinted by permission.

Questions to Use

in Social Values

Analysis of

Rhetorical Acts

1. What values exist in opposition? What elements in the rhetorical situation create tension between the values?

2. When does the value tension surface? What individuals or groups initially express concern over the value tension? At what point do others in the culture at large begin to question the prevailing value standard?

3. What message and media (films, political campaigns, television programming, speeches, songs, novels) express the symbolic value conflict?

4. Does value reorientation occur? If it occurs, is it a dialectical transformation or a dialectical synthesis?

5. Who is the change agent? Does the change agent possess the psychological prerequisites necessary to accomplish the value change?

6. What is the role of the audience? Are they aware bystanders who acknowledge the desirability of the value reorientation or active participants in accomplishing it?

synthesis was weak because it tried to erase all signs of tension rather than truly integrating the opposing values. Like Travolta's *Urban Cowboy,* Ronald Reagan was safer than a "real cowboy," which was acceptable to the electorate because Americans wanted the appearance of a hero and not the real thing (Rushing, 1983).

The Social-Values Model and Critical Evaluation

The results standard is the primary judgmental criterion used to evaluate rhetorical acts by the social-values model. The critic wants to know whether or not value change occurred, what type of change occurred, and how the change influenced the culture. The ethical standard can also be used to evaluate the role of the change agent in the value reorientation in terms of their credentials for championing the value transformation or synthesis. The truth standard can be applied to the role of the audience in determining how they perceived the proposed value change and why they responded in the way they did. An active audience might be judged to have perceived truthfulness in the proposed value change. Finally, the aesthetics standard could be applied to judge the artistic qualities of rhetorical acts such as films that affirm or question cultural values.

The social-values model assumes that the collective consciousness of a culture is made up of patterns of values in opposition and that a culture deals with its problems either by choosing one value over another or by synthesizing opposing values. The model is useful when a critic wants to examine a rhetorical act as the verbal, symbolic representation of value conflict. It is particularly well suited to the rhetorical evaluation of products of the mass media. Pseudoevents, fictionalized accounts of actual events, and the creation of images are all means the mass media use to convey cultural values. The social-values model gives critics a way to determine how values function rhetorically and to analyze and evaluate how social change occurs.

Jungian Psychological Model

The Jungian psychological model offers a system for analyzing and evaluating the way a succession of images involve an audience and draw perceptual, affective, and cognitive responses from them (Davies, Farrell, and Matthews, 1982). The model, which uses Carl Jung's theory of the human psyche as the source of its analytical questions, was developed for rhetorical criticism of film.

Jung investigated the unconscious by interpreting dreams. The Jungian psychological model posits that film is similar to the dream state in that films often express archetypal images and symbols found in the collective unconsciousness. We experience films as we do dreams, as primarily visual in dreamlike subdued lighting or darkness, and film technology can create surrealistic effects similar to those we experience in our dreams. Although dream imagery is individual, film imagery is public and frequently rhetorical (Rushing and Frentz, 1980).

Jung described the human psyche as a self-regulating system that tries to achieve balance between the conscious and the unconscious. The *persona* is the public self; it presents the socially acceptable side of the self. The *shadow* is the dark, socially unacceptable side of the self, against which each individual struggles. The shadow contains images of the evil, unacceptable tendencies in human behavior. Each person experiences the struggle between the persona and shadow sides of self (Rushing and Frentz, 1980).

The self is at the center of the public, conscious persona and the hidden, unconscious shadow. Consciousness is individual, made up of the ideas and feelings we are aware of. Unconsciousness is forgotten and subliminal, personal elements and impersonal, universal archetypes that seem to be innate in all people. Because these archetypes are unconscious, we do not know them, but they still emerge in the symbols and motifs of dreams, myths, folktales, and artistic works. These archetypes do not seem to be bound by time, culture, or individual differences. They make up the collective unconsciousness.

Understanding one's self occurs when a person comes to terms with these unconscious images (Davies et al, 1982). Berke Breathed's comic strip *Bloom County* featured a character named Binkley and his "closet of anxieties," which contained the images of Binkley's unconscious. Binkley's anxieties frequently emerged and took the form of monsters and prominent public figures, the archetypes of his unconscious experience of American culture.

Davies et al (1982) suggest that critics apply Jung's concepts to film as they would to dreams, treating the film as a whole and analyzing the interaction of its parts—story, characters, the progression of scenes, special effects, cinematography, sound, and editing. This means examining each element of the film and discovering the archetypes derived from the interaction of its parts. This kind of analysis can reveal the bond created between a film and its viewers and aids in accounting for the relevance or popularity of a particular film or film genre.

Because the goal of this model is to provide greater understanding of the archetypal themes that an audience experiences when viewing a film and the psychic role of a film or film genre, the model focuses on Jung's list of the most frequently recurring symbols from the shadow side of self found in dreams: the animal, the wise old man, the anima (female elements of the male unconscious), the animus (male elements of the female unconscious), and the mother and child. Jung grouped these symbols into four content categories (Davies et al, 1982):

1. The *mother* or *origin* consists of symbols for females, animals, places of darkness, the primeval time.
2. The *spirit* consists of symbols that serve as sources or places that provide renewal, energy, and guidance.
3. The *transcendence* symbols include heroes, the experience of being reborn, initiation rituals, and images of flight.
4. The *wholeness* symbols are mandalas or circle configurations, stones, and treasures.

These symbols commonly occur as paired opposites: male and female or light and dark. These juxtapositions are symbolic of the search for balance between the rational outer world and the irrational inner world. In Jung's theory, finding one's self is a matter of striking an appropriate balance between persona and shadow; as applied to film, symbols offer viewers a way of coping with the exigences of their time.

Stanley Kubrick's film *The Shining*, based on a Stephen King novel, has been examined by using Jung's theory of dreams. The film is set at the deserted Overlook Hotel, which is closed for winter. In its vast emptiness, this setting serves as a maze archetype of the unconscious. As the central character's shadow overwhelms his persona, *The Shining* moves the viewer from the reality of a pleasant sabbatical from work through a series of increasingly bizarre episodes culminating in a nightmarish chase through the hotel's garden maze during a blizzard. The message of *The Shining* is that when we ignore our inner self we risk calamity because our unconscious shadow inevitably exerts influence over our outer self or persona (Davies et al, 1982).

The Jungian Model and Critical Evaluation

The chief limitation of the Jungian psychological model is that it is used only to interpret. Jung provides no means for critically evaluating the dream, just a system for interpreting what happened in it. As a critic, you need to reach beyond the Jungian model to discover something about the message and its medium that can be evaluated. For example, you might apply this model to a science fiction film and discover that special effects influence the ability of the audience to interact with the symbol. You could then extend the model to make an aesthetic judgment about the film's ability to provide its viewers with coping behaviors for their problems.

Alternatively, the results standard might be used to determine the film's impact on the culture, its effect on the public psyche. The ethical standard might be used to evaluate characterization in the film, whether the major and minor characters demonstrated moral or immoral behavior. The truth standard could be used to judge the film against other rhetorical acts that use the same or similar symbols. What you add to the Jungian model depends on what you discover about the message and its medium in your description of the text of the rhetorical act. The model need not be limited to film study. You can test the soundness of the model by applying it to other rhetorical forms such as speeches, songs, or cartoons to determine how well it is suited to such acts.

Ideological Models

Ideological criticism has its roots in the revolutions and revolutionary thinking of the eighteenth and nineteenth centuries, when events were viewed in terms of a political struggle. Ideological critics of this period questioned the morality of mass culture and the rhetorical acts that promulgated the views and values of the ruling or economically dominant class.

An ideological model identifies what is considered to be good and right from the perspective of a particular political philosophy. The contemporary ideological critic believes that criticism of culture and communication can lead to a wider recognition of good reasons for right actions. The ideological critic sees truth as contained in his or her world view and in opposition to the world view of those vested interests that control important social, political, or economic institutions (Wander, 1981, 1983). An ideology may be the target of criticism; for example, conservativism could be studied to judge its usefulness or dangers. The critic operates out of a clearly articulated ideology and takes an activist stance.

Rather than using an established theory of rhetoric or trying to discover the social values inherent in a rhetorical act, ideological criticism goes directly to a political ideology and a historical context for its model. Any political ideology may serve as the basis for an ideological model by applying historical-political perspective to evaluate rhetorical acts within a culture. The critic confirms his or her conclusions by examining rhetorical acts that legitimize the actions and policies of society, including the facts as well as the silence, or negation, that surrounds important issues (Wander, 1984). Feminism and Marxism are the two predominant ideological models presently in use. A feminist critic focuses on issues of gender, a Marxist critic on issues of economic domination.

Feminism

The goal of feminism as a political ideology is to gain equality for women in all aspects of culture (Foss, 1989; Humm, 1986; Steeves, 1987). Although feminist theories and assumptions about communication and human behavior have long been part of the history of Western civilization, using these theories and assumptions as a basis for rhetorical criticism is a contemporary development. Feminist theories, which explain how a culture devalues women, begin with the assumption that women are devalued in society (Steeves, 1987).

An important concept in feminist ideology is gender. *Gender* is the cultural term used to identify the traits and roles society ascribes to men and women (Foss, 1989). Feminist ideology explains how society devalues the feminine gender by assigning the more desirable traits and roles to men. "Men's gender includes traits such as independent, competitive, logical, skilled in business, and financial provider, while women's gender includes traits such as emotional, gentle, graceful, concerned with appearance, and nurturing" (Foss, 1989, p. 151).

Feminist ideology argues that men have controlled critical theories and focused communication scholarship from an exclusively male perspective for too long (Foss, 1989; Humm, 1986; Mura, 1983). As the names associated with other approaches discussed in this book suggest, the study of rhetorical theory and activity does appear to be male dominated. The significance of this point for feminist criticism emerges from two assumptions: Men and women experience things differently and language reflects the male gender (Foss, 1989).

Feminism holds that men and women do not experience the world in the same ways and that it is meaningless for women to accept male-generated theories of communication and explanations of reality as equally applicable to them. However, the gender-language problem is the key tenet in feminist ideology and criticism because, as we indicated in Chapter 1, rhetorical acts are primarily verbal. Language creates gender inequality by assigning roles and characteristics on the basis of gender alone.

Men may be affected by this problem, but women are victimized by it because our language excludes the feminine gender entirely in its use of the generic "he," "man," and "mankind" to refer to both men and women. Sensitivity to this problem is the reason why publishers of textbooks such as this provide their authors with techniques for avoiding gender bias in their writing.

English also creates gender inequality in its use of sex-role descriptors such as "lady doctor" or "male nurse." Gender inequality arises as a consequence of common English usage as well. The tendency to add the suffixes "ette," "ess," or "ix" to masculine terms produces nouns such as "bachelorette," "actress," and "aviatrix," which trivialize the female state of being (Mura, 1983).

The problem created by gender inequality in language, regardless of its source, is that there is a relationship between the language people use to discuss something or someone and their perceptions of that which is being discussed (Mura, 1983). If "rhetor" were used to refer exclusively to male communicators and "rhetoress" or "rhetorix" to refer to female communicators, but all published materials on rhetorical theory used the term "rhetor" generically, you might perceive a person called a "rhetoress" or "rhetorix" as less important. When the language system is male dominated, female perceptions, experiences, and meanings may go unheard because they fail to fit the dominant language pattern (Foss, 1989).

These ideological assumptions—differential experience and gender inequality in language—transcend variations that exist across the spectrum of feminism: radical feminism, liberal feminism, Marxist feminism, and socialist feminism. Where these variations on the feminist theme differ from each other is in their explanation of the origins of and reasons for society's continuing devaluation of women. These differences are produced when elements of feminism are combined with elements of other political ideologies.

Radical feminism is rooted in the biological differences between men and women. The primary assumption of radical feminism is that women must take control over their reproductive systems away from men. Radical feminists reject suggestions that individual actions or social change will solve the gender problem. Only through radical collective action, such as complete separation from men and the creation of a completely feminine language system, can the devaluation of women be overcome (Steeves, 1987).

Liberal feminism applies liberal political ideas to the devaluation problem. These feminists appropriate the ideological position "that rational mental development is the highest human ideal and that the state should act to assure equal opportunities for all in pursuing this goal and associated ones from political liberalism" (Steeves, 1987, p. 100). Liberal feminists seek change within the framework of the political system. The right to vote and own property were goals of liberal feminists in nineteenth-century America that were not fully realized until early in the twentieth century. Contemporary liberal feminists pursued the equal-rights amendment, albeit unsuccessfully.

Marxist and *socialist feminism* are based on economic theories that view capitalism's oppression of the laboring class as a key element in explaining the oppression of women. Marxist feminists believe that society must change by throwing off the domination of capitalist rulers before women can change their situation. Socialist feminists use criticism of society to expose the oppression and domination of women caused by language and popular culture's imposition of social patriarchy. They embrace many of their Marxist sisters' ideas about capitalist exploitation of the lower classes but take a different approach in explaining the sources and causes of the devaluation of women (Steeves, 1987).

The goal of all feminist criticism, regardless of its political agenda, is consciousness raising, that is, to use rhetorical criticism to alert women specifically and society in general to the problem of devaluation. Political orientation influences the activist stance the critic takes in proposing how to deal with the problem. Feminist critics evaluate rhetorical acts that have importance for women, either because they offer women's perspectives or because they are male-centered, exclude women's perspectives, and further contribute to the devaluation of women. Feminist critics interpret how gender is reflected in a rhetorical act.

If you take a feminist perspective on rhetorical activity, you are most concerned with the issue of gender and how both the rhetor and the audience conceptualized it. You begin with the ideological assumption that a rhetorical act reflects the gender orientation of the rhetor, male-centered, female-centered, or androgynous, and offers a conceptualization of gender consistent with that orientation to the audience. Certain questions are fundamental to criticism using the feminist ideological model (see box below).

A feminist criticism of *The Shining* might view the concept of gender in terms of the issue of male violence and female victims, particularly a husband's abusive acts against his wife. The central character, Jack Torrence, acts out his frustration with his inability to make progress on his novel in increasingly neurotic and violent acts against Wendy, his wife, culminating in attempted murder as he stalks her and their son through the hotel maze. To the feminist critic, the film confirms what is seen as a typical masculine trait: holding women responsible for men's every failure rather than taking responsibility for themselves; the film also confirms a male belief that women are powerless to do anything about abuse by showing Wendy as unable to save herself and her son. It is only through divine intervention, a blinding snow storm and the sudden appearance of a superman with mystical, clairvoyant powers that she survives. *The Shining*, based on a novel

---

Questions to Use

in Feminist

Analysis of

Rhetorical Acts

1. What is the gender orientation of the rhetor? Is the experiential view male, female, or androgynous?

2. What cultural ideals of masculinity and femininity are presented?

3. Does the rhetorical act provide evidence that one gender is devalued? Are standards of behavior, personal attributes, important issues, or valuable qualities portrayed as masculine or as feminine?

4. Does the rhetor's use of language symbols devalue women?

5. What can be done to improve the status of women?

by a man and turned into a movie by the male-dominated movie industry clearly expresses a belief that women are the weaker sex.

The Feminist Ideological Model and Critical Evaluation

The truth standard is the principal means of evaluating rhetorical acts in feminist criticism. The critic is interested in how the rhetorical act conceptualizes the role of women in a culture. If it reflects gender equality, the act may be evaluated as true; if it devalues women, the critic may judge it to be misleading at best and deceitful or wrong at worst. The results standard may also be used by feminist critics to evaluate rhetorical acts in terms of whether or not they have changed, or have the potential to change, the valuation of women. The ethical standard may be applied to judge whether a rhetor expresses feminist ideology or contributes to the problem of the devaluation of women. Aesthetic evaluations are also customarily made of rhetorical acts by women whose work expresses feminist ideology because the artistic qualities of the work are evidence of the worth of women communicators.

Feminist ideological critics are concerned with how rhetorical acts and rhetorical theory perpetuate the devaluation of women. By studying the gender orientation of rhetorical acts and theories, these critics become activists who seek to expand the boundaries of how we define rhetoric by including women's perspectives. They are also activists in that their goal is gender equality in human communication. A feminist ideological perspective holds that the world view and experience of women must be given equal value in the study of rhetorical activity.

Marxism

The Marxist ideological model is based on the work of Karl Marx, a nineteenth-century social critic who is best known for his economic interpretation of history. Marx viewed economic forces as the most important factor in understanding a culture because the production and exchange of goods and services that support human life are the basis for all social processes and institutions. Marx's own cultural experience, nineteenth-century Europe with its rigid class system based on wealth and social standing, is reflected in his writings. He described the world as dominated by the industrial, capitalist societies in which ownership of the means of production was the key to their history. The owners (capitalists) made rules, set social standards, determined core values, and controlled all aspects of life. Cultural products—law, education, art, literature, and mass media—were all intended to maintain capitalism (Ebenstein, 1964).

Marxism is an ideology of class struggle. Because it is human nature to want an equal share of what society has to offer, labor, those who produce, would inevitably come into conflict with owners, those who control the means of production. Not wanting to give up what they saw as rightfully theirs, owners would unquestionably resist change (Ebenstein, 1964). For Marxists, the capitalist ideology was a false ideology because it did not represent the interests of the working class. Because it was false, it should be overturned. From the Marxist perspective, social change could only be brought about through revolution.

Contemporary Marxist critics view society as a complex network of divided groups that struggle for social power. Over and above the original Marxist notion of division by social class, the struggle for dominance today goes on among groups divided by gender, race, ethnic or national origin, political affiliation, and various other demographic factors. Society experiences struggle almost constantly as one group or another tries to ensure that its message, its meaning, be the dominant one (Fiske, 1987a).

Hegemony, the process by which a dominant group gains the willing consent of subordinate groups to that which maintains their subordination, is the key concept in contemporary Marxism. The dynamic nature of culture means that this winning of consent is an ongoing process. Hegemony, once attained, is not a constant, and culture is the locus of the struggle between those who have social power at the moment and those who have allowed them to have it (Fiske, 1987a).

When IBM entered the personal computer market in the early 1980s, its product was built around components that were widely available. IBM also made detailed specifications of the machine public, and it was readily cloned by a number of manufacturers who had previously produced machines incompatible with what became the de facto standard for a large segment of the industry. Only the unwillingness of Apple and a few other manufacturers to follow suit prevented absolute IBM hegemony in the personal computer industry.

Although many contemporary Marxists do not see revolution as the natural, inevitable outcome of these divisions, they do see society as being constantly defined and redefined through representations by the group in power. In such a group-dominated environment, the individual is a social subject who is constructed by, and constructs, systems of representation. Television is one system of representation. As individuals we are shaped by television to the extent that we use what we see as a model for our behavior and rely on what we hear for our information. We also shape television by choosing to view or not view certain programs. Contemporary Marxists describe such systems of representation as *epistemic,* and the point of criticism is to understand the epistemic nature of the system and determine how it offers a way of knowing or experiencing the world (M. White, 1987).

Close on the heels of the personal computer explosion came the personal computer magazine explosion. Today, multiple titles address the specific interests of owners of IBM, Apple, Commodore, or Atari computers. This epidemic on the newsstand is epistemic because each publication seeks both to inform its readers and to shape their behavior, directly or indirectly reassuring them that their choice of a computer was the right choice. Having watched the shift over time in the editorial thrust of some of these publications and having been left holding the unfilled bag of subscriptions to at least two publications that did not survive, we can assure you that these publications not only shape, but are shaped by, their readers.

The Marxist ideological model views the mass media as especially important because they are the chief means of social control in contemporary cultures. As such, Marxist critics do not separate communication theory from social theory. Each medium of communication has to be considered in its historical context along with the social, political, and economic forces in that context. Therefore, a Marxist critically evaluates both communication and society. The goal of the Marxist critic is to identify rhetorical acts that legitimize the hegemonic views of the group in power, regardless of whether they are the acts of that group or the acts of other groups that directly or indirectly preserve the powerful group's hegemony.

In the marketplace of products, rather than ideas, advertising is clearly an attempt by groups in power to retain hegemony, and the publication of computer-specific magazines might be viewed as a direct attempt by others to support their efforts. However, because it is not unusual for publishers to put out both an IBM and an Apple magazine, for example, an alternative explanation of their behavior might be that they are themselves locked in a battle for hegemony, or at least shelf space at your local newsstand. Be that as it may, indirect support for hegemony is easy to see if you are an avid moviegoer or television watcher. Have you ever noticed what kind of computers they used at the Blue Moon Detective Agency on *Moonlighting*? Apple hopes you did.

The Marxist ideological model asks questions to study the hegemonic orientation of a rhetorical act (see box below). A Marxist evaluation of *The Shining*

Questions to Use

in Marxist

Analysis of

Rhetorical Acts

1. What is the social, political, and economic context in which the rhetorical act exists?

2. Does the rhetorical act reflect the ideology of the dominant group or class? Does it articulate it? Does it support or legitimize it in some way?

3. What evidence of the subjugation or exploitation of classes or groups does the rhetorical act provide in its use of symbols, issues, and attempts to redefine or fragment a group?

4. Does the rhetorical act attempt to create imaginary unity, to incorporate subordinate classes or groups into the hegemonic ideology? In what way does the rhetorical act perpetuate the hegemonic ideology?

5. What can be done to change society, change the subjugation of the less powerful by the powerful, or improve their lot?

might focus on Jack Torrence as a victim of the Overlook Hotel, a materialistic pleasure palace. It has elegant furnishings, scenic panoramas, and the distinctive garden maze for its guests' amusement. The hotel is a haven for the wealthy, a place where weary capitalists go to escape the rest of the world. At the beginning of the film, we learn that the hotel has a history of violence and tragedy. It is not only a symbol of materialistic, capitalistic society, but it is also a foreboding place. Although the exterior looks luxurious and spacious, the hotel is ugly and rotten at its core. The inner evil of this magnificent hotel, a retreat for presidents and all the "best people," brings out the worst in ordinary people, especially Jack Torrence. It drives him to madness. Rather than rewarding his labors as its caretaker and faithful servant, the hotel exploits him. To the Marxist critic, the film's message confirms that the apparent opulence and splendor of materialistic capitalism corrupts and ultimately destroys those who are seduced by capitalism and its material pleasures.

The Marxist Ideological Model and Critical Evaluation

Contemporary Marxist criticism has focused on studying mass media, especially film and television, because they have the potential to raise people's consciousness. Much of the published Marxist criticism has been done by British scholars who focus on mass communication in the United Kingdom. These Marxist critics want to reform their society, and their critical analyses are intended to help achieve that goal. Their evaluations have commonly used the truth and aesthetic standards of judgment in evaluating the veracity of the class consciousness of the mass media and the artistic qualities of their productions. They believe their research will help people in Britain better understand class conditions and realize the kinds of change that are necessary (Becker, 1984).

Other political ideologies, such as humanism, liberalism, conservatism, or spiritualism, could serve as the basis for an ideological model. Criticism is ideological when it evaluates rhetorical activity to discover how the powerful, vested interests in a society benefit from policies that harm others in some way. Ideological criticism analyzes both the rhetorical act and the role of the vested interest. Whenever criticism recognizes and espouses the preferability of a course of action different from that supported by these powerful, vested interests, it becomes ideological (Wander, 1983).

Ideological Models and Critical Evaluation

Ideological criticism emphasizes the truth standard of evaluation, judging rhetorical acts by a definition of truth that is derived from the tenets of a particular ideology. The social value of the rhetorical act as true or untrue, worthwhile or worthless, is determined by the goodness of fit between the content of the act and the view of truth contained in the ideology used to critique it. Ideological critics may also use the ethical standard of judgment to evaluate the rhetor's credibility. To the extent that a rhetorical act supports the critic's stance, the rhetor may be deemed wise, just, or fair-minded. The results standard may be used to evaluate the impact of rhetorical acts in advancing the political agenda of the adherents to the ideology. The aesthetic standard may be used to evaluate the artistic properties of acts.

Ideological criticism does have utility. It can call attention to injustices, as the feminist critics have attempted to do. It can also increase the political and social awareness of the critic. Taking an ideological perspective may help you better understand your own political views.

To develop your own ideological model, you pose questions following a pattern similar to those offered by the feminist and Marxist models. The idea is to phrase questions that challenge the rhetorical act and measure it against the tenets of the ideology you have selected. Obviously, you must have a thorough knowledge of that ideology before you can even attempt to phrase such questions effectively.

Ideological criticism has certain limitations. Ideological critics tend to assume that the truth has been revealed to them, and they may become disciples of this truth. As an ideological critic, you run the risk of becoming a partisan, persuaded by a rhetorical act because it confirms your point of view or offended by it because it does not, so that you lose all objectivity. In either case, you are rendered at least partially incapable of giving full and fair attention to the rhetorical act that is the object of your criticism.

Social-Movement Model

During the 1960s and 1970s, communication criticism often focused on the rhetorical behavior of social movements as America's social structures were challenged by the civil rights movement, the student rights movement, antiwar activists, and the feminist movement. Each movement was based on its own ideology, had a political agenda for cultural change, and produced significant rhetorical activity. Although some historical social movements were studied, current history certainly provided the impetus to study movements rhetorically, and communication critics developed models to explain and evaluate the existence and impact of social movements.

We classify movement criticism with other cultural approaches because it always takes into account the cultural forces that are contemporaneous with the movement being studied. Social-movement criticism uses historical description of fact and negation, analyzes how a movement developed and communicated its ideology to members and the culture it challenged, and evaluates the impact the movement had on that culture. In particular, this type of criticism focuses on the history of a movement's ideology: how it evolved, how the ideas it contained were used, and how those ideas were operationalized in its rhetorical activity.

Although critics are certainly free to use their own ideological perspectives to evaluate a social movement, such as taking a feminist perspective on the antiwar movment, movement criticism differs from ideological criticism in that the critic usually does not become involved in the politics of the movement. A critic involved in pure movement criticism studies the rhetorical behavior of the social movement in its cultural context and evaluates the ability of the movement to achieve its goals.

The Nature of Social Movements

A social movement emerges out of the confrontation between a dissident group and established status-quo groups that define the limits of culturally acceptable belief or behavior. The key term is *confrontation*. Establishment rhetors and their ideologies are enjoined by the contrarian rhetorical acts of the movement. In the rhetorical sense of the term, a *group* becomes a *social movement* when it uses rhetorical acts to demand change.

The Berkeley free-speech movement of 1964 involved the confrontation between a small vocal group of University of California students and the school administration over rules and regulations governing political activity on campus. The students demanded these rules and regulations be changed so that they would have greater freedom to express their political views. Confrontation took the form of mass rallies of approximately seven thousand students, protest meetings, silent vigils, and sit-ins in the administration building (D.E. Phillips, 1985). In examining the details of the rhetorical situation in a case like this, locating and describing the nature of the confrontation and the form it took is essential to criticism because it helps identify the exigence in the situation.

Culture is dynamic, a social process that continually exerts pressure on institutions. Sometimes the pressures are weak, other times very strong. Why does a group find itself in conflict with the establishment? Because competing groups coexist in the context of a force field in which four categories of influence come into play:

> *Social-psychological forces* are clusters of beliefs and
> perceptions that determine how people will behave in a
> situation (Gronbeck, 1973). These forces shape the
> emotional climate and determine which values will be
> engaged by the conflict. In the case of the Berkeley
> free-speech movement, students valued freedom over
> order while the university administration held opposite
> values.
>
> *Political-institutional forces* are reflected in established
> institutions that act as a source of influence (Gronbeck,
> 1973). These forces represent the goals, practices, and
> experience of the culture as a whole; they usually
> represent the views of most people. In the Berkeley
> free-speech movement, the university's educational
> mission, long tradition, and its code of student conduct
> were the source of political-institutional forces.

Philosophical-ideological forces are a product of facts, values, and ideas (Gronbeck, 1973). These forces are the doctrines and intellectual structures that comprise the conventional wisdom of the culture. In 1964, students at Berkeley challenged the role of the university as a pseudoparent who had the right and ability to exercise control over most aspects of their lives. The free-speech movement also challenged the mainstream ideology that social change should be achieved by working through the means that government provides for the redress of grievances.

Rhetorical forces are the acts of communication favorable or unfavorable to the status quo (Gronbeck, 1973). Both movement and establishment rhetors engage in rhetorical activity by presenting their sides of the controversy. Free-speech rhetors at Berkeley used speeches, songs, slogans, posters, silent vigils, and sit-ins to express their dissatisfaction with the university's rules.

The mere presence of these four force-field elements does not guarantee the emergence of a social movement. Society and its institutions are not static. Change is always occurring as a natural consequence of these forces, though it is sometimes so gradual that it is not obvious in the short term. Social movements come into being when the need for change is perceived by some people and society's institutions seem to be resisting change or changing too slowly.

When social movements come into being, they seek one of three types of change relative to cultural norms, values, or the power structure: reform, revival, or resistance (Stewart, 1980). *Reform* movements seek a change in the status quo, ranging from limited change to a complete restructuring of society. Their goal is to take the culture where it has never been. *Revival* movements seek a return to the past that will either limit further social change or return society to some idealized earlier time. Their goal is to take the culture back to where it was. *Resistance* movements oppose a change that society is either predisposed to make or is in the process of making. Their goal is to keep the culture where it is.

A social movement, regardless of type, always constitutes a subculture or a counterculture. Even though it may gain a significant number of members, may be successful in fund raising, and may have a mastery of rhetorical skills, a movement does not possess the symbolic and physical resources necessary to place it on an equal footing with the institutions of the cultural mainstream (Cathcart, 1980). This defining characteristic of movements explains why the rhetorical force they are capable of generating is so important. The only way a movement gains power and makes progress toward its goal is by its ability to create doubt about the legitimacy and morality of the norms, values, and power structure of the established culture (Cathcart, 1980). This is also why *confrontation* is the key term in social-movement criticism.

Social-movement criticism focuses on the messages generated by movement rhetors and examines the confrontation between the movement and the established culture. The causes and consequences of those messages, along with analysis of the psychological, sociological, political, and historical impact of the movement, are the core of social-movement criticism (Bowers and Ochs, 1971). The object of movement criticism is to understand the movement's ability or inability to achieve its goal. To accomplish this, the critic analyzes the functions of rhetorical activity and the use of rhetorical tactics.

Functions of Rhetorical Activity

Social movements share similar life cycles characterized by inception, rhetorical crisis, and consumation (Gronbeck, 1973). As you consider the rhetorical acts of a movement, analyze how each act functioned and from which stage in the movement's life cycle it emanated.

In the *inception* phase, movement leaders define the exigence for those who share their ideological point of view and identify others who are either likely candidates for membership or likely to be sympathetic to their goal. Rhetorical activity in this phase is characterized by statements of ideology that define the movement, the change it ultimately seeks, and the actions members must undertake in pursuit of this goal. The movement is presented as a legitimate alternative to what exists or what will exist.

Although a social movement uses rhetorical force to change society, it must first solidify its internal power base. It must recruit new members and maintain the involvement of those who believe in the ideology and are willing to work to achieve its operationalization in a changed culture. In studying the rhetorical behavior of a social movement, you need to look for rhetorical acts that are directed toward gathering new members and retaining original members.

The *rhetorical crisis* phase of the movement's life cycle is characterized by rhetorical activity directed at both internal and external audiences. To be successful, a movement must expand its power base by convincing others in the mainstream culture that its ideology is sound, that the exigence is grave, and that the proposed change is feasible. To do this, the movement must become highly visible, marching, singing, talking, and demonstrating on behalf of the cause it promotes. The rhetorical crisis phase represents the high-water mark of rhetorical activity by a movement; this is the time that most of the action takes place as the campaign to reform, revive, or resist is articulated.

The purpose of a movement is to change political and/or social institutions. To achieve this, change in social-psychological predispositions of the established culture must take place. The social-psychological belief and value clusters of a culture influence whether people in the mainstream will accept or reject the movement's ideology. In examining the rhetorical behavior of a movement, you should look for acts that are directed at the cultural mainstream, the general public.

Social movements also direct rhetorical acts at the political and/or social institutions they seek to change. These rhetorical acts are sometimes less vehement than those used to reaffirm movement ideology to members, taking more of the form of reasoned arguments. Rhetorical acts aimed at establishment leaders may present the ideology as a set of principles, or solutions to problems, that leaders of the established order will find sufficiently compelling to allow them to accept them as a basis for change (Gronbeck, 1973). However, these rhetorical acts may also have a strong emotional component, as is the case when rallies, picketing, sit-ins, strikes, and other verbal and nonverbal symbols are used.

In the *consumation* phase, the movement goes into decline, regardless of whether it has succeeded or failed. If the movement was successful, its leaders can claim victory; but if it failed they must explain the reasons for failure to the members. Sometimes the movement only achieves a partial victory. Some change occurred in response to movement demands, but it was less than had been hoped for. Sometimes a movement does not gain immediate victory, but change eventually results from the actions of its members.

Use of Rhetorical Tactics

In doing social-movement criticism, you should focus on the content and form of the rhetorical activity of a movement. When a group determines that society and its institutions are resisting change or changing too slowly, various tactics, verbal and nonverbal, are used to apply rhetorical force. John Bowers and Donovan Ochs (1971) catalogued the tactics commonly used by social movements (see box below). As you describe the rhetorical act, examine rhetoric for evidence of any or all of these tactics.

Rhetorical Tactics

of Social

Movements

1. *Petition* is addressed to establishment leaders as speeches and other forms of discourse that use reasoning and argument to present the case for the change demanded by the movement.

2. *Promulgation* is used after demands have been rejected. This tactic takes the form of informational picketing, displaying posters and banners, passing out leaflets and handbills, holding mass protest rallies, and exploiting the mass media by staging pseudoevents and arranging interviews with movement leaders.

3. *Solidification* tactics are used primarily inside the movement to produce and reinforce commitment

continued

to the movement's ideology and goal. Solidification tactics help create unity of purpose and spirit through skits, songs, slogans, visual symbols, and internal publications.

4. *Use of a flag issue* singles out one establishment policy for attack. The flag issue becomes something for everyone to rally around. The refusal of the university administration to allow students to participate in the university governance process was a flag issue for the free-speech movement.

5. *Use of a flag individual* singles out one member of the establishment to hold personally responsible for the exigence. The flag individual becomes the lightning rod for disaffection. Naming the university president as the villain responsible for the problem was a tactic of the free-speech movement.

6. *Invention of derogatory jargon* enables the movement to create symbols to demean actions they object to and individuals they hold responsible. The symbols created are usually unique to a particular movement. Common derogatory jargon of the 1960s labeled police as "pigs," blue-collar workers as "hardhats," and Richard Nixon as "Tricky Dick."

7. *Nonviolent resistance* occurs when members of the movement deliberately and publicly violate the law or custom they oppose. Sit-ins at segregated lunch counters and burning draft registration cards are examples of nonviolent resistance. Boycotts and strikes are also forms of nonviolent resistance. In some cases, the resister hopes to provoke a violent response to prove the illegitimacy or immorality of the political or social institution whose law or custom has been violated.

8. *Escalation* tactics provoke the establishment into overreacting to, or overpreparing for, the confrontation and thereby appearing foolish. The use of rumor, an underground press that predicts the worst possible outcome, threats of disruption of "normal business," nonnegotiable demands, verbal and nonverbal obscenities, and token violence is a common escalation tactic (BOWERS AND OCHS, 1971).

Questions to Use

in Social-

Movement

Analysis of

Rhetorical Acts

1. What are the situational variables, the social-psychological, political-institutional, philosophical-ideological, and rhetorical forces that produced the movement?

2. Who are the leaders? What rhetorical behaviors do they engage in? What rhetorical tactics do they favor? How are they perceived by the establishment?

3. What function of rhetoric, relative to the movement's life cycle, does the rhetorical act fulfill? What phase is the movement in: inception, crisis, or consumation? Is the rhetorical act directed at maintaining membership, recruiting new members, challenging the establishment, or explaining success or failure?

4. What substance and form do the rhetorical tactics of the movement take? How does message content influence the ability of the movement to achieve its goal? How does the movement attempt to exploit the media and influence the content and reception of the message?

5. What is the social, psychological, political, and historical impact of the movement on its members, its leaders, the immediate history of the culture, and subsequent events in the culture?

Social-movement criticism examines the forces that produced the movement, its life cycle, and the tactics used in its rhetorical activity, by asking certain questions (see box above).

The Social-Movement Model and Critical Evaluation

Social-movement critics attempt to determine the impact of a movement on its culture. Therefore, the results standard of judgment is most commonly used to evaluate these rhetorical acts. Because our history records the successes and failures of movements in changing society and social institutions, macroscopic judgments about the role of a movement and microscopic judgments about how a particular rhetorical tactic worked are made in terms of results.

Of all the approaches to cultural criticism discussed in this chapter, social-movement criticism most closely resembles those approaches based on communication theories discussed in the four preceding chapters because its focus is on rhetorical tactics. Typically, social-movement critics discuss the forces that produced the movement and describe its rhetorical behavior. Concepts from one of the other approaches, particularly dramatism and fantasy theme analysis, are then used to evaluate that rhetorical behavior. Thus, social-movement criticism can extend beyond evaluating a movement by results to include evaluation using the ethics, truth, or aesthetic standards, as would be appropriate in terms of dramatism or fantasy theme analysis.

Social-movement criticism can increase your knowledge of history if you elect to use it to study movements that have influenced our culture or those that fell by the wayside. One of the principal difficulties in movement criticism is the extensive research required before the critic is able to explain events in a movement's life cycle. The civil-rights movement of the 1960s involved hundreds of acts, thousands of people, several notable leaders, and extensive coverage by the mass media. Simply assimilating, organizing, and judging the significance of the information on a movment like this before writing your criticism of it is a massive undertaking.

Summary

Cultural approaches draw their critical questions from some aspect of the culture in which the rhetorical act took place. Because culture is a complex of ideas, rules, customs, and values, many possibilities are available to the critic who is interested in creating a new model. In this chapter, we have discussed several examples of cultural criticism that you might elect to follow in your own critical efforts or that might inspire you to create your own model.

The *social-values model* bases evaluation on the existence of values in opposition and how the culture reorients its values through dialectical transformation or synthesis.

The *Jungian psychological model* uses psychological theory to analyze rhetorical acts analogous to a dream state. Archetypal themes and images in dreams serve as a category system for analyzing the rhetorical act. This model provides no means for evaluating the rhetorical act; it serves only as an analytical device.

Ideological models such as feminism and Marxism focus on the critic's ideological belief system, which defines the truth that serves as the basis for evaluating rhetorical acts.

Social-movement criticism focuses on ideology and cultural values more neutrally while examining the forces that bring social movements into being: the movement's life cycle and the tactics used by movement rhetors.

Regardless of whether you choose one of these models or create your own, doing cultural criticism requires a thorough understanding of the social, political, and economic forces that shape society.

Suggested Readings

Examples of Criticism

COX, J.R. (1974).   Perspectives on rhetorical criticism of movements: Anti-war dissent, 1964–1972. *Western Speech, 38,* 254–268.

> Cox uses the rhetorical situation created by the Vietnam War to discuss the antiwar movement. This article is a good example of movement criticism and provides an extensive discussion of the constraints on rhetorical acts by movement leaders. The antiwar movement is analyzed in terms of its collective behavior, reform goals, the credibility of its leadership, and rhetorical tactics directed at mainstream American culture.

DUNCAN, R.D. (1976).   Rhetoric of the kidvid movement: Ideology, strategies, and tactics. *Central States Speech Journal, 27,* 129–135.

> This article defines the ideology of the kidvid movement in terms of the various groups whose goal it is to improve the quality of children's television. This is an excellent example of using movement criticism to explore a group's ideology.

SOLOMON, M. (1983).   Stopping ERA: A pyrrhic victory. *Communication Quarterly, 31,* 109–118.

> This essay combines elements of feminist ideological criticism and social-movement criticism. The focus is on the results of the STOP ERA movement and the actions of its leader, Phillis Schlafly. Solomon's conclusions reflect her ideological position that the STOP ERA movement and other rhetorical acts by its leader created divisiveness among women and social friction that fuels the fire of gender inequality.

TRUJILLO, N., AND EKDOM, L.R. (1985).   Sportswriting and American cultural values: The 1984 Chicago Cubs. *Critical Studies in Mass Communication, 2,* 262–281.

> The authors did an inductive analysis of *Chicago Tribune* stories on the Cubs. They concluded that sports stories integrate conflicting values and that readers can extend this integration to help them cope with value conflict in their own lives. This is a well-written article and a good example of how a critic inductively creates a model by examining rhetorical acts for evidence of cultural values.

WANDER, P. (1984).   The rhetoric of American foreign policy. *Quarterly Journal of Speech, 70,* 339–361.

> The author claims that the rhetoric of American foreign policy "protects" the American voter from reality and provides an extensive discussion of the voter as an audience for foreign policy. Wander's own ideological bias is that rhetorical critics have the responsibility to confront real issues and deprogram voters. He evaluates the truthfulness of Eisenhower's "prophetic dualism" and Kennedy and Johnson's "technocratic realism" as presidential ideologies used to sell intervention, incursion, and war to the American voter as acceptable foreign policy options.

Resources for Doing Criticism

ALLEN, R.C. (1987). *Channels of discourse*. Chapel Hill, NC: University of North Carolina Press.

> This book is an anthology of essays on various cultural models used in television criticism. Each article offers a theoretical perspective and examples of criticism. The essays cover feminist, Marxist, and other ideological perspectives, the way in which television is ideological, and the aesthetic properties of television. An essay on narrative criticism is also included.

DAVIES, R.A., FARRELL, J.M., AND MATTHEWS, S.S. (1982). The dream world of film: A Jungian perspective on cinematic communication. *Western Journal of Speech Communication, 46*, 326–343.

> This article develops the Jungian model for rhetorical criticism of film. It provides a thorough, clear explanation of how Jung's theory of dreams can be applied to film. It not only sets up the critical model in detail but also provides a good discussion of the relationship between Jung's concepts of archetypal images and themes and the aesthetic properties of film.

FRENTZ, T.S. AND RUSHING, J.H. (1978). The rhetoric of "Rocky": Part Two. *Western Journal of Speech Communication, 42*, 231–240.

> This is the second of a two-part series that developed the social-values model presented in this chapter. The model is applied to the film *Rocky*, and the rhetorical situation of the 1976 presidential campaign is used to explain the value synthesis of both the film and James Earl Carter.

RUSHING, J.H. AND FRENTZ, T.S. (1978). The rhetoric of "Rocky": A social-value model of criticism. *Western Journal of Speech Communication, 41*, 63–72.

> This is the first of the two-part social-values model series explaining the popularity of *Rocky* and the election of President Carter. The authors argue that film has the potential to be more than an entertainment medium. Value-change patterns in film reflect changes in social values in America. The article develops the social-values model.

STEWART, C.J., SMITH, C.A., AND DENTON, R.E. (1984). *Persuasion and social movements*. Prospect Heights, IL: Waveland Press.

> This book offers a comprehensive discussion of social movements as rhetorical entities. It examines the properties of social movements in terms of their collective natures, ideological structures, and life cycles. The rhetorical tactics of using music, slogans, and obscenity are considered in detail. Case studies include the John Birch Society and the pro-life movement's response to the pro-choice movement.

8

The

Rhetoric of

Public Speaking

A record of our nation's past is found in public speeches. Sermons, legislative advocacy, political campaigning, lectures, and ceremonial orations all reveal important past exigences, in the words of people who experienced them. Today the public speech is even more important. Business, political, religious, educational, and other leaders acknowledge that to accomplish anything, it is necessary to build public consensus, and the most effective way is through public speaking.

In his 1925 essay, "On the Literary Criticism of Oratory," Herbert Wichelns opened the way for rhetorical criticism of public speeches. He believed the study of public speeches past and present was imperative given our culture, with its democratic government that operates on debate, inquiry, and political speech making. Wichelns felt most speech making had political overtones because leaders who set policies and standards, who made democracy function, all relied on public speaking (Wichelns, 1925).

On the surface, the formal properties of a speech seem simple compared with those of the other genres discussed in this book. As a genre, public speaking involves rhetorical acts that feature a speaker, an audience, and an oral message intended to influence the audience. The complexity of the genre is found in the variations of the speaker-message-audience relationship. Ancient Greek scholars identified three patterns that seemed to recur: *deliberative* rhetoric, speaking in the legislative assembly; *forensic* rhetoric, speaking in the courts; and *epideictic* rhetoric, speaking on ceremonial and social occasions. Each placed unique demands on the speaker, and a body of rhetorical theory developed as teachers and students explored how best to meet those demands.

Today, there is no similar master list of speaking situations. Even though the sweep of events is great, there are some limits on the number of situations that confront speakers, and the constraints imposed by the rhetorical situation limit the ways they can respond (Black, 1965). One of the greatest difficulties in categorizing speeches is that though critics want to find these recurring patterns, they recognize that each rhetorical situation is in some way unique (Jamieson and Campbell, 1982). Public speaking in America was shaped by the earliest rhetorical situations in our history which were religious. Our discussion of the public-speaking genre begins with a view of the colonial influence on American public address.

In the seventeenth century, the Puritans, middle to upper middle class educated people who were loyal to king and country, objected to the state religion of England. Persecution caused them to leave England for Holland where, although free to believe as they chose, they began losing their English identity. They decided to establish a colony across the western ocean, and other religious sects—Quakers, Roman Catholics, Huguenots, Moravians, and Presbyterians—followed them to the new world. These colonial groups were led by learned, eloquent men whose oratorical skills gave these groups the determination to leave their homelands, abandon the comforts of civilization, and create new social-religious communities in the wilderness. From sermons, they drew strength and learned to see themselves as the new Israelites who, like the followers of Abraham, had abandoned all but the Word of God to build a new Jerusalem in the wilderness (Bosley, 1969).

In religious speaking, the "priest" speaks of what a community believes to be true or real. The power of the priestly voice lies in the community's belief in extrahuman origins. The priest is an interpreter, not the originator, of messages. Priestly rhetoric is top-down, ordained by God, which gives it special potency. The persona of the priest plays an important role, disclosing the mystery of religious institutions.

> The priest, as a gatekeeper positioned at the outward frontiers of his professional world, seeks out and admits those initiates needed to replenish the life of the religious community and, at the same time, is entrusted with policing those boundaries dividing the sacred world from the profane. (LESSL, 1989, pp. 186–187)

Whatever the occasion, colonial preaching followed the same format, and sermons customarily lasted an hour or more. The sermonist began with a biblical text, then an exposition of the text to instruct the audience in its meaning. This was followed by the doctrinal part of the message, frequently the longest part, which presented propositions and proofs, usually biblical references. The sermon concluded with an application of the doctrine to the audience.

Although many of our tenets of democracy—freedom of speech and thought, individual rights, self-government, and separation of church and state—are inherited from these colonists, the Bible was their most cherished document, and the task of the sermonist was to interpret it.

> By means of analogies (frequently far-fetched) the preacher would find a reassuring word for them in hours of crisis: during famine, under Indian attack, when threatened by civil strife, when facing an election. The Election Day Sermon was, second only to Easter, the occasion for solemn and helpful scripturally based admonitions as to the kind of men needed to govern the new Israel. (BOSLEY, 1969, p. 27)

After a century of colonization, the religious establishment had begun to stagnate, and the evangelism of Wesleyan Methodism became a popular social force in America. The established churches responded, and religion as a personal experience was explored by leading New England preachers. Johnathan Edwards, one of the most famous preachers during the "Great Awakening," first delivered "Sinners in the Hands of an Angry God" at Enfield, Massachusetts in 1741. It was repeated, printed, and became one of the best known examples of Puritan preaching. Edwards preached a call to be born again to avoid the wrath of an angry God:

> So that, whatever some have imagined and pretended about promises made to natural men's earnest seeking and knocking, 'tis plain and manifest, that whatever pains a natural man takes in religion, whatever prayers he makes, till he believes in Christ, God is under no manner of obligation to keep him a moment from eternal destruction.
>
> So that thus it is, that natural men are held in the hand of God over the pit of hell; they have deserved the fiery pit, and are already sentenced to it; and God is dreadfully provoked, his anger is as great towards them as to those that are actually suffering the executions of the fierceness of his wrath in hell, and they have done nothing in the least to appease or abate that anger. . . .
>
> This that you have heard is the case of every one of you that are out of Christ. (ANDREWS AND ZAREFSKY, 1989, p. 25)

A concern for the Word of God as found in the Bible was typical of all sermons. Governments in the colonies of Massachusetts and Connecticut were elected annually by enfranchised citizens, and it was the custom to have a sermon precede these elections. Eventually governments throughout New England adopted the custom. Even though delivered once a year, these sermons had tremendous political influence because the chosen minister's sermon was also printed. On election day, the sermon explained the Word in terms of community as it marked the passage of an important point in time (Kerr, 1962).

Election sermons used biblical texts to connect political instruction to religious themes. Samuel Danforth's "A Brief Recognition of New England's Errand into the Wilderness" was the Massachusetts election day sermon in 1670. His theme was that colonists, like John the Baptist, had been sent into the wilderness by God for a purpose, and his arguments were biblically based; freedom was sanctioned by God, and the mission in the wilderness was to create a godly form of government.

Over time such sermons became a springboard for democracy. Echoing John Locke's philosophy of the social contract, they established the definition of what constituted the best form of government for America, collectively endorsing representative government. By the mid-eighteenth century many of these sermons had a revolutionary tone and the British government and King George III were judged according to this biblical standard.

Jonathan Mayhew, a liberal Unitarian minister in Boston, was popular with colonial leaders agitating for change. Samuel Adams considered his sermons an important part of the campaign against British rule. "Unlimited Submission and Non-Resistance to the Higher Powers" was a Sunday sermon delivered in 1749 or possibly 1750. Mayhew interpreted New Testament doctrine concerning submission to civil authority as Christian duty and argued that St. Paul was not advocating blind obedience to all rulers. He told his congregation that the apostles did not say a Christian had to submit to a ruler who acted against the people's welfare. In fact, they were obliged to resist such a ruler as a matter of Christian duty.

> [I]f the end of all civil government be the good of society; if this be the thing that is aimed at in constituting civil rulers; and if the motive and argument for submission to government be taken from the apparent usefulness of civil authority—it follows, that when no such good end can be answered by submission, there remains no argument or motive to enforce it; and if, instead of this good end's being brought about, and the ruin and misery of society effected by it, here is a plain and positive reason against submission in all such cases, should they ever happen again. And therefore, in such cases, a regard to the public welfare ought to make us withhold from our rulers that obedience and submission which it would otherwise be our duty to render to them. If it be our duty, for example, to obey our king merely for this reason, that he rules for the public welfare (which is the only argument the apostle makes use of), it follows, by a parity of reason, that when he turns tyrant, and makes his subjects his prey to devour

and destroy, instead of his charge to defend and cherish, we are bound to throw off our allegiance to him, and to resist. . . . Not to discontinue our allegiance in this case would be to join with the sovereign in promoting the slavery and misery of that society, the welfare of which we ourselves, as well as our sovereign, are indispensably obliged to secure and promote, as far as in us lies. (POTTER AND THOMAS, 1970, pp. 521–522)

Colonial New England was an amalgam of protestant groups who believed God intervened directly in their lives through good and bad harvests, successes and failures in business, and events such as fire, flood, and Indian attack. Any event could be an occasion for fasting and penitence or feasting and thanksgiving. "Fast and thanksgiving sermons were, therefore, concerned with the secular consequences of wickedness and holiness more often than not" (Kerr, 1960, p. 373). As the colonies moved toward rebellion, these sermons, which celebrated a point in time in a manner responsive to natural and social forces, took on a more political tone.

Days of fast or thanksgiving were ordered by the civil government, and normal activities were curtailed. On fast days people were to attend services and spend the remainder of their time in solemn contemplation of the event. Thanksgiving days were festive, sometimes combining public and religious celebrations. Even during the Revolution, days of fast and thanksgiving were a part of life. The Continental Congress proposed the first national fast day for 20 July 1775, asking the people to petition God to preserve the unity of the twelve colonies. "Later in the war, careful wording of fast and thanksgiving proclamations by Sam Adams and others encouraged ministers to discuss subjects which leaders of the nation wanted brought before the public and to avoid subjects which it was expedient to forget" (Kerr, 1960, p. 380).

Religious speaking in colonial America contributed to the form and content of contemporary speaking. The jeremiad is an outgrowth of the Puritan influence on rhetorical style and the organization of speeches. The Puritan jeremiad consisted of

1) a general theme of sin-repentance-reform; 2) a rigid organizational pattern that developed its theme; 3) the application of religious doctrine to secular, even political affairs; 4) an assumption that the American Puritans were God's chosen people with a special mission and destiny; and 5) a minister who spoke as a scolding prophet—a voice in the wilderness—but who was at the same time a part of the community. (RITTER, 1980, p. 157)

The idea of a nation forged in the wilderness, with special responsibilities ordained by heaven, was the foundation of the American dream for early colonists.

The jeremiad has evolved into a more generalized version of the American dream, with competing moral and material strains:

> In the moralistic version of the dream, Americans have the God-given rights of life, liberty, pursuit of happiness, and equality of opportunity. With the consent of the governed, government functions to secure these rights. Values to be actualized are tolerance, charity, compassion, regard for individual dignity and worth, equality of treatment by public institutions, and cooperation to help the unfortunate. In the materialistic component of the dream, the bedrock is the Puritan work ethic. Primary values include effort, persistence, initiative, self-reliance, achievement, material success, competitiveness, and self-interest. (JOHANNESEN, 1985, pp. 160–161)

The moralistic myth contains those freedoms expressed in the Declaration of Independence, and appears in rhetorical acts that seek reform, critique society, or cast blame on someone or something. The materialist myth is the foundation of the American sprit of competitiveness, the way we determine "personal worth, the free enterprise system, and the notion of freedom, defined as freedom from controls, regulations, or constraints that hinder the individual's striving for ascendancy in the social-economic hierarchy of society" (Fisher, 1973, p. 161).

The tradition of public speaking that we inherited from colonial times is the product of eloquent men whose education and social position made them the focal point of community life. The idea of a speaker's social status, combined with the need for a fitting response to the exigence in a rhetorical situation, suggests that speeches are most appropriately classified and easily understood by identifying the single force that placed a particular speaker before a particular audience delivering a particular message. As a result, the remainder of this chapter examines speeches that are a product of the speaker's public persona, speeches that celebrate a point in time, and speeches that are precipitated by social forces.

Public Persona Speeches

Senator Edward Kennedy found it necessary to address the people of his home state after an automobile accident claimed the life of a young woman and his subsequent behavior damaged his reputation. His speech was an attempt to restore his public persona. Lee Iacocca addressed the annual meeting of the American Bar Association not because of his standing as a legal scholar, but because of his shining reputation as the savior of Chrysler Corporation. He used the "bully" pulpit this afforded him to comment on and attempt to shape social forces.

The fact of the matter is, had Iaccoca been a worse manager, or Senator Kennedy a better driver, neither speech would have occurred. Though their speeches are as different as night and day and represent subcategories within the broader category of speeches that are a product of the speaker's public persona, they were alike in that both were about character. They differ only to the extent that Kennedy attempted to restore public perceptions of character whereas Iacocca attempted to capitalize on those perceptions.

Apologia

Any rhetorical situation that calls into question the reputation, moral qualities, behaviors, motives, or character of an individual or an organization requires an act of self-defense. *Apologia* is the term that describes rhetorical acts performed in response to situations in which the rhetor felt directly or indirectly damaged by charges of inappropriate behavior or poor judgment (Kruse, 1981).

> Typically a public person has been found in such an embarrassing dilemma that his effectiveness in public life is threatened. He then has made a single speech, reviewing the circumstances, defending his motives, and reminding the audience of his previously unblemished reputation and achievements, using almost-standardized methods and strategies to do so. He seeks in effect to redeem himself in the eyes of the public. (GOLD, 1978, pp. 307–308)

To be successful, apologia must answer the charges on the basis of morality and ethics and must be shaped in such a way that it repairs the character of the speaker (Kruse, 1981). The speaker's values are a key constraint in rhetorical situations that produce apologia. A speaker, particularly a politician, who appeals to, or adopts the values of, the audience has a better chance of succeeding (Hoover, 1989). The speaker reestablishes his or her reputation through a speech of self-vindication or self-justification using one or more of four strategies: denial, bolstering, differentiation, and transcendence (Ware and Linkugel, 1973).

A speaker can deny facts, feelings, emotions, or relationships, or deny any intent of wrongdoing. *Denial* is effective when it does not contradict what the audience already believes to be true. *Bolstering* is the opposite of denial. The speaker determines what the audience already believes, or values highly, and attempts to establish or reinforce his or her relationship to it. In *differentiation,* the speaker separates himself or herself from what the audience perceives negatively by redefining reality. The speaker takes what the audience presently thinks and puts a different spin on it to create a positive perception. *Transcendence* directs the audience's thinking away from the particulars of the alleged wrongdoing and toward a more abstract concept. Transcending rhetoric explains "what really happened" in a broader context (Ware and Linkugel, 1973).

Apologia seeks one of four outcomes. *Absolution* uses denial and differentiation to gain "forgiveness." The speaker denies any wrong was done and differentiates his or her behavior from that which the audience disapproves of. *Vindication* goes beyond the immediate situation to argue that the accused is more worthy than his or her accusers. Transcendent strategies are commonly used. *Explanative* apologia attempts to make the audience think of the speaker's transgression as good, just, or moral. The most defensive posture in apologia, it uses bolstering and differentiating strategies. *Justification* seeks the audience's understanding of the reasons for a wrongful act through bolstering and transcending strategies (Ware and Linkugel, 1973).

Clarence Darrow was one of America's greatest trial lawyers, nationally known for his eloquence in representing defendants in cases with social significance: a group of communists charged with conspiring to overthrow the government; Richard Loeb and Nathan Leopold, confessed murderers of a fourteen-year-old boy; and John Scopes in the famous "monkey trial" that pitted him against William Jennings Bryan. Cases arising out of labor–management turmoil became his chief occupation during the late nineteenth and early twentieth century, as he defended Eugene V. Debs, William Haywood, and other labor figures. His career as a labor lawyer culminated in his indictment for jury tampering in 1912.

On 1 October 1910, the offices of the *Los Angeles Times* were bombed and twenty people died in the explosion. The head of the Iron Workers Union and two union members were arrested. Reluctant to take the case, Clarence Darrow was persuaded by American Federation of Labor President Samuel Gompers to defend the men. In preparing for the trial, Darrow became convinced of their guilt, but a guilty plea would undermine organized labor and the defendants' status as symbols of oppression. The prosecution wanted to embarrass Darrow and at a crucial moment arrested, on a charge of attempting to bribe a juror, the detective that Darrow had employed to investigate prospective jurors. Because the detective was his agent, Darrow was also charged and brought to trial on 12 May 1912.

Although he did not conduct his own defense, Darrow did make the final plea to the jury. His objective was justification, and his arguments were primarily transcendence arguments that his trial was not about jury tampering but about the larger questions of the rights of labor. While he asked the jury to believe he was really on trial for defending labor and unionism, he also engaged in bolstering by associating himself with several virtues. "I believe if you went to my native town, that the rich would tell you that they could trust not only my honor, but my judgment, and my sense of justice and fairness" (Graham, 1970, p. 32). Darrow's work as a labor attorney had been part of the national climate of violence that accompanied the unions' struggle for legal rights, higher wages, and better working conditions for their members. His transcendence arguments put this climate in perspective for the jury, illustrating the principle of going from the particular to the abstract in apologia.

> I have loved peace, all my life. I have taught it all my life.
> I believe that love does more than hatred. I believe that
> both sides have gone about the settlement of these
> difficulties in the wrong way. The acts of the one have

> caused the acts of the other, and I blame neither. Men are
> not perfect. They had an imperfect origin, and they are
> imperfect today, and the long struggle of the human race
> from darkness to comparative civilization has been filled
> with clash and discord and murder and war, and violence
> and wrong, and it will be, for years and years to come.
> But ever we are going onward and upward toward the
> sunshine, where the hatred and war and cruelty and
> violence of the world will disappear. (GRAHAM, 1970,
> p. 33)

Richard Nixon's Checkers speech, mentioned in Chapter 1, was also an example of an apologia, but one in which the speaker sought absolution from wrongdoing. The then vice presidential candidate denied that he had made personal use of $18,000 in political contributions while he was a senator. "Not one cent of the $18,000 or any other money of that type ever went to me for my personal use. Every penny of it was used to pay for political expenses that I did not think should be charged to the taxpayers of the United States" (Ryan, 1983, p. 115). The speech was a success and saved Nixon's candidacy in 1952, in part because of an appeal differentiating the acceptable personal use of a contribution from the unacceptable:

> One other thing I probably should tell you because if we
> don't they'll probably be saying this about me too, we did
> get something—a gift—after the election. A man down in
> Texas heard Pat on the radio mention the fact that our
> two youngsters would like to have a dog. And, believe it
> or not, the day before we left on this campaign trip we got
> a message from Union Station in Baltimore saying they
> had a package for us. We went down to get it. You know
> what it was.
>
> It was a little cocker spaniel dog in a crate that he sent
> all the way from Texas. Black and white spotted. And our
> little girl—Tricia, the 6-year-old—named it Checkers.
> And you know, the kids love that dog and I just want to
> say this right now, that regardless of what they say about
> it, we're gonna keep it. (RYAN, 1983, pp. 119–120)

Apologia is prompted by an exigence concerning perceptions of the rhetor's character or behavior (Kruse, 1981), and its appeals are intended to repair his or her reputation. When a rhetor's reputation is not in need of repair, but is instead an asset, an opportunity exists. The Puritan work ethic holds that if people used their talents and knowledge diligently they would be rewarded. Speakers of exceptional reputation have capitalized on their assets, and have been amply rewarded.

Enterprise Speaking

Public lecturing, the professionalization of public speaking through the lyceum and chautauqua movements, began early in the nineteenth century. Some speakers emerged as national celebrities, and most of what went on was fairly commercial, intended to make money and win the audience's admiration (Oliver, 1965). Others, such as abolitionists and advocates for women's suffrage, temperance, and other social causes, used the public lecture platform to express their views to a national audience, focusing both urban and rural attention on issues of the day (Hance, 1944).

The first lyceum lecture program was organized in 1826 by Josiah Holbrook, a manufacturer who wanted to establish an adult education system. The lyceums flourished, and by 1834 there were three thousand town lyceums organized by local volunteers. These early efforts were intended to fill an educational and informational void, because public education was limited to the primary grades, and the only sources of public information were partisan newspapers that resembled propaganda sheets and an occasional, poorly produced, magazine (Hance, 1944; Oliver, 1965).

After the Civil War there was renewed interest in public lectures, and James C. Redpath and George L. Fall organized the Boston Lyceum Bureau to supply talent to local lyceums. Redpath was the most successful organizer of public lectures, managing most American lecturers from 1867 to 1875. He made the best, most famous speakers—including such notables as Wendell Phillips, William Lloyd Garrison, Charles Sumner, John B. Gough, Ralph Waldo Emerson, John Greenleaf Whittier, Elizabeth Cady Stanton, Susan B. Anthony, Anna Dickinson, Henry Ward Beecher, and Charles Dickens—available to cities and small towns across the nation. These people were the stars of the lecture circuit and famous in their own right as religious, political, and social leaders, or as explorers, authors, and scientists (Hance, 1944).

In 1874 the chautauqua movement was born at Lake Chautauqua, New York. John H. Vincent, a leader in the Methodist church, and Lewis Miller, a prominent manufacturer with an avocation for Sunday school work, developed an institute to train Sunday school teachers. Their idea was to mix work and play, enriching the intellectual and spiritual lives of the participants. They hired leading academics, clergy, and famous lyceum speakers and provided concerts, fireworks, and games for lighter entertainment. The idea spread across the country, and Vincent organized traveling chautauquas that, like circuses, moved from town to town, spending a week in each (J.E. Gould, 1961; Oliver, 1965). The arrival of the chautauqua was a major event in most rural communities from the 1880s until radios became inexpensive and network programming expanded to take over the task of informing and entertaining the nation.

Although the inspirational elements of its Sunday school origins never entirely left chautauqua, it quickly turned secular, a way to hear the most famous national and international lecturers, see actors and singers, and experience culture. Russell Conwell, a captain in the Union Army and founder of Temple

University, was among the most popular inspirational speakers on the circuit. His lecture "Acres of Diamonds," a series of stories linked to the theme that everyone had golden opportunities in their own backyard and only needed to work hard to be successful, was presented over six thousand times.

Conwell's lecture was popular because it fitted the times, a period of extremes of wealth and poverty, and audiences wanted to find out how they could get a piece of the American dream. Conwell reassured them that money and morality were not incompatible.

> You ought to make money. Money is power. Think how much good you could do if you had money now. Money is power and it ought to be in the hands of good men. It would be in the hands of good men if we comply with the Scripture teachings, where God promises prosperity to the righteous man. (ANDREWS AND ZAREFSKY, 1989, p. 337)

Conwell was adept at using a humorous story to reveal a moral or principle. On the secret of making money, he told an anecdote about one of the richest men in America, John Jacob Astor, who foreclosed on a hat shop and then became the previous owner's partner.

> After he entered into partnership, he went out and sat down on a bench in the park. . . . As he sat upon that bench if a lady passed him with her shoulders thrown back and her head up, and looking straight to the front, as though she didn't care if all the world did gaze on her, then John Jacob Astor studied the bonnet she wore; and before it was out of sight, he knew the shape of the frame, and the curl of the lace, and crimp of the feathers, and lots of intricate things that go into a bonnet which I cannot describe. Then he went to his millinery store and said: "Now put in the show window just such a bonnet as I describe to you, because I have just seen a real lady who likes just such a bonnet." Then he went and sat down again. Another lady, with another form and complexion came, and, of course she wore another style of bonnet. He then went back and described that and had that put into the window. He didn't fill his show windows full of hats and bonnets to drive the people away, and then sit back in the store and bawl because people went somewhere else to trade. He didn't have a hat or a bonnet that some lady didn't like. That has since been the wealthiest millinery firm on the face of the earth. . . . Now John Jacob Astor made the fortune of that millinery firm not by lending them money, but by finding out what the ladies liked for bonnets, before they wasted any material in

> making them up. And if a man can foresee the millinery
> business, he can foresee anything under Heaven!
> (ANDREWS AND ZAREFSKY, 1989, p. 341)

Along with inspiration and entertainment, chautauqua was a forum for populist ideas. William Jennings Bryan was "King of the Chautauqua," speaking to as many as four million people in a single year. Although ultimately unsuccessful in the general election, his popularity on the chautauqua circuit, where he presented his "Prince of Peace" lecture about three thousand times, helped him gain the Democratic party's presidential nomination on four occasions (Oliver, 1965). Its theme was primarily religious, the Bible and the Ten Commandments were the best codes of conduct, but Bryan also managed to weave two salient late nineteenth-century issues into the fabric of the speech. Having told the audience that the most fundamental commandment was to "love thy neighbor as thyself," he proceeded to apply this concept to the issues of labor relations and the distribution of wealth:

> First let us consider the question of capital and labor. This is not a transient issue or a local one. It engages the attention of the people of all countries and has appeared in every age. The immediate need in this country is arbitration, for neither side to the controversy can be trusted to deal with absolute justice, if allowed undisputed control; but arbitration, like a court, is a last resort. It would be better if the relations between employer and employee were such as to make arbitration unnecessary. Just in proportion as men recognize their kinship to each other and deal with each other in the spirit of brotherhood will friendship and harmony be secured. Both employer and employee need to cultivate the spirit which follows from obedience to the great commandment.
>
> The second problem to which I would apply this platform of peace is that which relates to the accumulation of wealth. We cannot much longer delay consideration of the ethics of money-making. That many of the enormous fortunes which have been accumulated in the last quarter of a century are now held by men who have given to society no adequate service in return for the money secured is now generally recognized. While legislation can and should protect the public from predatory wealth, a more effective remedy will be found in the cultivation of a public opinion which will substitute a higher ideal than the one which tolerates the enjoyment of unearned gains. No man who really knows what brotherly love is will desire to take advantage of his neighbor, and the conscience when not seared will admonish against injustice. (GINGER, 1967, pp. 149–150)

The lyceum, chautauqua, and lecture bureaus had different purposes and reached different audiences. Lyceums operated during the winter and usually reached an educated, socially elite audience, even though their original purpose had been to provide general public education. By 1875, the lyceum system had been overtaken by the more commercial public lecture bureau. Chautauqua operated during the summer in both large cities and rural areas. It reached an audience with little education and lower social status. The public lecture bureaus acted as booking agents, taking a commission for their services and placing speakers across the country. The lecture bureaus operated year-round and were exclusively profit making enterprises (Oliver, 1965). They continue to do a lucrative business today, placing celebrity speakers before community, business, and professional audiences.

A relatively recent development in this sort of enterprise speaking has been the emergence of the chief executive officer (C.E.O.) as a spokesperson. Stockholders and employees expect to see good judgment and long-range planning, and the public expects to see good corporate citizenship. For much of our history, business leaders have had access to government and could exert political influence. The Great Depression significantly reduced their influence. Because of the loss of confidence in business, labor leaders, scholars, and the intellectual elite were able to exert the kind of rhetorical influence previously wielded by big business (Corn, 1981).

The rhetorical problems of big business were compounded by the perception of a corporation as "faceless." Business leaders have come to realize the importance of speaking out on issues and serving as a living symbol of the corporation. As spokesperson, the business leader symbolizes and articulates the goals, activities, and values of an organization (Seeger, 1986). Chief executive officers now seek opportunities to give commencement speeches, participate in public forums, address community and special interest groups, testify at Congressional hearings, and speak to other audiences of opinion leaders (Tarver, 1987).

Lee Iacocca became an American folk hero, credited with saving Chrysler Corporation. His leadership offered Americans object lessons in how to act in a crisis, maintain their values, and work as a team to be successful (Dionisopoulos, 1988). His celebrity as the C.E.O. who took the big gamble that paid off translated into an opportunity to address the annual meeting of the American Bar Association in 1987. He told the legal profession that product safety litigation seriously threatened our nation's ability to compete because it discouraged corporate risk taking:

> A small company in Virginia that made driving aids for handicapped people went out of business because it couldn't afford the liability insurance. Too risky.
>
> There used to be 18 companies making football helmets in this country, but the liability crisis has pared them down to just two. Nobody makes gymnastics equipment or hockey equipment anymore. Too risky.
>
> We've virtually stopped making light aircraft in this

> country. The biggest production cost is the liability
> insurance. Too risky.
>
> One of these days we're going to wake up and say "the
> hell with it—*competing* is just too risky!" . . . I'm afraid
> we're beginning to punish some of the normal risks that
> simply can't be avoided when you produce almost any
> kind of product. And when we do that—when we punish
> *normal* risk—then we're also punishing *competitiveness,*
> and we're punishing *progress.* (IACOCCA, 1987,
> p. 747)

Like Lee Iacocca, Michael Eisener, chairman and C.E.O. of The Walt Disney Company, has gained national visibility and become an active speaker. In 1987, he was invited to address an ABC Television Network conference on how television portrays business. He advised his audience that they might improve the image of, and stimulate confidence in, American business through quality programming, a value synonymous with the organization he guides:

> These attitudes probably stem as much from TV news as
> they do from TV drama, but in either case, they underline
> once again the power of the medium and remind us that
> we who are responsible for TV's content must assume our
> share of responsibility for its impact.
>
> Too often, perhaps, the unfair or inaccurate portrayal of
> business may be the result of a malady that plagues our
> entire society today—a general relaxation of quality
> standards that once made our country famous. . . .
>
> Today, sad to say, it seems to me that too many
> television offerings are falling into the same trap as too
> many businesses in America who have forgotten the
> quality standard and are increasingly in a race to the
> bottom. By that I mean competing at any cost, producing
> at the lowest common denominator, doing anything for a
> short-term solution. . . . In television, these marathons of
> mediocrity often take the form of using business or other
> handy stereotypes in place of creativity and thoughtful
> characterization. (EISENER, 1987, p. 667)

Labor leaders use the occasion of Labor Day to discuss the status of organized labor. University presidents begin each academic year by speaking with the assembled faculty and staff about campus and community issues. But these speeches are not restricted to products of the speaker's public persona, these are speeches celebrating a point in time. The C.E.O.s of a variety of entities other than publicly held corporations engage in these "state of the organization" rhetorical acts.

Point-in-Time Speeches

In addition to speaking for their organizations as corporate citizens, chief executive officers also perform rhetorical functions similar to those of United States presidents. Employees expect regular reassurances that the business is prospering, and businesses are legally obligated to report to their stockholders annually. The annual meeting provides an occasion for the C.E.O. to speak, justifying or explaining the past year's activities and results and laying out future plans.

The U.S. Constitution established that the president should report to Congress on a regular basis, and the first State of the Union message was delivered by George Washington at the opening session of Congress in 1790. He congratulated North Carolina for endorsing the Constitution and observed that the past actions of Congress seemed to have been favorably received by the American people. He then turned to important issues he believed Congress must consider, particularly the defense budget, beginning the tradition of using the State of the Union speech to hector Congress for legislative action. In George Washington's America, the enemy was Indian tribes; in Ronald Reagan's America it was the Soviet Union. His 1987 State of the Union speech continued the tradition and told Congress and the American people that a vote for his defense budget was a vote for a safer world.

Arthur Gashbow, chief executive of the Mille Lacs Band of Chippewa Indians, delivered the "State of the Band, January 14, 1989" to members of the Mille Lacs Band and federal officials. Opening with a lengthy account of the loss of tribal lands over the preceding one hundred years, he outlined his plan to regain these lands, the problems the Band faced, and what they must do to overcome them:

The non-Indian people who live within our reservation boundaries are not our enemies. The United States and the State of Minnesota are not our enemies either.

The true enemies of the Mille Lacs Band are those aspects of humanity that ruin the world: greed and ignorance.

We lost our land because of greed. Greed caused the injustice of the last century. Mainly it was the greed of timber companies, but it was also the greed of America itself.

Our enemy in this century is ignorance. The United States forgets what it did to us. The State of Minnesota does not understand that we are a sovereign government.

Of the two enemies, ignorance is the more dangerous.

To combat these enemies, greed and ignorance, we must always take the high road.

We must fight for our rights, but we must do so in

> a decent, honest and legal manner as our ancestors
> taught us.
>   We must follow the principles of Midewewin. We must
> be honest, we must respect others and we must be hard
> working. (GASHBOW, 1989, p. 410)

His speech ended by echoing words John Kennedy had spoken in his inaugural address: "Let the word go forth from this time and place, to friend and foe alike, that the torch has been passed to a new generation of Americans" (Reid, 1988, p. 711).

> For now let the word go forth from this time and place,
> the state of this Band is sound and let friend and foe alike
> know that we are on the offensive.
>   We will not back down.
>   We are on the attack.
>   There is no retreat.
>   There is no surrender. (GASHBOW, 1989, p. 413)

Commemorative Speaking

Celebration of national holidays, particularly the Fourth of July, and commemoration of historical events have helped create and sustain nationalism. Around the nation, audiences expected that the anniversaries of important events would be marked by a speech (Larson, 1940; H.H. Martin, 1958).

> Audiences took in whole communities, especially on the
> frontier, where the national anniversary was one of those
> infrequent chances for social intercourse. And out of these
> ceremonial gatherings emerged an image of America and
> its uniqueness that seems to have been the unifying
> element in American group life. (H.H. MARTIN, 1958,
> p. 401)

The Fourth of July symbolized what was sacred to all Americans: our mission as a democratic nation to serve as a political and moral standard for the world, the benefits of a classless society in which hard work was the measure of one's worth, and the foundations of our political, economic, and cultural values as set forth in the Declaration of Independence (H.H. Martin, 1958).

Independence Day has been celebrated since 1777. On that occasion, Reverend William Gordon delivered a speech at Roxbury, Massachusetts that compared the newly declared republic to the division of the tribes of Israel after the death of Solomon and compared George III to the tyrant Rehoboam (Larson, 1940). In the first half-century of our history as a nation, Fourth of July speeches expressed pride in the country and its democratic institutions. As time passed, these speeches began to talk of the nation's manifest destiny to expand its territory. For nineteenth-century speakers and audiences, the Fourth of July oration defined and maintained American values and kept alive a popular tradition of celebrating an important occasion with a speech (Larson, 1940; H.H. Martin, 1958).

Both before and after the American Revolution, one of the most frequently commemorated events was the Boston massacre, an altercation between a Boston mob and some British soldiers in which a few civilians were killed. The "massacre" was held up as a symbol of British tyranny to stir up patriotic fervor and anti-British sentiments. John Hancock, a gifted patriotic orator, was selected to give the commemorative speech at Boston in 1774. His account shows how events were interpreted:

> It was reasonable to expect that troops, who knew the errand they were sent upon, would treat the people whom they were to subjugate, with a cruelty and haughtiness which too often buries the honorable character of a *soldier*, in the disgraceful name of an *unfeeling ruffian*.
>
> The troops, upon their first arrival, took possession of our senate-house, and pointed their cannon against the judgment-hall, and even continued them there whilst the supreme court of judicature for this province was actually sitting to decide upon the lives and fortunes of the king's subjects. Our streets nightly resounded with the noise of riot and debauchery; our peaceful citizens were hourly exposed to shameful insults and often felt the effects of their violence and outrage. (REID, 1988, pp. 101–102)

Hancock's avowal of the willingness of Bostonians to sacrifice themselves used the flowery, evocative language expected in ceremonial speaking at the time:

> Death is the creature of a poltroon's brains; 'tis immortality to sacrifice ourselves for the salvation of our country. We fear not death. That gloomy night, the pale-faced moon and the affrighted stars that hurried through the sky, can witness that we fear not death. (REID, 1988, p. 103)

Today, it is tempting to dismiss speeches commemorating national holidays as excessive, a style of speaking that is no longer good form. We seldom gather to listen to speakers on these occassions, but the tradition and the need to commemorate our history still exists. On Memorial Day, 29 May 1989, the NBC morning news program commemorated those who died in the Vietnam War by showing viewers the objects and letters left at the Washington D.C. monument to these veterans. We carry on the commemorative tradition, albeit in different ways.

Eulogy

Eulogies are an especially important type of speaking to mark a point in time. Death by accident, assassination, untimely illness, or circumstances other than old age can significantly disrupt the social order. The assassination of a president or national leader, or a tragedy such as the explosion of the space shuttle *Challenger,* disrupts the sense of community and creates the expectation of a fitting response. A eulogy must memorialize the dead, console the living, and restore the sense of community.

Research into how the terminally ill and their families cope with death has revealed a five-stage process: denial, anger, bargaining, depression, and acceptance. A eulogy can be judged in terms of how well it was adapted to the constraints imposed by these stages:

> The constraints of eulogistic rhetoric can be viewed as responding to these reactions and rehearsing the transition through these stages. While denial can be a useful buffer after receiving unexpected, shocking news . . . it is only a temporary defense. Public acknowledgment and transformation of the relationship with the deceased forces the bereaved toward final acceptance. Mourners may attempt to bargain with God to reverse the course of events as they confront the truth. Easing their terror of mortality and arguing that the dead live on reduces the stakes (and the need for bargaining) and soothes their anger and depression. As the bereaved come to accept death, eulogies reknit the community in the deceased's absence. (MISTER, 1986, p. 159)

Sometimes the eulogist calls for social action, however such a call must be consistent with the views of the person being memorialized. For example, Senator Hubert Humphrey's death from cancer brought calls for more cancer research, and Senator Robert Kennedy's assassination was followed by eulogies demanding stricter gun control. Had Humphrey been against increased spending for medical research or Kennedy against gun control, using the occasion of their deaths to demand such actions would have been not only inappropriate but disrespectful. Though the political or ideological opponents of the deceased may memorialize them, they obviously do not call for actions that would be counter to their own views (Jamieson and Campbell, 1982).

Adlai E. Stevenson was noted for his eloquence as a eulogist. In 1961 he was appointed ambassador to the United Nations by President John F. Kennedy. Four days after Kennedy's assassination, Stevenson delivered the eulogy at the United Nations, demonstrating the properties of this type of speaking. He spoke of the fallen president as a man of his times and memorialized his beliefs in a series of "We shall not soon forget" statements:

> President Kennedy was so contemporary a man, so involved in our world, so immersed in our times, so responsive to its challenges, so intense a participant in the great events and the great decisions of our day, that he seemed the very symbol of the vitality and the exuberance

that is the essence of life itself. . . . We shall not soon forget that he held fast to the vision of a world in which the peace is secure, in which inevitable conflicts are reconciled by pacific means, in which nations devote their energies to the welfare of all their citizens, and in which the vast and colorful diversity of human society can flourish in a restless, competitive search for a better society.

We shall not soon forget that, by word and by deed, he gave proof of profound confidence in the present value and the future promise of this great organization, the United Nations. (GRAHAM, 1970, p. 123)

Stevenson concluded by casting President Kennedy's death as a tragic ending, while at the same time reassuring his listeners of the underlying continuity of American political institutions and support for the United Nations:

Now he is gone. Today we mourn him. Tomorrow and tomorrow we shall miss him. And so we shall never know how different the world might have been had fate permitted this blazing talent to live and labor longer at man's unfinished agenda for peace and progress for all. Yet for the rest of us, life goes on. Our agenda remains unfinished. Minutes after his spirit departed, Lyndon B. Johnson took his oath of allegiance to the permanent institutions of this country, institutions which outlast violence and outlive men. These hours of mourning are then but a pause in a process, not a break in purpose or in policy. . . .

So my friends, we shall honor him in the best way that lies open to us, and the way he would want it to be, by getting on with the everlasting search for peace and justice for which all mankind is praying. (GRAHAM, 1970, p. 124)

Presidential assassination places special demands on the vice president. Upon President Kennedy's death, Lyndon Johnson had to symbolically vacate the office, laying Kennedy to rest, before he could state his own intentions and political agenda. This placed organizational constraints on his eulogy which had to fulfill some of the functions of an inaugural address, establishing continuity and legitimizing his presidency, as well as stating his own policy goals (Jamieson and Campbell, 1982).

Commemorative speeches and eulogies usually concentrate on making value judgments about a person, place, event, idea, or action. The occasion, audience, and character of the speaker are very important in judging the effectiveness of such speaking. The degree to which the audience does or does not become involved in the message is determined by the speaker's ability to select the right themes. Commemorative speeches and eulogies reveal much about the culture shared by speaker and audience and about social values at the time. Successful commemorative speakers and eulogists are those able to tap into salient audience beliefs and attitudes and address appropriately the exigence created by the occasion.

Political Campaign Speaking

Until the mid-nineteenth century, leading politicians picked the presidential candidates, and relatively few people were enfranchised to vote. Eventually, the two-party system as we know it emerged, and the rituals of campaigning began to evolve. In the nineteenth and early twentieth centuries, candidates made public appearances, taking their campaigns to the voters. Printed texts of their speeches, journalists' accounts of these speeches, and editorials in politically partisan newspapers helped deliver the candidate's message to those not in attendance. Technological progress allowed a wheelchair-bound Franklin D. Roosevelt to use radio to reach the public.

In the latter half of the twentieth century, campaigns have been changed by television. Televised coverage of preconvention campaigning, the nominating convention, candidate debates, and political advertising now bring political oratory into the voter's home quadrennially. Dwight Eisenhower used television commercials and was the first nominee of a national convention covered gavel-to-gavel by television. Although the process of political campaigning involves a wide variety of rhetorical activities, we will focus on two of the more interesting forms of public speaking, keynotes and acceptances, which mark the psychological beginning and end of the nominating convention.

Keynote Speeches

The concept of the keynote speech emerged from the 1896 Democratic convention, in which the party was split over an economic issue, the gold standard versus the free coinage of silver. The "Silver Democrats" challenged the party chair, a "Gold Democrat," and had their man make a speech keynoting the crusade for silver (Miles, 1960). This first keynote speech was eclipsed when William Jennings Bryan spoke on the same issue the next day, but the idea of an opening, keynote speech caught on and has become part of the convention ritual. The keynote speech must whip the delegates' enthusiasm, set the tone or theme for the convention, and showcase a leading son or daughter of the party. Keynote speeches are extravagant, bivalued speeches which praise the keynoter's party and castigate the opposition.

At the time of the 1988 presidential elections the Democratic party had been defeated by Ronald Reagan twice. Ann Richards, state treasurer of Texas, was selected as the keynote speaker. Her speech was typical of the bivalued style of keynoting. She described Republican policies that were "wrong" and characterized the Democratic party as the embodiment of right thinking:

They've told farmers that they were selfish, that they
would drive up food prices if they asked the Government
to intervene on behalf of the family farm, and we watched
farms go on the auction block while we bought food from
foreign countries. Well, that's wrong.

They told working mothers it's all their fault that
families are falling apart because they had to work to keep
their kids in jeans, tennis shoes and college. And they're
wrong.

They told American labor they were trying to ruin free
enterprise by asking for 60 days' notice of plant closings,
and that's wrong. . . .

Now we Democrats believe that America is still the
country of fair play, that we can come out of a small town
or a poor neighborhood and have the same chance as
anyone else, and it doesn't matter whether we are black or
Hispanic, or disabled or women.

We believe that America is a country where small-
business owners must succeed because they are the
bedrock, backbone, of our economy.

We believe that our kids deserve good day care and
public schools. We believe our kids deserve public schools
where students can learn and teachers can teach.
(RICHARDS, 1988, pp. 647–648)

The 1988 Republican keynoter, Governor Thomas Kean of New Jersey,
responded with an equally bivalued attack on the Democrats' ability to preserve
national symbols. Noting their choice of colors at their convention, he called his
audience's attention to the flag.

You see this flag of red, white, and blue? It symbolizes the
"Land of the Free" and the "Home of the Brave." Well,
their media consultants in Atlanta said they didn't think
the colors looked good on television. So they changed red
to pink, blue to azure, and the white to eggshell. Well I
don't know about you, but I believe Americans, Democrat
and Republican alike, have no use for pastel patriotism.
(KEAN, 1989, p. 7).

Keynoting is a difficult task because partisans expect a sustained attack on the
opposition, and members of the opposing party find such attacks offensive.
Democrat Barbara Jordan's 1976 keynote address was unique in that it succeeded
with both groups (Thompson, 1979).

I could easily spend this time praising the
accomplishments of this party and attacking the
Republicans but I don't choose to do that.

I could list the many problems which Americans have. I
could list the problems which cause people to feel cynical,
angry, frustrated: problems which include lack of integrity
in government; the feeling that the individual no longer
counts; the reality of material and spiritual poverty; the
feeling that the grand American experiment is failing or
has failed. I could recite these problems and then I could
sit down and offer no solutions. But I don't choose to do
that either.

The citizens of America expect more. They deserve
more than a recital of problems. We are a people in a
quandary about the present. We are a people in search of
our future. We are a people in search of a national
community. (RYAN, 1983, pp. 227–228)

Her speech fit the expectations of partisans and nonpartisans alike because of the
value clusters she used to characterize national leadership, patriotism, cooperation, and pioneer morality. The motive appeals were set in nonpartisan contexts
and cast philosophically. Praise for the Democratic party was tempered with
constructive criticism, and Jordan's personal credibility and skill in delivery
conveyed sincerity (Thompson, 1979).

Acceptance Speeches
Grover Cleveland made the first modern acceptance speech at a rally after his
nomination in 1892, and Franklin D. Roosevelt established the modern tradition
of making an acceptance speech at the convention. These speeches enable the
nominee to publicly accept the mantle of party leadership, to attempt to unify the
party behind this leadership, and to send a message of party and personal
ideology to a national audience. Acceptance speeches are a political ritual and
have a predictable structure and style:

Similar to Aristotle's notion of Epideictic speech, such a
ritual is characterized by a rhetoric structured and styled
to produce physical rather than intellectual response from
the audience, by a dynamic, often almost rhythmical,
pattern of statement-response between the speaker and his
auditors, by a verbal content which appeals to the mass
rather than to any limited faction, and by an implied or
explicit credo which is absolute in its rightness and denies
the validity of all others. (NORDVOLD, 1968, p. 34)

John F. Kennedy's 1960 acceptance speech established his credo, the theme
of "The New Frontier."

I tell you the New Frontier is here, whether we seek it or
not. Beyond that frontier are uncharted areas of science
and space, unsolved problems of peace and war,

> unconquered pockets of ignorance and prejudice, unanswered questions of poverty and surpluses.
>
> It would be easier to shrink back from that frontier, to look to the safe mediocrity of the past, to be lulled by good intentions and high rhetoric—and those who prefer that course should not cast their votes for me, regardless of party.
>
> But I believe the times demand invention, innovation, imagination, decision. I am asking each of you to be new pioneers on the New Frontier. My call is to the young in heart, regardless of age—to the stout in spirit; regardless of party. (KENNEDY, 1960, pp. 611–612)

In acceptance speeches, a variation of the Puritan jeremiad surfaces when the challenger is trying to prove that the incumbent has not kept faith with America.

> Americans are warned that they have deviated from the abiding principles of the American Dream; their present suffering is a sign of their infidelity to the past. The presidential candidate offers to lead the people through repentance back to their fundamental national values and, thereby, restore America to its former greatness. Like the Puritan form, the modern jeremiad both laments America's present condition and celebrates the prospect of its ultimate fulfillment. It glorifies America's special status as man's "last best hope," and constantly warns Americans of their failure to live up to that ideal. (RITTER, 1980, p. 159)

Ronald Reagan's 1980 acceptance speech indicted the Democrats and President Carter for just these failures. He told conventioneers and the viewing audience that he considered his candidacy a promise.

> I want my candidacy to unify our country; to renew the American spirit and sense of purpose. I want to carry our message to every American, regardless of party affiliation, who is a member of this community of shared values.
>
> Never before in our history have Americans been called upon to face three grave threats to our very existence, any one of which could destroy us. We face a disintegrating economy, a weakened defense and an energy policy based on the sharing of scarcity.
>
> The major issue of this campaign is the direct political, personal, and moral responsibility of Democratic Party leadership—in the White House and in the Congress—for this unprecedented calamity which has befallen us. They tell us they've done the most that humanly could be done.

> They say that the United States has had its day in the sun,
> that our nation has passed its zenith. They expect you to
> tell your children that the American people no longer
> have the will to cope with their problems; that the future
> will be one of sacrifice and few opportunities.
>
> My fellow citizens, I utterly reject this view. (REAGAN,
> 1980, p. 642)

Acceptance speeches typically conclude with some reference to the choice between parties and candidates. In 1940 Franklin D. Roosevelt broke with the custom established by George Washington by seeking a third term as president. With war raging in Europe and Japanese expansion in the Pacific, Roosevelt's acceptance speech barely acknowledged the other candidate, speaking only of "untried hands." His closing suggested that a much more compelling choice faced the electorate:

> We face one of the great choices of history. It is not alone
> a choice of government—government by the people
> versus dictatorship. It is not alone a choice of freedom
> versus slavery. It is not alone a choice between moving
> forward or falling back; it is all of these rolled into one. It
> is the continuance of civilization as we know it versus the
> ultimate destruction of all that we have held dear—
> religion against godlessness, the ideal of justice against the
> practice of force, moral decency versus the false lullaby of
> appeasement. (F.D. ROOSEVELT, 1940, p. 613)

Initiation Speaking

Delivering a speech can serve as a rite of passage, marking the point at which the speaker's life changes. The significance of the moment is reinforced by the fact that such speaking occurs even when no audience is present. One of the customs of the U.S. Senate is that new members do not take an active part in debate and the business of the Senate until they have presented a "maiden speech," which few people may actually hear. The custom is a legacy from the British House of Commons, where the maiden speech determined the viability of the member's political career. Unlike their British counterparts, U.S. senators seldom regard the maiden speech as so momentous an event (O. Peterson, 1984). The other form of initiation speaking we shall examine, the inaugural speech, is considered both momentous and worthy of an audience.

The Maiden Speech

Maiden speeches actually are important for a senator's constituency. They are reported in the press and signal those issues the speaker regards as important. On 7 June 1983, freshman New Jersey Senator Frank R. Lautenberg gave his maiden speech to an almost empty Senate chamber. Only the majority and minority leaders of the Senate and members of the press actually listened to the speech, but his subject, the challenge of the information age, was potentially interesting to many. He had three audiences who could be reached through coverage of the speech after the fact.

Senator Lautenberg's first audience was his constituency, whom he acknowledged in the introduction. "I am deeply grateful to my fellow citizens in the State of New Jersey for entrusting me to serve them in this great center of debate and decision" (O. Peterson, 1984, p. 28). His second audience was the American people, acknowledged by their occupations. As was customary, he addressed these remarks to the president pro tem of the Senate, the vice president of the United States, who is the elected representative of all the people.

> Mr. President, not very long ago, our nation entered what many call the information age, a period during which information-service industries have become predominant in our economy. They have eclipsed manufacturing, just as manufacturing surpassed farming decades ago. The change has been gradual, but undeniable. Some 60 percent of our work force is employed in creating, storing, processing, or distributing information. Who does that include? Office workers, salespeople, secretaries, people at work in telecommunications, computers, in education, research and science, financial services, and insurance to name a few. People applying information technology to make the production of goods more efficient.
> (O. PETERSON, 1984, pp. 28–29)

Even though most of his Senate colleagues were absent, they were Senator Lautenberg's third audience. His speech would be available in the *Congressional Record,* and he referred to them obliquely in signaling his legislative agenda:

> I am proud that New Jersey has been the home of many of the inventions that are the foundation of this new age. But New Jersey was also the birthplace of American manufacturing—and many of its factories and plants are in decline. New Jersey was third in the nation in new patents last year. But it lost 46,000 jobs in manufacturing. For those workers there is no end to recession.
>
> The suburbs of my state are enjoying great growth, tied to service- and research-based industries on the rise. But New Jersey's cities are being stripped of the industry around which they were built. The unemployment in some of our cities is about the highest in the nation. . . . I pledged to the people of my state that one of my main missions would be to work to provide employment and economic opportunity. We must work to insure that

everyone shares in what is to come. Already we can
identify the tasks that lie ahead, to insure that the
promises of the future are promises for all of us.
(O. PETERSON, 1984, p. 29–30)

The Inaugural Speech

The inaugural address sets the tone and expectations for a new administration
or one returned to office. George Washington's inaugural address set the pattern
for subsequent presidential inaugurals. His first inaugural was shaped by the
situation he faced as the first president under the new Constitution. Washington
spoke of his concern over his ability to measure up to the office, but the heart of
his speech admonished Congress not to let sectionalism and local prejudice
interfere with their ability to discharge their responsibilities. An issue raised in
state ratification conventions had been the absence of a bill of rights in the new
Constitution, and Washington endorsed the idea of adding amendments to
correct the problem. He also requested he not be given a salary but be reimbursed
for his expenses instead. Responding to issues of immediate concern established
the pattern for first inaugural speeches.

In his second inaugural speech, Washington was brief, acknowledging his
reelection in 135 words, so it fell to Thomas Jefferson to set the pattern for second
inaugural speeches. During his first term the seventeenth state had been added to
the Union, the Louisiana Purchase had added substantial new territory to the
frontier, and a successful military expedition to Tripoli had resolved the problem
of the Barbary pirates. Jefferson's second inaugural reflected a nation at peace, the
success of his policies, and his philosophy of government.

On 4 March 1861 Abraham Lincoln was sworn in as president of a nation
from which seven states had seceded. His inaugural address opened with a
reaffirmation of the right of each state to determine its own position on slavery
and a summary of the Constitution's provision for returning fugitive slaves.
Because seven states had already seceded, slavery was an issue secondary to the
legality of secession. The heart of Lincoln's speech was his argument for
the preservation of the Union, in that the Union of the States had preceded the
Constitution.

Although secession had raised the prospect of civil war, Lincoln indicated he
hoped to avoid it. "In doing this there needs to be no bloodshed or violence, and
there shall be none unless it be forced upon the national authority" (Lott, 1961,
p. 119). Lincoln was known for his plain speaking and his ability to get to the core
of any matter.

A husband and wife may be divorced and go out of the
presence and beyond the reach of each other, but the
different parts of our country can not do this. They can
not but remain face to face, and intercourse, either
amicable or hostile, must continue between them. Is it
possible, then, to make that intercourse more

> advantageous or more satisfactory *after* separation than *before?* Can aliens make treaties easier than friends can make laws? Can treaties be more faithfully enforced between aliens than laws can among friends? Suppose you go to war, you can not fight always; and when, after much loss on both sides and no gain on either, you cease fighting, the identical old questions, as to terms of intercourse, are again upon you. (LOTT, 1961, p. 121)

Four years later, Lincoln's second inaugural was a masterpiece, expressing compassion for the losses suffered on both sides and the need to make the nation whole again.

> With malice toward none, with charity for all, with firmness in the right as God gives us to see the right, let us strive on to finish the work we are in, to bind up the nation's wounds, to care for him who shall have borne the battle and for his widow and his orphan, to do all which may achieve and cherish a just and lasting peace among ourselves and with all nations. (LOTT, 1961 p. 126)

Inaugural speeches such as Lincoln's stand out as particularly memorable or significant because they provided a fitting response to a rhetorical situation that found the nation in peril. They were more than speeches celebrating a point in time, they were also speeches precipitated by social forces.

Social Forces Speeches

By tradition, political attention often focuses on the president of the United States. In crisis situations, when the president tells the nation what will be or has been done, justificatory techniques are often used; this has been a frequently used form of presidential speaking in the years since World War II. The principal argument has been that the United States must assume free-world leadership in opposition to a totalitarian communist threat (Rasmussen, 1973). The United States fights unavoidable, "just" wars of self-defense or collective support for an ally. Justification may include an expression of reluctance to have gone to war against a savage enemy and a plea that it was necessitated by the imperatives of policy. "The usual strategy is to construct the image indirectly through contrasting references to the adversary's coercive, irrational, and aggressive attempts to subjugate a freedom-loving, rational, and pacific victim" (Ivie, 1980, p. 284).

Justificatory Speaking

World War I began in Europe in 1914, and it was President Woodrow Wilson's great hope that the United States could remain neutral. On the occasion of welcoming newly naturalized citizens in 1915, he characterized the United States as above the conflict, "a nation being so right that it does not need to convince others by force that it is right" (Brandt and Shafter, 1960, p. 301). American neutrality proved impossible to maintain, and on 2 April 1917, he asked Congress for a declaration of war, justifying his request on the basis of unrestricted submarine warfare by Germany:

> Vessels of every kind, whatever their flag, their character, their cargo, their destination, their errand, have been ruthlessly sent to the bottom without warning and without thought of help or mercy for those on board, the vessels of friendly neutrals along with those of belligerents. Even hospital ships and ships carrying relief to the sorely bereaved and stricken people of Belgium, though the latter were provided with safe conduct through the proscribed areas by the German Government itself and were distinguished by unmistakable marks of identity, have been sunk with the same reckless lack of compassion or of principle. . . . The present German submarine warfare against commerce is a warfare against mankind. (BRANDT AND SHAFTER, 1960, p. 302)

Justificatory speaking is also used to mobilize support for nonmilitary policy goals. President Lyndon Johnson had declared war on poverty in 1964. Later, against the backdrop of mass demonstrations in Selma, Alabama, he addressed a nationally televised joint session of Congress on 15 March 1965 concerning the need to pass the Voting Rights Bill, giving what was probably his best speech (Matson, 1967). The speech was a declaration of war on racial discrimination. "These are the enemies: poverty, ignorance, disease. They are our enemies, not our fellow man, not our neighbor. And these enemies too—poverty, disease and ignorance—we shall overcome" (Matson, 1967, p. 151). The president asked those present, and those watching on television, many of whom had already served their nation in time of war, to join him in a war against intolerance:

> As we meet here in this peaceful historic chamber tonight, men from the South, some of whom were at Iwo Jima, men from the North who have carried Old Glory to the far corners of the world and who brought it back without a stain on it, men from the East and from the West are all fighting together without regard to religion or color or region in Vietnam. Men from every region fought for us across the world 20 years ago. . . .
>
> And I have not the slightest doubt that good men from everywhere in this country, from the Great Lakes to the Gulf of Mexico, from the Golden Gate Bridge to the harbors along the Atlantic, will rally now together in this cause to vindicate the freedom of all Americans. (MATSON, 1967, pp. 151–152)

The orderly processes of government have been facilitated by presidential speaking. These speeches have articulated motives, principles, and arguments by which they have managed national consensus and provided leadership in response to the nation's needs. The legislative branch of government has also been an active participant in the process and has developed its own rhetorical practices.

Legislative Speaking

Colonial legislative assemblies and New England town meetings extended English parliamentary practices to the new world. The people's elected representatives freely debated trade policies, banking laws, and how to deal with Indian tribes, raise money for defense, and encourage industrial development (Bohman, 1943). Later these bodies became forums for agitation against British rule. The Continental Congress was the first national legislative body, declaring independence and raising revenue to conduct the revolution. Afterward, the Continental Congress began the process of drafting a constitution for the new nation.

The Continental Congress, the state assemblies, and later the new Congress, established by the Constitution, were dominated by powerful speakers. With relatively few participants, deliberations in Congress were spirited and lengthy. Both the House and Senate frequently met as a committee of the whole, with few restrictions on debate, and the visitors' galleries were packed. Copies of speeches were rushed into print, and thousands were distributed through the congressman's franking privilege.

For students of public speaking, one of the most interesting periods in our legislative history is the forty-year period when Daniel Webster, Henry Clay, and John C. Calhoun dominated Congress. Meeting first in the House of Representatives in 1813, they came together again in the Senate in 1832. All three were known for their speaking ability, their political determination, and their intellect. They dominated political life and political thought, culminating their careers in shaping the debate over the Compromise of 1850 (M. Peterson, 1987).

Henry Clay, from Kentucky, was a founder of the Whig party and Speaker of the House early in his legislative career. He was known as the "great compromiser" because he wanted to keep the Union together despite the struggle between the North and the South, precipitated by slavery and economic differences, which challenged the Constitution. In 1850, Clay returned to the Senate at the age of 73 and submitted a series of proposals he believed would strike a balance between the demands of the North and the South.

> First, the admission of California as a free state. Second, organization of the balance of territory acquired from Mexico, that is New Mexico and Utah, without restriction to slavery. Third, adjustment of the boundary between Texas and New Mexico. Fourth, assumption of the pre-annexation Texas debt, which had been premised on a revenue from imports. Fifth, non-interference with slavery

> in the District of Columbia. Sixth, prohibition of the slave
> trade in the District. Seventh, a more effective fugitive
> slave law. Eighth, congressional disavowal of authority to
> interfere with the slave trade between slaveholding states.
> (M. PETERSON, 1987, p. 456)

Clay's point was that the territories themselves, not Congress, should determine whether they were to be free or slave in applying for statehood.

> The first resolution, Mr. President, as you are aware,
> relates to California, and it declares that California, with
> suitable limits, ought to be admitted as a member of this
> Union, without the imposition of any restriction either to
> interdict or to introduce slavery within her limits. Well
> now, is there any concession in this resolution by either
> party to the other? I know that gentlemen who come from
> slaveholding States say the North gets all that it desires;
> but by whom does it get it? Does it get it by any action of
> Congress? If slavery be interdicted within the limits of
> California, has it been done by Congress—by this
> Government? No, sir. That interdiction is imposed by
> California herself. And has it not been the doctrine of all
> parties that when a State is about to be admitted into the
> Union, the State has a right to decide for itself whether it
> will or will not have slavery within its limits? (BRANDT
> AND SHAFTER, 1960, p. 11)

Hard-liners from both the North and the South condemned Clay's proposal, but it succeeded because it offered southern Whigs an alternative to either secession or domination by northern interests. Clay's proposal seized the initiative, "centered it in the Senate under his leadership, and set the legislative agenda for the country" (M. Peterson, 1987, p. 459).

South Carolina's John C. Calhoun was the voice of the South and one of the leading political scholars of the nineteenth century. In addition to his terms in Congress, he served as vice president under John Quincy Adams and Andrew Jackson and also served as secretary of state and war. He resigned his vice presidency under Jackson over the issue of a state's right to nullify a law it found unconstitutional and accepted a Senate seat (senators were appointed by state governments at the time) to speak against Jackson's proposals for federal monetary policy and tariff laws.

Calhoun was against any form of compromise. He saw the issue of territorial admission as the test of state sovereignty. His speech on 4 March 1850 analyzed the exigence and the possible outcome of disunion and opposed the sentiment for compromise that Clay's speech had aroused. Calhoun was too ill to deliver the speech himself; it was delivered by James Mason of Virginia. Writing it and attending some of the Senate's meetings were Calhoun's last acts. He died on 31 March 1850 (M. Peterson, 1987).

His speech argued that the primary cause of southern discontent was the loss of influence "found in the fact that the equilibrium between the two sections, in the government as it stood when the Constitution was ratified and the Government put in action, has been destroyed" (Brandt and Shafter, 1960, p. 46). Calhoun argued that the North, through admission of new states, would totally control the government, and he opposed Clay on the issue of which agency should have sovereignty in deciding the admission status of territories as states. He contended that Congress, rather than the people in a territory, possessed sovereignty in territories gained through treaty.

> The recent movement of individuals in California to form a constitution and a State government, and to appoint Senators and Representatives, is the first fruit of this monstrous assumption. If the individuals who made this movement had gone into California as adventurers, and if, as such, they had conquered the territory and established their independence, the sovereignty of the country would have been vested in them, as a separate and independent community. In that case, they would have had the right to form a constitution, and to establish a government for themselves, and if, afterwards, they thought proper to apply to Congress for admission into the union as a sovereign and independent State, all this would have been regular, and according to established principles. But such is not the case. It was the United States who conquered California and finally acquired it by treaty. The sovereignty, of course, is vested in them, and not in the individuals who have attempted to form a constitution and a State without their consent. All this is clear, beyond any controversy unless it can be shown that they have since lost or been divested of their sovereignty. (BRANDT AND SHAFTER, 1960, p. 62)

Daniel Webster was one of the greatest speakers in American history. A skilled lawyer, he tried many important cases, including several before the Supreme Court. A Federalist, he believed in a strong federal government. Webster served first in the House, as a representative from New Hampshire, and later as a senator from Massachusetts. The expectation was that he would rise in the Senate and deliver a great speech defending the Union; instead he defended Clay's compromise on 7 March 1850.

His goal was to preserve the Constitution and the Union at all costs. Although he was vehemently opposed to slavery, he defended, as the price of preserving the Union, the right of southern states to maintain slavery but argued that the South should not consider slavery and the locus of sovereignty an issue in territories such as California and New Mexico:

> I hold slavery to be excluded from those territories by a law even superior to that which admits and sanctions it in

Texas. I mean the law of nature, of physical geography, the law of the formation of the earth. . . . California and New Mexico are Asiatic in their formation and scenery. They are composed of vast ridges of mountains, of great height, with broken ridges and deep valleys. The sides of these mountains are entirely barren; their tops capped by perennial snow. . . . What is there in New Mexico that could, by any possibility, induce any body to go there with slaves? There are some narrow strips of tillable land on the borders of the rivers; but the rivers themselves dry up before midsummer is gone. All that the people can do in that region is to raise some little articles, some little wheat for their tortillas, and that by irrigation. And who expects to see a hundred black men cultivating tobacco, corn, cotton, rice, or anything else, on lands in New Mexico, made fertile by irrigation? (BRANDT AND SHAFTER, 1960, p. 97–98)

Webster's speech was hailed around the nation, but especially in the South, as a masterpiece of statesmanship, although many northerners condemned him for selling out. Abolitionist preacher Theodore Parker spoke at an anti-Webster rally at Faneuil Hall in Boston, saying Webster was running for the presidency with this speech (M. Peterson, 1987).

Clay's resolutions were grouped together in an Omnibus Bill, which President Zachary Taylor threatened to veto. Taylor died of a sudden illness on 9 July 1850, and his successor, Millard Fillmore, favored Clay's proposals (Oliver, 1965; M. Peterson, 1987). The Texas–New Mexico boundary dispute was settled separately, but the essence of Clay's proposal passed. The fugitive slave law proved to be its fatal flaw. The North continued to disregard it, and abolitionists stepped up their agitation. By 1858, Abraham Lincoln used a biblical phrase favored by Webster, "a house divided," to characterize the state of the nation.

After the Civil War the practice of legislative speaking began to change. There were still examples of extended debate in the manner of Clay, Calhoun, and Webster, but these became the exception. As the nation expanded, Congress grew, the business of government became more complex, and the committee system evolved to the point where much Congressional work was done in relatively small groups. Today, bills are "reported out" to the House and Senate with opinions for and against them in majority and minority reports. Most debate takes place at the committee level. Limited debate still takes place on the floor of the House and Senate, along with the practice of "reading into the record" statements not actually made in committee or before Congress.

Issues concerning the basic rights of citizenship have continued to concern Congress. In 1984, Congress considered proposals to pay reparations to Japanese Americans deprived of property and sent to internment camps during World War II. The House Subcommittee on Administrative Law and Governmental Relations of the Committee on the Judiciary held hearings on three bills. Joan Z. Bernstein, chair of the Commission on Wartime Relocation and Internment of Civilians, testified concerning the circumstances leading up to the order for internment.

> The Commission found that the decision to exclude the Japanese-Americans from the west coast cannot be traced to any single simple cause. There was a long and ugly history on the west coast of discrimination and agitation against the ethnic Japanese which gained new vigor with the start of the war. After Pearl Harbor, there was a deep reaction of fear and anger against Japan which was often focused on the Japanese-Americans because of our repeated failure to distinguish between Japanese ethnicity and allegiance to Japan. There was a failure among both military leaders and civilian public officials on the west coast and in Washington to calm the fears and rumors which followed Pearl Harbor and to make a searching test of the reasons propounded for these mass exclusions. . . . These events were unique in our history. In simple terms, 120,000 people lost the right to live where they chose, and a large majority were held in detention for more than 2 years in the absence of any criminal charge. (JAPANESE-AMERICAN AND ALEUTIAN WARTIME RELOCATION, 1984, p. 30)

California Representative Norman Mineta explained why, after so much time had passed, Americans of Japanese ancestry were seeking redress.

> When we were first released from camp, Americans of Japanese ancestry did not think primarily of our legal rights. Our main goal was to rebuild our lives, rebuild our businesses, and regain our standing in the community. We were shamed and held up to public humiliation by the internment. Frankly, we just did not want to think or speak about it. All our energies went into rebuilding. That rebuilding process began to end in the early 1960's— that is, it took 20 years for us to get back what this Government had taken away from us in 1942.
>
> And then we began to think about what had happened to us. Our children began to ask questions about the missing years, the silent years that were never discussed at home. The movement for redress began slowly and built up steam. In the 1970's we obtained passage of two bills, providing Social security and civil service retirement protections for those interned.

>But one problem remained. Our Government had labeled us—and by us, I do mean all 120,000 of us—as vaguely untrustworthy and a danger to the republic.
>
>Mr. Chairman, on behalf of all Americans of Japanese ancestry who were interned, I ask and entreat this subcommittee to give us back our honor. Give us back the dignity and the pride that this Government so unnecessarily took from us in 1942. Every citizen of this land will benefit from our rededication today to equal justice. (JAPANESE-AMERICAN AND ALEUTIAN WARTIME RELOCATION, 1984, p. 74)

Contemporary legislative speaking combines traditional floor debate with committee testimony by expert witnesses, with statements by the representatives of various governmental agencies and commissions, and with statements read into the record—which produces an interesting rhetorical stew. Unlike the president who can speak with one voice, provided his appointees are well disciplined, the two-party system and the range of liberalism and conservatism present in each party make legislative discourse varied and lively. However, not all voices and points of view are represented equally, and some are not represented at all. They are not rhetorically disenfranchised because our system of government allows political dissent.

Dissent

Dissent has been part of the tradition in American public speaking from the very beginning. The Puritans left England for religious liberty. Roger Williams emigrated to the Massachusetts Bay Colony in 1631 and began dissent against the Puritan theocracy. Our nation was the product of dissent over the role of the colonists in regulating colonial affairs. Americans have dissented over slavery, civil rights for blacks and women, the rights of labor, appropriate male and female roles, the consumption of alcohol and other drugs, and our involvement in wars, particularly Vietnam.

Dissent is expressed through *agitation,* "a persistent and uncompromising statement and restatement of grievances through all available communication channels, with the aim of creating public opinion favorable to a change in some condition" (Lomas, 1968, p. 2). Agitation employs both verbal and nonverbal communication, but in a society that protects freedom of speech, it is most frequently a product of acts of public speaking.

Agitation succeeds only if large numbers of people pay attention to the agitator. Therefore, success depends on the existence of social or political conditions simultaneously favorable to the agitator's role but unfavorable to his or her purpose. First, there must be evidence of injustice or apparent injustice, a perceived exigence. Second, the power structure must be implacable and resistant to change. Third, the agitator must be able to gain the ear of an audience capable of acting as change agents. Both the channel of communication (free speech, free press) and the ability to gather an audience (first amendment freedom of assembly) are important. In addition to these situational factors, dissent requires a spokesperson with rhetorical abilities (Lomas, 1968). Inept, bland, unexciting speakers usually do not attract a following.

The American Revolution was the product of successful agitation. In colonial America, most citizens considered themselves Englishmen, sent their sons to England to be educated, engaged in active trade with England, and fought for England in the French and Indian War. Without Samuel Adams to fan the flames of discontent, there would have been no rebellion (Oliver, 1965). He was the premier propagandist of the Revolution, staging demonstrations, organizing groups, such as the Sons of Liberty, to encourage the revolt, and creating and sustaining a campaign of revolutionary agitation through newspapers, pamphlets, songs, and much impromptu oratory.

At issue in the debate over independence was whether or not the colonial charters were binding. An important part of Adams' propaganda campaign was the rejection of contracts made by previous generations as no longer meaningful in the present circumstances. His speech to the Continental Congress in July 1776 reprised his theme of the irrelevancy of past contracts and charters:

> Ye darkeners of counsel, who would make the property, lives, and religion of millions depend on the evasive interpretation of musty parchments; who would send us to antiquated charters of uncertain and contradictory meaning, to prove that the present generation are not bound to be victims to cruel and unforgiving despotism, tell us whether our pious and generous ancestors bequeathed to us the miserable privilege of having the rewards of our honesty, industry, the fruits of those fields which they purchased and bled for, wrested from us at the will of men over whom we have no check. (ANDREWS AND ZAREFSKY, 1989, p. 69)

Adams was at the height of his powers as an agitator in describing the violence visited upon the colonies by the mother country:

> [W]hen I am aroused by the din of arms; when I behold the legions of foreign assassins, paid by Englishmen to imbrue their hands in our blood; when I tread over the uncoffined bodies of my countrymen, neighbors, and friends; when I see the locks of a venerable father torn by savage hands, and a feeble mother, clasping her infants to her bosom, and on her knees imploring their lives from her own slaves, whom Englishmen have allured to treachery and murder; when I behold my country, once the seat of industry, peace, and plenty, changed by Englishmen to a theatre of blood and misery, Heaven

> forgive me if I cannot root those passions which it has
> implanted in my bosom, and detest submission to a
> people who have either ceased to be human, or have not
> virtue enough to feel their own wretchedness and
> servitude! (ANDREWS AND ZAREFSKY, 1989, pp. 69–70)

Dissent seeks one of several outcomes, and critics evaluate agitational speaking as a fitting response based on the end sought and whether or not it was achieved. The simplest form of agitation seeks specific, short-range, immediately attainable goals that the authorities have the power to grant and that will not produce any noticeable change in the social or political structure (Lomas, 1968). For example, a group of parents agitate for a park in their neighborhood, petitioning the city council as it rezones an adjoining tract of unused land for residential use.

A second type of outcome is predicated on specific long-range agitation intended to produce incremental change in political or social structures. Action can take the form of an informational campaign to change society through education. Such action can be the product of political or economic conditions, and agitation occurs through extensive debate and discussion (Lomas, 1968). Such agitative speaking has been used in the quest for civil rights.

Frederick Douglass was born into slavery, escaped to New York, and became a leading abolitionist speaker. Beginning with an impromptu speech at a meeting in 1841, he gave hundreds of addresses throughout the North and in Europe and was much in demand as a speaker at abolitionist gatherings. His address, "American Slavery," demonstrated his skill with language and his ability to help his audience visualize the evils of slavery.

> In law, the slave has no wife, no children, and no home.
> He can own nothing, possess nothing, acquire nothing,
> but what must belong to another. To eat the fruit of his
> own toil, to clothe his person with the work of his own
> hands, is considered stealing. He toils that another may
> reap the fruit; he is industrious that another may live in
> idleness; he eats unbolted meal, that another may eat the
> bread of fine flour; he labors in chains at home, under a
> burning sun and a biting lash, that another may ride in
> ease and splendor abroad; he lives in ignorance, that
> another may be educated; he is abused, that another may
> be exhaulted; he rests his toil-worn limbs on the cold,
> damp ground, that another may repose on the softest
> pillow; he is clad in coarse and tattered raiment, that
> another may be arrayed in purple and fine linen; he is
> sheltered only by the wretched hovel, that a master may
> dwell in a magnificent mansion; and to this condition he
> is bound down as by an arm of iron. (ANDREWS AND
> ZAREFSKY, 1989, pp. 171–172)

The third outcome is based on revolutionary agitation that attempts to change the political and social order completely, to reverse the balance of power between the group presently in power and the agitators or the group championed by the agitators (Lomas, 1968). William Lloyd Garrison was a militant abolitionist. A white newspaper editor, he helped set the pattern for antislavery speaking and writing that condemned the South, the U.S. government, and all those who supported the institution of slavery. Garrison's speeches always had a religious theme. In "No Compromise with Slavery," delivered at the New York meeting of the Anti-Slavery Society in 1854, his rejection of slavery carried with it a religious condemnation of the Compromise of 1850 and a call for a revolt against the government that produced it.

> God never made a human being either for destruction or degradation. It is plain, therefore, that whatever cannot flourish except at the sacrifice of that being, ought not to exist. Show me the party that can obtain supremacy only by trampling upon human individuality and personal sovereignty, and you will thereby pronounce sentence of death upon it. Show me the government which can be maintained only by destroying the rights of a portion of the people, and you will indicate the duty of openly revolting against it. (WRAGE AND BASKERVILLE, 1960, p. 174)

The fourth and final outcome is based on counteragitation or diversionary agitation that focuses on an external threat to the existing political and social order. The goal is to direct attention away from what is happening inside the political and social structure to an external cause for the problem addressed by the agitators (Lomas, 1968). The decade of the 1960s saw nationwide dissent on college campuses, agitation for fewer restrictions on student behavior by college administrations, and protests against the Vietnam War, a movement labeled the New Left.

Tom Hayden, one of the most vocal leaders of the movement, helped organize antiwar demonstrations at the 1968 Democratic national convention in Chicago and was arrested for conspiracy to incite a riot. In 1970, he had the opportunity to address government officials, university administrators, and student leaders at a conference in St. Louis. Using counteragitational tactics, he discussed violence in terms of the acts of those in power against agitative movements throughout American history. Claiming that the only violence antiwar demonstrators committed was calling policemen "pigs," Hayden called attention to more serious violence in Chicago, suggesting that what was identified as an act of violence had more to do with politics than public safety.

> There was an electrical workers strike in Chicago before the convention, if we want to talk about comparative violence. Electrical workers took guns and shot down the

> cables leading to the Nike-Zeus system on the eve of the
> convention, thus exposing the good citizens of Chicago
> and the Democrats to a Russian missile attack. . . . There
> was no grand jury looking for the scoundrels who had
> done this. There was no great investigation; nothing
> happened whatsoever. You know why? Not because of the
> issue of violence or methods, but because Mayor Daley
> knew he had the electrical workers' union leadership in
> his pocket and could settle the strike any time he
> wanted. (D.E. PHILLIPS, 1985, p. 298).

Concern for social issues and political activism has been part of the tradition of religious speaking in America. Antislavery sermons helped the abolitionist movement. After the Civil War the "social gospel" raised an urban voice in religious speaking that urged cooperation between labor and management. Religious speakers campaigned for temperance and eventually helped pass the Volsted Act which outlawed the production and sale of alcoholic beverages. Black ministers helped found the Civil Rights Movement.

Public Theology

Today we label such activism "public theology," a combination of religious and political concerns that produces

> theologically-based discourse intentionally targeted for
> mass audiences in an attempt to influence the attitudes,
> beliefs and values of both religious and secular publics on
> public policy. . . . An audience attracted to the God of
> these rhetors will experience a God very much caught up
> in present issues, who mandates specific programs in the
> political arena, all of which are legitimated by partisan
> theological and political values. (GOLDZWIG, 1987,
> p. 130–131)

Three features characterize discourse on public theology: expedient simplicity, existential content, and action rituals.

> "*Expedient simplicity* is the rhetor's invocation of a univocal
> and partisan God who not only mandates how one is to
> worship and serve others, but also determines whom
> one should support politically and what ideology is
> most acceptable" (Goldzwig, 1987, p. 135). God
> endorses one, and only one, candidate, policy, or world
> view, and the rhetor tells the audience what or who it is
> that God has sanctioned. To depart from this view is to
> disown God.

"*Existential content* describes a discourse laced with current
problems and concerns" (Goldzwig, 1987, p. 138).
Public theology directly addresses a current exigence,
and individual morality becomes a matter of getting
involved and doing the right thing. The rhetor makes
solving present problems a matter of doctrine. There is
no separation of church and state, because the morality
of public theology dictates that God must be the source
of solutions to social problems.

"*Action rituals* include the distinctive formal symbolic
enactments which help to link the public theologian
with the audience" (Goldzwig, 1987, p. 142). Ritual, in
the form of services, broadcasts, and other ceremonies,
provides a channel for getting the message to the
public. These rituals always feature one or more
symbols, which combine abstract religious themes with
specific details of public policy proposals. Rhetors
organize the message simply, feature only a few themes,
and repeat them frequently.

Public theology has been associated with the religious speaking of Catholic
leaders. In recent years, the National Conference of Catholic Bishops has confronted national issues in a series of pastoral letters on public policy, position
statements on the relationship between church doctrine and government policy.
Their content is reprised in sermons and other speeches. In 1983 the Bishops
attacked President Reagan's defense policy, and in 1984 they commented on the
American economy, stating that the inequality in income that left so many
Americans in poverty was morally wrong.

Many religious and political leaders attacked the 1984 letter, saying it discussed matters beyond the Bishops' ministry. Joseph Cardinal Bernardin defended the letter on the grounds that church involvement in secular matters dated
back to biblical times. "The prophets asked questions in Israel about patterns of
land ownership and wages, about the rules and customs used to design the social
life of the nation" (O. Peterson, 1985, p. 179). Cardinal Bernardin also specified
what church involvement in government policy should be:

First, the delivery of some social services is best done in a
decentralized local mode. For many social services today,
only the taxing power of the state can raise sufficient
funds to meet human needs. But the state is often not the
best agency to minister services to people in need. The
church and other voluntary agencies can often deliver, in
a humane and compassionate way, services that only the
state can fund. Second, the church's agencies of direct
social service should be not only a source of compassion
but also creativity. Public bureaucracy is not known for

creative innovation. Its size and complexity often prevent
it from acting in anything but routine patterns. In every
field from housing to health care to hospices, there is
room for new creative methods of public-private
cooperation to feed the hungry, shelter the homeless and
heal the sick. (O. PETERSON, 1985, pp. 179–180)

Contemporary speaking by nationally known clergy also reflects the traditions of colonial preaching. Reverend Jerry Falwell has made political statements about school prayer, *Roe vs. Wade,* the relationship between church and state, and the kind of leaders Americans should elect. His 1982 speech to the Christian Life Commission of Southern Baptists concluded that there are three divinely ordained institutions in America: the family, government, and church. In developing his point on government, he used the same biblical text, Romans 13, that Jonathan Mayhew had used in 1749.

[T]here are three institutions in God's society, clearly
mandated in Scripture. . . . The second one, of course, is
the state or civil government. The powers that be—the
President, the members of Congress , the governors, the
legislators, the powers that be are ordained of God in
Romans 13. They are ministers of God, whether they
know it or not, you're supposed to know it. And,
therefore, we are to respect them and to obey them and
the only time we have any right to disobey a law of man
is when that law of man demands that we disobey a law
of God and then we ought to obey God rather than man
and pay the consequences. But in America that hasn't
happened yet. In America you can obey God's laws
without defying the laws of man. (RYAN, 1983, pp. 262–
263)

Doing Rhetorical Criticism of Speeches

Public speaking has been such an integral part of American history that you have a variety of options available if you choose to focus your rhetorical criticism on this genre. You may choose to study a single speech, several speeches by a single rhetor, or a series of speeches on a single issue by a number of rhetors. The texts of speeches are available from a variety of sources. Several general anthologies of speeches are available as well as specialized compilations of particular types of speeches such as sermons or the collected works of an individual rhetor. From the records of the Continental Congress to the most recent hearings, any speech made in Congress is available through *The Congressional Record* and government documents that report hearings conducted by the various committees of the House and Senate.

Two anthologies, which are continually updated, can also prove useful. Since 1937, the Reference Shelf series has published annually *Representative American Speeches,* a volume of selected speeches that includes not only the speech text but also an overview of the rhetorical situation and biographical information about the speaker. The editors of this series select speeches for inclusion in each volume on the basis of the rhetorical situation, that is the important issues of the year. *Vital Speeches of the Day* is a biweekly periodical that publishes the texts of speeches. The series began in 1929 and includes speeches by political and business leaders, as well as speeches by less well-known individuals, on important contemporary issues. A recent trend is the video anthology. Being able to see and hear the speech as it was delivered allows you to observe delivery and audience response. The list of video collections is not yet extensive and tends to be focused on political speaking at the national level.

Much of the historical record of political speaking is devoted to national issues and includes the rhetorical activity of presidents and leading national politicians. This is not to say that local and state elections and governmental actions at the grass-roots level are unimportant. Many issues, such as gun control, auto insurance, abortion funding, and education standards, are debated and determined at the state and local level.

Whatever theory you choose to apply in making your evaluation, criticism of public speaking always focuses on aspects of the relationship between speaker, message, and audience. You may decide to focus on a single aspect, such as the style of the message or how the message was shaped to respond to the audience's beliefs about the speaker, or you may decide to cover all aspects of the speaker-message-audience relationship. The categories used to describe speaking in this chapter may help you choose your focus.

Because theories of communication developed as a consequence of the needs of speakers, the traditional approach to rhetorical criticism is particularly useful for studying public speaking. This approach gives you a system for evaluating how various constraints in the rhetorical situation imposed by the rhetor, the audience, and the message were managed. Using the traditional approach also allows you to narrow your focus. For example, if you want to study an individual confronted with the need to do apologia, or a group of speeches that constitute a particular type of apologia, your focus would be on the rhetor's destroyed reputation, and how repairs were attempted. Concepts of ethos and argument from the traditional approach would provide useful insights to guide your endeavors.

Because we have such an extensive record of public speaking in America, it is also possible to use the traditional approach to study how definitions of what constitutes effective speaking, the fitting response, have evolved. Characteristics of style and the concepts of argument are particularly useful in making comparisons across historical periods. Colonial style differs considerably from contemporary style as you may have noticed in reading the speech excerpts, even though the subject matter may not have changed much. Considering how and why a given style influenced audience reaction to a speaker's message helps determine standards of appropriateness. Style is related to argument in that what constituted acceptable proof has also changed over time. You might inquire into whether or not the elaborate use of metaphor and allegory found in early congressional speaking remains appropriate to decisionmaking today.

Although the truth, ethical, and aesthetics standards are important judgmental criteria for doing criticism of speeches, the results standard is often the most important to the critic: Did the speaker accompish what he or she set out to do? This is a question you should ask, regardless of your approach to criticism. Since the traditional approach has a strong orientation toward the results standard of judgment, determining how one or more aspects of the rhetor-message-audience relationship influenced the outcome of the speech can be useful to making your final judgment about the speech.

The success or failure of a speech may be influenced by the extent to which an audience perceived it as truthful. Because so much public speaking has been issue oriented, the rhetor's ability to argue the probable truth of an issue is also of great importance in critically evaluating speeches. Probability is created through the use of logical argument, and more than any other genre of communication, public speaking features the use of argument as a part of message development. Choosing an approach that will help you assess the strength of a speaker's arguments is important to doing a thorough, meaningful job of criticism.

Dramatism has been the approach of choice for many critics because the concept of identification provides a way of determining how a speaker attempts to become one with an audience and manage his or her differences with them. The pentad can be used to understand how a speaker created identification by manipulating the ratios between its elements. Certain types of speaking are ritualistic, eulogizing the dead, installing a new leader, or seeking absolution and the restoration of a speaker's reputation. The processes of guilt, purification, and redemption are useful for examining such public rituals.

The fantasy theme approach also emphasizes the results and truth standards of rhetorical evaluation. Speaking in a political campaign frequently makes a hero of one candidate and a villain of his or her opponent. Using fantasy theme analysis to discuss success and failure in campaign speaking enables you to reveal whose rhetorical vision was most believable to the voters. Those rhetorical visions that catch on and become part of our larger public consciousness are the ones that offer the most salient interpretations of reality. The politician, agitator, preacher, or other speaker whose message catches on is the one who provides the most acceptable view of probable truth in the rhetorical situation. This message may then be picked up and repeated by others, as was the case in the development of Fourth of July oratory in the eighteenth and nineteenth centuries. Any speech may be analyzed in terms of its rhetorical vision and of how the fantasy themes of character, setting, and plotline were developed.

A narrative approach to criticism can be useful when the speaker used anecdotes or stories to develop content. Legislative speeches on policy proposals, such as Japanese-American reparations, inaugural speeches, such as Lincoln's first, and enterprise speeches, such as "Acres of Diamonds," used anecdotes and stories to interpret the future. Analyzing the narrative fidelity of arguments based on such devices can help you determine the quality of arguments in a speech. A single speech or group of speeches, such as Fourth of July oratory, can also be viewed in terms of how myth is created and perpetuated. Speeches that celebrate American history and heroes tell a story of this country. Using the narrative approach to criticism can help you discover more about our national mythology.

Selecting one of the cultural approaches to criticism allows you to view public speaking in terms of how speeches function to create and maintain culture. The social values, Marxist, and feminist approaches each offer methods of analyzing what and who society values. Agitative speaking is particularly related to the social movement model of cultural criticism, since agitators are often the spokespersons for movements. The great social movements of American history—Abolitionism, women's suffrage, progressivism, civil rights, and the student movement—produced many examples of public speaking by dynamic, dedicated individuals.

In this chapter we have discussed the characteristics of public speaking, one of the most important forms of rhetorical activity that has shaped our society. Our core values were formed during periods of peril and prosperity and articulated in speeches by leaders and dissenters responding to these exigences. Viewing the record of public speaking in America rhetorically is a way of understanding both history and the people who shaped our culture. Studying the speeches of yesterday and today is one way to understand the power of the spoken word and the dynamics of situations in which attitudes are influenced and action inspired by a compelling speaker addressing a receptive audience.

Suggested Readings

Examples of Criticism

BIRDSELL, D.S. (1987). Ronald Reagan on Lebanon and Grenada: Flexibility and interpretation in the application of Kenneth Burke's pentad. *Quarterly Journal of Speech, 73,* 267–279.

> This article analyzes President Reagan's first speech to the nation after the bombing of the Marine compound in Lebanon and the U.S. invasion of Grenada. Birdsell applies the pentad to each event separately as discussed in Reagan's speech. This article discusses the rhetorical situation and applies the pentad clearly. Birdsell provides an especially nice explanation of how the assignment of terms of the pentad by a critic is arbitrary—what one critic calls "act" another may call "agent."

BROMMEL, B.J. (1969). Eugene V. Debs: The agitator as speaker. *Central States Speech Journal, 20,* 202–214.

> This article uses the traditional approach to criticism to examine the speeches of labor leader Eugene Debs, a good example of criticism focused on the collected speeches of an individual. Brommel concentrates on Debs' invention, particularly how Debs created ethical appeals and attracted a large group of committed listeners. This article demonstrates how concepts about agitation can be combined with the traditional approach to criticism.

CARLSON, A.C. (1988). Albert J. Beveridge as imperialist and progressive: The means justify the end. *Western Journal of Speech Communication, 52,* 46–62.

> This article uses concepts from social movement criticism and dramatism to analyze the speeches of Senator Albert Beveridge. Beveridge began as a champion of American imperialism and later became an advocate for progressive causes, two seemingly incompatible positions. Carlson concludes that this shift was really a redefinition of Beveridge's belief in America's Anglo-Saxon tradition and superiority. This is an excellent example of organic criticism that combines approaches into a framework for criticism, and a good model of criticism of political speaking.

LARSON, B.A. (1978). *Prologue to revolution: The war sermons of the Reverend Samuel Davies.* Falls Church, VA: Speech Communication Association.

> This 50-page monograph is part of a Bicentennial series analyzing communication and the American Revolution. Through her examination of sermons advocating war, Larson explains how colonial Americans changed from loyal British subjects to militant revolutionaries. Fantasy theme criticism demonstrates how Samuel Davies used sermons as a propaganda device. Because this monograph is longer than the standard journal article or anthology essay, it demonstrates how a critic can bring depth to the discussion of the rhetorical situation and the application of a critical approach. It is well written and provides good detail on colonial preaching.

LING, D.A. (1970). A pentadic analysis of Senator Edward Kennedy's address to the people of Massachusetts July 25, 1969. *Central States Speech Journal, 21,* 81–86.

> This critcism uses dramatism, particularly the pentad, to study an example of apologia. Ling analyzes how Senator Kennedy described the events surrounding the death of Mary Jo Kopechne for the voters of Massachusetts. Scene was the controlling factor in Kennedy's explanation, and he cast himself as a victim of some awful family curse. In the speech's final appeal, Kennedy focused on the people of Massachusetts as the agents who must decide if he was morally fit to continue as their senator. This article is a good example of using dramatism to evaluate apologia.

SOLOMON, M. (1988). Ideology as rhetorical constraint: The anarchist agitation of "Red Emma" Goldman. *Quarterly Journal of Speech, 74,* 184–200.

> Criticism can reveal why a rhetor failed. This article critiques the failure of Emma Goldman to gain public support, even though audiences were attracted to her public lectures and though her magazine, *Mother Earth,* had thousands of subscribers. Solomon combines concepts from several critical approaches to discuss Goldman's ideology and why her rhetorical vision was unappealing even though she was able to attract an audience. The article also investigates the ideology of anarchism, focusing on the kinds of rhetorical strategies used by anarchists and why these strategies cannot be effective with American audiences.

STRICKLAND, W.M. (1982). The rhetoric of removal and the trail of tears: Cherokee speaking against Jackson's indian removal policy, 1828–1832. *Southern Speech Communication Journal, 47,* 292–309.

> By 1828 the Cherokee nation no longer had the resources to physically resist the expanding frontier, so they waged a war of words to preserve their lands and tribal status with the federal government. Strickland analyzes the recorded speaking and traditions of the Cherokee nation, both internal and external tribal rhetorical activity.

This article uses an organic approach, applying concepts of narrative, traditional, and social values criticism to the examination of a lost cause. This is a good model of criticism. It is well written and offers fascinating insights into the mythology of the Cherokee people.

Resources for Doing Criticism

ANDREWS J., AND ZAREFSKY, D. (1989). *American voices: Significant speeches in American history 1640–1945.* New York: Longman.

> This is an anthology of speeches organized chronologically. The sections are: Colonial America: Making a Revolution; Foundations of Government; The Young Republic; Ordeal of the Union; Challenges at Home and Abroad; The Trouble Decade (1930s); and America in the Global Conflict. The introduction reviews the traditional approach to criticism. Each speech text is presented with an overview of the historical context and details of the speech setting. The appendix provides brief biographical information on, and a bibliography of resources related to, each speaker. These bibliographies are relatively up to date and a great aid to research. A second anthology, covering post–World War II to the present, is planned.

BRIGANCE, W.N. (Ed.). (1943). *A history and criticism of American public address,* Vol. I. New York: McGraw-Hill.

> This is the first of a three-volume series of essays on public speaking. Criticism follows the traditional approach, and though these essays might serve as models of the traditional approach, their content is more often historical detail on speakers and speeches. We recommend this series as reference material rather than as models of criticism because it has more description of history than critical evaluation of speeches. This first volume has good overview material on types of speaking during the colonial period, the early national period (1788–1860), and the later national period (1860–1930). There is also an overview of women speakers and the teaching of rhetorical theory in colonial America. Essays on speakers include Jonathan Edwards, Theodore S. Parker, Henry Ward Beecher, Phillips Brooks, Wendall Phillips, Robert G. Ingersoll, Henry W. Grady, Booker T. Washington, Rufus Choate, Jeremiah S. Black, and William Everts.

BRIGANCE, W.N. (Ed.). (1943). *A history and criticism of American public address,* Vol. II. New York: McGraw-Hill.

> The second volume in the series has essays on Ralph Waldo Emerson, Charles W. Eliot, Edwin A. Alderman, Samuel Gompers, Patrick Henry, Henry Clay, John C. Calhoun, Daniel Webster, William Yancy, Charles Sumner, Stephen A. Douglas, Abraham Lincoln, James G. Blaine, William Jennings Bryan, Albert J. Beveridge, Robert M. La Follette, and Woodrow Wilson.

DUFFY, B.K. AND RYAN, H.R. (Eds.). (1987). *American orators of the twentieth century.* New York: Greenwood Press.

> This anthology provides information on fifty-eight prominent political speakers of the twentieth century, from Spiro Agnew to Woodrow Wilson. Each selection provides the speaker's biography, style as a speaker, issues and themes in speeches, and bibliographic sources. This is an excellent research source because it provides a capsule view of each speaker and his or her work. Greenwood Press indicates there will be additional volumes for the nineteenth century and colonial America.

HOCHMUTH, M.K. (Ed.). (1955). *A history and criticism of American public address* Vol. III. New York: Longman.

> This is the third volume in the series begun under Brigance's editorship. This volume offers essays on Alexander Hamilton, Thomas Hart Benton, Susan B. Anthony, George William Curtis, Lucius Q. C. Lamar, Dwight L. Moody, Clarence Darrow, Theodore Roosevelt, William E. Borah, Harry Emerson Fosdick, and Franklin D. Roosevelt.

HOLLAND, D. (1973). *American in controversy: History of American public address.* Dubuque, IA: William C. Brown.

> This anthology examines debate over issues in American history chronologically. The twenty-four selections begin with colonial America and end with the antiwar movement of the 1960s. Each essay considers the historical framework and speaking on both sides of issues. This is an excellent resource on controversial issues such as the Puritan treatment of Indian tribes, the Congressional compromises to keep the North and the South together from 1828 to 1850, labor agitation, agrarian protest movements, the social gospel, science versus Christian fundamentalism, anticommunism, and the civil-rights movement at various times in American history.

JAMIESON, K.H. (1988). *Eloquence in an electronic age: The transformation of political speechmaking.* New York: Oxford University Press.

> We know from looking at speech texts that styles of speaking have changed considerably from the days of Webster, Clay, and Calhoun. Jamieson provides an in-depth treatment of how political speaking has evolved from the grand oratory of Daniel Webster to Ronald Reagan's appellation as "the great communicator." Jamieson discusses what constitutes eloquence in public speaking and how electronic media have changed the concept of eloquence. She provides both information and criticism on modern political campaigns by winners and losers from Harry Truman to Ronald Reagan.

OLIVER, R.T. (1965). *History of public speaking in America.* Boston: Allyn & Bacon.

> Oliver begins with the premise that our nation's history is found in the words of its speakers. He discusses speakers and situations, from the arrival of the Pilgrims through the presidency of Woodrow Wilson. Written as a history and one of the best references for background information on speakers of the time covered, Oliver tried to get inside the minds of speakers and audiences, so there is a wealth of information about audiences and the outcomes of speaking. Although dated, there is an extensive bibliography of sources on approaches to criticism, speech anthologies, and resources on individual speakers.

REID, R.F. (1988). *Three centuries of American rhetorical discourse: An anthology and a review.* Prospect Heights, IL: Waveland Press.

> This anthology spans history from the Puritan preachers to the Reagan presidency. Reid provides a representative group of significant speeches in American history, with an especially good selection of speeches from the abolitionist movement, compromise efforts to save the Union, and the era of reconstruction. The emphasis is on political oratory, although there are a few examples of other types of speaking. Reid provides excellent overviews on each speech and lists the source from which the speech text was taken.

The

9

Rhetoric of

Film

Since the beginning of the twentieth century, movies have been a chief means of creating and sharing our culture. By 1895 the movie camera had been developed to the point that making and showing films was commercially viable. The American film industry began, and continues to exist, as a business that satisfies the desire of people willing to see movies and pay for the experience. Can a medium whose chief purpose is making money be considered rhetorical? Before you dismiss film's persuasive power, consider that after seeing Clark Gable sans undershirt in *It Happened One Night,* American men stopped buying undershirts and that U.S. Navy enlistments went up significantly after *Top Gun* exposed young men to the glamour of being a navy pilot. Therefore, even a film intended only to entertain can become rhetorical when an audience infers a message from it.

Film provides a way of visualizing the past, gaining insight into the present, and speculating about the future. Because certain films and film genres have influenced our beliefs and behaviors, they are a form of rhetorical activity. In the twenties, films stimulated moviegoers with visions of fads, fantasies, romanticism, and escapism. During the Depression, movies were a source of comfort, a way for people to forget their problems for a few hours. During World War II, filmmaking became part of the war effort, encouraging people to have faith and do their part. After the war, "monster" movies and Westerns explored the consequences of, and suggested codes of conduct for, living in the nuclear age.

The collective experience of going to the movies allows us to share dominant cultural images and enables us to find out who we are, to an extent not possible in earlier times. Film tells and retells the stories, the myths and folklore, that make us Americans. Film gives us a visual-aural record of the aspirations, fears, and desires that affect our national psyche (M.D. Bryant, 1982).

This chapter examines the rhetorical functions of film and presents three concepts for undertaking film criticism. Although we shall discuss documentary films, this chapter is primarily concerned with Hollywood films that are commercial, made for a mass market, and usually labeled "entertainment." These films are an important part of the rhetorical history of our culture, and they perform several functions: exposing past and present events, raising future issues, defining social trends, analyzing social issues, and serving as metaphors for our experience (Palmer, 1987).

First, films expose events of the present or past. They bring information to the viewer's attention. By showing issues that have been suppressed or lain dormant, films explore and expose the social history of a culture (Palmer, 1987). Frank Capra was involved in making films for the government during World War II, the most famous of which were the *Why We Fight* series. However, *The Negro Soldier in World War II,* though less widely known, was an exemplary piece on the contribution of African-Americans.

This film, originally intended only for black troops, became mandatory viewing at many training centers during the latter stages of the war because of the defacto integration of the military. *The Negro Soldier in World War II* was as much a chronicle of African-American dignity, achievement, and an espousal of the values common to all Americans as it was a film about black soldiers. Eventually, the film found its way into civilian release and was used by civil-rights groups after the war. African-American leaders acclaimed it as one of the most positive achievements in film (Cripps and Culbert, 1983). Although the U.S. government continued to make films, and is still one of the leading producers of documentaries, its films never again approached the level of influence achieved during World War II.

The government is not the only maker of propaganda films. Two antiwar activists, Bert Schneider and Peter Davis, decided to make their case against Vietnam on film. *Hearts and Minds,* which captured the 1975 Academy Award for best documentary, is a powerful piece of persuasive filmmaking because of its style and content. Schneider and Davis used a "tapestry of war footage, interviews, clips of old war movies, antiwar demonstrations, PTA meetings, and high school football games" (Cagin and Dray, 1984, p. 140) to argue that U.S. involvement in Vietnam was linked to common American cultural rituals and beliefs. The film's condemnation of the war uses such devices as the voice of General William Westmoreland, suggesting that Asians do not value human life as much as Americans do, over the image of Vietnamese civilians mourning their dead at a cemetery.

Second, films raise future issues. Films sound warnings by interpreting present events and speculating on what might happen if certain steps are, or are not, taken (Palmer, 1987). John Kennedy's victory in 1960 brought liberals into power. Stanley Kubrick combined satire with dark humor in *Dr. Strangelove, or How I Learned to Stop Worrying and Love the Bomb* (1964) to attack the liberal political consensus, which held that technology and expertise were the answers to all problems (Maland, 1983): All you had to do to solve a problem was identify it and formulate a program to solve it. Technology, appropriately applied, would provide the solution. The chief international problem confronting sixties liberals was communism, and using U.S. nuclear capability to deter Soviet expansion became the cornerstone of American foreign policy.

Stanley Kubrick's films frequently featured the theme that "one of the greatest dilemmas of modern industrial society [is] the gap between man's scientific and technological skill and his social, political, and moral ineptitude" (Maland, 1983, p. 194). Kubrick purchased the rights to *Red Alert,* a serious novel about accidental nuclear war, with the intention of making *Dr. Strangelove* as a "straight" film, but the more he thought about it, the more the absurdity of nuclear deterrence struck him (Suid, 1978). Kubrick saw international relations and nuclear deterrence as madness; building bombs to preserve peace creates the paradoxical circumstances in which nuclear war ultimately becomes possible.

In *Dr. Strangelove,* Kubrick has the Soviets develop a doomsday device that will destroy the planet by automatic activation of the Soviet nuclear arsenal if anything attempts to destroy it. A rabidly anticommunist U.S. Air Force general attacks the Soviet Union on his own initiative. The American president joins forces with the Soviet premier to stop him, but they are too late. Kubrick's warning to America was sent by Major King Kong, one of the attacking pilots, who literally rides his nuclear weapon to doomsday at the film's end.

> Kubrick has Kong go through the contents of a survival kit. It includes, among other items, a pistol, nine packs of chewing gum, several pairs of nylon stockings, a miniature combination Bible and Russian phrase book, and, of course, an issue of prophylactics. Besides parodying what every soldier shot down over enemy territory might need, the scene reasserts that Kong is fighting another war at another time, never having realized that if his bomber goes down after dropping its atomic load, the crew will not have to worry much about survival, to say nothing of survival kits. (MALAND, 1983, pp. 200–201)

Third, films define social trends by highlighting what is important, crucial, or unique. A film or group of films can examine social values (Palmer, 1987). The comedy-film formula typically followed during the Depression was "screwball," derived from a type of Broadway play in which rich people confront being poor. In a screwball comedy, the idea of a rich person living behind a mask of wealth and privilege and having it stripped away gives audiences a look at social values. The "good" rich proved they were "poor at heart," or classless, and the poor hero or heroine was rewarded in the happy ending by becoming rich (Bergman, 1971; Wead and Lellis, 1981).

Screwball comedies were the ultimate escape for Depression audiences, allowing people to laugh at misfortune, to believe that future prosperity was a possibility, and most importantly, to continue to believe that America was still the land of opportunity. Frank Capra was king of the screwball comedies, establishing the formula with *It Happened One Night* (1934), the story of a spoiled rich girl who is temporarily without funds and a poor reporter who teaches her the values of being poor. The screwball comedy formula has been applied to contemporary themes, and the concept of the reversal of fortunes is still used rhetorically. One example is the sex role reversal in *Tootsie* (1982), in which the title character's experiences taught him and us something about how society treats women.

Fourth, films analyze social events and issues, educating the viewer about how society works and giving meaning to events. A film can make an otherwise imponderable event accessible to the viewer (Palmer, 1987). One of the most political films of the 1930s was King Vidor's *Our Daily Bread* (1934). Vidor, a successful director at MGM, had made two popular message movies, *The Big Parade* (1925), an antiwar film, and *The Crowd* (1928), about a man and a woman trapped in the "heartless" city. In the midst of the Depression, he wanted to make a "documentary flavored" film showing how the characters from *The Crowd* find cooperation and community in rural America (Bergman, 1971).

MGM and the other studios were opposed; they did not think the project was commercially viable. Vidor was determined to make the film and finally secured bank loans, backed by Charlie Chaplin, to produce and distribute the film himself. His message to America was that people should take responsibility for each other and return to community values to "get the job done." *Our Daily Bread* tells the story of a young couple from the city who, just when things are at their worst, inherit a farm. As city folk, they have no skills or knowledge of farming, so they take in a farmer and his family who have lost their own farm. As other skills are needed, more dispossessed people become part of the community, and it thrives (Bergman, 1971; Maltby, 1983). *Our Daily Bread* met with mixed reviews and did not capture the imagination of movie fans the way that a later film about the Depression, *The Grapes of Wrath* (1940), would.

Fifth, a film can serve as a metaphor for a larger social issue (Palmer, 1987). Stanley Kramer's *High Noon* (1950) was the story of Marshal Will Kane and his confrontation with a man he sent to prison four years earlier. Its theme was fear and how it paralyzed a community. At the end of the film, Marshal Kane stood alone, deserted by the townpeople and even his bride, facing the men who came to kill him.

The film must be viewed in the context of the rhetorical situation of the early 1950s, specifically the accusations by Senator Joseph McCarthy that America, and particularly Hollywood, was riddled with domestic communists. Kramer had been asked by a United Nations representative to make a film about that organization. He and Carl Foreman, the author of *High Noon's* script, decided to do something allegorical, set in the old West, that would be less obviously propagandistic. Foreman had originally intended to use the Western myth of a community pulling together in the face of danger as a metaphor for the United Nations; but while he was working on the script, he expected to be called to testify before the House Un-American Activities Committee (HUAC) (Behlmer, 1982). The theme of *High Noon*, one man with courage facing fear ·without caving in, might be interpreted more as a parable for members of the film industry facing HUAC and charges of being communists than as a plea for world unity.

Making a film involves more than recording images and dialogue. The processes of script writing, character interpretation, directing, and editing combine to produce a narrative statement. Film communicates by combining verbal and visual elements simultaneously and in sequence to produce a whole. This gives film its own grammar of sight and sound, in which each has meaning in terms of the other. Taken together, the grammatical elements of a film can be used to determine its aesthetic properties and how it functions rhetorically.

Aesthetics are important in judging a film's value. The plot line of any film can be reduced to a couple of sentences that make it sound like a hundred other films we have seen. What turns the cliché into a significant experience is the artistry of filmmaking found in the combination of script, characters and the actors' interpretation of them, the editing of scenes together, and the special effects that enhance scene and action (Bywater and Sobchack, 1989). "The many aspects of a film are meant to contribute to the total effect without drawing attention to themselves" (W.H. Phillips, 1985, p. 61).

The grammar of a film also helps to determine meaning and message. A film offers the viewer a self-contained world that sometimes seems more real than life. Although our real lives may seem to be a jumble of discontinuous, confusing events and people, the world on film is an orderly one in which heroes demonstrate their ultimate mastery over circumstances and all elements—visual, aural, and action—are unified (M.D. Bryant, 1982). One of the reasons that films are rhetorical is because they provide answers to our dilemmas and solutions to our problems.

> Thus heroes are presented as those who have learned the secrets of technique which give power over the world in a way far beyond our ordinary abilities; we are implicitly led to affirm the orientation of our technological civilization and to grant to it the ability to overcome disorder and achieve the order we so desperately desire. (M.D. BRYANT, 1982, p. 112)

Finding order comes from experiencing a film's pace, sensuousness, feeling, symbol, and meaning in toto (W.H. Phillips, 1985).

A film's *pace* is its sense of moving through time. Does the story seem to move swiftly or slowly from one event to the next? Pacing quantifies a film's action level. Action-adventure films are characterized, as the label suggests, by lots of story movement. Pace is also determined by the interspersing of action with periods of relative calm, breathing space for the audience. Romantic interludes in action-adventure films slow the pace. Pace is also influenced by the number and length of conversations between characters, the speed at which objects and people move, and the frequency of scene changes in the film (W.H. Phillips, 1985).

The *sensuousness* of film is found in how it encourages viewers to use their senses. You might think film only engages our senses of sight and sound, but it can also stimulate memories of taste, touch, and smell. The sight of a meal can make us taste food and drink mentally. We might recall the scent of flowers or woodsmoke if we see a perfect rose filling the screen or a welcoming blaze in a fireplace. We can almost feel the heat of a desert scene or the bone-chilling cold of the arctic. Sensuousness is achieved by visual and aural elements that awaken memories of sensory experience (W.H. Phillips, 1985).

If you have ever had tears in your eyes, felt uplifted or emotionally exhausted after seeing a film, or wanted to live in a movie's world, you've experienced the *feeling* a film can stimulate. Although not everyone who sees a film has the same emotional experience, the topic, story development, characterization, and technical properties of filmmaking are used to encourage a particular emotional response by the viewer (W.H. Phillips, 1985).

The power of a film may be found in how it creates *symbols* for the viewer to identify with or use to interpret its message. Film extends our ability to create and use symbols by making things, people, places, and events seem real. Because film is a highly visual medium, its symbols are frequently visual: objects, places, persons, and events. Aural symbols, musical themes, spoken phrases, and special effects sounds may also be used. Symbols are usually prominent and function symbolically because they are thrust upon the viewer's consciousness repeatedly. In determining symbolism, you need to consider both the obvious, overt displays and the hidden, covert ways in which something might serve symbolically (W.H. Phillips, 1985).

The final element of a film's ability to create order is found in its *meaning*. Meaning is the key element in how a film functions as a rhetorical act, how it influences the viewer to believe or behave in a partciular way. One of the reasons film is a popular medium of communication is that, when a film entertains, it fulfills a desire we all share, the chance to feel heroic. The meaning of a film, something the viewer must interpret from the characters' words and deeds, is ultimately found in how we translate this feeling into our own lives (W.H. Phillips, 1985).

Meaning is a composite of the values and predispositions the viewer brought to the experience and saw on the screen, which explains why not everyone responds to a film in the same way. The problem of meaning is compounded for the critic who looks at a film from another era. You must try to see the film from the historical, cultural, and sociopolitical perspective of its intended audience. When we show *Easy Rider* (1969) to classes in 1990, many students are disappointed. They have heard so much about the film, but it does not strike a responsive chord or create order for them. Although the explanation, "You had to be there," may not be very satisfying, understanding why *Easy Rider* had an impact on millions of "baby boomers" requires the critic to analyze it in terms of that audience. Your research concerning the rhetorical situation, the historical setting, issues and events, exigences, and audience expectations when they went to see the film enables you to "be there" with them.

Even though identifying pace, sensuousness, feeling, symbol and meaning is crucial to the critical process, the fact that these qualities are present in every film means that they are useful to you only after you have made a fundamental decision about a focus for undertaking film criticism. There are three ways to begin film criticism. First, the critic can look at film as a rhetorical act: *message-movie criticism*. Second, the critic can examine the films of a particular director or star: *auteur criticism*. Third, the critic can focus on films that tell one type of story: *genre criticism*.

Message-Movie Criticism

The message-movie critic begins by selecting a film, no easy task when you consider how many films you have to choose from. You might want to select a film that professional critics consider praiseworthy. Film criticism has become an industry itself, with newspaper columns, magazines, and television programs devoted to making judgments about good and bad films. Although these reviewers may touch on the rhetorical qualities of a film, their judgments are usually restricted to the artistic or qualitative domain, so you can learn what constitutes a great or timeless film from their work.

Film critics generally agree that the best films are those that reveal what it means to be human. Regardless of whether it is a comedy or a tragedy, a documentary or fiction, realistic or surreal, "films of the highest order are those in which the spectator learns something about the complex nature of human existence, finds a world represented that makes one think of the world outside the theatre, shows us the way the world really is, and not simply the way we'd like it to be" (Bywater and Sobchack, 1989, p. 37).

As a business, filmmaking has operated on a multitiered system, and during the days when major studios dominated the business, "A" and "B" films were produced and distributed. To get an A film, a theatre also had to take the B films, so lots of B movies have been produced. Like the products of any other artistic media, some films are judged great art and others are pure "schlock." A film in the latter category does not lack rhetorical properties. *Godzilla* (1955), with its bad special effects and worse English dubbing, is as surely rhetorical as it is surely not great art.

Every film tells a story by showing the tension between its characters' points of view. Point of view is disclosed by bits of verbal and visual information set in a particular emotional climate (Harrington, 1973). Selecting a point of view is the filmmaker's first task, and identifying that point of view is the message-movie critic's first task. When films draw points of view from events happening in the viewer's world, they may be classified as *documentary films,* or *realism*. What distinguishes the former from the latter is the filming of non-actors or the use of footage of events that actually happened. Realistic films do not use real people or historical footage because they are often made after the fact, but still they draw their theme or thesis from actual events. Films that draw their theme or thesis elsewhere are *fictional*.

Some filmmakers see themselves as scientists, filming socially relevant subjects and offering viewers a "slice of life" rather than a partially or wholly fictional point of view (Wead and Lellis, 1981). The documentary film best illustrates the concept of scientific filmmaking. Shooting life as it happens, without a script, actors, sets, or any artificial rearrangement of the mise-en-scène, Frederick Wiseman's "public affairs" approach is an example of this school of thought. His films, *High School* (1968), *Hospital* (1970), *Basic Training* (1971), *Juvenile Court* (1973), and *Canal Zone* (1977) are case studies, nonfiction accounts of social problems presented simply, from which the harm is to be inferred.

Many documentaries fall into the slice-of-life category, in which a story exists only to the extent that the film follows a group of people over a period of time. In this kind of documentary, which often concentrates on members of the lower class, concern for people or their cause is a common theme. The activities of the rich are seldom a subject for this kind of filmmaking unless they disclose sources of oppression or social injustice (Wead and Lellis, 1981). Most slice-of-life documentaries are made by independent filmmakers and do not get widespread theatrical release. The filmmaker often takes responsibility for distribution, taking the film from group to group, showing it in church basements, town halls, and such places.

Documentaries of particularly high quality often find a larger audience on cable television. *Union Maids* (1971) by Julia Reichert and James Klein, *Attica* (1973) by Cinda Firestone, and *Harlan County* (1977) by Barbara Kopple and Hart Perry are examples of critically acclaimed documentary films that reached audiences initially through distribution by their makers and later through television.

Union Maids told the story of the growth of organized labor in the 1920s and 1930s. It focused on the experiences of three women who were union organizers and included interviews, music, and newsreel footage of the time to communicate its message about class struggle. *Attica* presented views of inmates of the New York State Prison at Attica both before and after the September 1971 riots. The uniqueness of this film lay in its use of footage shot by state troopers as they stormed the prison in an attempt to free hostages. *Harlan County* was a slice-of-life in a Kentucky coal mining town during a thirteen-month strike, made from the point of view of the miners, their families, and other townspeople (Rosenthal, 1980).

Realistic filmmakers see themselves as scientists because the films they produce are true: accurate, objective works documenting human actions and events. *Silkwood* (1983) was a realistic film based on the life and death of Karen Silkwood, a real person who worked in the nuclear industry and became concerned about the safety of producing fuel for nuclear power plants. In the film, the late Ms. Silkwood was portrayed by a professional actress, and events from her life were re-created. The film questioned the safety and honesty of the nuclear power industry.

An earlier film, *The China Syndrome* (1979) had a similar thesis but was completely fictional. Professional actors portrayed the news reporters and a nuclear plant supervisor, who might have resembled real people but were characters drawn entirely from the script writer's imagination. Ironically, dangerous events occurred at Three Mile Island, a nuclear power station in Pennsylvania, the week that *China Syndrome* began playing in theaters, indicating that the line between realism and fiction is sometimes hard to distinguish.

One of the first things the message-movie critic must determine is what point of view—documentary, realistic, or fictional—the object of criticism represents. This question has signficant critical implication. For example, as a scientist, the rhetor-filmmaker brings a sense of invention to his or her work, by considering the facts and determining what is important. The scientific aspect of documentary filmmaking may cause the director to be nonselective, presenting everything and allowing the viewer to determine what is important. Realistic films often contain an enormous amount of detail that would be absent in fictional films (Wead and Lellis, 1981). The truth criterion, as discussed in Chapter 2, is important in the rhetorical criticism of message movies, particularly documentaries such as Frederick Wiseman's. No filmmaker can produce an absolutely true film because deciding such matters as what to film, how many cameras to use, and where to place them influences what the film finally becomes.

Documentaries, realistic, and purely fictional films are often termed *propaganda*. In general, a propagandist tries to direct the viewer to a particular conclusion. The realist may show sympathy for the subject but does not try to steer the viewer toward one conclusion more than another (Maynard, 1975). The United States government has produced propaganda films, the high-water mark coming during World War II.

Frank Capra, one of the most successful filmmakers of the 1930s, known for his sentimental films about small-town America and its values, was asked to make a series of films by Army Chief of Staff General George C. Marshall. Capra recalled Marshall's charge in his autobiography:

> Young Americans, and young men of all free countries, are used to doing and thinking for themselves. They will prove not only equal, but superior to totalitarian soldiers, *if*—and this is a large if, indeed—they are given answers as to *why* they are in uniform, and *if* the answers they get are *worth* fighting and dying for. And that, Capra, is our job—and your job. To win this war we must win the battle for men's minds. . . . I think films are the answer, and you are the answer to such films. Now, Capra, I want to nail down with you a plan to make a series of documented, factual-information films—the first in our history—that will explain to our boys in the Army *why* we are fighting, and the *principles* for which we are fighting. (CAPRA, 1971, p. 372)

Capra recalled his previous notion of documentaries: "ash-can films made by kooks with long hair" (Capra, 1971, p. 328).

He began preparing to make what came to be called the *Why We Fight* series by watching the Nazi documentary *Triumph of the Will* by Leni Riefenstahl. He was overwhelmed by the power of imagery and mood in her film but believed he could use the enemy's own films to expose them for the "bastards" they were. The result was a series of seven, fifty-minute training films to be used during the induction of men and women into the military.

The first three films, *Prelude to War, The Nazis Strike,* and *Divide and Conquer,* depict the rise of fascism, its early military successes, and the impact of earlier appeasement in the face of Hitler's threats as factors that set the stage for the invasion of Poland. By the end of the third film, western Europe is under Nazi occupation. The next three films, *Battle of Britain, Battle of Russia,* and *Battle of China,* show the terrible price our allies in Europe and Asia were paying as they gallantly and succesfully defended the skies over London, the gates of Moscow, and the Asian mainland against Germany and Japan. The final film, *War Comes to America,* celebrates the themes of diversity and unity at home. Although we were all immigrants, or the sons and daughters of immigrants, and had mixed feelings about whether we should become involved in events overseas, once we came to the realization that anything that threatened the freedom of other people threatened our own freedom, we all united behind the war effort.

Frank Capra may have been one of the few people in American history to actually make government policy with a movie camera. General Marshall had instructed him to make factual films and use his own judgment in telling army inductees what constituted U.S. policy, why they were going to be fighting. Although commissioned for use by the U.S. Army, the films were also used by other branches of the service and other countries. The British, Canadian, Australian, and New Zealand armed forces used them as training films, the Russians showed *Battle for Russia* in theaters, and Winston Churchill had all seven films shown to the British public. Regardless of what U.S. policy might have been, by the time so many people had seen Capra's films, his version of American policy was what the government endorsed as its policy (Capra, 1971; Maynard, 1975).

Through videotape and cable television, many World War II propaganda films are finding new audiences. Today, we recognize the overt attempts of these films to manipulate emotions and beliefs. Any film may be labeled propagandistic if it directly or indirectly affects the viewer, shaping attitudes and inducing change in belief or behavior; but those influenced are less likely to label it as propaganda (Wead and Lellis, 1981). Commercial Hollywood films frequently reflect our culture and reaffirm its ideology and values. The rhetorical nature of these message movies is implicit whereas that of a propaganda film is explicit. Consider, for example, a film based on one of the most controversial and talked-about novels since *Uncle Tom's Cabin.*

Depending on the reader's politics, John Steinbeck's *The Grapes of Wrath* was either seen as left wing, New Deal liberalism, or revolutionary socialism. John Ford saw in it the potential for an epic film about the Depression, though focused more on people than political issues. Where Steinbeck's novel was angry, harsh, concerned with politics and the relationship of people to the land, Ford wanted to produce a film about how the Depression affected families (Behlmer, 1982). Script writer Nunnally Johnson described the adaptation of the novel for the film:

> [The script] simplified the narrative of *The Grapes of Wrath,* eliminating most of the material that did not concentrate specifically on the Joad family and their trek. The religious satire inherent in the book was eliminated and the politics muted. Dropped entirely were the author's sometimes angry interludes and explicit indictments. The profanity was deleted and the dialog heavily pruned. (BEHLMER, 1982, p. 121)

Ford's film even changed the ending to make it more upbeat, and he focused on the strength of the family rather than the politics of the dispossessed. *The Grapes of Wrath* (1940) was a rare message movie, a film everyone wanted to see; it got great reviews and also made money.

Because most films are moneymaking ventures, their subject must be something the viewer is willing to pay to see. The films we like most, the films we see over and over again and recommend to our friends, are those films that capture our own values, ambitions, desires, and beliefs in some way. In this sense, every successful film—documentary, realistic, or fictional—communicates something.

Many science fiction films are distinctly rhetorical, making statements against the abuse of science, the irresponsible uses of technology, the rape of the environment, and the curtailment of individual rights. *The Andromeda Strain* (1971) suggested that materials brought back from space might be dangerous. *A Clockwork Orange* (1971) warned that behavior modification destroyed freedom of choice. *Fahrenheit 451* (1966) showed what happens when freedom of speech is limited and learning is considered dangerous. *Silent Running* (1972) was a fable about one man's fight to save what, in the story, was left of the environment. *Brother from Another Planet* (1984) and *Enemy Mine* (1985) discussed racism.

Once you have determined whether the film you have selected has a documentary, realistic, or fictional point of view, the critical process begins with description of the rhetorical act and selection of an appropriate methodology. The wholeness of a film, the order it shows or makes for us out of the discontinuity of human affairs, is accomplished through the technical aspects of filmmaking. Pace, sensuousness, feeling, symbol, and meaning are achieved technically through a process understood in terms of the basic film concepts (see box on next page), which should prove helpful in describing the rhetorical act. The box is not an all-inclusive list, but it gives you a working vocabulary for describing and analyzing film. The suggested readings at the end of this chapter include more detailed information on the technical aspects of filmmaking. This vocabulary is also useful if you decide to do auteur or genre, rather than message-movie, criticism.

Basic Film

Concepts

Frame: a single cell or photographic image on film. Think of a snapshot as one frame. Ordinarily you cannot detect a single frame in a motion picture unless a technique called *freeze frame* is used to stop apparent action for dramatic effect.

Shot: one uninterrupted sequence of action recorded with a single camera. Several shots are edited together to produce a film. *Shot* also refers to particular kinds of shots: Establishing shot or extreme long shot is action seen from a distance, taking in what surrounds it; long shot, medium shot, closeup shot, and extreme closeup shot refer to the diminishing distance between the camera lens and the focal point of action.

Scene: a single shot or series of shots taking place over a continuous time period at the same location. A scene may be brief or cover several minutes.

Sequence: several scenes linked by character, story line, or some other device. A sequence is a narrative or dramatic unit similar to a chapter in a novel.

Mise-en-scène: the detail, particularly the background detail of props and setting, that add "realness" to a scene. Set decoration, costuming, makeup, hair styling, the positioning and movement of primary and secondary characters, and visual perspective are all elements of mise-en-scène.

Sound: dialogue, narration, singing, background talk, and legends appearing on screen. It also includes music written for the film to highlight, emphasize, or signal scene changes. Music is frequently selected to represent the film's historical period. Ambient sound, naturally occuring background noise, also contributes to film realism.

Special effects: images and sounds unobtainable using "regular" techniques. Imaginary creatures, stunts, motion beyond the range of what is presently technically possible, historical re-creation, combination of animation and live action, explosions and natural disasters, and montage camera shots all fall under the heading of special effects.

Auteur Criticism

We have talked about filmmakers in a general way, but you might decide to focus criticism on the person who might properly be said to be the film's rhetor. The body of work on film criticism has produced the *auteur theory,* an approach that focuses on the person most responsible for creating the film. Factors apart from the film itself—the auteur's personal history, political views, degree of control over the film, and the body of films he or she has made—are important (Bywater and Sobchack, 1989).

If you choose to focus on the rhetor, auteur theory should be followed. It identifies the director or the "star" as the rhetor for a film's message. The director can be viewed as rhetor because he or she determines what images and sounds are filmed and how everything that contributes to the message of a film is to be interpreted and presented. It is the director's world view, biases, prejudices, and value system that are reflected in the film (Ellis, 1985). However, the film's star, particularly one with the powerful screen presence of a Humphrey Bogart or a John Wayne, can also be considered the auteur.

In using auteur theory, consider whether or not a body of work exists that develops a certain theme. Although characters, scenes, or plots may not be duplicated exactly, the work of certain directors and stars is identifiable, and their influence over their films reveals much about their personal beliefs. John Ford, Frank Capra, Howard Hawks, Alfred Hitchcock, Stanley Kubrick, Woody Allen, Robert Altman, Francis Ford Coppola, Martin Scorsese, Steven Spielberg, George Lucas, and Oliver Stone are among those director-auteurs whose films bear their personal imprint as surely as David Wark Griffith's bore his.

By 1912 there were 12,869 movie theatres in America, with nearly 500 in New York alone. Even small towns of 6000 people might have as many as four places to show films. D.W. Griffith and other early filmmakers assumed that fourteen minutes, the length of film to a "can," was the length of an audience's attention span. Because copyright was not a factor in early script development, famous novels, plays, and epic poems were condensed into fourteen minutes of action and emotion (Lynes, 1985).

Griffith was the first great innovator in the history of American film, the first to recognize what could be done with a movie camera. He introduced the idea that the shot, rather than the scene, was the basic unit of film and that several shots should be edited together to create a scene (Ellis, 1985). Other filmmakers approached moviemaking as though they were filming a play on a stage: point the camera in the right direction and let the film roll.

Griffith also revolutionized filmmaking by using multiple points of view. He moved the camera in for closeups and pulled it back for long shots, focused on single objects to set the scene, cross-cut between scenes to show action on two fronts, and invented the flashback (Lynes, 1985). He liked to use *irises* as connective devices, small figures of light on a dark screen that gradually opened to reveal the full picture (Ellis, 1985).

As a director, Griffith changed the way actors performed to fit his camera techniques. Actors who were trained for the theatre often used broad pantomime: Even an aging actor could get away on the stage with playing a young girl because the audience was seated too far away to see her face plainly. Griffith's use of the closeup required that subtley of movement and expression become part of the actor's craft in film (Lynes, 1985).

In April 1913, the Italian film *Quo Vadis* opened in New York and gave Americans their first chance to see a feature-length film. Running about two hours, *Quo Vadis* told the story of decadent Rome. It featured a cast of thousands, blood-thirsty lions, and a nude girl perched on the back of a charging bull (Lynes, 1985). Inspired by the success of *Quo Vadis,* Griffith was determined to film "the greatest picture ever made."

For his story, he used the plot of *The Clansman,* Thomas Dixon's 1905 novel about the Civil War and Reconstruction. D.W. Griffith was from Kentucky and considered himself a son of the old South. His own values and prejudices were embodied in Dixon's novel, the story of two families, one northern and one southern, whose children had met at school in the North shortly before the war (E. Carter, 1983).

The novel offered a mythic view of the old South, the culture and serenity of plantation life, aristocratic gentle white men and women and happy negroes existing in a feudal society. After the war, this tattered aristocracy struggled to preserve their values during Reconstruction. Dixon's "Clan," based on the extended family tribalism of the Scots' clans, had as its purpose the defense of white southern aristocracy (E. Carter, 1983). In the real world of early twentieth-century America, the Knights of the White Camelia had evolved into the Ku Klux Klan, an antiblack, anti-Jewish, and anti–Roman Catholic hate organization.

Griffith used Dixon's story but filmed *The Clansman* from his own southern point of view. The film "became a visualization of the whole set of irrational cultural assumptions" (E. Carter, 1983, pp. 11–12) that white southerners believed about themselves and the inferiority of blacks. After west-coast showings, Dixon suggested that the title be changed to *The Birth of a Nation* to better represent the epic scope of the film (Ellis, 1985).

The Birth of a Nation was the first film shown in the White House. Upon seeing it, President Woodrow Wilson became an instant film fan, declaring: "It is like writing history with lightning" (Knock, 1983, p. 88). The film was not received that way by all audiences. Liberals, including social reformer Jane Addams, university presidents, and the NAACP called the film racist and bigoted. Not wanting to be thought a racist, Wilson later claimed he had praised the film for its technical rather than its topical merit (Mast, 1981). In Boston, the film incited a riot, and Griffith's press agents used the incident to promote the film. It was a box office success, as much for its notoriety as its spectacle.

The Birth of a Nation should be recognized for its innovation as the first American feature-length film and the first film to display the art of editing and camera work. It should also be recognized as racist, based on a view that blacks are inferior. "Good" blacks were childlike and dependent; "bad" blacks, frequently of mixed blood, were deceitful or misguided by whites (Ellis, 1985). The film is a record of D.W. Griffith's personal prejudices as well as his art as a filmmaker.

In the wake of criticisms of *The Birth of a Nation,* Griffith made *Intolerance* to show he was on the side of morality and social justice. He combined an unreleased feature about a violent labor movement conflict, *The Mother and the Law,* with three other historical stories, a re-creation of the fall of Babylon, selected scenes from the life of Christ, and the massacre of French Huguenots in 1572, to show how love and charity constantly battle hatred and intolerance (Ellis, 1985).

Griffith's artistry may have run amok in *Intolerance.* Instead of telling each story in sequence, he intercut among them so that the final product was an amalgam of ever more rapid scene shifts. Audiences found the film confusing and exhausting. Griffith had invented the montage film in which a generalized emotion or idea, rather than plot, presents the message. With its lavish sets, huge cast, and the enormous cost of production, *Intolerance* ruined Griffith financially (Ellis, 1985).

Darryl F. Zanuck, a legendary director of the 1930s, believed that going to the movies should be educational as well as entertaining. He was known for "biopics," films about the great people who had a significant impact on history (Knock, 1983). He made several successful films of this type: *Disraeli* (1929), *The House of Rothschild* (1934), *The Story of Alexander Graham Bell* (1939), and *Young Mr. Lincoln* (1939). In making these films, Zanuck tried to re-create history faithfully, at least insofar as the entertainment value of the film was not sacrificed.

Perhaps the best, most message-oriented, of Zanuck's bio-pics was *Wilson* (1944). Zanuck wanted to make a film about President Woodrow Wilson, in part because Wilson had been a great movie fan but also because Zanuck believed there was a lesson in the Wilson administration's failure to ensure world peace at the end of World War I. *Wilson* used the past to interpret the present and to offer a solution: the idea of a global organization for world peace. Filmed in the new technicolor process, *Wilson* was remarkable in its depiction of history. It re-created the 1912 Democratic convention, was shot on sets that faithfully reproduced the interior of the White House and Capitol Hill, and used Wilson's recorded speeches and other documents for its script (Knock, 1983).

Film critics and analysts called it an important picture, one that would save the next generation from repeating the mistakes of the past.

> [I]t was among the first American films which attempted to raise public consciousness. Released just as World War II was coming to an end, during a period when over half the American population went to the movies each week, *Wilson* was pregnant with meaning for its audiences because of its theme of peace and its implied plea for the future of the United Nations. (KNOCK, 1983, p. 89)

As with so many films, *Wilson* was only a partial success. Seen and praised by millions of Americans on both coasts, it was a failure in middle America. It was perceived as too controversial (Knock, 1983). Although nominated for ten Academy Awards, it lost to the widely popular and noncontroversial *Going My Way*.

If you have an image of World War II, it may be soldiers raising the flag atop Mount Suribachi on Iwo Jima. That image might come from a monument in Washington D.C., but more likely it comes from a film. *The Sands of Iwo Jima* (1949), a film entwined with the image of John Wayne as an all-American soldier-hero, followed a small group of Marines from boot camp through the war in the South Pacific. John Wayne played Sergeant Stryker, the film's central character, as a tough but caring leader who took a group of raw recruits and turned them into a fighting machine. Stryker's devotion to the Corps cost him his wife and son, so he became father and teacher to his men. The film culminates on Iwo Jima where, although Stryker is killed by a sniper's bullet, his men are inspired to go on and take Mount Suribachi.

With the cooperation of the Marine Corps, John Wayne turned himself into a Marine for the film. Marine heroes David Shoup and Jim Crowe helped re-create their experiences for the film, and the three surviving members of the flag-raising detail, including Ira Hayes, re-created that now famous scene (Suid, 1978). The film was one of the most popular of 1950, and the Marines praised its spirit and true portrayal of the Corps. For decades, Marine recruiters acknowledged the effectiveness of *The Sands of Iwo Jima* in attracting recruits. In this film and many others, John Wayne epitomized the American fighting man, "representing the traditional American ideal of the anti-intellectual doer in contrast to the thinker" (Suid, 1978, p. 102). If John Wayne reached his zenith as a war hero in this film, he may have found his nadir in *The Green Berets* (1968).

Robin Moore had written a popular novel of the same name in 1965, about the exploits of special forces advisers in Vietnam. John Wayne contacted President Lyndon Johnson to ask for the defense department's cooperation in making the film.

> He explained that while he supported the adminstration's Vietnam policy, he knew the war was not popular. Consequently, he thought it was "extremely important that not only the people of the United States but those all over the world should know why it is necessary for us to be there. . . . The most effective way to accomplish this is through the motion picture medium." He told Johnson he could make the "kind of picture that will help our cause throughout the world." While still making money for his company, he could "tell the story of our fighting men in Vietnam with reason, emotion, characterization, and action. We want to do it in a manner that will inspire a patriotic attitude on the part of fellow Americans—a feeling which we have always had in this country during times of stress and trouble." (SUID, 1978, p. 222)

The Green Berets told the story of a special forces unit, commanded by Wayne, and the skeptical liberal journalist who follows them to Vietnam to do a story. In the course of the film, the journalist is won over and sees the "rightness" of American involvement in Vietnam. The film was only marginally successful at the time of its release.

Auteurism is most closely connected to traditional views of rhetoric although organic criticism would allow inclusion of concepts from other approaches as well. Auteur criticism enables the critic to examine a series of rhetorical acts by a single director or star to discover how the nature of these acts was influenced by, and influenced, the rhetor's persona.

The final way to focus film criticism is to study a series of rhetorical acts linked, not by a common rhetor, but by a set of common characteristics.

Genre Criticism

Genre criticism describes and categorizes films by their narrative patterns, similar story lines, and ability to offer the viewer a relatively predictable experience. Westerns, crime dramas, and slapstick comedy were the first film genres, and we shall examine these and other genres in the pages that follow. The relationship between a film representing a particular genre and the social and political conditions of its time is important. Critics typically look at salient economic, political, and ideological forces in the culture to discuss a genre's popularity and how it has changed over time.

The Western

The Western, the one truly American film genre, embodies the conflict between community values and individual values that is inherent in our society. This value conflict, usually the source of dramatic tension in Westerns, makes them uniquely American because our expansion was accomplished by imposing a series of codes of legal, philosophical, ethical, and economic behavior on the wild frontier (Wead and Lellis, 1981). In a Western, civilization always confronts chaos.

The Western is also about a place. Even if you have not seen a Western lately, you probably have a mental image of the landscape: hot, harsh, rugged, dusty, mountainous, and generally inhospitable. There is always a town in a Western, symbolizing the encroachment of civilization, the boundary between the savage wilderness and the communal interdependence of city life.

Westerns primarily feature male heroes and villains; women play secondary roles, in which their purpose is to humanize and to bring the values of civilization to the wilderness. The hero may have a wife or romantic interest, but she seldom plays an important role in resolving the conflict.

The Western hero has certain characteristics that set him apart, something from his past—a mistake, a deep hurt, an as yet unresolved incident—that makes him a loner (Solomon, 1976). The hero is also a survivor, with the courage and skills to handle his environment, who may seem priestlike in his separateness (Marsden, 1982). The plot always forces the hero to confront his past and symbolizes the conflict between civilization and the wilderness. The hero confronts the threat to civilization, frequently resorting to the violence of the wilderness to conquer it.

The badman or outlaw is the other important character in the Western. He may also display certain virtues because, unlike the ostentatious wealth of urban gangsters, the Western outlaw has no wealth; he depends on his skill and daring and is also a survivor in a harsh environment. Frequently, the only thing that separates outlaw from hero is a single criminal act or a life outside the law forced on him by circumstance. Ultimately, the outlaw always loses, outnumbered or outgunned by law and order (Solomon, 1976).

How officers of the law are characterized in Westerns ranges from hero to outlaw to supernumerary. The local sheriff or marshal may be empowered by the townspeople to act on their behalf, may be in the employ of a wealthy cattle-baron villain, or may be simply one of the secondary characters who gather around the hero at the conclusion.

The plot of the Western frequently features the journey motif: a cattle drive, wagon train, stage coach crossing Indian or bandit territory, or a lawman or bounty hunter bringing an outlaw to town. The journey is a movement through danger, culminating in the hero's confrontation with his past (Solomon, 1976). What does this motif mean in terms of our culture? It symbolizes our national journey from the raw, uncivilized, quasitribal, autonomous collection of towns in earliest colonial America to present civilization.

The West on film is a romanticized West, the West as it ought to have been (Marsden, 1982), and John Ford's *Stage Coach* (1939) is one of the best films of the genre. The film was shot in Monument Valley, a common location for Hollywood Westerns. Its harsh yet majestic scenery is the image most of us have of the wild west. *Stage Coach* was a benchmark film defining the journey motif and John Wayne as a Western hero. It tells the story of a group of people traveling through Indian country, who we recognize as the stereotypes present in every "group-of-strangers" film. *Stage Coach* celebrated cooperation and the ability of ordinary people for heroic and noble behavior in trying circumstances. It is important to recognize the impact of this film on audiences in 1939, ordinary people being tested by the Depression and the growing war in Europe, and to speculate why it was more successful at the box office than *Our Daily Bread,* a film with a similar theme.

Crime Dramas

The crime drama is related to the Western because it also focuses on the conflict between the law and those outside it. Crime dramas are set against an urban landscape, and the outlaw is someone out to succeed in the big city. Most crime dramas are based on some aspect of the American dream run amok. Marxist criticism of crime films concludes that the genre reflects class struggle in America; crime is a logical consequence in a society that measures individual worth in terms of material possessions.

There are four types of criminals: the gangster or syndicate member, the concealed criminal, the prisoner, and the thief or swindler (Solomon, 1976). Differences among types are accommodated by variations in the basic plot line. For example, the gangster, mobster, or syndicate member is an overt criminal, part of a large family or organization. Edward G. Robinson in *Little Caesar* (1930), James Cagney in *The Public Enemy* (1931), and Humphrey Bogart helped established the genre by creating compelling characters.

Lawmen in early gangster films were often inept and sometimes corrupt themselves. The film industry was charged by the Catholic church and other concerned groups with promoting immorality and responded by establishing production codes and making films that portrayed law enforcement in a more favorable light. One technique was to have a popular gangster star do a turnaround. In *G-Men* (1935), James Cagney portrayed a man who joined the FBI. The popularity of *G-Men* apparently led the House of Representatives to vote a budget increase for the FBI (Bergman, 1971). Edward G. Robinson also did a turnaround in *Bullets or Ballots* (1936), playing a double agent who worked his way up in a gang in order to destroy it.

Gangster films remain popular. Francis Ford Coppola's *The Godfather* (1972) and *The Godfather, Part II* (1974) are films as much about organizational change in a changing world as they are about crime. Both films tell the story of the Corleone family as leadership passes from one generation to the next. Michael Corleone must reshape the family crime business in the face of competition or lose everything, a choice not unlike that facing many business leaders in the 1970s.

Another form of the crime drama is found in films about private investigators who inhabit a world of criminals. These *film noir* (black film) dramas always have a sinister element—a looming threat, fear, the feeling of helplessness—a trend first popularized in American filmmaking in the 1940s as a counterbalance to the patriotic zeal of wartime filmmaking.

> As opposed to the idealism of the society fighting together to combat the political evil of facism, film noir dealt with individuals conspicuously antisocial in their greed and selfishness, driven to betrayal, violence, and crime (usually including murder) out of an incurable sickness (often ending in death or incarceration). Their malaise was presented as endemic to the human species, and the world they inhabited was a dark one literally as well as morally. The films seem to take place mostly at night, in seedy furnished apartments and on rain-washed streets of big cities. A jungle atmosphere was created in those studio sets (a human jungle, an asphalt jungle, a neon jungle), with predators stalking prey and danger lurking in the shadows, intermittently revealed by flashing signs. (ELLIS, 1985, p. 219)

Humphrey Bogart's portrayal of Sam Spade in *The Maltese Falcon* (1941) established the archetypal noir hero. Spade is not heroic, he is cynical, sardonic, and world weary, but he lives by a code that says "a man's got to do the right thing." For him, that means finding out the truth about his partner's death, even though he didn't really like the guy and even though it means turning in a woman who offers him love and wealth (Wead and Lellis, 1981). In Sam Spade's hierarchy of values, professionalism as an investigator is more important than personal gain.

In Roman Polanski's *Chinatown* (1974), Jack Nicholson played Jake Gittes, a private investigator trying to figure out what is going on and why. "Forget it, Jake, it's Chinatown," the last line of the film, became a catch phrase to explain the unexplainable. William Palmer interpreted the rhetorical significance of *Chinatown* at the time:

> We all lived in a Chinatown world where nothing was ever what it seemed, where reality was so layered and complicated that it could never be grasped, where any natural impulses were doomed to failure, where innocence was but a naive dream in the face of the sinister and brutal nightmare known as reality . . . that last line also implies all of the futility and hopelessness of the film and of the seventies decade. In the course of the movie, "Chinatown" has become more than just a sinister L.A. neighborhood. It has become a way of life, a mode of thinking, a symbol of all that is opaque, sinister, and ultimately, dangerous. "Chinatown" becomes a symbol of the futility of attempting to grasp and interpret reality. Those who listened to what was left of the Watergate tapes, who sat throughout those interminable Watergate hearings, must have felt the same frustration with grasping reality that Jake felt in Chinatown. Those who examined their conscience about Vietnam, either incountry or at home, faced the same problem of understanding what they were doing that Jake faced in Chinatown. (PALMER, 1987, pp. 118–119)

The Comedy

Although films in other genres can be comedies, we classify comedy as a separate genre based on its specific elements of structure and characterization. More will be said about humor as a rhetorical form in Chapter 12, but we shall describe the rhetorical aspects of the comic film briefly here. All comedy works rhetorically by showing the arbitrariness and perversity of codes of social conduct. The structure of comedy disrupts one or more of these established patterns and then resolves the disruption in a "happy ending." Comedy films have followed one of three basic formulas to produce the disruption: slapstick, satire, and the previously described screwball.

Slapstick comedy is visual, emphasizing physical humor, pratfalls, pie throwing, and broad, exaggrated gesture. Slapstick began in silent films, which adapted the comic traditions of vaudeville and combined them with the antics of the circus clown. The Marx Brothers (Chico, Groucho, Harpo, and Zeppo) combined physical humor with verbal comedy. Language took on a slapstick quality in their films. Logic blurred with illogic, malapropisms, confused dialects, and punning (Bergman, 1971) in *Cocoanuts* (1929), *Animal Crackers* (1930), *Monkey Business* (1931), *Duck Soup* (1933), *A Night at the Opera* (1935), and *A Day at the Races* (1937). Although each film had elements of social criticism, the most rhetorical was also the least popular at the time of its release.

Duck Soup is one of the finest examples of rhetorical comedy (Bergman, 1971), but it was out of step with the "can do" spirit of Franklin D. Roosevelt's government and did not strike a responsive chord with audiences in 1933. Slapstick and the verbal anarchy typical of Marx Brothers films was used to show the inherent dangers of nationalism. With its political, antiwar message, *Duck Soup* told the story of Freedonia and Sylvania, two nations governed by absurdists, in which the only game was the war game.

As it evolved, film satire was not particularly controversial, gently attacking social conventions. Satire became more relevant and frequently more rhetorical in the 1960s and 1970s. Woody Allen's *Take the Money and Run* (1969), *Bananas* (1971), *Play It Again Sam* (1973), and *Annie Hall* (1977) treated everything from Latin American revolutions to the complexities of relationships with a biting satirical wit. Mel Brooks satirized Broadway, other film genres, and auteurs in *The Producers* (1967), *Blazing Saddles* (1974), *Young Frankenstein* (1975), *Silent Movie* (1976), and *High Anxiety* (1977).

Science Fiction and Horror Films

Films in this genre feature the unknown or the challenge of technology. Danger, frequently in the form of a "creature," is the genre's unifying element. In the science fiction film, the danger has a physical, technological source that comes from outside (Solomon, 1976) and that can usually be dealt with, or at least explained, by appropriate application of "science." The horror film is psychological; the danger lies within the human mind and soul and cannot be removed by any quick technofix.

Although some silent films forecast the future, science fiction films, frequently B movies with low budgets and cheap special effects, gained broad exposure during the 1950s. Many featured invasions or visitations from other worlds, sometimes friendly, frequently hostile. The alien visitors in *The Day the Earth Stood Still* (1951), one of the better films of the era, brought a message about world peace whereas the pod people in *The Invasion of the Body Snatchers* (1956) were menacingly McCarthyesque, seemingly normal on the outside but driven by sinister intent.

Creatures with superhuman powers or strengths were born in the German expressionist cinema of the early days of silent film. Folk tales and gothic novels inspired films about vampires, werewolves, and manmade monsters that warned of the beast that resides in each of us just waiting to come out. We each had the impulse to violence (Solomon, 1976). In the fifties, creatures were more frequently the product of external factors, such as nuclear radiation or toxic waste, which produced *Them!* (1954) and *The Incredible Shrinking Man* (1957).

The earliest films about creatures, such as *Frankenstein* (1931), were aimed at an adult audience. Vampires, werewolves, and other film creatures have lived on in popularity though there has been a gradual shift to a more adolescent audience. One reason for the fascination of young audiences with monster movies may be that they help adolescents come to terms with the transition from the security of childhood to the sexuality of adulthood. Like the werewolf undergoing physical transformation, adolescents are changing physically as well as psychologically (Evans, 1982).

War

The message of a war film depends on when it was made. In wartime, the emphasis is on morale whereas after the war the focus is frequently on moral issues questioning the motives that got us into the war (Wead and Lellis, 1981). War films, whether they address morale or morality, are extremely popular. Peace won at the point of a gun makes good movies. The first film awarded the best-picture "Oscar" was a war film, *Wings* (1929). Films in this genre also disclose the essential contradiction in our national character. Although we see ourselves as peaceloving, our nation was born in violent revolution and continues to exercise military force.

As the earlier discussion of Frank Capra's propaganda films suggests, the film industry helped fight and win World War II. In 1942, it cost thirty-five cents to go to the movies and approximately ninety million tickets were sold. Hollywood preparedness films—*Flight Command* (1940), *I Wanted Wings* (1941), and *Dive Bomber* (1941)—combined romance with footage of training and practice missions by the navy and army air corps. Other prewar films were intended to create patriotic feelings and unite America behind the arsenal of democracy policy.

Two prominent isolationist senators, Gerald Nye and Champ Clark, convened a hearing to investigate Hollywood films as propaganda that violated interstate commerce legislation. They claimed that *Sergeant York* (1941), the story of a World War I hero, and *Confessions of a Nazi Spy* (1939), the story of a spy ring in New York City, were stirring people into a war frenzy. The Japanese attack on Pearl Harbor occured before the hearing concluded, and their point became moot.

In 1941, a historical film captured the attention of American moviegoers. Alexander Korda's *Lady Hamilton* (1941), about British hero Lord Nelson and the battle against Napoleon, depicted the British as heroes fighting for freedom against a dictator. Winston Churchill loved the film and, much to the dismay of his staff, viewed it frequently (Shindler, 1979). The success of *Lady Hamilton* paved the way for William Wyler's *Mrs. Miniver* (1942).

Mrs. Miniver and *Wake Island* were the two big hits of 1942. *Mrs. Miniver* struck a responsive chord with American moviegoers, and got Academy Awards for best picture, best actress, and best director. Today, it may seem a bit silly, but at the time it was a fitting response to a strongly felt exigence. Its story concerned a middle-class British family during the blitzkrieg and the heroism of the British people. Throughout the film, the message was that, in fighting the war, the British people had broken the bonds of their rigid class system. England was truly a democracy. A flower show and a contest for best rose was the vehicle for this message.

At the beginning of the film, the stationmaster asks Mrs. Miniver if he can name his new rose after her, and much of the film's early exposition involves the debate over whether or not he should even be allowed to have an entry in the village flower show. The local gentry, in the person of Lady Beldon, has traditionally won the prize for best rose. Lady Beldon ultimately shows herself to be a democrat. Even though the judges award her the prize, she bestows it on Stationmaster Ballard. The flower show is hit by an air raid in which Lady Beldon's daughter and Ballard are killed. The final scene takes place in the village church, another setting for democracy, where all are equal in the eyes of God.

> As the congregation files in it is apparent that several people are missing. The camera pans over the people and then slowly points upward revealing a huge hole in the roof. The minister begins his sermon: "We in this quiet corner of England have suffered the loss of friends." George West, a young choir-boy killed. James Ballard, Stationmaster, dead just one hour after winning the rose competition. And, most tragically Carol Beldon. "Why, in all conscience, should these be the ones to suffer?" he asks. "I shall tell you why! Because this is not only a war of soldiers in uniform. It is a war of the people—of all the people—and it must be fought not only on the battlefield but in the cities and in the villages, in the factories and on the farms, in the home and in the heart of every man, woman, and child who loves freedom. . . . This is a people's war! It is our war! We are the fighters!" As the sermon concludes the camera moves from the minister to the hole in the church roof. With "Onward Christian Soldiers" playing on the sound track, the sky is suddenly filled with English fighter planes going off to battle. (KOPPES AND BLACK, 1987, p. 229)

Mrs. Miniver is an example of the fitting response to a rhetorical situation. American moviegoers and critics loved it. Franklin D. Roosevelt thought it gave the war effort an enormous boost. The press thought it was more powerful than any propaganda film and that it showed the meaning of war rather than heroics on the battlefield (Koppes and Black, 1987). Films that were a fitting response during a war may seem less meaningful when viewed even a short time later. *Wake Island* demonstrates why.

> *Wake Island* was a film for 1942. Three years later it seemed like ancient history. The battle scenes were unrealistic, as were the preachments in the trenches about fighting for democracy. As one combat veteran observed years after the war, "I remember those Hollywood films where people sat in their trenches and had ideological discussions about the beauties of democracy at home. Oh, bullshit! I remember those movies. They were stupid." *Wake Island* was popular in 1942 because it fed the public's desire for anything about the war. The battle scenes had a sanitized quality that made war seem more like a big football game than a mortal encounter. Three years later, when audiences knew much more about the reality of war, *Wake Island* seemed like a naive period piece. (KOPPES AND BLACK, 1987, p. 254)

Throughout most of 1942, American forces had been losing the war, and the audience at home was desperately in need of hope. During that time, Hollywood tried to boost morale and aid the war effort. The attack on Pearl Harbor, the fall of the Philippines and Wake Island, and other events in the south Pacific were turned into inspirational films, featuring the various branches of the service. The message was that America had superior morality, men, and machines. Because these films were intended for a national audience, the stories, which often focused on the actions of a small group of men, each representing a different ethnic group, were films the audience could identify with. The formula for World War II films "was based on the coincidental but fortuitous composition of the typical platoon which inevitably comprised the tough sergeant, the rich kid, the ex-con, a Jew, a Polish-American, an Italian-American, and a Black" (Shindler, 1979, pp. 40–41).

During the crucial years of the war, moviegoers experienced the scope of the fighting. *Bataan* (1943) told the story of the final days of thirteen American soldiers during the Japanese invasion of the Philippines. At the film's end, the last man alive buries the others, digs his own grave, and prepares to machine gun as many of the enemy as he can. The last image the viewer saw was his silent machine gun barrel with a wisp of smoke curling from it. In *Sahara* (1943), Humphrey Bogart played a tank commander, fighting the Nazis in north Africa alongside our British allies, and the story of submarine warfare was told in *Destination Tokyo* (1943).

General Hap Arnold of the army air corps and Jack Warner of Warner Brothers collaborated to produce the quasidocumentary *Air Force* (1943), which followed the exploits of a bomber crew and their plane, "Mary Ann," in the Pacific. Directed by Howard Hawks, *Air Force* was an archetypal World War II movie, containing all the elements audiences had come to expect in a war film.

> The crew of the "Mary Ann" consisted of a heterogeneous cross section of the nation, except for a black, of course. The plane's crew chief, a crusty old sergeant, provided a father figure to the younger men. The pilot's wife and copilot's girlfriend served as the faithful women, waiting loyally at home. And the mascot, an all-American mutt who raged at the mention of Tojo, provided some comic relief. While one of the gunners, a washed-out pilot, becomes a temporary malcontent, the "crew takes care of each other" and everyone does his assigned job for the good of the plane. The final didactic message is related through a fighter pilot. Along for the ride to the Philippines, he learns how important bombers are for the war effort, and by the time he reaches Australia, he is ready to fly a B-17 for the duration. (SUID, 1978, pp. 41–42)

Films of this period always portrayed the enemy as absolute evil. The characterization of the Japanese in *Air Force* was typical.

> [T]he Japanese are all characterized as sneaky and treacherous and throughout the film are referred to in derogatory terms. This message is constantly reinforced beginning with the opening scenes. On the way to Hawaii, the crew hears a news broadcast that a Japanese peace envoy was planning to meet with Secretary of State Hull on the morning of December 7. When the plane lands at Pearl Harbor, the crew is immediately told of Japanese sabotage of American planes before the attack (historically untrue). The Japanese are portrayed as fighting unfairly, attacking without warning, and shooting at a helpless flier as he parachutes from his disabled plane. . . . The message stands out clearly: the United States will win the war, we may have lost the first round through deceit, but victory will be ours. (SUID, 1978, p. 42)

Early in the war, Hollywood also produced a series of pro-Russian films. Franklin D. Roosevelt asked Jack Warner to make a movie based on *Mission to Moscow,* a book by former American ambassador Joseph E. Davies. Released in 1943, the film stirred up controversy because it whitewashed repression under Joseph Stalin. Most Americans found it completely unbelievable. The other studios also made pro-Russian films, most released in 1943. MGM had the musical salute to the Russian people, *Song of Russia.* United Artists made *Three Russian Girls* and Columbia countered with *Boy from Stalingrad* (Koppes and Black, 1987).

Films about the heroic actions of resistance fighters were also popular, and *Casablanca* (1943) became a film classic. Originally to star Ronald Reagan and Ann Sheridan following their success in *King's Row,* the script, based on the failed Broadway play *Everybody Comes to Rick's,* was not ready, and Reagan and Sheridan had other commitments (Koppes and Black, 1987).

Set in December 1941 just before Pearl Harbor, it opens with the local police questioning refugees. A German courier has been killed, two letters of safe-conduct are missing, and a German officer, Major Strasser, has come to Casablanca to arrest the head of the Czechoslovakian resistance, Victor Laslo. Most of the action is set in Rick's Cafe Americain. Rick, played by Humphrey Bogart, is a cool expatriate who seems to have no cause but his own. As the film unfolds, we learn that Rick really is a patriot at heart.

Although Casablanca is governed by the collaborationist French Vichy government, the French, symbolized by Captain Renault, dislike the Germans. A confrontation occurs at Rick's that shows their animosity.

> [A] Frenchman yells at a woman for going with a German officer. The men start to argue and Rick breaks it up. As the Frenchman leaves he mutters: "Sale boche, un jour nous aurons notre revanche!" (Dirty German, some day we'll have our revenge!) Renault, who along with Strasser has overheard the conversation simply shrugs: "My dear Major, we are trying to cooperate with your government. But we cannot regulate the feelings of our people."
> (KOPPES AND BLACK, 1987, p. 289)

To make sure the point was not lost on the audience, the scene continued:

> Several German soldiers, drinking too much and nostalgic for the Fatherland, start singing "Horst Wessel." Everyone else remains sullen and silent. Laslo tells Sam to play "La Marseillaise." Sam hesitates, then looks to Rick, who gives him an almost imperceptible nod of approval. Slowly the entire cafe begins to sing louder and louder until the Germans are isolated and humiliated. The scene was one of the most powerful and memorable in World War II films. The Germans might be conquerors but they could not crush the people's desire for freedom. (KOPPES AND BLACK, 1987, p. 289)

After the war, films about it continued to be popular. *Twelve O'Clock High* (1950) was the story of the command decisions made by General Frank Savage in carrying out the air war over Europe, a study of leadership and the burden of command. The general takes over the 918th bomb group after it loses a very popular commander. The men are dispirited by the losses they have suffered in daylight-bombing missions over Germany. General Savage pushes himself and his men to be survivors through seemingly endless training and iron discipline. The drama focuses on how the men react to his leadership. By the final mission, the strain of command has taken its toll on General Savage, but he has achieved his goal and his men are able to succeed without his supervision.

Antiwar

An antiwar film does not make war look attractive, exciting, or justifiable.

> Good antiwar films sift through the rubble of history in search of images and ideas that will shake us from our complacency. They show the callousness of power and the power of callousness. They unmask war's political causes and its cultural consequences. They show the dark secrets of human character and how war exploits them. They examine how—beyond mere death—war maims the lives of its makers and victims. They explore human self-destructiveness, the myth of the hero, the meaning of memory, and sometimes they even point out the perils of pacificism. And to top it all, a great antiwar movie must do this all with panache, in an original yet fitting style. (POWERS, 1985, pp. 63-64)

A film that meets these criteria is Robert Altman's *M*A*S*H* (1970). Although ostensibly set in Korea, most viewers at that time interpreted it as being about Vietnam. Altman was ambiguous about the meaning of the film, saying that war just happened to be the setting for a story about people interacting within the confines of a structured bureaucracy (Shindler, 1979). *M*A*S*H* was a dove-liberal fantasy that the military was the real enemy and that the individual had to maintain his values in the face of such an irrational institution (Cagin and Dray, 1984).

Following on the heels of *M*A*S*H*, other films such as *Apocalypse Now* (1977), *The Deer Hunter* (1978), and *Coming Home* (1978), have given movie audiences ample opportunites to rethink and refight the Vietnam War and to reconsider its effect on those who fought it and those who waited or protested back home. These films demonstrate how American filmmakers and audiences have used the medium to come to terms with the only war we have ever lost.

Doing Rhetorical Criticism of Film

The videocassette recorder has expanded opportunities for rhetorical critics who are interested in film. Thousands of titles can be purchased or rented inexpensively, and each month many older, "classic," films are released on videotape. If the film you want to study is not available locally, make inquiries about its availability through the University of California at Los Angles (U.C.L.A.) film school; U.C.L.A. and other universities archive films and make them available to scholars.

If you choose to do rhetorical criticism of film, you must recognize certain constraints peculiar to the medium. Like any other rhetorical act, a film is part of a rhetorical situation. In doing a rhetorical analysis and criticism of film, you need to think in terms of its historical context. The theme or topic of a film, its characterization, its stars, and its technical properties are all influenced by the period in which it was produced, and the "movie world" of a another era cannot always be replicated (Jarvie, 1978) by watching the film on videotape today.

The Hollywood film was and is meant to be seen on a large screen in a darkened movie theatre with many other people sharing the experience. Unlike movies on television that are constantly interrupted by commercials, viewing a film in this way focuses our attention from start to finish. The text of a film is a combination of its plot, characters, themes, and technical properties. What kinds of symbols are overt and covert in a film? How does the filmmaker get a message across to the audience? What is his or her world view?

We have used the terms *story, story line,* and *plot line* on several occasions in this chapter, suggesting the relationship between the narrative approach and the rhetoric of film. Because Hollywood depends on narrative structures to tell a story, the narrative approach is appropriate for doing rhetorical criticism of films. Because films helped create the mythology of various episodes in our history, the Great Depression, World War II, or Vietnam, narrative analysis can provide insights into both the process and the product of mythmaking.

When you are able to identify a rhetor, termed an *auteur* in film studies, and his or her rhetorical purpose, concepts from the traditional approach may become important in doing criticism. The auteur's background and intentions, the persuasive case made in the story, and the audience's response may all be examined within the framework of the traditional approach. Films can be examined as arguments that offer visual and verbal proofs. As such, they can be studied by asking such questions as how does film function as an enthymeme and how is reasoning accomplished? The truth and results criteria of judgment are particularly important relative to documentary and realistic films, and the traditional approach may help you render these judgments.

At the beginning of this chapter, we described some of film's grammatical elements that correspond to the concepts of style, arrangement, and invention of the traditional approach. A film or group of films may also be judged aesthetically in terms of these concepts, but they are particularly useful in categorizing films as a genre. For example, horror films popular with adolescent audiences may share elements of style, arrangement, and invention that not only make them unique but also help explain their popularity.

Because films of a particular genre also comprise a set of cultural artifacts, the use the audience made of these artifacts and the ability of a film to serve as a source of cultural influence can be explained through fantasy theme analysis. The experience of seeing a film is a fantasy experience. Because fantasy theme analysis focuses on how an audience gives meaning to a rhetorical act, this approach can be particularly useful in film criticism.

Film can provide a cathartic experience, as demonstrated by the popularity of films about Vietnam fifteen years after the American withdrawal. Dramatism can be used to examine film as a vehicle for purification and redemption. The pentad (scene, act, agent, agency, and purpose) and the ratios among its elements can be particularly helpful in discovering important symbols in a film or group of films. Because dramatism conceptualizes "literature" as equipment for living and films are a form of literature, this approach can be used in determining how a film came to be a metaphor for how to conduct one's life.

Because some of the examples in Chapter 7 were drawn from film studies, you may already have concluded that elements of the cultural models are applicable in rhetorical criticism of film. The social-values and Jungian models were created specifically for film analysis and offer excellent systems for criticism. One of the ways to extend these models is to apply them to film genres that are different from those to which they have already been applied. As we have suggested, films visualize ideology. Therefore, ideological criticism, particularly the development of ideological models beyond Marxism and feminism, is possible if you select other political, economic, religious, or social-belief systems as your basis for evaluating popular films.

In this chapter we have tried to give you a sense of the rhetorical properties of film. Both limited distribution documentary films and nationally released commercial entertainment films afford the critic the opportunity to study a form of communication that provides us with information, social criticism, and interpretations of our culture. As a result of experiencing life on film, we may do things differently, change our minds about some person, place, or event, and ultimately extend the boundaries of our consciousness. As a result of engaging in film criticism, you will expand your understanding not only of this medium but also of the specific rhetorical properties of a single-message movie or the films of a particular auteur or genre.

Suggested Readings

Examples of Criticism

FRENTZ, T.S., AND FARRELL, T.B. (1975).   Conversion of America's consciousness: The rhetoric of *The Exorcist. Quarterly Journal of Speech, 61,* 40–47.

> *The Exorcist* was one of the most popular films at the time of its release and one of the top-ten moneymakers in film history. Frentz and Farrell conclude that its popularity can be explained in terms of how it represented a value change for Americans. This is an excellent example of how to apply cultural concepts to a film to discuss its appeal and how a critic draws conclusions about a film.

RUSHING, J.H. (1983).   The rhetoric of the American western myth. *Communication Monographs, 50,* 14–32.

> Rushing is one of the best, most-productive rhetorical critics of film; any of her works can serve as models for doing rhetorical criticism. This article contains a

complete history of the rhetorical aspects of Westerns, the most comprehensive rhetorical analysis of the traditional Western film and the paradox of community versus individual values available. If you want to study any film genre rhetorically, we recommend this article as a starting point to see how it's done.

RUSHING, J.H. (1989). Evolution of "the new frontier" in *Alien* and *Aliens*: Patriarchal co-optation of the feminine archetype. *Quarterly Journal of Speech, 75*, 1–24.
> Rushing applied some of her earlier views on the Western myth, combined with feminist concepts and religious myths, to analyze popular science fiction films rhetorically. In the traditional Western, women played secondary roles. In *Alien* and *Aliens,* elements of the frontier of the old West exist but the male hero has been replaced. Rushing traces the evolution of a dominant feminine archetype in religious mythology and applies it to the character Ripley in the two films, discussing a hybrid of the frontier myth and religious myth found in the new frontier of outer space.

WILLIAMS, D.E. (1984). *2001: A Space Odyssey*: A warning before its time. *Critical Studies in Mass Communication, 1,* 311–322.
> Williams uses dramatism to analyze Stanley Kubrick's *2001*. This article is an excellent example of how to use Kenneth Burke's concepts of hierarchy and the redemptive process to interpret a film rhetorically. Williams concluded that *2001* was a warning to humans to not be too dependent on the technology they have created and that the final sequence of the film offered a religious vision to transcend this dependence.

Resources for Doing Criticism

BYWATER, T., AND SOBCHACK, T. (1989). *Introduction to film criticism: Major critical approaches to narrative film.* New York: Longman.
> This is a textbook about different types of film criticism: humanist, auteurist, genre, social science, historical, and theoretical-ideological. The book explores why film criticism is done in various academic and professional disciplines, how a critic from each discipline approaches film, and what uses are made of the resulting criticism. Excellent and varied examples illustrate each approach to criticism. A complete glossary of film terms and a comprehensive bibliography of materials on criticism are included.

CAGIN, S. AND DRAY, P. (1984). *Sex, drugs, violence, rock 'n' roll, and politics: Hollywood films of the seventies.* New York: Harper & Row.
> This book is an account of Hollywood's brief golden age of political movies of the late sixties and the decade of the seventies, a running analysis of the rhetorical properties of films made during a volatile period of American history. Background and "insider" information about films and the people who made them, the authors' comments on the politics and social movements of the era, and their interpretations of well-known films—in light of events happening at the time—make this a useful source and a good read.

ELLIS, J. C. (1985). *A history of film* (2nd ed.). Englewood Cliffs, NJ: Prentice-Hall.
> Many books of this type are available. Most do a good job of describing the development of the medium, but we chose this one because it discusses film history in terms of events, issues, and beliefs that were current when each film was produced. This excellent general reference source includes international and third-world films and has excellent bibliographies for each segment of film history.

HARRINGTON, J. (1973). *The rhetoric of film*. New York: Holt, Rinehart, & Winston.
This book explains how the various grammatical elements (shots, scenes, themes, narrative voice, and the like) are used by the viewer to draw meaning from a film. The examples are not drawn from actual movies but from material Harrington had shot because he wants the reader to be able to use these film concepts as a basis for understanding the viewing experience, rather than just assimilating his interpretations of familiar films. This is one of the most comprehensive discussions of the grammar of film available.

MARSDEN, M.T., NACHBAR, J.G., AND GROGG, S.L. (1982). *Movies as artifacts: Cultural criticism of popular film*. Chicago: Nelson-Hall.
This anthology of articles on film covers the early days of film, the nature of the film industry, the Hollywood star system, movies as signs of attitudes and value change, and how movies are used by viewers to understand the nature of being human. Well-known films such as *Gone with the Wind* and some film genres are covered. This is a good background source on American film as a cultural artifact.

PALMER, W.J. (1987). *The films of the seventies: A social history*. Metuchen, NJ: The Scarecrow Press.
This is an excellent example of in-depth film criticism from a social-rhetorical perspective. The chapter on movie villains of the seventies is a fascinating discussion of the corporation as a villain. In particular, we recommed reading Chapter Seven, "The Forgotten Vietnam War Film," an analysis of *Go Tell The Spartans*, which Palmer says was the most accurate portrayal of the Vietnam War. This book is written in a straightforward, nonacademic style that produces effective criticism that is interesting to read.

PHILLIPS, W.H. (1985). *Analyzing films: A practical guide*. New York: Holt, Rinehart, & Winston.
This is a textbook on how to do film analysis. Its value lies in its complete guidelines for doing descriptive analysis of film. Phillips includes a section on writing, with many examples of ways to turn description into a written analytical statement. Chapter Six, "Viewer Responses," has a good discussion of symbolism in films.

ROLLINS, P.C. (1983). *Hollywood as historian: American film in a cultural context*. Lexington, KY: The University Press of Kentucky.
In this anthology, each article offers a historical interpretation of a particular film. Documentaries and entertainment films are included. Although the book is not a comprehensive source, each article provides good examples of how a film was used by audiences at the time of its release and how it now serves as part of the history of a period. Each article is thorough and well written and usually addresses some aspect of the rhetoric of the film.

SOLOMON, S.J. (1976). *Beyond formula: American film genres*. New York: Harcourt Brace Jovanovich.
This book begins with an explanation of genre as a legitimate category of film study, providing a good explanation of what is meant by film genres and the difficulty of categorizing films. Solomon's generic categories include Westerns, musicals, horror, crime, private eyes and police, and war. This is an excellent source on the narrative structures of different genres.

The

10

Rhetoric of

Television

Television is the youngest but possibly the most ubiquitous genre of communication we shall examine. The word *television* first appeared as part of a caption in a report by the International Congress of Electricians on 25 August 1900. By the end of 1922, Edward Belin had given a public demonstration of "tele-vision" in Paris. Only three years later, Charles Francis Jenkins demonstrated the first television that could send pictures more than a few feet, a system based on a mechanical process of spinning discs. By 1929, John Baird had started regular television service in London, and twenty-six stations were operating in the United States, but programming was spotty (Castleman and Podrazik, 1982). From these humble beginnings, television grew quickly into such an important medium of communication that only half a century later the number of American households with at least one television set was approaching ninety million, more than the number of American homes estimated to have a shower.

What explains the attraction that television holds for millions of Americans? What are its rhetorical properties? Television is an entertainment medium that combines the visual experience of going to the movies with the personal experience of listening to a favorite radio program in the comfort of your living room.

> Unlike any previous form of entertainment, television brought lifelike images directly into homes throughout the country by the mere flick of a switch, allowing people

> thousands of miles apart to see, share, and learn the same
> things together. (CASTLEMAN AND PODRAZIK, 1982, p. v)

Television is neither movies shrunk to fit inside a box nor radio with pictures added. To understand television's rhetorical properties, it is first necessary to understand how it differs from film and other forms of rhetorical activity.

Television and Other Genres of Communication

Like most films, television programming is designed to make money for the companies that produce it. This is done by selling commercial advertising time to sponsors or by selling programming directly to viewers in the case of premium cable channels. The predominance of the former approach means that, unlike the film audience, the television audience shares its influence over the content of the rhetorical act with advertisers. Also, because broadcast signals travel through the public airwaves, the government regulates certain communication practices through the Federal Communications Commission (FCC). These groups, in addition to television networks themselves through executive decision making, influence the content of television.

Sponsors may be the most powerful group because their decisions ultimately determine what gets on the air.

> Reginald Rose's 1954 drama Thunder on Sycamore Street,
> for Studio One, sponsored by Westinghouse, was based
> on a real racial incident in Chicago in which a black
> family moved into an all-white housing project and the
> whites stoned them. Westinghouse refused to allow the
> family to be black. Rose converted the blacks to the family
> of a white ex-convict to satisfy the advertiser's
> demands. (HIMMELSTEIN, 1984, p. 168)

This is not to suggest that the networks are without power. Like the producers of films, the networks do affect program content. Although the networks are frequently accused of having a liberal bias, during the Vietnam War, political expression on entertainment programming that opposed it was carefully monitored. We shall discuss the problems this posed for the popular Smothers Brothers program in Chapter 11. Network decision making reflects not only the tastes and political ideology of executives but also their concern for the tastes and ideology of sponsors. These executives realize that to make their product enticing to sponsors, they must deliver the largest possible audience for their commercial messages.

> Television is, above all else, a popular culture medium.
> The economics that determine its production and

> distribution demand that it reaches a mass audience, and a mass audience in western industrial societies is composed of numerous subcultures, or subaudiences, with a wide variety of social relations, a variety of socio-cultural experience and therefore a variety of discourse that they will bring to bear upon the program in order to understand and enjoy it. For its own purposes television attempts to homogenize this variety so that one program can reach as many different audiences as possible. (FISKE, 1987b, p. 37)

The third mediating audience, government, also shapes television. Unlike films, the form and to some extent the content of what we see and hear on television is regulated by the government. Through the FCC, government regulates such things as the length and placement of blocks of commercial air time. Television is really a format, a combination of program genre, length, and scheduled air time. Whenever the FCC changes its rules on commercials, it indirectly changes the look of television programming (Eliot, 1981).

Television programming is highly segmented, so much so that the "television time out" had to be invented to enable the networks to cover sports such as football, basketball, and hockey. The flow of these sports made them difficult, if not impossible, to cover within the framework of government regulations on the timing and placement of commercials. The plots of entertainment programs are structured into "12 minute acts, each with a climax, and a happy ending" (Himmelstein, 1984, p. 160) so that the requisite "message from our sponsor" can be fit in.

These commercial breaks are more than merely annoying, the structure they impose produces a predictability unlike anything we find in film. The typical structure of a one-hour program, whether it is a cowboy story, a doctor story, a detective story, or some other genre, was described by Himmelstein (1984): The program's prologue reveals the basic crisis or conflict that the plot will center around and then cuts to a commercial break. Tension begins to rise in the next program segment as subplots or complications are introduced into the situation developed in the prologue, and another commercial break takes place. When we return from the advertisements, tension continues to rise. While headway is made in resolving the plot's central crisis, additional complications crop up, followed by a pause for a "message from our sponsor." Plot development culminates in the denouement in which tension is brought to its peak and resolved. After the final commercial break, the epilogue and credits produce in the audience a sense of relief and closure.

Obviously, this format is not universally followed. Soap operas never reach a point of closure in their story lines and for this reason do not have a point of equilibrium from which they begin each day (Fiske, 1987b). This makes them unique because, as Silverstone (1988) points out, "[t]he chronologic is the logic of the logic of the individual story. The beginning, middle, and end of it; the functional logic of the hero, of test, of search, of success and failure" (p. 33). The simplicity of this basic story form makes the individual stories told on television easy to grasp.

Nowhere is the difference between film and television as storytelling media more graphically apparent than in the relative effectiveness of the made-for-television movie.

> One reason the made-for-TV movie is more effective on commercial television than the theatrical film is that the former has been hierarchically constructed with commercial breaks in mind. Plot action thereby occurs in a way that will not be harmed (and may even be helped) by the interposition of spot clusters. Created initially for uninterrupted movie house or pay cable exhibition, the feature film, on the other hand, has not been written to breaks. When a commercial network injects advertisements, these often come at inopportune moments and sever the stair step pattern of rising tension. (ORLIK, 1988, p. 192)

Therefore, the first major difference between television and other forms of rhetorical activity, particularly film, lies in the impact of mediating audiences, sponsors, network censors, and government agencies. What the audience for television rhetoric sees and hears has been constrained by forces that do not impinge on film in the same way.

The manner in which the audience attends to the rhetorical activity on television is also different. Unlike the audience for a film, concert, or public speech, at least in the days before television, the television audience is made up of small groups separated from each other and the rhetor by great distances. As a result, they are much freer to devote different levels of attention to the rhetorical act. Some watch and listen with rapt attention, others may have television on while they do something else. The predictable structure of television makes this sort of inattentive viewing possible. For this latter group, their full attention is gained only by something out of the ordinary.

> This is another way in which television differs from film, which has to cater for only a single mode of watching and does not have to compete for the viewer's attention. . . . Television is normally viewed within the domestic familiarity of the living room, which contrasts significantly with the public impersonal place of the cinema. In going out to cinema we submit to its terms, to become subject to its discourse, but television comes to us, enters our cultural space, and becomes subject to our discourses. (FISKE, 1987b, p. 74)

Although the filmgoer can certainly get up and leave, or an audience member at a public speech can tune out a boring speaker, neither of them is capable of doing what the experienced television viewer can do. Because of the predictable structure of television and the availability of competing viewing options, the experienced viewer can elect to watch several programs simultaneously, a process called *zapping*. The zapper uses knowledge of the media to fill in the gaps produced by switching back and forth.

> Zapping allows the viewer to construct a viewing experience of fragments, a postmodern collage of images whose pleasures lie in their discontinuity, their juxtaposition, and their contradictions. This is segmentation taken to the extreme of fragmentation and makes of television the most open producerly text for it evades all attempts at closure. It is a form of scratch video that produces an individualized television text out of its mass-produced works. (FISKE, 1987b, p. 105)

As a consequence, the concept of the audience for television rhetoric, both as it relates to audience use of the rhetorical act and the meaning they create for it, differs from that of other communication genres.

A third way in which television differs from film is in its visual properties. The almost square aspect ratio of the much smaller television picture obviously differs from the huge rectangular movie screen. Differences in aspect ratio are most significant for critics who use videotaped copies of movies to do rhetorical criticism of film. Part of what the movie audience saw in a theater will be missing on television unless the videotape was produced using a technique called "letter boxing." When a film is letter boxed, a portion of the top and bottom of the television screen is blacked out so that the aspect ratio of the image is correct. Few films are letter boxed. Most are reedited onto videotape using a process called "panning and scanning." This technique changes the film substantially because the camera moves back and forth across the scene to pick up action in ways that bear no resemblance to the original. The camera may also remain fixed on one part of the scene ignoring the rest. A film that has been badly panned and scanned can be laughable or unintelligible, but in either case the critic's ability to make intelligent judgments about it is compromised.

The most important visual difference is the comparative lower resolution of the television picture. Television images are of lower quality and are less capable of rendering fine detail at a distance than motion picture film. As a result:

> television is particularly well suited to representing human action in human terms—its small screen and comparatively poor definition lead it to concentrate on midshots and close-ups of people acting, reacting, and interacting. Its repetition and its origin in studios rather

> than exterior locations lead it to rely on familiar interior
> settings of a human domestic scale that fit comfortably
> into the family room within which it is usually
> viewed. (FISKE, 1987b, p. 22)

It will be important to keep television's low-resolution images in mind when we discuss aspects of its technical properties in the next section of this chapter.

Style of editing and the level of apparent action also create visual-image differences between television and film. Coupled with the predictability of its format, the smaller size and lower quality of the television picture requires careful editing to capture and hold the audience's attention.

> Motivated editing, which developed as the classic
> Hollywood realist style, tries to make the work of the
> editor and director as invisible as possible. It does this by
> giving the impression that the edits are always required or
> motivated by the events in the "reality" that the camera is
> recording; they are never the result of the desire to tell a
> story in a particular way. This produces the effect of
> seamlessness, of a continuous flow, with no manufactured
> joins or edges. Of course this is, in practice, all
> nonsense—television is heavily edited, with cuts occurring
> on average about every seven or eight seconds. This
> maintains a high degree of visual stimulation—constantly
> changing signifiers is a televisual characteristic—and
> seems to be required by television's less than imposing
> visual image and its typical mode of repetition. (FISKE,
> 1987b, pp. 26-27)

Finally, television rhetoric differs from that of other genres of communication in that it can provide its own contextual basis for interpretation. Television audiences, like the audience for any other form of communication, can create meaning for its visual and verbal symbols by grounding them in patterns of previous experiences. Television helps create and maintain the mythology of our culture. "In helping to pattern the relationships among basic beliefs, values, and behaviors that organize social interaction, myths produce common social under-standings of new social conditions" (Breen and Corcoran, 1982, p. 128). Television, however, provides its own microscopic and macroscopic contexts, which the audience frequently uses in interpreting its mythology.

On the microscopic level, the contextual basis for understanding television's rhetorical acts is found in previous iterations of the acts. Television programming is primarily episodic and follows either the *series* or *serial* format. Series, such as *Magnum P.I.* and *Charlie's Angels,* are a programming format in which the main characters and their situation remain the same from episode to episode, each of which tells a complete story. A serial, such as *Dallas* or *Hill Street Blues,* preserves not only the main characters and their situation from episode to episode but continues their story as well (Ang, 1982).

Because situations really do not change much from week to week, the audience—though free to interpret single episodes in isolation—gains deeper understanding by interpreting subsequent episodes in the context of previous ones. Television series repeat underlying principles through characterization, plot lines, and topical themes. Those principles are easier to grasp after seeing them repeated. The main characters become "exemplary models for a whole society in a process that translates a single life-history into an archetype, thereby setting up patterns for imitation" (Breen and Corcoran, 1982, p. 129).

Much television programming is not only repetitive but imitative as well. Television features "simple stories, easily recognizable, continually reiterated, and remarkably similar in form and content not only to each other but to other stories in other cultures at other times" (Silverstone, 1988, p. 22). The spin-off, a program that takes characters from a well-established series and relocates them in a series of their own, is a programming staple.

The actors who played George Jefferson and Maude Findlay, two of Archie Bunker's well-defined antagonists on *All in the Family,* were spun off to create *The Jeffersons* and *Maude. Happy Days* was largely recast after being derived from a story entitled "Love in the Happy Days," which aired on the anthology *Love, American Style.* The actresses who played Laverne DiFazio and Shirley Feeney, two relatively minor *Happy Days* characters, ended by starring in the spin-off *Laverne and Shirley,* and Erin Moran and Scott Baio landed in the short-lived *Joannie Loves Chachi.*

Spin-offs involve characters from successful programs because broadcasters and sponsors hope the audience will follow them from the original show to the situation created in the new show. In part, viewers who tune in the new show do so because they found the characters interesting before, but they also watch because they know what to expect from the characters in their new shows. On the microscopic level, a spin-off has a context for understanding provided by its parent show. Principles of characterization, plot, and themes may be carried over from the parent show. Depending on how the spin-off is scheduled, macroscopic contextuality may also come into play.

On the macroscopic level, the context for understanding television as rhetorical activity is provided by the flow of the television medium itself. Fiske (1987b) suggests that even though the flow of television is interrupted by commercials, the medium possesses flow in the sense that it is continuous, never ending, and some stations broadcast twenty-four hours a day. The time and date that a program is aired provide a context for understanding it. Programming flow is designed by network executives for economic rather than ideological reasons. A program is scheduled to realize its potential to deliver the biggest audience to the sponsor.

> In the USA two sorts of strategy have evolved to promote
> flow and encourage channel loyalty, one of scheduling,

and one of promotion. Scheduling strategy designs the
sequence and choice of programs in an attempt to build
and hold a large prime-time audience whose
demographics are desired by advertisers. It will typically
use a strong "lead-in" program to begin prime time and
attract the audience that must be held. Then two
alternative, or alternating, strategies are used. "Tent-
poling" consists of placing a strong, popular program at
the peak of prime time and "hanging" less popular ones
on either side of it. "Hammocking" consists of suspending
a weaker or newer program between two strong, well-
established ones. Both strategies, as their metaphorical
names suggest, aim to tie programs together into an
unbroken flow and to produce equivalently unbroken
viewing in the audience. This scheduling strategy is then
supported by the promotional, in which "promos" for
programs later in the evening are inserted early into the
flow, so that later programs are tied in to earlier
ones. (FISKE, 1987b, p. 102)

Network executives consider flow in scheduling. Essentially, they are concerned with whether the program length is right for its subject, if the time of day
chosen is one that can deliver the desired audience, how the program stacks up
against the competition, and how it relates to the programs that precede and
follow it (Orlik, 1988). Location is everything in determining how well a particular televisual "property" will sell and how it will be viewed.

When CBS scheduled *Cagney and Lacey* after *Magnum* on a
Thursday evening, it rated poorly. But when rescheduled
on a Monday following *Scarecrow and Mrs. King, Kate and
Allie* and *Newhart* it topped the ratings. Monday became
known as "women's night" and *Cagney and Lacey* was
shifted away from the masculine generic relations with
Magnum and towards more feminine ones. Because *Cagney
and Lacey* shows a particularly even mix of generic
characteristics, its prime genre was in some doubt, and so
scheduling was able to tip the balance away from
masculine cop show towards soap opera or woman's
show. (FISKE, 1987b, p. 113)

The regulative, image quality, audience attention, and contextual differences
between television and other communication genres all influence the ability of
television to function rhetorically. How the medium encodes messages—the
technical properties of lighting, camera work, and editing—also influences its
ability to function rhetorically.

Television's Technical Properties

Lighting, camera work, and editing are the technical properties of television programming through which a televised rhetorical act is cocreated in the work of script writers, set designers, head costumers, makeup artists, and directors. Lighting, camera work, and editing encode messages, adapting to the constraints of television's low-resolution visual image.

Lighting

Light is the primary technical element of television; television, quite literally, could not exist without it. Its visual image is composed by illuminating points of light on the screen. *Notan lighting* provides a level of illumination that flattens out the images of the actors and the set. Under such lighting conditions, if a character is to stand out or be emphasized, a particular kind of camera shot is selected. Actors can also attempt to overcome the constraints of lighting by attracting the viewer's attention through characterization.

The other form of lighting is *chiaroscuro lighting,* which was an important part of black and white filmmaking, particularly in film noir, in the 1930s and 1940s. It "is concerned not only with illumination but also with the way it can determine and contrast with shadow . . . an important element for pictorial composition and mood enhancement" (Orlik, 1988, p. 88).

The link between black and white film technology and television is that, with the exception of old series presently in syndication, today's television programming is almost entirely in color. Given its lower resolution compared with film, the mechanics of light and shadow differ between the two media. Television can literally swallow up characters standing in deep shadow, rendering its visual image even less imposing. Mood and tone, easily established by lighting in film, are created more by camera placement and editing in television.

Camera Work

Camera location exists in a horizontal and a vertical plane relative to the scene. Characters can be seen head on, in profile, from behind, and from an almost infinite variety of intermediate compass points. When the subject faces and addresses the camera, the psychological effect is one of making the viewer part of the action (Orlik, 1988). It can also have the effect of producing metatelevision, as occurred on *Moonlighting* whenever the leading characters would turn and address the audience directly, commenting on what was going on in the show. Metatelevision is used to stimulate viewer involvement, but overuse breaks the viewer's sense of television's communication rules.

When the camera-subject relationship places the viewer face-to-face with one of the characters, it does not usually do so in a way that suggests the viewer is literally taking the place of one of the show's other characters. Not only would this seem an inappropriate invasion of the viewer's home, it would also make the viewer's position ethically ambiguous and uncomfortable. Although we are amused, entertained, or intrigued by the plot twists in series or serial television, a program's self-generated contexts for understanding mean that viewers know roughly what will happen and that it will happen within the next thirty or sixty minutes. This sense of omniscience allows for inattentive viewing but also requires a program to engage viewers' attention without involving them directly. "The omniscience given us by this dominant discourse of the camera depends also upon our position as an invisible eavesdropper-voyeur who can hear, see, and understand all without the characters' knowledge. 'Reality' is laid bare before us," (Fiske, 1987b, p. 28).

The composition of the image captured by the camera lens can produce a variety of meanings. Closeups suggest intimacy, and medium or full shots suggest personal or social relationships. Long shots provide the context for the action. Editing techniques such as fades, dissolves, and cuts serve as the signifiers of beginnings, endings, simultaneity, and excitement (Berger, 1981). Because most programming is produced on sound stages, and with the limitations of television's visual image, television emphasizes closeups, medium, and full shots of people talking. "Two and three shots establish identities, spatial relationships, and location, and then the camera moves in on the individual," (Fiske, 1987b, p. 149). Editing creates the impression of motion in an otherwise static scene.

Editing

The durations of shots and the rapidity with which transitions are made between scenes determine the program's pace. Other techniques create the illusion that what is essentially a two-dimensional medium actually has a third dimension, making what is fairly static appear dynamic. Graphic, index, and motion vectors can create the impression of action even when the camera remains stationary (Zettl, 1981).

A *graphic vector* gives the impression of a third dimension. It is established when stationary elements are arranged in such a way that they lead our eyes in a certain direction, as does a line of telephone poles receding into the distance. This third dimension is also suggested when characters are placed closer to, or farther from, the camera. *Index vectors* include such nonverbal signifiers as a person looking or pointing in a direction, drawing the viewer's attention toward the apparent focus of their attention. *Motion vectors* are also nonverbal signifiers, but they involve action that crosses the camera's field of vision, such as a person running or a car driving by.

Editing knits everything together. If a speaker and an audience index their apparent relationship by looking to the left and right, respectively, in two separate shots, editing them together would imply they are looking at each other. The motion indexes of a suspect fleeing to the left, pursued by a police officer running to the right, when edited together would signify a pursuit that will probably end in failure because the characters appear to be going in different directions. If the officer were to appear suddenly with the suspect in custody, the earlier misconvergence of their respective motion indexes would undermine the audience's sense of reality in what they were seeing.

Getting these details right is important to television's ability to serve a rhetorical purpose. How a program is crafted determines the audience's willingness to watch. Orlik (1988) suggests that viewers experience television on sensuous, expressive, and productional-technical planes. The sensuous plane involves the pleasure the viewer derives from experiencing the sights and sounds of television. The expressive plane relates to the meaning audience members derive from the viewing experience. But the productional-technical plane "includes not just the recording and manipulation of sound, illumination, and substance, but also the skills and techniques that writers, actors, directors, and technicians bring to the program property. The most adroit manipulations will not even be noticed by the audience, but their absence or mishandling would be widely felt" (Orlik, 1988, p. 68)

When television gets the details right, it creates a sense of reality that is sufficiently convincing to engage the audience's attention and to expose them to whatever rhetorical acts it transmits. "We can thus call television an essentially realistic medium because of its ability to carry a socially convincing sense of the real" (Fiske, 1987b, p. 21). This sense of reality is seen in various types of television programming.

We begin by examining the rhetorical properties of what you might think of as televised "real events": news, sports, and documentary programming. Following discussion of this type of programming, we shall consider fictional-entertainment programming offered by series and serial television. Finally, we shall examine narrow-casting, television channels devoted to a single programming focus such as music television.

News, Sports, and Documentary Programming

Programming of this type, especially news and sports, creates a tremendous impression of reality because much of it is broadcast in "real time." The development of satellite technology affords television the opportunity to cover stories around the world and to bring visual information into the viewer's living room almost instantaneously. With the exception of live coverage of anticipated events such as inaugurations, press conferences, and the Super Bowl, television broadcasting is rarely raw footage of events as they happen.

When the unanticipated occurs, such as an attempted or successful presidential assassination or the explosion of the space shuttle *Challenger,* networks may break into their regular programming and cover events as they unfold in real time. But this is a rarity. More often the network returns to regular programming and breaks in from time to time "as more details become available." Rhetorically, this means that "television news is a symbolic expression of a social construction of reality" (Bantz, 1975, p. 125). The productions of network news departments do not mirror reality; they interpret reality through production values such as camera angles. The reality of television news is influenced by editorial decisions about what to include in the newscast and where to place it.

News Coverage

News must be thought of as more than factual information because the television networks think of it as more than that. They view it as a commodity: something that costs them a lot of money to gather and distribute and something that they must be able to sell to advertisers (Fiske, 1987b). From this perspective, and given the placement of the newscast at various points in the broadcast day, it should not be surprising that "one of the guiding objectives of the newscast is to hold the attention of as large a proportion of the afternoon viewing audience as possible and begin building an audience for evening programming. This objective constrains the forms of the newscast, which are shaped so they are congruent with the audience expectations for the later shows" (Gregg, 1977, pp. 223–224).

As a result, the news must not only inform but entertain as well. This, coupled with time limits and the limitations of a primarily visual medium on communicating information, imposes several constraints on the typical newscast. These constraints shape the rhetorical properties of newscasts. With the exception of networks devoted to news, time becomes the first important constraint. The typical newscast is only thirty minutes long and must include several commercial breaks. As a result, only a minute or two can be devoted to all but the most significant breaking stories, and the diversity of events in a typical news day produces an amalgam of stories.

> Consequently, the interrelatedness of matters in a larger context drops by the way and viewers are hard pressed to understand how unemployment relates to shifting ecological priorities, or the birth rate twenty years earlier. . . . Further, the segmentation of time on the typical newscast creates a kind of flatness to the overall news presentation, a giving of equal weight to the discussion of a natural disaster in Bolivia which causes widespread death, the remarks of a presidential candidate carried in a *Playboy* interview, and the opportunity to start the day with a breakfast cereal which is full of health giving bran fibers. (GREGG, 1977, pp. 224–225)

The second constraint imposed on television news is the visual nature of the medium. With so many stories to choose from and so little time to tell them, stories with a strong visual dimension tend to be favored. The highly visual story is both easier to tell and more in keeping with the entertainment imperative of the news. Cross (1983) suggests the term D.G.S.N.W., "dull government shit nobody watches," is used by network news insiders to describe events that lack a visual hook to hang the story on.

Presuming the event has sufficient visual appeal to attract the interest of the news department, it must meet four other tests as well. First, it must have occurred recently, preferably within the last twenty-four hours. Second, it should concern people with whom the audience is already familiar, either as individuals or as the representative of some group. Third, it should relate to public rather than domestic events unless the domestic event can serve as a metaphor for a larger social issue. Fourth, it should be negative. Negative events are more rhetorically powerful than positive events in the view of television newscasters because they possess tension and dramatic conflict (Fiske, 1987b).

The key in news story selection is whether a story can be personalized in its telling. "Personalization tends to get depicted in two presentational forms which are sometimes intermingled: the 'cast of characters' form and the form of 'argon' which stresses conflict, gamesmanship and strategy" (Gregg, 1977, p. 229). Personalization afforded by a familiar cast of characters results in focusing on newsmakers, the person associated with the story. Argon (a form of news story in which events are cast as a game or conflict) results in casting events into a simpler storyline. Thus, a woman who shoots her abusive husband becomes televisually newsworthy if her action is discovered almost immediately. She can be characterized to represent a group (abused women) or a social problem (spouse abuse), and her story is negative because it shows a tear in the otherwise apparently perfect fabric of society.

The ability to tell the story so soon after it happens contributes to the sense of apparent objectivity and authenticity engendered by its telling. "The instantaneity implies that there has been no time for editorializing or reworking, that television brings us events-as-they-happen" (Fiske, 1987b, p. 289). This is obviously false. Television is words as well as pictures, and it is a rare occasion indeed when the visual image is left to stand on its own, without comment, in news, sports, or documentary programming.

The way in which the verbal content of news coverage is chosen reflects the fourth constraint. The necessity of having entertainment value in news broadcasts influences how the rhetorical act unfolds. "Entertainment is the supra-ideology of all discourse on television. No matter what is depicted or from what point of view, the overarching presumption is that it is there for our amusement and pleasure," (Postman, 1985, p. 87). The most egregious examples of news-as-entertainment probably occurred when so-called happy news, in which the on-air talent engages in cheerful banter between stories, came into favor.

The real impact of the entertainment imperative is on how news stories are told. Cross (1983) suggests that news stories are constructed like plays, using elements that Aristotle would have labeled as incitement, complication, and resolution. The play begins with a line that grabs our attention but does not actually tell us what happened, the *incitement*. Next comes the story itself, which focuses on some tension or conflict, the *complication*. "Newswriters generally try to wrap up their brief story-dramas with a 'snapper closer' . . . a sense of resolution so viewers can relax and stop worrying, at least for one day, about the problem" (Cross, 1983, p. 66), the *resolution*.

Fiske and Hartley (1978) have suggested that television functions like the bard in earlier times, articulating cultural values, implicating members of the culture in its value system, and celebrating the achievements of individual representatives of the culture. If that is true, what significance does it impart to the role of television news anchor? Those individuals—who are more modestly called "news readers" in England—become, like their print counterparts, the living symbols of the truthfulness of their own work. "These journalist heroes allow viewers to vicariously watch the unapproachable bureaucrat or the arrogant general (who never answered letters of complaint or phone calls) brought to his knees by the crafty and efficient journalist, the modern-day personification of the Homeric epic hero" (Himmelstein, 1984, p. 203). There are two potential problems with this characterization, both of which are related to the entertainment imperative.

The first problem has to do with the way some news stories are recorded and edited. Recall our earlier discussion of television editing and how reaction shots are used to signify interaction. This has conditioned viewers to recognize certain conventions about the way conversation occurs on television. An interview is a form of televised conversation. For entertainment, or possibly for political or ideological reasons, this same editing technique that is used in fictional entertainment is used in news coverage.

> In news or current affairs programs location interviews are normally shot with a single camera trained on the interviewee. After the interview is finished, the camera is then turned on the interviewer who asks some of the questions again and gives a series of "noddies," that is, reaction shots, nods, smiles, or expressions of sympathetic listening. These are used to disguise later edits in the interviewee's speech. When a section of this speech is edited out, the cut is disguised by inserting a "noddy," thus hiding the fact that any editing of the speaker's words has occurred. Without the "noddy," the visuals would show an obvious "jump" that would reveal the edit. (FISKE, 1987b, p. 29)

The second problem relates to the implications of selecting anchors and other on-air personalities on the basis of entertainment rather than journalistic criteria. Christine Craft was fired from her news job with a Kansas City television station because viewers did not like the way she looked, a decision that represents issues of taste and style winning out over content. Serious implications are contained in the notion "that the perception of truth of a report rests heavily on the acceptability of the newscaster" (Postman, 1985, p. 101).

Although the entertainment imperative and other constraints on television news may impair its ability to cover certain kinds of stories, there is no denying the potential rhetorical power of television news coverage. Although the debate over who lost the war in Vietnam continues, some people feel that television coverage played a major role in changing public opinion. Unlike previous wars, Vietnam was a television war, brought into the nation's living rooms by the nightly network news. For many people, television was the primary source of information about the war. As a result, people across this country watched what television showed them instead of listening to what their leaders told them about Vietnam (Castleman and Podrazik, 1982).

Television news remains an important source of information. It has "achieved the status of 'meta-medium'—an instrument that directs not only our knowledge of the world, but our knowledge of *ways of knowing* as well" (Postman, 1985, pp. 78–79). Pseudoevents staged by national leaders to attract news coverage are efforts to shape public opinion by focusing attention on something. They are covered with the same care and attention as those events that mark important historical milestones and transmit the cultural values of security and involvement that were part of the tradition of the Celtic bard. Commenting on coverage of Ronald Reagan's 1980 inauguration, Cross (1983) noted that "Reagan even included television directions on the advance text of his inaugural address so cameramen would be sure to maximize the majesty of the moment" (pp. 188–189).

Television news is constrained by time, the visual nature of the medium, and the entertainment imperative. Sports coverage is similar in many ways. Like the news, entire cable networks are devoted to sports. Like the news, some sporting events are broadcast in real time, and others are edited and shown after the fact. Like news, sports is entertainment. However, sports coverage is sufficiently different from news coverage in its rhetorical properties to warrant separate consideration.

Sports Coverage

Sports is certainly an important part of every network's schedule. The national interest in baseball, basketball, and football almost insures an audience, making televised sporting events easy to sell to sponsors. The question remains, is television coverage of sports rhetorical? We believe coverage in real time is definitely rhetorical and delayed coverage, using edited versions of the action, has the potential to be rhetorical. Our focus is on live coverage because the rhetorical properites of after-the-fact coverage as storytelling are similar to those of the nightly news and series entertainment programs.

Live sports coverage is rhetorical because it must attract and hold its audience. The sports broadcasters must persuade the audience to "stay tuned." People would probably continue to watch a Super Bowl tied 10–10 going into the fourth quarter no matter how inept the coverage, but most games are not the Super Bowl, nor are the scores that close. Most games face competing rhetors on other networks offering potentially more interesting contests.

The attraction of live televised sports lies in the rhetorical properties of its visual and verbal images. Visually, the game on television is different from anything spectators in the stands see. For spectators at the game, the action is continuous, without instant replay except in those stadiums that have installed facilities to mimic television. When basketball is televised,

> the action usually begins with a standard mid-court shot from high in the stands and thereafter action is segmented by switches to different camera shots . . . several separate viewpoints which rapidly move us closer to the action and isolate details central to the action. Also, we might see a dramatic postscript: a close-up profile of the player who slam-dunked the ball; shots showing elated fans' reaction to that play. (MORRIS AND NYDAHL, 1983, p. 200)

The visual images are more stimulating on television than in the stands, compensating the television viewer for the loss of the visceral stimulation of being part of the crowd at the arena.

Because the rhetorical act of live sports coverage occurs in real time, it is visually and verbally extemporaneous, unscripted, and unrehearsed. Even though preproduction meetings can discuss the range of possibilities that might occur after the game begins, and well-prepared sportscasters can do their homework on both teams, nothing is certain until play begins. The sportscaster contributes to the rhetorical properties of sports coverage by creating verbal images to accompany the visual images. The sportscaster can be an asset or a liability, depending on his or her verbal facility and preparation.

Unlike the stadium announcer who merely chronicles what has occurred on the field, the sportscaster is a cheerleader, not for either team, but for the game. The sportscaster is required to give an account of what is happening and, more importantly, to elaborate on it in order to intensify the drama of athletic competition. Keeping the audience tuned in for messages from the sponsors of the telecast is the real purpose. Intensifying competitive drama is rhetorically most important when the score is lopsided, but it is also rhetorically most difficult then. Holding the audience during a game that is "no contest" is the primary rhetorical purpose and the measure of excellence for the sportscaster-rhetor. The sportscaster who fails to invent dramatic devices to hold the audience will lose them to a more exciting contest.

Morris and Nydahl (1983) identify the kinds of statements sportscasters use to accomplish this purpose. In describing the action, the sportscaster makes objective statements of fact about what happened, offers expert interpretation of it, and places it in historical or statistical perspective. Elaborating on what has happened to intensify excitement is more complex and includes speculating about the motive of a coach or player for an action, the direction the game is taking, and the possible impact of an event on the final outcome.

The effective melding of the visual and verbal images of live televised sportscasting can contribute to achieving the purpose of attracting and holding the audience. The initial success of *ABC's Monday Night Football* may be attributable in part to the byplay between Don Meredith and Howard Cosell that accompanied Frank Gifford's play-by-play announcing. The commercial viability of later radio coverage of the Monday night games may also suggest that some people were watching with the sound turned off. In either case, live sports coverage constitutes a unique form of rhetorical activity.

Coverage of sporting events after the fact and coverage of pseudosports such as professional wrestling may also have rhetorical properties, but nothing distinguishes these forms of rhetorical activity from other televised entertainment. The documentary in its various permutations is different and represents a form of programming in which a significant amount of rhetorical activity takes place.

Documentary

The documentary film was examined in Chapter 9. We revisit documentaries in this chapter because the medium of television affords opportunities not available to the filmmaker. The term *television documentary* suggests reality programming. *Documentary* implies a connection to nonmediated events outside the usual scope of television news (Silverstone, 1988). Although television networks have produced documentaries, they have also documented significant events by literally turning over control of the airwaves to nonnetwork sources.

In 1951, the hearings of the Senate Crime Commission, more popularly known as the Kefauver Commission after its chairman Senator Estes Kefauver, ran live during daytime hours. The hearings drew audiences twenty times larger than the networks normally attracted with their daytime programming. In 1954, the DuMont Network covered the Army-McCarthy hearings in a similar manner (Castleman and Podrazik, 1982). This is a fundamentally different rhetorical experience for the audience than that which they would have received from exposure to network news coverage of these events or to subsequently produced documentaries about them.

The purpose of the television documentary in the classical sense of the term is to present "socially useful information to a public" (Bluem, 1965, p. 14), not merely to inform them but to influence or persuade them. Although television news may have the effect of persuading, that persuasion is largely a by-product of the constraints imposed on network news departments and by the medium itself. The documenting of events by making the airwaves available to nonnetwork sources places the responsibility for defining the persuasive purpose in the hands of rhetors such as Senators Kefauver and McCarthy, whereas producing a documentary by editing footage of actual persons and events places that decision in the hands of network researchers, writers, and directors.

Historically, documentaries produced by or for television could be classified as representing one of two types. The first type is the *thematic documentary*, a series of programs that deal with various aspects of one event or trace an individual's life and accomplishments in detail. The second type of documentary can best be described as part of an anthology. The *anthology documentary* is the product of a network decision to set aside time in its schedule each week for in-depth analyses of significant issues. Frequently produced by members of the news department, anthology documentaries have the look of a news report but the length of a thematic documentary.

The classic example of the thematic documentary is the twenty-six half-hour episodes chronicling U.S. naval operations during World War II, *Victory at Sea.* Aired first on NBC in 1952–53, these episodes were conceived by Henry Salomon who "brought to his art the gentleness of time remembered and an enlarged sense of humanity—a compassion in terms of the pictorial record of war's brutality" (Bluem, 1965, p. 146). This thematic documentary series was produced by reviewing over sixty million feet of film and editing sixty thousand feet of it into twenty-six episodes, each with an original score by Richard Rodgers. Each episode had a point of view or treated a specific part of naval operations, and the series was focused to make an "emotional statement about men and nations at war. This was evoked in different ways, as both aural and visual communication combined to transmit the artist's representation of life" (Bluem, 1965, p. 148). Available on videotape, *Victory at Sea* received widespread critical acclaim as both a rhetorical and an aesthetic accomplishment.

All of the major networks have produced anthology documentaries. The tradition of anthology documentary on CBS began with the series *See It Now,* which ran through *CBS Reports* and continues today in *60 Minutes* and *48 Hours.* Begun in 1951, with more of a televised newsreel than a documentary format, *See It Now* did not find its documentary voice until its third season. The series "built its largest audience . . . with its deliberate choice of those social conflicts which define the course of a free society, and thereby were of compelling interest to most Americans" (Bluem, 1965, p. 97). The program is best remembered for host Edward R. Murrow's famous confrontation with Senator Joseph McCarthy, but its more lasting contribution to the genre was the refinement of the cross-cut interview technique. The series ended in 1958 and reemerged as *CBS Reports* one year later (Castleman and Podrazik, 1982).

In 1960, *CBS Reports* produced *Harvest of Shame,* considered the most dramatic documentary of any of those produced by the networks that year. In his role as host-narrator, Edward R. Murrow won for himself and CBS as much attention as he had six years earlier in his confrontation with Senator Joseph McCarthy. Characterized as "an updated Grapes of Wrath" (Castleman and Podrazik, 1982, p. 142), it demonstrated the plight of America's migrant farm workers and the deplorable conditions in which they lived and worked, and it suggested specific legislative action to correct the problem. The growers' side of the issue was acknowledged, but the program was neither balanced nor impartial. It was aggressively rhetorical in its purpose and was criticized for its lack of impartiality. "The lessons of 'Harvest of Shame' had been observed, however, and thereafter most of its [*CBS Reports*] programs did seek to present impartial consideration of all issues" (Bluem, 1965, p. 107).

Television documentarists, especially those with strong ties to the network news department, face a challenge that their film counterparts do not. The journalist's ethic of telling the audience a story can come into conflict with the documentarist's ethic of telling the audience what the story means. When the documentary's rhetor—its host, narrator, or lead reporter—is normally seen in the role of news anchor or on-air personality, the potential for audience confusion over whether to create a meaning for the documentary as fact or as editorial opinion abounds.

Another source of confusion potentially exists in a new form of television documentary rooted in realistic filmmaking, the *docudrama*. "Docudramas are simply accurate re-creations of events in the lives of actual persons, as in the 'pure example' of *Missiles of October*" (Hoffer and Nelson, 1980, p. 150). The form may not be all that new since some of earliest television dramas were loosely based on actual events. The danger lies in the use of the term *docudrama* and the meaning that viewers may create for it by confusing fiction with fact and thinking of a docudrama in the same way they think of the news.

The worry about such confusion is not due to some elitist academic disdain for the common sense of the average television viewer but to the looseness with which the term *docudrama* is used in describing and promoting programming. The key terms in Hoffer and Nelson's (1980) definition of docudrama are *re-creations, events,* and the *lives of actual persons.* Their analysis of the types of programming aired as docudramas over a twelve-year period indicates wide disparity in what these key terms actually signify about programming.

Programs such as *Will Rogers USA,* which re-created events in an actual person's life through his own documented words, and *Missiles of October,* which re-created documented events surrounding the Cuban missile crisis, with an emphasis on the events rather than the people involved, are both docudramas. Unfortunately, the term is also applied to *Washington Behind Closed Doors* and *The Trial of Lee Harvey Oswald.* The former program was loosely based on events similar to those of the Watergate break-in and the subsequent cover-up which lead to President Richard Nixon's resignation, although actual persons were not identified. The latter program identified actual persons and speculated about what might have happened if President John F. Kennedy's alleged assassin had come to trial instead of being gunned down in the basement of the Dallas police station by Jack Ruby (Hoffer and Nelson, 1980).

News, sports, and documentary television programming all shape the viewer's reality because they mediate it. These types of nonfiction programming do not simply present information, they choose and mold it. The rhetorical properties of news are a consequence of adaptation of information to media constraints. Sports broadcasting, especially live coverage, uses the capability of television to heighten the excitement that normally surrounds athletic competition. Television documentaries can give viewers access to experiences in real time and information that they would not otherwise have, persuading viewers and possibly causing social change.

The tenuousness of the connection between some docudramas and the mediated reality that ties news, sports, and documentary together may cause you to wonder why we chose to discuss them here rather than in the following section, Fictional Entertainment. The choice is arbitrary because successful fictional-entertainment programming is also concerned with reality, or the appearance of reality. Fictional-entertainment programs make reality rather than mediating information drawn from the world of events and experiences found in nonfictional programs.

Fictional Entertainment

Because fictional-entertainment programming is largely formulaic and self-imitative, it is possible to discuss its rhetorical properties in terms of easily identified character types, locations, and plots. This is the approach we used in discussing film genres in Chapter 9. The same generic categories—Western, crime drama, comedy, science fiction, and war—can be used to do criticism of television's fictional-entertainment programming. Not all films and not all television fiction fit conveniently into generic classifications. Significant programs such as *All in the Family* and *Hill Street Blues*, do not so much fit into genres as restructure them by stretching or violating their conventions (Orlik, 1988).

In this chapter, we provide an alternative means of describing and evaluating fictional entertainment that can be used in doing film as well as television criticism. We approach fictional entertainment on television by asking two questions about it: What is its rhetorical format and what is its rhetorical vision?

Rhetorical Format

The format that makes televised fictional entertainment capable of functioning rhetorically is a product of three factors: television's place in society, the viewer's relationship to it and means of creating meaning for its messages, and the persuasive logic of the types of stories it tells. "Television, through its use of a powerful language comprising, images, words, gestures, clothing, settings, music, and sounds, has become one of our society's principal repositories of ideology" (Himmelstein, 1984, p. 3). Ideology both explains reality and functions normatively when it is repeated and reinforced through rhetorical activity.

Viewers use television for one or more reasons: "entertainment/time punctuation, information/surveillance, escapism/nostalgia, companionship/conversation building, problem solving, personal enrichment and development, and catharsis/tension release" (Orlik, 1988, pp. 115–116). The uses are numerous and varied, and the viewers may be unable to identify the specific reason for watching a particular program or the type of gratification they receive from watching it. Nevertheless, what they watch becomes rhetorical, either by the process of revelation or the process of accretion.

Watching television exposes the viewer to the persuasive messages of entertainment, and she may experience a *revelation* if the program touches an issue that concerns her. The revelation makes the viewing experience a significant emotional event and the program memorable as a rhetorical act. For instance, in an episode of *Kate and Allie,* Kate finds a condom among her pubescent son's possessions, agonizes over what to do, and finally confronts the problem successfully. A parent who has been wondering how to confront this, or any other, situation concerning sexuality as their son or daughter approaches puberty, or who is actually facing such a family crisis, might create meaning for the program in terms of the relevelations it provides. This viewer might use the program to ask and answer such questions as

1. How is our physical environment constituted?
2. What is society like?
3. What consequences flow from our actions?
4. What are our responsibilities?
5. What are the standards by which we should evaluate ourselves?   (ORLIK, 1988, pp. 201–202)

Although these questions were suggested by Orlik as a means by which the television critic could decode the content of a television program, which may or may not be concerned with all of them, they also represent the locus of rhetorical activity in prime-time programming for viewers who create meaning on the basis of accretion. *Accretion* is a process by which something builds up as material is added to it over time. It is not the significant emotional event of a single viewing experience that functions as the rhetorical act but rather the accumulation of multiple viewing experiences. A regular viewer of *Kate and Allie* would not remember and be persuaded by any one episode but by the show in toto. Whatever the program's message, it accumulates with messages from other favorite shows into a sense of how one ought to think and act. This is because of the underlying redundancy in prime-time programming.

Chesebro (1986) has argued that fictional-entertainment programming follows one of five communication systems. Each system represents a different view of the source of and the appropriate means for resolving social tension or conflict, and each reinforces a different social value system. *Kate and Allie* is mimetic, a term that will be explained shortly. The mimetic communication system is used in many popular prime-time programs. Therefore, the *Kate and Allie* fan has the opportunity to choose a number of shows that share its underlying perspective on social values, and the viewer who dislikes that show has a good chance of being exposed to its rhetorical vision in a show they do like. From the perspective of accretion, the rhetorical significance of redundancy in formulaic prime-time television lies not in genre but in the logic of plot types which cross traditional classifications of genre.

The audience for prime-time television's rhetoric, like the audience for any other genre of rhetorical activity, creates meaning for it.

> Any messages "communicated" by television series lie not
> so much "in" the program or "in" the intent of the
> producers, directors, writers, actors, and editors. Rather,
> the messages lie in the culture and codes which are shared
> by all these people—and their viewers. The program is
> but a series of cues that create viewer expectations—that
> "engages" an audience formally and substantively—and
> then, if the program is well-executed, satisfies and
> confirms those expectations. Different groups of viewers,
> of course, will be engaged on different levels or in
> different arenas-of-meaning, depending upon their
> sophistication, experiences, and the like . . .
> communication, in television as elsewhere, simply could
> not occur were it not for the presence of shared stocks of
> knowledge—knowledges of things, of cultureways, of
> signs and their related signifieds—which can be called up
> symbolically or iconically. (GRONBECK, 1984, p. 10)

This shared stock of knowledge comes from several places, only one of which is television.

Not everyone who watched Archie Bunker verbalize his prejudices every week on *All in the Family* thought he was wrong. The way some people read the show made him their hero, although most viewers got producer Norman Lear's point. More important from the perspective of accretion, however, is the fact that as television watching increases, less time is available for other pursuits that might provide information contradicting the self-confirming messages of fictional-entertainment programming. Gordon Shumway, better known as *ALF*, makes this point in the extreme. Everything he knew about our society before crashing into the Tanner family's garage, and much of what he has learned since then, comes from television. The trouble he gets into because of his literal reading of television is amusing, but it should also be taken as cautionary (Rybacki and Rybacki, 1989).

Unlike Gordon Shumway, most television viewers do not take what they see on prime-time television literally. They may, nevertheless, be persuaded to think and act in certain ways by the accretion of messages that support certain social values. Before turning to the question of what prime-time television's rhetorical vision might contain, it is necessary to examine the communication systems it uses and the underlying value orientation inherent in each.

Ironic Television

The *ironic communication system* has been termed "the rhetoric of the loser" (Chesebro, 1986, p. 497). The central figure in television programs that employ this communication system is, or gives the appearance of being, ignorant of social rules or the norms that ought to govern conduct in a situation. Because the central character is the source of tension or conflict in the situation, others in the cast take steps to try to solve the problem. Fortunately for the continuation of the show, but unfortunately for the other characters in it, the central figure regains control over the situation before the show ends, thus ensuring that the drama will reoccur the following week.

If you said that sounds just like Archie Bunker on *All in the Family,* you have a grasp of the ironic communication system. Archie unknowingly violates rules of grammar with his frequent malapropisms and his insensitivity, "I'm not prejudiced, I'm not blaming you for being Black!" Despite the efforts of his family and neighbors, Archie remains Archie. The ironic communication system is not restricted to comedies. *Columbo,* a detective series starring Peter Falk, operates on the same communication system with one exception. Unlike Archie Bunker, whose ignorance is real, we are never certain whether Lt. Columbo is faking ineptitude or really is a dolt. Fake or real, every week the guilty party becomes overconfident, slips up, and Columbo cracks an otherwise airtight alibi.

Chesebro (1986) suggests that the ironic communication system equates with the value system of existentialism, which concerns our freedom and responsibilities as human beings. Inconsistency is at the heart of the ironic communication system, by means of which viewers hear the central character, either intentionally or out of ignorance, say one thing and have it mean another, thus isolating themselves from the characters around them. To the central character, this isolation from family, peers, or co-workers seems totally undeserved if their behavior is a result of ignorance, or unavoidable if their behavior is calculated to separate him from the other characters. In either case, the audience sees or senses the frustration and grief this causes the central character (Chesebro, 1986). With the exception of those for whom he is a hero, no one wants to be Archie Bunker. Although viewers respect his success as a law enforcement officer, few respect or want to be thought of as a Lt. Columbo type of person.

Mimetic Television

The *mimetic communication system* focuses on "the common, the ordinary, or those 'slices of life' all of us experience" (Chesebro, 1986, p. 487). The central-character in the mimetic system is someone like ourselves, our friends, ourneighbors, or someone we knew in high school. The central character is as intelligent as we are, something we cannot say with certainty about the ironic "hero." The tension or conflict created by the central figure in the mimetic communication system comes from breaking, often intentionally, some minor rule for personal reasons. As the story unfolds, the central figure admits his guilt, is mildly punished for his sin, and emerges older and wiser for the experience. The mimetic communication system resembles the slice-of-life documentary because the characters and plots seem to come from the viewer's own experiences.

Happy Days, and more recently *The Wonder Years* are examples of situation comedies in the mimetic tradition. Richie Cunningham and Kevin Arnold, the central figures, are struggling with life in high school and junior high school, respectively. Actually, they are both struggling with their hormones and peer pressure, which cause them to do things they wish they had not done. This is the appeal of mimetic stories: the pathos created by recognition of the weakness that causes the central figure to act as he does and the sense of frustration with personal weakness that we share with him. Although Richie and Kevin suffer for their transgressions, the harm is not permanent and they learn from their experiences. The knowledge gained is handled quite didactically on *The Wonder Years* because the viewer gets to eavesdrop on the grownup Kevin's reflections about his adolescent life. The mimetic communication system equates with the value system of individuality and the uniqueness of people going about their everyday lives (Chesebro, 1986).

Leader-Centered Television

The *leader-centered communication system* differs from the mimetic, not in the situations the characters find themselves in but in the personal qualities of the central figure. Unlike the mimetic central figure, who makes mistakes and creates problems because of personal inadequacy, the central figure in a leader-centered story takes charge of situations and solves problems. Problems arise from the actions of peripheral characters in the story. Their behavior violates the central character's sense of right and wrong. The story revolves around how the central character regains control of the situation and accomplishes what he or she set out to do in the first place.

Hill Street Blues and *The Cosby Show* represent leader-centered fictional television. Captain Frank Furillo and Dr. Cliff Huxtable dominate the action in their shows. Dr. Huxtable has to deal with the problems created by his children and their friends. The show is made complex by the characterization of his wife. Clair Huxtable is also a professional, a lawyer. In those shows in which her character is featured, she emerges as her husband's equal or occasionally his superior. Captain Furillo is a more complex character than Dr. Huxtable because of his publicly known status as a recovering alcoholic. This gives the character a flaw that could interfere with his ability to control events at Hill Street Station. The show is also significant for its simultaneous development of multiple plots and extending plot development across several episodes.

The leader-centered communication system equates with values of authority. It views

> symbols of authority, influence, and power over others as necessary, effective, and useful modes of human interaction. Authority can be viewed as a set of skills, resources, and so forth that allows one to control. Or, authority can be viewed as a relationship in which one agent's behavior causes or is allowed to cause another's behavior. In either case, those in authority examine the situation or scene, consider the materials available and the material outcomes of decisions, and attempt to develop

> and secure support for an idiom that will allow one to
> move "logically" from one issue to the next in proper
> syllogistic order until the solution emerges. (CHESEBRO,
> 1986, p. 507)

The value system of authority is a logic of good reasons that, depending on the ideology of the leader, can support liberal or conservative outcomes.

Romantic Television

The *romantic communication system* is invoked when the central character is not that much smarter or stronger than the average person; however, he or she is confronted with a situation filled with "almost overwhelming elements of unknown danger and risk as well as requiring remarkable levels of human power, intensity, dedication, and capacity. We almost expect that the ordinary laws of nature must be suspended if these dramas are to be successfully resolved" (Chesebro, 1986, p. 492). The romantic hero not only sees the problem and understands its scope and cause better than anyone else but also has the skills necessary to solve the problem. By the end of the romantic story everyone recognizes the hero's special qualities.

Both *Miami Vice* and *The A-Team* follow the pattern of the romantic communication system although viewers may find *Vice* somewhat closer to reality as they know it. Crockett and Tubbs work to preserve law and order in society. The members of *The A-Team,* themselves wrongly accused and convicted of breaking the law, pursue justice for others while staying one step ahead of their own pursuers. Crockett and Tubbs achieve success through dedicated police work and by putting their lives on the line in their daring undercover work. *The A-Team* triumphs through team work that capitalizes on each member's unique skills, careful planning, and precision execution. As their leader, Colonel Hannibal Smith, is fond of remarking, "I just love it when a plan comes together." The romantic communication system equates with an idealistic value system that celebrates individual genius and personal greatness (Chesebro, 1986).

Mythic Television

The *mythic communication system* is a form of fictional entertainment in which "the central character transcends the mundane world of the audience and is confronted with a mystical experience" (Himmelstein, 1984, p. 79).

> A myth is a fabricated, invented, or imagined story of
> historical events in which universal struggles concerning
> truth, beauty, and patriotism are depicted. In an almost
> sacred or timeless order (ritual or dream), a hero or
> heroine embarks on a long, unknown, and difficult
> journey in order to retrieve a "precious object" that is
> guarded by unusually powerful counter-agents.
> (CHESEBRO, 1986, p. 494)

The problem that leads to the tension and conflict is one that is inevitable or at least could not have been anticipated. As a result, unlike other communication systems, the mythic communication system is one in which no one is to blame for the problem, but it is so overwhelming that personal heroic action is required to confront it. If the central character succeeds, a new society emerges. Complete resolution of the problem may occur in a film, but in series television the outcome is normally left in a state of flux at the end of each episode. The immediate crisis is resolved but the basic problem remains unresolved.

Battlestar Galactica was television's attempt to capitalize on the popularity of the first *Star Wars* film. It "opened with a three-hour premier that so effectively captured the *Star Wars* techniques and rhythm that 20th Century-Fox sued Universal for copyright infringement" (Castleman and Podrazik, 1982, p. 28). *Battlestar Galactica* was the story of a group of space colonists fleeing the ravaging hordes of Cylons, a race of robots, who had destroyed their planet and would not be satisfied until they had wiped out the human race. The colonists' destination—Earth. The mythic communication system equates with a theological value system. "[T]he essence of theology is its reliance on some kind of god or divinity. Whether the divinity be religious or otherwise, its will is assumed to create and to regulate the natural, human, and ethical laws controlling all human beings" (Chesebro, 1986, p. 509).

Rhetorical Vision

Fictional programming is persuasive. Entertainment and persuasion, long considered to be at opposite ends of the communication continuum, may actually be at the same end (Chesebro, 1986). The sheer volume of rhetorical activity in prime-time television precludes a complete assessment of its rhetorical vision, but let us sample aspects of it.

Whether by providing its viewers with revelations or, more probably, through the process of the accretion of images, some examples of the persuasive agenda of entertainment are found in the roles that individuals representing various groups in our society are allowed to portray. "Television dramas and advertisements sometimes portray a world in which men are doctors but not nurses and women rarely plumbers or lumberjacks. Thus, television often 'persuades' by its presentation of diverse social groups in fictional dramatic roles" (M.J. Smith, 1988, p. 259). In assessing the rhetoric of fictional entertainment on television, consider what kinds of people are cast as ironic losers, the central figures in entertainment based on the leader-centered communication system, or who portray the mythical heroes.

Beyond role assignment, entertainment programming is persuasive in how it constructs reality. In prime-time America, poverty is not so bad and affluence is not so good (Gould, Stern, and Adams, 1981). Analysis of one week of prime-time network programming indicated that the hardships of urban and rural poverty were downplayed: Poor people were shown to be more healthy and active than middle- and upper-class people in shows such as *Little House on the*

Prairie. On the other hand, affluent white-collar professionals were shown to be experiencing hardship: the emotional costs of career advancement and the grind of putting in long hours on shows such as *Trapper John, M.D.* and *Lou Grant*.

> [W]e discovered a fairly coherent and prevalent message: that economically deprived people should not strive, at least not to make money. Those who did not usually led wholesome, fulfilling lives, so long as they remained content with their fates. Occasionally deprived mildly (*inconvenienced* almost might be a better word) by their "poverty," they learned to get by with less and still to be happy. Affluent people, on the other hand, often were beset with hardships, including financial ones; and those wealthy people who were engaged actively in acquiring capital were typically amoral or tormented by their own greed. (C. GOULD ET AL., 1981, p. 314)

Social values are inherent in this kind of rhetorical vision, and communication systems work to reinforce them. The repetition of these messages in shows that cross typical generic lines of categorization can be powerfully persuasive. Mimetic, leader-centered, and romantic programming, with their attendant values of individualism, authority, and idealism, have dominated prime-time television for more than a decade (Chesebro, 1986). Taken together, the underlying messages of these systems are that people who want what they do not have or do what they are not supposed to do get in trouble (mimetic); that people should respect the wishes of those in authority and appreciate the angst that accompanies leadership (leader-centered); and that only uniquely gifted individuals or groups, magnanimous enough to forsake personal safety or comfort, can solve society's major problems (romantic).

Some evidence suggests that audience members do ground their perceptions of reality in a fictional world that resembles the world of entertainment television. Heavy television viewers overestimate the probability of being a victim of serious crime (Gerbner, Gross, Signorielli, Morgan, and Jackson-Beeck, 1979). This should not be surprising since crime has been a staple of prime-time series television, providing as it does dramatic tension: the conflict between right and wrong. Because of the need to reach a point of closure at the end of each episode in a series, the theme represented is actually crime *and* punishment. Whether told through the ironic (*Columbo*), leader-centered (*Dragnet*), romantic (*Perry Mason*), or mythic (*The Six Million Dollar Man*) communication system, the message is the same, the system works: Crime is all around us, but the guilty suffer punishment for their deeds. *Hill Street Blues* differs from these programs primarily in its serial restructuring of rhetorical activity, which adds layers of complexity and uncertainty to the outcome.

On *Columbo*, punishment is assured as the consequence of crime in two ways: the humiliation of the criminal by being unmasked by the bumbling detective, and the criminal's confession, which assures conviction. On *Dragnet*, punishment is shown in its signature epilogue—"in a moment the results of that trial"—which informs the viewer of the length of the criminal's sentence and where it will be served. On *Perry Mason,* wrongly accused defendants are exonerated as the guilty admit their sins in court, often in emotional outbursts of repentance and contrition. On *The Six Million Dollar Man,* punishment is metaphoric as Colonel Steve Austin either prevents the criminals from possessing the "sacred object" they covet or retrieves it from their clutches if they have succeeded in gaining control of it.

Thus, the rhetorical properties of fictional-entertainment programming lie in the underlying value systems that the five basic plot types support and the recurring persuasive messages that these value systems are used to encode. Prime-time programming is based on ironic, mimetic, leader-centered, romantic, and mythic communication systems. These systems frame rhetorical acts by rhetors that have differing views of the sources of, and the appropriate solutions to human problems. In this manner, fictional-entertainment programming espouses values of existentialism, individualism, authority, idealism, and theology. These value systems in turn suggest appropriate patterns of belief and sources of human behavior. Other advice on how to think and act is found in the rhetorical potential of narrow-cast cable television services.

Narrow-Casting

Narrow-casting is programming aimed at a particular audience defined by a commonality of taste, interest, age, religious preference, or one of a host of other psychographic or demographic characteristics. In a sense, you could say that every program that we have discussed represents narrow-casting of a sort because networks have the ability to deliver a particular audience to their sponsors by scheduling a partiuclar show in their line-up. Narrow-casting, as considered here, refers to an entire network or channel that is devoted to serving the programming desires of a particular group. Eternal World Television Network, Nickelodeon, and MTV are narrow-casting services, though the promotion of reruns of old comedy series as part of "Nick at Night" suggests that Nickelodeon is attempting to broaden its child-oriented base to include adults.

Narrow-casting represents the confluence of technology, economics, and history. Technologically, the development of the communication satellite made narrow-casting commercially feasible. Prior to the placement of satellites in geosynchronous earth orbit, the typical television set had thirteen channels, many of them unused by broadcasters because they found it too difficult and expensive to reach national audiences. The networks dominated national programming. Although they might pick up a local show such as *American Bandstand* out of Philadelphia and broadcast it in the afternoon, they had neither the desire nor the resources, nor for that matter the commercial need, to provide special programming aimed at a narrow audience. Communication satellites changed that.

Technology also provided the economic impetus for manufacturers to produce sets capable of receiving more channels and for cable television services to expand. Availability, coupled with a decline in the cost of television sets relative to most people's standard of living, made ownership of more than one set possible for many families. The use of television as an "electronic babysitter" has been widely criticized, but it is a fact of life in many households, as is the trend toward the kids having a set in their own room. This not only changed the sociology of viewing, the family no longer gathered in the living room to watch *Gunsmoke,* but also redefined the typical audience. Individual preference, rather than that of the family and its collective (more likely Mom's or Dad's) preferences, became the concern of broadcasters.

The third force that influenced the development of narrow-casting is historical. We are not sure whether life really does imitate art, but in writing this chapter we have become convinced that television imitates everything, especially itself. Religious programming had long been a staple of Sunday morning programming and Catholic Bishop Fulton J. Sheen was a hit in the 1950s, so why not a religious network or several religious networks? Children's programming worked for part of the schedule, why not make it all of the schedule? The list of possiblities seems almost endless. To give you an idea of the rhetorical potential of narrow-casting we look at music television.

Music Television (MTV)

The recession of the late seventies and early eighties brought a slump in record sales, and the music video was born out of the necessity to stimulate consumption (Lynch, 1984). The idea of providing visual accompaniment for music was not new. In the 1950s, the popular radio program *Your Hit Parade* was turned into a staple of television. Every week, the cast acted out skits that were supposed to convey a sense of the lyrics. People tuned in to see what new goofy way Snooky Lansen and the rest of the gang would use to visualize "Shrimp Boats Are a Comin'."

Several films made in the sixties were, for the most part, footage of popular rock groups singing and playing their instruments. Conceived as a means to sell more Beatles albums and more paraphernalia with The Beatles pictures plastered on it (as if it was necessary), *A Hard Day's Night* was shot cheaply, in black and white, in six weeks (Ward, Stokes, and Tucker, 1986). Just as this film was nothing more than a Beatles commercial, music videos are commercials.

MTV is almost synonymous with music video today. It is patterned after radio, broadcasts twenty-four hours a day with a rotation of popular videos and occasional "oldies," and segments with rock personalities doing interviews and guest appearances. MTV has "vee-jays" who introduce songs, announce concert dates, and chat with the audience. MTV even has its own game show, or a parody of television game shows, *Remote Control,* which features questions on television trivia.

As a commercial, the music video gets the viewer into a consumer mode for record buying (Levy, 1987). However, unlike commercials for other consumer goods, "music video never delivers a hard·sell, never identifies the record or tape or group as a product. Instead, it equates the product with an experience to be shared, part of a wonderous leisure world" (Aufderheide, 1986).

Most music videos are not message oriented in the same way that message songs are (Chapter 11), but they are rhetorical acts. Their purpose is to persuade the viewer to do something, actually to buy something. Music videos can also function as rhetorical acts in other ways. As with earlier nonvisual rock songs, music videos are a form of expression that comments on society and offers a world for the viewer to enter. "One of music video's distinctive features as a social expression is its open-ended quality, aiming to engulf the viewer in its communication with itself, its fashioning of an alternative world where image is reality" (Aufderheide, 1986, p. 57–58).

Videos sometimes employ a narrative structure similar to that of films or episodic television programs: heroes battling villains and saving fair maidens, heroes battling monsters and saving themselves, two people meeting and falling in love.

> The parallels between dream structure and music video structure have fascinating implications for the form. Music videos offer a ready-made alternative to social life. With no beginnings or endings—no history—here may be nightmarish instability, even horror. But there can be no tragedy, which is rooted in the tension between an individual and society. (AUFDERHEIDE, 1986, p. 66)

Music video is the present-day continuance of the message of alienated youth, with many videos offering examples of rock as statements of rebellion. Parents, teachers, police, businessmen (though seldom businesswomen), and other authority figures are characterized as oppressors. Indeed, the world of music video is a sexually stereotypical world: "Male images include sailors, thugs, gang members, and gangsters. Female images include prostitutes, nightclub performers, goddesses, and servants" (Aufderheide, 1986, p. 69).

The rhetorical properties of MTV are interesting for two reasons. The first relates to the rhetors that MTV competes with for its audience's attention: radio and the music the viewer already owns on records, tapes, and compact discs. The second relates to the meaning that viewers create for the rhetorical acts of MTV.

Other television programming competes with non-television forms of entertainment for the viewer's attention, but once the viewer decides to watch television, the medium competes only with itself. As Fiske (1987b) has indicated, watching television is a part of, and is integrated into, the daily lives of many viewers. This would suggest that these viewers do not decide between watching *Dynasty* or reading *War and Peace;* they decide between watching *Dynasty* or watching something else. MTV forces its viewers to decide, consciously or unconsciously, among itself, the aurally similar experience of radio, and the personal control afforded by listening to their own music on record or disc. This means that MTV, more than any other form of programming on this highly visual medium, relies on its visual images to gain a rhetorical edge over competing rhetors.

The visual symbols of music videos not only give them this edge, but the manner in which the audience creates meaning for them may differ from other visual and verbal rhetorical forms. Music videos are brief, unlike movies and fictional television entertainment, which may last for two hours or more. They can employ only the established symbols of the mythology of particular genres such as the Western frontier myth, but the genre of a video, if there is one, is enigmatic at best. The rhetoric of music videos is based on the intertextual reading of iconic images.

> The theory of intertextuality proposes that any one text is necesarily read in relationship to others and that a range of textual knowledges is brought to bear upon it. These relationships do not take the form of specific allusions from one text to another and there is no need for readers to be familiar with specific or the same texts to read intertextually. (FISKE, 1987b, p. 108)

As an example of intertextual reading, Fiske discusses Madonna's *Material Girl* music video, which parodied Marilyn Monroe's performance of the song "Diamonds are a Girl's Best Friend" in the movie *Gentlemen Prefer Blondes*. Creating intertextual meaning for the video does not depend on specific knowledge of the film, something which none of the Madonna "wannabe's" of 1985 would have been likely to have. Intertextual reading of the video only requires knowledge of our culture's iconic image of the sexy blonde who capitalizes on her looks and men's desires.

> The meanings of *Material Girl* depend upon its *allusion* to *Gentlemen Prefer Blondes* and upon its intertextuality with *all* texts that contribute to and draw upon the meaning of "the blonde" in our culture. Intertextual knowledge preorients the reader to exploit television's polysemy by activating the text in certain ways, that is, by making some meanings rather than others. (FISKE, 1987b, p. 108)

Although all television programming is polysemic because it is designed to reach the widest possible audience, it need not be read in the same ways that music videos must be read. The characters Chrissie (played by Suzanne Sommers on *Three's Company*) and Jennifer Marlowe (played by Loni Anderson on *WKRP in Cincinnati*) were in many ways iconically "the blonde" and could have been intertextually understood in that way alone. However, because of the ongoing nature of series television, viewers were able to confirm, refine, or change their reading of these two attractive young women by watching what they did and listening to what they said every week.

Meanings created for a particular music video are reinforced by repeated viewings and may or may not contribute to understanding the next video by the same recording artist because it may be based on drastically different iconography. Individual music videos may be studied as rhetorical acts, with their own special properties of visual and verbal discourse.

Doing Rhetorical Criticism of Television

Doing rhetorical criticism of television may seem easy: There are so many rhetorical acts to choose from, and you can videotape your selection and watch it over and over again. You can even look at rhetorical acts from the past because so many shows are being rerun on cable channels, and classics such as *I Love Lucy* are available prerecorded. There are two cautionary rules for choosing television material as the subject of your rhetorical criticism.

First, you must decide whether your choice is a rhetorical act or merely your favorite show. Not all communication is rhetorical, so review the discussion of the properties of a rhetorical act in Chapter 1. Some programs, such as the classic *CBS Reports* documentary *Harvest of Shame*, are clearly rhetorical.

Nothing is inherently wrong with choosing a favorite show as your object of criticism. We happen to love *ALF* and think of that program as a rhetorical act warning of the dangers of too much media consumption. Does that make it a rhetorical act, or have we merely found a convenient academic justification for a guilty pleasure?

In some cases, the writers, directors, or producers of a show have described their reasons for making it. Norman Lear has certainly not been bashful in talking about *All in the Family* or his other shows. In some cases, however, you will be unable to look inside the rhetor's head and will have to rely on the program itself for indications of its rhetorical properties. Having said that, doesn't that mean that our reading of *ALF*, an audience use, makes it a rhetorical act?

Most television programs may have the potential to function rhetorically. How a specific program can be said to function rhetorically must be explained by your criticism of it. To develop our thesis about the rhetoric of *ALF*, we were required to prove how the show functions as a source of values, ideas, or arguments for its viewers. In doing criticism of a favorite show, you must go beyond what you find appealing and judge its rhetorical properties.

The second cautionary rule for choosing televised rhetorical acts as objects of criticism concerns audience use. If the way an audience uses a television program is your criterion for claiming that it functions as a rhetorical act, you need to be aware of the difficulty involved in establishing how an audience actually uses it. The audience for television is more remote and ill defined than that for speeches and films. Determining audience use for any communication genre can be the most difficult task a rhetorical critic faces. We have no certain way of knowing the meaning people assign to a speech, especially when their knowledge of it is limited to reading or hearing about it after it was given. Equally, we have no certain knowledge of the impact of movie reviews on whether or not people decide to see a film.

The remoteness of the audience, combined with their already discussed ability to create an individual viewing experience by zapping from one program to another, makes television criticism challenging. Should you decide to accept that challenge, a range of critical approaches is potentially appropriate to your endeavor and can help solve the problem of explaining how an audience might have used a particular television program.

Because news, sports, documentary, and fictional-entertainment programming all involve telling a story, the narrative approach is appropriate. The techniques used by television storytellers to create the impression of reality suggest that the criteria of narrative rationality and fidelity can be used to test how well this purpose is accomplished. Look first at the story, its characters, setting, and plot, and then see how it is told. In examining the telling, be sensitive to how lighting, camera work, and editing contribute to the finished product. The narrative approach may also be appropriate to examining music videos because some critics claim these have an underlying narrative structure, at least in their visual properties.

The dramatistic approach can also be applied to television. The dramatistic process of pollution, guilt, purification, and redemption and the management of critical ratios of the pentad can reveal the lessons taught by a variety of television programs. News stories about public wrongdoers, hard-hitting documentaries, and even comedies such as *Gilligan's Island* follow an underlying pattern that is dramatistic. Every week Gilligan commits some mistake, throws the island into chaos, but ultimately is welcomed back into the arms of his fellow castaways after some act of contrition. The lead-in for *ABC's Wide World of Sports,* extolling "the human drama of athletic competition," is not entirely hype. Television sports coverage, particularly of athletes making successful comebacks, is heavily Burkean.

Because many cultural approaches to criticism were developed to look at the impact of mass media on society or the rhetorical strategies used to attract media attention by those attempting to change it, the approaches to criticism found in Chapter 7 are particularly appropriate for doing television criticism. A social-values model was used to explain the lessons of newspaper sports coverage, so an interesting comparison might be made by looking at television sports coverage to discover if it reflects similar value oppositions. Because fictional-entertainment programming is heavily value oriented, and the tension in night-time serials such as *Dallas* and *Dynasty* is a product of value opposition, the Rushing and Frentz model of value change might be an appropriate critical concept to apply to prime-time television.

Because the Jungian model was developed to facilitate the interpretation of the visual images in film, it would also be appropriate to use it in interpreting television's highly visual rhetorical form. Jungian concepts may have the greatest usefulness to those interested in exploring the rhetorical properties of music videos. The Jungian approach provides no vehicle for evaluation, only a means of interpretation. You might find an appropriate context for evaluation in one of the ideological approaches to criticism.

Feminist criticism is concerned with the devaluation of women in society and how rhetorical activity perpetuates it. Marxist criticism focuses on class differences in society and how rhetorical activity serves the hegemonic interest of the upper class. Music videos are by and large sexist, and New Wave groups certainly challenge hegemonic interests, at least those of the mainstream of the music industry. The Jungian approach might provide a useful interpretive system on which to base feminist or Marxist criticism of music videos, but these two approaches could also be used in their own right to evaluate other forms of television programming.

Feminist criticism could be applied to news and documentary programming to see how issues about women in society are portrayed and might even be applied to sports: We have long wondered why golfers on the LPGA tour are referred to as "the girls" whereas members of the PGA and Senior's tour are never called "the boys." Fictional-entertainment programming is also populated by women. *Charlie's Angels* ushered in the age of "jiggle TV," now largely departed, but it was not the first nor will it be the last time female characters are portrayed in a way that reinforces the second-class status of women.

Marxist criticism can be applied to the entire range of television programming. Largely developed in Great Britain as means of critiquing television in that country, Marxist criticism holds that hegemony is maintained and social change prevented because of rhetorical activity by those in power. Because television is a commercial medium, and what is shown is often changed to suit the interests of the sponsor, it should not be surprising that fictional-entertainment programming seldom rocks the boat. When it contains messages that suggest that the poor may be better off than the wealthy, public acceptance of that message obviously serves the hegemonic interests of the upper class and impedes social change. News and documentaries can also be approached from a Marxist perspective, examining and evaluating how social problems such as homelessness or social unrest are portrayed.

Criticism of social movements focuses on the rhetorical strategies used by a movement during the various stages of its life cycle. Part of what a movement must do to survive is grow and gain support. To succeed, a movement must make the institution or individual it opposes look bad. Both of these ends can be accomplished by attracting television news coverage. The ability of television to bring supporters of a movement together vicariously and to encourage them to keep up their efforts has been capitalized upon by both the pro-life and pro-choice sides of the abortion controversy.

A worthwhile extension of movement study might relate to the role of narrow-casting and the use of public access channels to build and sustain a movement. Although we would not necessarily classify certain fundamentalist religious groups as social movements, their rhetorical activity seems to be directed toward revival of past values and resistance to social change. The contribution of the "electronic church" to these efforts could prove an interesting topic of study.

Fantasy theme analysis is also a useful approach for doing television criticism. The electronic church has a clearly articulated rhetorical vision; and it has a large enough audience and list of contributors to not only sustain it on the air but also to suggest that many people have adopted the vision as their own. Religious programming is not the only form of programming with a regular following. Any time you can identify a program that people just will not miss and will videotape if they must miss it, whether it is a game show, soap opera, prime-time melodrama, or situation comedy, you have identified a program with a compelling rhetorical vision. The Nielsen ratings and your own common sense tell you that a program that has lasted for more than one season has attracted adherents to its vision.

In examining fantasy theme and fantasy type, be sure to consider the program in the context of programming flow. The preceding and following programs can affect the way a program is read. Do not assume that the fantasy theme approach is only appropriate to analyzing hit shows; it can tell you something about failures as well. If you are evaluating a Nielsen loser, look at the competing rhetorical visions in its time slot. Why were their visions more compelling? Also look at the shows that preceded and followed it and how they may have shaped the reading of the fantasy. Fantasy theme analysis is also useful in the evaluation of news and sports coverage, which tend to be filled with heroes and villains, tragedies and conspiracies.

On the surface, the traditional approach to criticism may seem the least appropriate to television, but there are several possibilities for using the traditional approach to do television criticism. Obviously, if the rhetorical act is a televised speech, you would consider using the traditional approach to examine how it was adapted to the constraints imposed by television. Ronald Reagan was the first president in our memory to adapt visual aids in his televised speeches.

The traditional approach's concept of ethos, rhetor credibility, is particularly appropriate for analyzing and evaluating how a sports commentator, newscaster, or other on-air personality gains celebrity status and viewer approbation. Why is Willard Scott's weather report, complete with birthday salutes, a factor in the popularity of NBC's morning news program? Which network news anchor is perceived most and least credible and why? These are the kinds of critical questions you can ask and evaluations you can make using the concept of rhetor in the traditional approach.

Analyzing and evaluating the rhetoric of sports programming is also possible using concepts from the traditional approach. In addition to considering the credibility of sportscasters and color commentators, you can also analyze and evaluate their use of invention. The most difficult rhetorical task in sports programming is holding the audience during an unexciting contest. What devices of argument, emotional appeal, and presentational style and delivery does the rhetor employ? Sports programming, particularly on ESPN, includes newscast-style coverage of events and issues in sports. How this coverage is framed can also be studied using the traditional approach to criticism.

Documentaries are arguments about events or people. The quality and sufficiency of the proof and reasoning they offer can be evaluated using the Toulmin model of argument. News stories are often framed metaphorically, the subject of the story representing part of the larger social picture, and they can be examined in the context of tenor and vehicle. Unlike the classic public-speaking situation, some of the logical proof or the argument's metaphoric content, along with practically all of the emotional proof, will come from the visual images. Consider the visual as well as the verbal elements in how television uses argument.

The stock the viewer places in a documentary or news report rests in part on the credibility of the rhetor and the medium. Who was the rhetor, what was his or her prior reputation with the audience, and what efforts were made in the context of the rhetorical act to enhance or maintain that credibility? Once again, visual elements can be very important in contributing to the rhetor's ethical appeal. The reporter on the scene, ducking bullets, may be risking life and limb. She augments the credibility of the report by being on the scene, rather than electing to be videotaped standing safely around the corner.

Television has been labeled a vast wasteland. If it is, it is a wasteland studded with rhetorical activity of various kinds. As a widespread medium of communication that has the public's attention, it is worthy of rhetorical criticism. The critic interested in television must recognize its differences from other communication media and take them into account in studying the rhetoric of television. Television creates the appearance of reality in everything it does: news coverage, fictional-entertainment programming, and the surrealistic quality of music television. Our exclusive focus on the visual message of MTV may have left you asking, but what about the words? They too have rhetorical properties and Chapter 11 will examine the rhetoric of music lyrics. The cross-over between music and television demonstrates the ubiquity of television. Today, television spills over into or envelops most communication genres.

Suggested Readings

Examples of Criticism

AUFDERHEIDE, P. (1986). Music videos: The look of sound. *Journal of Communication, 36,* 57–78.

> The author describes the world of music videos as an open-ended social system. Music videos have the potential to communicate a number of messages. The purpose of this article is to describe the content of music video, but Aufderheide also draws several conclusions about the persuasive abilities of music video. Of particular interest is his discussion of the "cause" video used to actuate audience members. This is a good example of sociological analysis of music.

CAREY, J.W. (ED.) (1988). *Media myths and narratives: Television and the press*. Newbury Park, CA: Sage Publications.

> As the title of this anthology implies, the primary critical focus is on the mythology and narrative structure of television. The book is divided into three parts: an overview of mythmaking, an analysis of entertainment programmming, and an evaluation of electronic journalism. Of particular methodological interest is the lead article in the second section, which traces the narrative themes created in one night of prime-time television by tracking programming within and across the three major networks.

CHESEBRO, J.W. (1986). Communication, values, and popular television series—An eleven-year assessment. In G. Gumpert and R. Cathcart (Eds.), *Intermedia: Interpersonal communication in a media world* (3rd ed.) (pp. 477–512). New York: Oxford University Press.

> The anthology that contains this essay includes a number of thought-provoking articles on television, but this one is singled out because of the clarity with which it relates concepts from dramatism to series television. Using the classifications of ironic, mimetic, leader-centered, romantic, and mythic communication systems developed earlier, the author explains how the dramatic progression, from pollution through guilt and purification to redemption, is articulated in each system. Popular television comedy and drama series are used as examples. The article points out how the proportion of prime-time network programming representing each communication system has shifted over time and discusses the underlying value systems associated with each system.

HIMMELSTEIN, H. (1984). *Television myth and the American mind*. New York: Praeger.

> The author looks at how television reflects the dominant myths in our culture and how, by reflecting them, it reinforces them. Himmelstein's treatment of the medium is wide ranging and critical, including analysis of advertising, situation comedy, drama, game shows, talk shows, sports coverage, religious shows, news, and documentary programming. His concern is that an uncritical acceptance of television's myths impedes social change. His essays on television's various subgenres are well-written examples of the critic exercising what he feels is a moral obligation to society.

SCHRAG, R.L. (1982). Teach your children well: Method and rationale in the criticism of adolescent oriented television programming. *Western Journal of Speech Communication, 46,* 98–108.

> This article looks at *The White Shadow*, a program about the white basketball coach of an inner-city high-school team, and identifies the three dominant fantasy themes it contains. Well written and interesting, the article is particularly useful in its illustration of the importance of stance for a critic. Schrag's article was stimulated by the charges of media critics that there is nothing of value on television for children and adolescents. Because the program he selected was one of the most popular with younger audiences, its themes of realization of significant others, alliance in action, and membership into personhood refuted those charges. The fact that the show, and others like it, had been canceled moved him to argue for the need to identify and support such programming in the future.

Resources for Doing Criticism

ADLER R.P. (ED.) (1981).   *Understanding television: Essays on television as a social and cultural force.* New York: Praeger.

> This book is a collection of thought-provoking essays on approaches to television criticism, various types of entertainment programming, and the news on television. Of particular use in understanding the visual language of television are the essays on semiotics and aesthetics. The section on programming includes essays that examine entire subgenres such as soap operas, situation comedies, and docudramas, as well as some that comment on specific programs such as *Dallas* and *Maude*.

CANTOR, M.G., AND PINGREE, S. (1983).   *The soap opera.* Beverly Hills, CA: Sage.

> For the critic interested in daytime television, this book is an excellent place to start. The authors define what is and is not a soap opera and chronicle the history of the genre on radio and television. Although many of the examples are drawn from British television, they examine how the "soaps" treat specific content issues such as sex, relationships, social status, and sex roles, and their application of various methods to reading television is intriguing. Be sure to look at their discussion of the audience for this type of programming, the reason for watching, and the effect it has on viewers, not only for the insight it can add to your own criticism but also for the insight it provides into how these questions can be pursued.

CASTLEMAN, H.H., AND PODRAZIK, W.J. (1982).   *Watching TV: Four decades of American television.* New York: McGraw-Hill.

> This excellent history of television is good reading for the television critic or any person interested in this medium of communication. The authors provide background on the development of television and, starting with the 1944–45 season, cover the prime-time schedule of the major networks through the 1980–81 season. They also discuss some major daytime programming events. In addition to capsule discussions of each year's network programming, the book provides scheduling grids that indicate which shows competed directly with each other for the audience's attention. Because many of the programs mentioned are now in syndication on cable channels, this book provides useful background information for the critic interested in examining them.

FISKE, J. (1987).   *Television culture.* New York: Methuen.

> Anyone interested in doing television criticism should take a look at this book. Fiske looks at the medium not only as a form of popular culture but also as an instrument that reinforces capitalist values. He examines how audiences become televisually literate by learning to create meaning from television's fundamentally polysemic text, unique narrative structure, and method of creating characters. Of particular interest are the chapters on gendered television, programming designed to appeal primarily to masculine or feminine viewers.

GROTE, D. (1983).   *The end of comedy: The sit-com and the comedic tradition.* Hamden, CT: Archon Books.

> Although we do not deal with prime-time entertainment programming in terms of genres, we have included this and another book on an important genre of prime-

time programming in the resources we suggest you might want to examine in doing television criticism. Situation comedies remain an important part of every network's programming, and many cable networks have gone to the trouble of developing their own comedies. Grote discusses situation comedy in relationship to classic Greek theories of the comic, to film, and to other mass media. His discussion of how this genre has evolved and changed over the years on television makes this book worthwhile reading for the television critic interested in the sit-com genre.

MacDONALD, J.F. (1987). *Who shot the sheriff? The rise and fall of the television Western.* New York: Praeger.

This is the other "genre" book we elected to include, not because the television Western is a big part of contemporary prime time but because of its place in television history. Many of the programs MacDonald discusses are being rerun on cable channels. MacDonald places the Western in the context of American mythology and discusses a wide range of programs, from the earliest Westerns such as *Hopalong Cassidy* (which were considered children's programming) to adult Westerns such as *Have Gun–Will Travel.* Of particular interest is his discussion of adult Westerns as legal, moral, and political dramas and the development and changes in the rhetorical vision of shows such as *Gunsmoke,* which spanned three decades in its run on CBS. As this material was being edited, Willie Nelson announced his plans to launch a "cowboy network" on cable, perhaps signaling a revitalization of interest in the Western genre.

The

11

Rhetoric of

Song

Music, its lyrics and melodies, is pervasive in contemporary culture. "Muzak" surrounds us while we shop in supermarkets, cash a check at the bank, wash clothes at a launderette, wait in the dentist's office, and when we are "placed on hold" while making a phone call. Music is a part of ceremonies and rituals in public and private life. "Hail to the Chief" announces the arrival of the president; "The Star Spangled Banner" is played before athletic contests begin; hymns mark religious festivals; the authors played "union" music and sixties folk albums to get in the spirit for writing this chapter. Portable radios and tape recorders make it possible for everyone to accompany their lives with a personal soundtrack. "We use music to change our behavior. We may play a recording or turn the radio dial to match or change our present mood" (Perris, 1985, p. 6).

But can music be a rhetorical act? Consider this: On his guitar, Woody Guthrie had inscribed, "This machine kills Fascists." Guthrie's protege, Pete Seeger, penned this sentiment on his banjo, "This machine surrounds hate and forces it to surrender." Music can create socially shared meanings in both the artistic and rhetorical sense.

That music has rhetorical properties was recognized by the earliest authors. Plato's *Republic* warned that the wrong kind of music could be a danger to the state. Aristotle's *Poetics* discussed the influential possibilities of verse. In 1703, Andrew Fletcher's treatise on government stated: "Give me the making of the songs of a nation and I care not who makes the laws" (Perris, 1985, p. 2). Music has played its part in all of America's wars from the Revolution to Vietnam. Music was a persuasive vehicle for those who protested the wars as well as for those who planned and fought them.

In examining music as a rhetorical genre, we are particularly concerned with the *message* song. Frequently, message songs are the folk or popular songs of an era. One of the characteristics of message songs is that most are time bound. After the rhetorical situation is resolved or decays, the message is no longer meaningful, and the song loses its popularity. However, this is not always the case. The folk-protest music of the sixties revived message music of earlier times, sometimes offering new interpretations of old lyrics. Message music pertains to its time period because its purpose is to create socially shared meanings for singers and listeners.

Because the purpose of a message song is getting a point of view across, the tune may not be a very important part of the rhetorical act. Message songs frequently adopt tunes that are already familiar to their listeners. Hundreds of song lyrics have been written to the tune of "John Brown's Body," which you may also recognize as "The Battle Hymn of the Republic." It is an easy song to sing, and everybody seems to know it. In viewing music as a rhetorical act, it is important to remember that message music is not necessarily "good" music by artistic standards.

Some of the world's greatest musicians have used their art for rhetorical purposes. Beethoven's only opera, *Fidelio,* was a statement of his concern for social issues. It tells the story of a political prisoner (Perris, 1985), and its story becomes contemporary when viewed against events in many Latin American countries. Many of the great composers intended their works to be nationalistic. Chopin, Wagner, Rimsky-Korsakov, and many others wrote musical scores that celebrated the ethnic and political ideals of their nations.

Light opera, musical drama, and comedy can also convey messages. The works of Gilbert and Sullivan addressed the ethnocentricities of Victorian Britain. Two popular musicals of Rodgers and Hammerstein, *Oklahoma* and *South Pacific,* communicated American values to audiences during World War II. *South Pacific,* in particular, because it was a story about people touched by the war, conveyed to its audience a message of pride, sacrifice, and hope for improving cultural relations. More recently, the musical drama *Zoot Suit,* based on a Los Angeles trial that took place during World War II, dealt with the hatred toward, and injustices suffered by, Chicanos.

Music, whether it is a single song or a long score, is a rhetorical act when it is used to influence opinion and behavior. The singer or artist intends to invoke some response from the audience. Music is also used for rhetorical activity by groups, social and political movements, and individuals, who are not necessarily the creators of the song. It is particularly true of folk music that no one "owns" a song; its use transcends the intention of the writer-composer (Denisoff, 1972a). When you, as a critic, study music as rhetorical activity, examine it in terms of the function it performs in the rhetorical situation.

The Persuasive

Functions of

Songs

1. Propaganda songs to solicit or arouse outside support and sympathy for the group
2. Propaganda songs to reinforce the value structure of the group's supporters
3. Propaganda songs to create and promote unity, morale, and offer an identity for a group
4. Propaganda songs to recruit new members
5. Propaganda songs to identify societal problems or group discontent, usually in emotive terms
6. Propaganda songs that activate by offering solutions to problems (DENISOFF, 1969, 1971, 1972a, 1972b)

Denisoff (1972a) describes message songs as "propaganda" or persuasion that "can only be perceived functionally when they are performing the requirements of invoking some form of reaction or interaction" (p. 2). Propaganda songs are either designed or used to communicate social, political, economic, or ideological values to listeners (Denisoff, 1972a; Ewen, 1977; Rodnitzky, 1976). Denisoff created one helpful classification system for the persuasive functions of music (see box above).

These notions about the intentional uses of music are useful analytical tools for the rhetorical critic. These classifications help categorize a song relative to the rhetorical situation and suggest outcomes that the users and creators of the song may have had in mind. Determining how the users intended the song to function helps the critic choose evaluation techniques appropriate to the message of the music.

In addition to classification by function, Denisoff (1969, 1971, 1972a, 1972b) also groups propaganda songs into two categories based on intent. *Magnetic* songs are designed to attract the uncommitted listener and to express the rhetor's ideology to an external audience. Magnetic songs are also used by group members to promote unity and improve morale. These songs appeal to both our emotions and our intellect. "Maryland, My Maryland," a Civil War song, was printed in a Baltimore newspaper to stimulate support for state secession and joining the Confederacy. "We Shall Overcome" was and is used by civil-rights activists to keep up the spirits and express the goal of those who protest racial discrimination.

Rhetorical songs describe social conditions, pose questions, express discontent, and attempt to influence public opinion. Sting's song "I Hope the Russians Love Their Children Too" is rhetorical; it proposes no solution to the problem of East-West relations, only a universal hope for peace in the future. Unlike the magnetic song, which is used to draw people into a group or movement, the rhetorical song does not advocate joining a movement or turning to a group to solve the problem.

Denisoff's use of the term *rhetorical* is somewhat narrower than our definition in Chapter 1. His purpose is only to categorize songs into those used for movement or group unification and those used to address society in a more general way. However, this distinction is useful for critical efforts that attempt to determine how the writer-composer or user of a song might have expected it to function rhetorically.

Throughout history, dissident groups and individuals have used music as a means of expressing their discontent. From Methodist church founder John Wesley's view that the devil should not have all the good songs to Karl Marx's view that art reflects social class, and to Joan Baez's use of her remarkable voice as a political instrument, songs have been a form of rhetorical activity.

In the next section, we focus on some of the uses of message songs in American history. Then we selectively examine two recent episodes: folk-protest and antiwar music of the sixties and seventies. Our exploration of the message song concludes with a quick look at rock music. In other words, our discussion is not meant to be an all-inclusive history of the message song but to acquaint you with some of the wide-ranging possibilities you have as a critic if you choose to examine music as a rhetorical act.

Historical American Message Music

The earliest message songs in American history were religious hymns. The "Separatists" (Pilgrims) had left Plymouth, England to preserve their religious beliefs. In addition to their Bibles, they brought with them Henry Ainsworth's *Psalter,* a book of thirty-nine psalms and hymns (Ewen, 1977). You may have sung some of those hymns or recognize tunes such as "Old 100," a melody common to many hymns still in use. Just ten years after the *Mayflower* arrived, the first "broadside" was sold in the new world. Broadsides were single sheets of lyrics and sold for a penny. They served as a convenient way to spread news and (later) propaganda of rebellion (Ewen, 1977).

Singing and lyric writing were key elements in the rebellion against Great Britain. One writer of patriotic verse, Joel Barlow, who later served as a chaplain in the revolutionary army, wrote in 1775:

> I do not know whether I shall do more for the cause in
> the capacity of Chaplain than I would in that of poet; I
> have great faith in the influence of song; and I shall
> continue, while fulfilling the duties of my appointment, to
> write one now and then, and to encourage the taste for
> them which I find in camp. One good song is worth a
> dozen addresses and proclamations. (EWEN, 1977, p. 13)

Propagandists James Otis and Samuel Adams recognized the value of song as a political instrument. They encouraged the singing of songs depicting events of the rebellion so that those not present could experience the act vicariously. Several accounts of the Boston Tea Party captured the essence of that act, but "Revolutionary Tea," by an unknown author, uses the parent-child metaphor common to many revolutionary songs:

> There was an old lady lived over the sea,
> And she was an island queen;
> Her daughter lived off in a new countrie,
> With an ocean of water between.
> The old lady's pockets were filled with gold,
> But never contented was she,
> So she called on her daughter to pay her a tax,
> Of three pence a pound on the tea,
> Of three pence a pound on the tea.
>
> "Now mother, dear mother," the daughter replied,
> "I shan't do the thing you ax;
> I'm willing to pay a fair price for the tea,
> But never the three penny tax."
> "You shall," quoth the mother, and reddened with rage,
> "For you're my own daughter, you see,
> And sure 'tis quite proper the daughter should pay,
> Her mother a tax on the tea,
> Her mother a tax on the tea."
>
> And so the old lady her servant called up,
> And packed off a budget of tea,
> And eager for three pence a pound, she put in
> Enough for a large familie.
> She ordered her servant to bring home the tax,
> Declaring her child should obey,
> Or old as she was and a woman most grown,
> She'd half whip her life away,
> She'd half whip her life away.
>
> The tea was conveyed to the daughter's door,
> And all down by the ocean side,
> And the bouncing girl poured out every pound,
> In the dark and boiling tide,
> And then she called out to the island queen,
> "O mother, dear mother," quoth she,
> "Your tea you may have when 'tis steeped enough,
> But never a tax from me,
> But never a tax from me."(WHITMAN, 1969, p. 2)

Because today's mass media probe so intimately into the lives of politicians and candidates, our elected leaders and would-be leaders may look with envy on the post-Revolution days as a time of political heroes. Songs of the era reveal that this was not always the case. Thomas Jefferson, author of the Declaration of Independence and hero of the Constitutional Convention, was America's third president. The opposing party, the Federalists, attacked Jefferson's personal life hoping to harm him politically. A plantation owner from the slave-state of Virginia, Jefferson owned many slaves; and Sally Hemings, a quadroon slave, was alleged to have borne Jefferson five children. During his presidency, the Federalist newspaper *Boston Gazette* published several abusive songs about Jefferson and Sally Hemings (Lawrence, 1975).

Sung to the tune of "Yankee Doodle," this untitled song, written by "The Sage of Monticello," appeared on 11 October 1802. Speaking as Jefferson's persona, it was used to cast doubt on Jefferson's democratic ideology. Then and now, it is particularly racist and offensive. We include it because it demonstrates Plato's concern that the wrong kind of music could pose a danger to the state and because it is a typical example of the use of songs in mudslinging politics.

Of all the damsels on the green,
On mountain, or in valley,
A lass so luscious ne'er was seen
As Monticellean Sally.

CHORUS
Yankee Doodle, who's the noodle?
What wife were so handy?
To breed a flock, of slaves for stock.
A blackamoor's the dandy.

Search every town and city through,
Search market, street and alley;
No dame at dusk shall meet your view,
So yielding as my Sally.

CHORUS

When press'd by loads of State Affairs,
I seek to sport and dally,
The sweetest solace of my cares
Is in the lap of Sally.

CHORUS

Let Yankee Parsons preach their worst—
Let tory Witling's rally
You men of morals! and be curst,
You'd snap like sharks for Sally.

CHORUS

She's black you tell me—grant she be—
Must colors always tally?
Black is love's proper hue for me—
And white's the hue for Sally.

CHORUS

You call her slave—and pray were slaves
Made only for the galley?
Try for yourselves, ye witless knaves—
Take each to bed your Sally.

CHORUS
(LAWRENCE, 1975, p. 175)

The War of 1812 produced our national anthem, which demonstrates one cultural factor of message music. Songs of this type function because the tune to which the lyrics were sung was already part of the culture. Many songs of the revolutionary war had been set to the tunes of popular British songs such as "God Save the King," "Heart of Oak," and "The British Grenadier." Both before and after Frances Scott Key's "The Defense of Fort Henry" was popularized as "The Star Spangled Banner," its tune, derived from the drinking song "To Anacreon in Heaven," was a frequent choice for lyricists (Ewen, 1977; Lawrence, 1975).

One of the most prolific eras for message songs was the Civil War. Abolitionist hymns, slave songs, and songs written specifically for the propagandistic purposes of the movement were key elements of the abolitionist's drive to free the slaves. When war broke out, its every aspect was treated through song. "Mother" songs, such as "Just Before the Battle Mother," spoke of the conscript's desire to be home. "Goober Peas," sung by both sides, spoke to the poor quality of food that both armies endured late in the war. Wives and sweethearts were fondly remembered in songs such as "Lorena," and families back home sang out their fear about "The Vacant Chair." Draft dodgers sang "Wanted—A Substitute."

The two most important uses of music in the Civil War were to draw converts to "The Cause" or to keep solid the union ranks, and to rally troops and keep morale high. As in the revolutionary war, these songs grew out of a common culture, and both sides used variations on the same songs. "Maryland, My Maryland" was one such song. Said to be the second-most important song to the Confederacy (Ewen, 1977), the lyric was written by a Baltimore professor of English, Ryder Randall. He saw a newspaper account of the fighting in Baltimore on 19 April 1861 when a union regiment was attacked by southern sympathizers, and Jennie Cary, a "pro-Confederate lady," sang his lyric to the tune of the popular Christmas song, "Tannenbaum, Oh Tannenbaum" (Ewen, 1977).

Initially a southern magnetic song, Randall's first verse was:

The despot's heel is on thy shore,
Maryland, My Maryland!

His touch is at thy temple door,
Maryland, My Maryland!
Avenge the patriotic gore
That flecked the streets of Baltimore,
And be the Battle Queen of yore,
Maryland, My Maryland.
(LAWRENCE, 1975, p. 360)

Randall's song became so popular that several northern imitations soon followed. Septimus Winner, a prolific songwriter of the era, published a version shortly after the Confederate victory at the First Battle of Bull Run. The first verse reveals that Winner was not very creative:

The rebel horde is on thy shore,
Maryland! My Maryland!
Arise and drive him from thy door,
Maryland! My Maryland!
Avenge the foe thou must abhor,
Who seeks thy fall, oh Baltimore,
Drive back the tyrant, peace restore,
Maryland! My Maryland!
(LAWRENCE, 1975, p. 360)

Another northern version appeared in *Beadle's Dime Knapsack Songster* in 1862; the first verse displays the bitterness northerners felt after the Confederate victory (Lawrence, 1975):

The rebel thieves were sure of thee,
Maryland! our Maryland!
And boasted they would welcome be,
Maryland! our Maryland!
But now they turn and now they flee,
With Stonewall Jackson and with Lee
And loyal souls once more are free!
Maryland! our Maryland!
(LAWRENCE, 1975, p. 361)

The songs of the South were acknowledged as good by both sides of the divided nation, but the songs of the North may have given them an edge. More significant than the songs that described the war from the noncombatants' point of view, the battle songs were the most important use of music in the war.

> In the battle of songs, as on the field of conflict, the North emerged victorious. Shortly after the surrender of General Lee, a few Northern soldiers performed a potpourri of Northern war songs for several Confederate officers. A Southern Major remarked: "Gentlemen, if we had had your songs, we'd have licked you out of your boots." (EWEN, 1977, p. 72)

Two popular songs demonstrate the Civil War's musical battle. You judge which song is more arousing. "The Bonnie Blue Flag," written by actor-comedian Harry Macarthy, was popular before "Dixie" became the "national anthem" of the Confederacy. First sung at musicals in the South in 1861, it was said to be so capable of stirring southern emotions that late in the war northern occupation troops forbade its being played or sung (Lawrence, 1975).

We are a band of brothers and native to the soil,
Fighting for the property we gained by honest toil;
And when our rights were threatened, the cry rose near and far:
Hurrah! for the bonnie blue flag that bears a single star.

CHORUS
Hurrah! Hurrah! for Southern rights! Hurrah!
Hurrah! for the bonnie blue flag that bears a single star.

As long as the Union was faithful to her trust,
Like friends and like brothers, kind were we and just;
But now, when Northern treachery attempts our rights to mar,
We hoist, on high, the bonnie blue flag that bears a single star.

CHORUS

First gallant South Carolina nobly made the stand,
Then came Alabama who took her by the hand;
Next, quickly Mississippi, Georgia and Florida,
All raised on high the bonnie blue flag that bears a single star.

CHORUS

Ye men of Valor, gather 'round the banner of the right,
Texas and fair Louisiana join us in the fight;
Davis, our beloved President, and Stevens, statesman rare,
Now rally 'round the bonnie blue flag that bears a single star.

CHORUS

And here's to brave Virginia, the old Dominion State,
With the young Confederacy, at length, has linked her fate;
Impelled by her example now other States prepare
To hoist, on high, the bonnie blue flag that bears a single star.

CHORUS

Then cheer, boys, cheer, raise the joyous shout—
For Arkansas and North Carolina now have both gone out;
And let another rousing cheer for Tennessee be given—
The single star of the bonnie blue flag has grown to be eleven.

CHORUS

Then here's to our Confederacy—strong we are and brave,
Like patriots of old, we'll fight our heritage to save;

And rather than submit to shame, to die we would prefer—
So cheer for the bonnie blue flag that bears a single star.

CHORUS
(LAWRENCE, 1975, p. 359)

President Lincoln's call for volunteer regiments inspired George Frederick Root to write the North's most popular battle song, "The Battle Cry of Freedom," in 1862. The power of this song was such that merely singing it could improve morale:

> It is hardly possible to exaggerate the influence that "The Battle Cry of Freedom" had on the fighting spirit of Union soldiers. When the morale of these men plunged to the depths of despair in 1863, a glee club sang it for some of the troops. One unidentified soldier remarked that the song "ran through the camp like wildfire. The effect was little short of miraculous. It put as much spirit and cheer into the camp as a splendid victory. Day and night you could hear it by every campfire in every tent." One Confederate soldier recorded, after hearing some captured Union soldiers sing it: "I shall never forget the first time I heard 'Rally 'Round the Flag.' It was a nasty night during the 'seven days' fight and if I remember it rightly it was raining. I was on picket when, just before taps, some fellow on the other side struck up the song and others joined in the chorus until it seemed to me the whole Yankee Army was singing. . . . I am not naturally superstitious but I tell you that song sounded like the knell of doom." (EWEN, 1977, p. 77)

Yes we'll rally round the flag boys, we'll rally once again,
Shouting the battle cry of Freedom,
We will rally from the hill-side, we'll gather from the plain
Shouting the battle cry of Freedom.

CHORUS
The Union forever, Hurrah boys, hurrah!
Down with the Traitor, Up with the Star
While we rally round the flag boys,
Rally once again,
Shouting the battle cry of Freedom.

We are springing to the call of our Brothers gone before,
Shouting the battle cry of Freedom,
And we'll fill the vacant ranks with a million Freemen more
Shouting the battle cry of Freedom.

CHORUS

We will welcome to our numbers the loyal, true, and brave,
Shouting the battle cry of Freedom,
And altho' he may be poor he shall never be a slave,
Shouting the battle cry of Freedom.

CHORUS

So we're springing to the call from the East and from the
West,
Shouting the battle cry of Freedom,
And we'll hurl the rebel crew from the land we love the best,
Shouting the battle cry of Freedom.

CHORUS
(LAWRENCE, 1975, p. 362–3)

One song from the Civil War has been the basis for hundreds of other message songs and continues to be used today, "The Battle Hymn of the Republic." The origin of its tune is obscure, said to be an old camp-meeting song popular with black congregations. At the beginning of the Civil War, "John Brown's Body" was sung to it, a song that lampooned the misfortunes of a sergeant in the Boston Light Infantry. The song was popularized by abolitionists in the mistaken belief that it was the story of the John Brown who staged the raid on Harper's Ferry on 16 October 1859 (Ewen, 1977; Lawrence, 1975). Late in 1861, a clergyman asked Julia Ward Howe, an early suffragette, to write more suitable words for the tune.

The Civil War ended after four bloody years, but the issues that divided North and South were not fully resolved. Reconstruction placed harsh strictures on the southern states, and rebellion continued in less overt ways. Songs expressed discontent. "I'm A Good Old Rebel", attributed to a Confederate major, Innes Randolph, it was quickly adopted by southern veterans who wanted to speak out against the oppressive measures of reconstructionist politics (Lawrence, 1975).

O I'm a good old rebel,
Now that's just what I am,
For this "Fair Land of Freedom"
I do not care a damn;
I'm glad I fit against it—
I only wish we'd won;
And I don't want no pardon
For anything I done.

I hates the Constitution,
This Great Republic, too,
I hates the Freedmen's Buro,
In uniforms of blue;

I hates the nasty eagle,
With all his brags and fuss,
The lyin', thievin' Yankees,
I hates them wuss and wuss.

I hates the Yankee nation
And everything they do,
I hates the Declaration
Of Independence, too;
I hates the glorious Union—
'Tis dripping with our blood—
I hates their striped banner,
I fit it all I could.

I followed old mas' Robert
For four year, near about,
Got wounded in three places
And starved at Pint Lookout;
I cotch the roomatism
A campin' in the snow,
But I killed a chance o' Yankees,
I'd like to kill some mo'.

Three hundred thousand Yankees
Is stiff in Southern dust;
We got three hundred thousand
Before they conquered us;
They died of Southern fever
And Southern steel and shot;
I wish they was three million
Instead of what we got.

I can't take up my musket
And fight 'em now no more,
But I ain't a going to love 'em,
Now that is sarten sure;
And I don't want no pardon
For what I was and am,
I won't be reconstructed
And I don't care a damn.
(LAWRENCE, 1975, p. 437)

In times of economic hardship, message songs are used to chronicle the hardships and make the burden seem easier to bear. "Work" songs from the slave era, the cattle drives, and the industrialization of the nation are part of our national heritage. Message songs have also been used to protest the plight of the working man and unite workers against their common enemy, the bosses (D.A.

Carter, 1980). During the first wave of unionism at the beginning of the twentieth century, the International Workers of the World (IWW), "Wobblies," brought new life to message singing.

The American Federation of Labor (AFL) had evolved from the Knights of Labor in the late 1800s. Its purpose was to organize skilled workers into separate craft unions. Standing in opposition to the AFL, the Wobblies wanted to organize all workers, skilled and unskilled, into "one great union." Wobbly politics were socialist-populist and not well received by the social order, but their music appealed to many. Wobbly organizing drives were patterned after the Salvation Army's street-preaching tactics, and Wobbly songs were often sung to the tune of well-known hymns.

> After the street meetings were over, the Wobbly band would strike up a lively tune and lead the crowd into the hall. Here it would play a medley of Wobbly and rebel tunes to which the audience would sing the words (in those days almost everyone in Spokane knew one Wobbly song or another); then a short talk or some announcements would be made . . . the original idea was to intersperse a little entertainment in order to break the monotony of long-winded speeches. It was a successful formula and drew large crowds. (BRAZIER, 1968, p. 63–64)

One of the innovations of the Wobblies was the creation of a labor songbook, *The Little Red Songbook*. The early years of the twentieth century were not an easy time for labor organizers. It was not uncommon for them to be seriously injured or even murdered in clashes with "the bosses." Eulogies and the stories of strikes were common themes in Wobbly songs. One of the original authors of the songbook, Joe Hill, was executed by the State of Utah on trumped-up charges. Hill was later immortalized in a song still popular among today's protesters.

Ralph Chaplin, a leader in the IWW during his youth, wrote what has been called the greatest Wobbly song, "Solidarity Forever." Sung to the tune of "John Brown's Body/The Battle Hymn of the Republic," it states the grievances of the working class and the value of a union organization. It is still a staple union song.

> *When the union's inspiration through the worker's blood shall run,*
> *There can be no power greater anywhere beneath the sun.*
> *Yet what force on earth is weaker than the feeble strength of one?*
> *But the union makes us strong.*
>
> CHORUS
> *Solidarity forever!*
> *Solidarity forever!*
> *Solidarity forever!*
> *For the union makes us strong.*

Is there aught we hold in common with the greedy parasite
Who would lash us into serfdom and would crush us with his
might?
Is there anything left for us but to organize and fight?
For the union makes us strong.

CHORUS

It is we who plowed the prairies; built the cities where they
trade;
Dug the mines and built the workshops; endless miles of
railroad laid.
Now we stand, outcast and starving, 'mid the wonders we
have made;
But the union makes us strong.

CHORUS

All the world that's owned by idle drones, is ours and ours
alone.
We have laid the wide foundations; built it skyward stone by
stone.
It is ours, not to slave in, but to master and to own,
While the union makes us strong.

CHORUS

They have taken untold millions that they never toiled to earn.
But without our brain and muscle not a single wheel can turn.
We can break their haughty power; gain our freedom while we
learn
That the union makes us strong.

CHORUS

In our hands is placed a power greater than their hoarded gold;
Greater than the might of armies, magnified a thousand-fold.
We can bring to birth the new world from the ashes of the old,
For the union makes us strong.

CHORUS
(GREENWAY, 1970, p. 181)

The International Workers of the World still exists, but its membership is small, and many of its members are American communists. Although it never gained power or respectability, it was the first labor organization to make singing an integral part of unionism. In the second wave of unionism, during the Depression, other unions used message songs in their efforts to organize workers. The Congress of Industrial Organizations (CIO) and the United Mine Workers (UMW) sang on the picket line, during the union organizing drives, and while in jail for "illegal" activities; they added many new songs to labor's hymnal.

More will be said about Woodrow Wilson Guthrie shortly, but he and a young man named Peter Seeger were two of the great message-song writers of the thirties and forties. Message songs written then were revived by the protest movements of the fifties and sixties. Woody Guthrie's songs described the Depression and provided encouragement to people at the bottom of the social structure, and they live on today.

> His songs reflected both the failures and possibilities of the nation. Guthrie was partisan, bawdy, erratic, and perhaps a naive ideological captive of the American left, but his simple, powerful ballads somehow rang true and captured aspects of the nation's glory and shame. (RODNITZKY, 1969, p. 38–39)

Some of Guthrie's best-known songs tell stories about people, stories with a message. "Jesus Christ" cast Jesus as a revolutionary who preached to working men and women. "Tom Joad" was written after Guthrie had seen the film, *The Grapes of Wrath*. Because the people who would identify most strongly with Steinbeck's story could neither afford the book nor admission to the film, Guthrie wrote the song so that they could hear the story (Rodnitzky, 1976). At one point, Guthrie was hired to write propaganda for the federal government. He was commissioned to write a series of songs about the Tennessee Valley Authority project and the Grand Coulee Dam. His best-known songs from this period are "Roll on, Columbia" and "This Land Is Your Land."

Labor lore was the basis for several of Guthrie's stories in song. The events of 1913 in Ludlow, Colorado and Calumet, Michigan were particularly bitter episodes in union efforts to organize miners. Guthrie used these stories to rekindle sympathy for miners and all unskilled workers in the thirties. "The 1913 Massacre" illustrates his ability to make a song interact with the audience, as the listener is made a participant in the tragedy (Greenway, 1970).

> Take a trip with me in 1913,
> To Calumet, Michigan, in the copper country.
> I will take you to a place called Italian Hall,
> Where the miners are having their big Christmas ball.
>
> I will take you in a door and up a high stairs;
> Singing and dancing is heard everywhere.
> I will let you shake hands with the people you see,
> And watch the kids dance round the big Christmas tree.
>
> You ask about work and you ask about pay;
> They tell you they make less than a dollar a day
> Working the copper claims, risking their lives,
> So it's fun to spend Christmas with children and wives.
>
> There's talking and laughing and songs in the air,
> And the spirit of Christmas is there everywhere.

Before you know it you're friends with us all,
And you're dancing around and around in the hall.

Well, a little girl sits down by the Christmas tree lights
To play the piano, so you gotta keep quiet.
To hear all this fun you would not realize
That the copper boss thugmen are milling outside.

The copper boss thugs stuck their heads in the door;
One of them yelled and he screamed, "There's a fire!"
A lady she hollered, "There's no such a thing,
Keep on with your party, there's no such a thing."

A few people rushed and it was only a few,
"It's just the thugs and the scabs fooling you."
A man grabbed his daughter and carried her down,
But the thugs held the door and they could not get out.

And then others followed, a hundred or more,
But most everybody remained on the floor.
The gun thugs they laughed at their murderous joke,
While the children were smothered on the stairs by the door.

Such a terrible sight I never did see;
We carried our children back up to their tree.
The scabs outside still laughed at their spree,
And the children that died there were seventy-three.

The piano played a slow funeral tune;
And the town was lit up by a Cold Christmas moon,
The parents they cried and the miners they moaned,
"See what your greed for money has done."
(LEVENTHAL AND GUTHRIE, 1976, pp. 174–176)

Causes, issues, and politics have been a part of American history since colonial times. The political nature of folk music increased during the Great Depression and World War II. The music was not necessarily popular or even approved by most of society. Songs written by Guthrie and Seeger were sung at communist party meetings, socialist party meetings, and in union halls, anywhere that the disenfranchised were likely to gather. Neither the singers nor their songs had access to the mass media (Denisoff, 1969). Folk-protest music would come into its own after World War II and become a part of popular culture on a scale never before possible.

Folk-Protest Music

There is not a great deal of agreement regarding the boundaries of folk music. "True" folk music is anonymous in origin, transmitted orally from one generation to the next, and altered in the transmission (Denisoff, 1972a). American folk music is an amalgam of music from different ethnic groups in our population. Folk songs reflect people's thinking at any given time. Folk music in its most rhetorical form underwent a massive change in the sixties.

The patriotic fervor of World War II had decreased the popularity of songs about strikes, capitalist bosses, and the sorry state of day laborers. The message in music of the war years urged Americans to "Praise the Lord and Pass the Ammunition," celebrated "Rosie the Riveter," and pleaded that wives and sweethearts "Don't Sit Under the Apple Tree With Anyone Else But Me." By the end of the war, folk music was being kept alive by a group of eastern, urban, hard-core folk artists who united around Woody Guthrie and Pete Seeger. America entered a period of postwar prosperity at home and deteriorating relations with the Soviet Union abroad.

Folk music became almost synonymous with domestic communism in the late forties and early fifties. The World War II allies had become cold warriors; and, with some accuracy, folk singers were branded as domestic communists. At the turn of the century, the members of the IWW had been socialists or members of the American communist party. Folk singers of the depression era had associated with the old socialist party of Eugene Debs or the international communist movement. The driving force behind many CIO unions had been American communists, and Guthrie and Seeger made no secret of their identification with working people. It is debatable whether either was actually a "communist" though to this day, Seeger describes himself as an American Marxist and invokes the political nature of folksinging:

> An artist, any kind of artist, is also a citizen and has a
> citizen's responsibilities. This means voting, among other
> things. . . . We have a duty to inform ourselves, and
> when you inform yourself, you want to communicate
> what you learn. I think it is a mistake to think *any* music
> doesn't have a message of some sort. (GALLANTER, 1986, p. 30)

The death knell for many folk singers of the Depression era sounded during the communist witch hunts of the McCarthy era. The entertainment industry in particular was singled out as a source of domestic communism. Already stricken with Huntington's chorea, Guthrie was spared from appearing before the House Un-American Activities Committee, but Seeger was called to testify in 1955 and defiantly asserted his radicalism and dissatisfaction with the government. When asked if he was a communist, he refused to answer and refused also to plead the fifth amendment to avoid self-incrimination. As a result he was convicted on ten counts of contempt of Congress. His one-year sentence was overturned on a technicality, and the charges were finally dropped in 1962 (Ewen, 1977; Spector, 1983). In the meantime, Seeger was blacklisted and had no media access.

> A small esoteric group of folk enthusiasts saw their
> folksinger heroes investigated by Congress and blacklisted
> by the media. On college campuses, there was little
> interest in folk music—topical or otherwise—and guitars

were definitely symbols of leftist agitation. (RODNITZKY, 1969, p. 41)

On 1 December 1955, a black woman named Rosa Parks became a catalyst for the civil-rights movement when she refused to give up her seat to a white man on a Montgomery, Alabama bus. The Montgomery bus boycott began a wave of nonviolent resistance throughout the South, protesting the Jim Crow laws, which were the aftermath of nineteenth-century reconstruction. Black students throughout the South joined Dr. Martin Luther King, Jr.'s Southern Christian Leadership Conference in "freedom rides" on buses, sit-ins at segregated lunch counters, registration at white-only colleges, and confrontations with law enforcement.

Dr. King's movement was a singing movement (Rodnitzky, 1969) that got plenty of media coverage because it was good drama, highly visual. Television news programs, newspapers, and magazines juxtaposed shots of people with arms linked, singing "We Shall Overcome," "The Battle Hymn of the Republic," and "We Shall Not Be Moved," with shots of police with fire hoses, billy clubs, cattle prods, and snarling dogs. As Pete Seeger is still fond of saying every time he sings "We Shall Overcome," "The most important verse is the one they wrote down in Montgomery, Alabama: We are black and white together, We shall not be moved." White college students joined black students in the Student Non-Violent Coordinating Committee, white liberals trekked South to become freedom riders and to help in voter registration drives, all the while singing songs of solidarity and brotherhood.

Folk-protest music might have been nothing more than the sound track for the civil-rights movement had it not been for one other phenomenon of the late fifties: Big record companies discovered that folk music was commercially viable. Phyllis Diller was unable to keep a commitment to perform at San Francisco's Purple Onion club, and three college friends who had been singing folk songs on campus got their big break (Ward et al., 1986). The Kingston Trio soon had a number-one pop hit with "Tom Dooley," a folk song about a convicted murderer, Tom Dula.

Part of the commercial success of folk-protest music was linked to the desire of college students to forge new identities when they left the reference groups and values of high school (Denisoff, 1969). The Kingston Trio was not, by any stretch of the imagination, political or protest-oriented, in fact, they purged folk songs of lyrics that might be perceived as radical. But they paved the way for the liberally aggressive Peter, Paul, and Mary and the politically irreverent Chad Mitchell Trio (Rodnitzky, 1969).

The election of youthful John Kennedy in 1960 forecast the new youthfulness of society. Because of the post–World War II baby boom, there were then more young people than at any time in American history. More of them were attending college than ever before, and there was a new affluence. Inspired by Kennedy, the new decade was marked by idealism, social commitment, and abounding energy.

The sixties also had means of mass communication that had never existed before. Earlier protest songs did not reach mass audiences. Distribution had been limited by the technology and economics of the music business to printing broadsides and songbooks, recording on little-known labels with small production runs, and almost no play on radio. The message had been largely confined to the singers and their audiences.

Commercial success changed that. Television took an archaic event, the hootenanny, and made it a prime-time feature. ABC's second-rated program in 1963 was *Hootenanny,* an anthology of folk songs and topical humor, recorded live on a different college campus each week. *Shindig* and *Hullabaloo,* variations on the theme, were offered by the other networks. Studio-produced, they never achieved the popularity of *Hootenanny,* which captured the essential spirit of folk singing. The blacklisting of Pete Seeger almost a decade earlier eventually caused the demise of *Hootenanny.* ABC refused to book him because he would not sign a loyalty oath, and some of the most popular folk acts—Bob Dylan; Joan Baez; Peter, Paul, and Mary; and the Kingston Trio—refused to appear on the show, in support of Seeger (Ward et al., 1986).

Among this younger generation of folk singers, Bob Dylan was the pivotal figure. Early in 1961, Robert Zimmerman left his home in Hibbing, Minnesota for New York to meet his hero, Woody Guthrie. A poet, songwriter, and rock-and-roll musician in high school, he changed his name to Dylan after the poet Dylan Thomas. In the early sixties, Dylan tried to re-create himself in Guthrie's image. His early hit songs, "Blowin' In the Wind" and "The Times They Are A-Changin' " used the musical pattern of Guthrie's "talkin' blues."

Dylan was the archetypal sixties protester. He was scruffy looking, projected the image of not caring what people thought about him, and a hip cool that said "don't follow leaders" (Rodnitzky, 1976). Dylan seemed to always be acting in opposition to something. "One could argue that Bob spent the first half of his life reacting to being a Jew in a small Minnesota town and the second half reacting to his growing role as a musical messiah for America's developing counter-culture" (Rodnitzky, 1976, p. 104). Dylan's protest songs of the early sixties did not offer any solutions, they simply described uneasiness with the culture.

Dylan was a pivotal figure in folk-protest music because by the mid-sixties he had violated a cardinal tenet of folk music—using only acoustic guitars—by electrifying folk and changing it into folk-rock. Dylan's work as a musician also reflected his eclecticism, incorporating country-western, blues, gospel, and other musical forms. Predominant in Dylan's music was the myth of the outlaw hero:

> Dylan, then, offers his cultural criticism through the illumination of ethical traits ascribed to the myth of the outlaw-hero, one whose life style is simple, who has integrity, and who openly opposes corrupted authority. These traits reflect the outlaw as a distinctive American folktype influenced by the legendary Robin Hood. What makes them unique is the way they are portrayed through the rhetoric of an American singer-song writer who continues to offer a cultural criticism. (MAKAY AND GONZALEZ, 1987, p. 179)

Whether singing his own compositions or writing songs for others, Bob Dylan profoundly influenced American music. He wrote the first anthem for the war between the generations in the sixties—"The Times They Are A-Changin'."

Joan Baez was a sixties folk singer in the mold of earlier artists, who continues to use her music to make a political statement. Where Dylan's voice was distinctive for its reedy, nasal quality, Baez's voice was sweet and clear. A singer rather than a composer, she follows the style of sing-a-little, talk-a-little. Whether singing a traditional folk ballad or a topical song, she uses narrative and exposition of current events to make her songs political statements. "Joe Hill," which she described as an "organizing" song at Woodstock is one of her perennial favorites. When she sings "Joe Hill," she uses it to transfer the specific arguments for justice for the worker to the general struggle for social change and human rights.

Baez accelerated her activism as the sixties went on. In 1964 she refused to pay sixty percent of her income taxes, that portion of the national budget allocated to defense spending. In the mid-sixties, she funded the Institute for the Study of Nonviolence which survives as an organization devoted to studying ways to resolve conflict (Crockett, 1986; Rodnitzky, 1976). She has also been a devoted activist for civil rights, drawing on her own experiences of cultural rejection as a child. The daughter of a Mexican-born physicist, she experienced the Anglo rejection of "ethnic-looking" people in Southern California during the fifties.

Baez has remained faithful to her use of music for advocacy. She continues to perform at concerts and rallies to raise funds, frequently for no fee. She has recently sung to protest nuclear power plants, the arms race, and to raise funds for the homeless and hungry. In 1985, she opened the Live Aid concert "and used the opportunity to pass the torch of protest to a new generation of musicians, saying, 'This is your Woodstock, and it's long overdue' " (Crockett, 1986, p. 73).

Phil Ochs, a former journalism major at Ohio State University, typified the college-student-as-protester of the sixties. Although most of his songs were antiwar, he was politicized like Dylan and Baez in the New York folk scene of the early sixties. Ochs was the all-American boy, the son of an army physician, who became a campus radical, eventually leaving school to join the folk-protest scene.

In "I'm Gonna Say It Now," he pointed out the inconsistencies college students saw in what they were taught in the classroom versus what was going on in the world. The lyric pungently asks how the student can read through the smoke caused by book burning? It warns that American students have learned the lesson of student protests abroad and says there's a time to study and a time to fight. Ochs wrote volumes of topical protest songs, but he never gained the stature of Baez or Dylan. "Ochs' talent was a biting, satirical missionary to guilt-ridden, affluent liberals and especially to their aimless children, but he yearned to be a hero of the left" (Rodnitzky, 1976, p. 63).

There were many folk-protest legends in the sixties. Paul Simon and Art Garfunkel produced a topical album, *Wednesday Morning Three A.M.,* which did not sell well at the time but included the song, "Sounds of Silence," which seemed to express the sense of isolation most young people felt. Several topical songs appeared on this album: "He Was My Brother," a eulogy for an older brother who was a freedom rider; Dylan's "The Times They Are a Changin'," sung so that everyone could finally figure out the words; a peace song, "Last Night I Had the Strangest Dream," the dream being an end to war; and "Go Tell It on the Mountain," a song favored by the civil-rights movement. Ironically, the album sells more copies today in re-release than it did in 1964 (Ward et al., 1986).

Simon and Garfunkel became one of the more popular folk duos of the sixties. Their *Parsley, Sage, Rosemary, & Thyme* album featured an innovative use of stereo technology. "7 O'Clock News/Silent Night" offered the traditional Christmas song from one speaker juxtaposed with an evening news cast from the other. Paul Simon continues to write protest songs and topical music. Most recently, his *Graceland* album combined African folk music with his own work to make a political statement about apartheid in South Africa.

Steven Stills and his group, Buffalo Springfield, described the alienation of youth from the establishment in "For What It's Worth," a song about police confrontations with teens on the Sunset Strip in Los Angles. The image of "something's happening here" and "a man with a gun over there" spoke of the us-against-them mentality that divided baby boomers from their parents. Stills later joined David Crosby, Graham Nash, and Neil Young to form one of the supergroups of the late sixties. "Wooden Ships," sung at the Woodstock festival, told the story of survivors of a nuclear holocaust, and Crosby's "Almost Cut My Hair" addressed the paranoia of sixties youth and the long hair they favored as a symbol of separation from the general culture.

Two songs by Crosby, Stills, Nash, and Young stand out as archetypal. Graham Nash's "Chicago" is the story of the clash between protesters, peace-activists, and Mayor Daley's police during the 1968 Democratic convention. The lyric held out the promise that the young people could "change the world, rearrange the world." In "Ohio," Neil Young responded to the clash between students at Kent State University and the Ohio National Guard in the spring of 1970, "four dead in Ohio." The recording was rushed to disk jockeys but was banned in many areas, especially in Ohio, because it was feared that it would provoke other confrontations.

The topical protest song had its heyday in the early sixties. By the mid-sixties, musicians began to realize that politics was no substitute for musical technique and aesthetics. Woody Guthrie and Pete Seeger had often played below their musical abilities so that the music would not get in the way of the message (Rodnitzky, 1976). When it became commercially viable, folk-protest music became popular music and subject to the bottom-line policies of record companies, the value system of "Top 40" play lists and album sales. The folk artists of the thirties and forties had aimed their music at a more historically minded audience, usually delivering it in person. Whether or not it would sell was not the point (Denisoff, 1969).

Folk-protest became folk-rock, usually once removed from the audience and aimed at a less historically minded record buyer.

> In attempting to be all things to all people, the compositions became do-it-yourself protest songs. One could read whatever one wanted into the lines. Stance became more important than goals. Whether or not the medium is always the message, the medium had obviously overtaken most protest ballads. However, although the song lyrics were increasingly hazy and thus less powerful, their influence was far more persuasive because of the simple weight of numbers and their matter-of-fact presentation. (RODNITZKY, 1976, p. 16)

Folk-rock had a different flavor from folk-protest. The growing youth counterculture became more concerned with existential resistance to the establishment, and songs reflected opposition to a society of parents, political leaders, and anyone over thirty. The folk-protest and folk-rock songs of the sixties addressed a number of issues: racial discrimination, the nuclear arms race, pollution and destruction of the environment, drug laws, police brutality, and especially the war in Vietnam.

Antiwar Songs

Although some Americans have protested the nation's involvement in any war, protests against American involvement in Vietnam stand out as an antiwar crusade in which music played a particularly important role. As the draft took more and more young men, attending college to gain a deferment or leaving the country to avoid the draft were the options some chose. On college campuses, commitment to the civil rights movement gave way to protests against the Vietnam War.

Singing was a natural way to express opinions for a generation who had learned the power of song. Folk and folk-rock were the musical styles that differentiated the antiwar activists from their parents and the establishment, whose image of the folk-singer was that of a scruffy, long-haired individual with an acoustic guitar and, most likely, a bomb in the guitar case (Denisoff, 1969).

Phil Ochs was one of the most prolific writers of antiwar songs. In 1964, his "I Ain't Marchin' Any More" chronicled the ordinary soldier's deeds in the country's previous conflicts and expansion. Adopting the persona of the soldier, the singer concluded that, though it might be called "peace" or it might be called "treason," he would not fight again. Rejecting the argument that the U.S. role in Vietnam was a police action against communism, Ochs wrote "Cops of the World" in 1966. The lyrics described an imperialistic military that was going to bring freedom and democracy to the world, even if it had to do so at gun point. Ochs decided to declare an end to the war in 1967. On 21 October, he stood on the steps of the Pentagon and sang "I Declare the War Is Over." Calling up images of the war on TV screens and the folly of believing that pride and patriotism were at stake, Ochs concluded that we are only what we believe and he chose to believe that the war was over.

Bob Dylan also wrote songs for antiwar activists, and many of his compositions were popularized by other artists. Dozens of versions of "With God on Our Side" were recorded. This song is still used by protesters to oppose American involvement in the Middle East and Latin America. It tells the story of America's wars and the shiftiness of claiming divine backing. The Russians were once our allies, with God on their side, while the Germans were our enemies and without divine favor. After World War II, the situation was reversed. The message of history seemed clear: become America's ally, and God will be on your side.

One song, so popular in the sixties that it was recorded by dozens of groups and individuals, was originally a prowar song from World War II. Woody Guthrie and one of the best known of the "old" folk groups, the Almanac Singers, wrote a song to commemorate the men who died when the U.S.S. *Reuben James* was torpedoed by a German submarine in 1941. The Almanac Singers were loosely affiliated with elements of the communist party in the United States in the thirties and forties. Hitler had signed a nonaggression agreement with the Soviets late in the thirties, but broke it in 1940 by invading Soviet territory. By 1941, the United States was sending war materials to Europe.

This series of events had a curious impact on communists in the United States. During the period of German-Soviet friendship, communist unions had tried to block President Roosevelt's efforts to send war materials to Europe. When Soviet territory was invaded, the communists suddenly became prowar. Songs were written to stimulate war production and to celebrate the men and women working for the war effort. The original version of "The Sinking of the Reuben James" was a chronicle of the men who died, their military specialties, and their virtues as fighting men. That version proved too cumbersome to sing at war rallies, so Guthrie streamlined the song.

The song was revived in the late fifties and early sixties by popular folk groups and became a staple on many albums. The Almanac Singers later added one verse that changed the whole message of the song. They noted that even though a long time had passed since the crew had died, war still meant the same thing: "The worst of men must fight and the best of men must die." So with a single verse, a song celebrating the great struggle against fascism in World War II was turned into an argument against the value of war.

One of the more eloquent songwriting duos of the late sixties, who kept much of the folk-protest quality in their music, was John and Terry Talbot. Like Phil Ochs, their group, Mason Profit, never gained the stature they sought as the musical voice of the antiwar movement. Nevertheless, their songs were powerful examples of the message song.

The title cut on their first album, *Last Night I Had the Strangest Dream,* was an older peace song by Almanac singer Ed McCurdy, and most of the rest of the songs contained antiwar messages. "Eugene Pratt" was a story-in-song about an antiwar activist on a college campus who is a mystery to fraternity men, whose purpose in life seems to be getting drunk. Written so that the singer assumes the persona of a frat man, the song concluded that maybe Pratt was the smartest of them all, even if he did go to jail for his beliefs. "Mother," a dying soldier's tribute to his mother, is evocative of the "mother" songs of the Civil War. The song tells of a high-school graduate whose cap and gown were exchanged for a uniform. He had been turned into a "rice paddy man," sent to kill Vietnamese but uncertain if he can. "Twenty-Four Hour Sweetheart" was a song about a Saigon brothel and a soldier's sense of loneliness in a foreign land.

One of the best-known antiwar songs was the "Fixin' to Die Rag," by Country Joe and the Fish. It was always preceded by the famous "Fish Cheer":

> *Gimme an F,*
> *Gimme a U,*
> *Gimme a C,*
> *Gimme a . . .*
> *What's that spell?*
> *What's that spell?*
> (COTILLION RECORDS, 1970)

Radio stations would not play the song, even though it was selling well. To get it on the air, this preamble was re-recorded to spell fish. "Fixin' to Die Rag" fit the mold of the classic protest song. The Fish Cheer involved the audience right away, the song's lyrics were easy to learn, and the audience was expected to sing along.

In addition to traditional folk songs, Joan Baez sang "Saigon Bride," a story-in-song about a South Vietnamese soldier leaving his bride for a war he thinks will never reunite them or his country. Buffie Sainte-Marie, a Cree Indian and former member of the Buffalo Springfield, wrote "Universal Soldier," which was popularized by the British folk singer Donovan. "Universal Soldier" claimed that blame could not be shifted to governments or national leaders. The individual soldier was the "weapon" of war, and his orders came from the individual citizens of the world.

John Fogerty of Creedence Clearwater Revival wrote "Fortunate Son," which focused on the basic inequities of military service. The sons of the poor fought the war while the "fortunate sons" could afford to go to college and get a deferment. The Doors recorded the "Unknown Soldier," which called up images of the soldier-as-statistic in the body count that had replaced the ability to gain and hold territory as the military's index of progress in Vietnam.

Arlo Guthrie has frequently employed the extended story-song as a protest technique. His classic antiwar song, "Alice's Restaurant Massacree," was an eighteen-minute, thirty-second narrative about an incident that actually happened to him.

> Arlo Guthrie's chronicle, "Alice's Restaurant Massacree,"
> written in 1968, is a beguiling protest against an officious
> and petty village police department, as well as the
> Vietnam War draft. Its long text is tongue-in-cheek from

> the beginning to end, but has been clearly understood as
> social criticism and heard by thousands of people in
> concerts and from the record album. The vocal style is
> simple, and the singer's ideas are assimilated
> effortlessly. (PERRIS, 1985, p. 5)

Arlo and some of his friends turned the song into a film, *Alice's Restaurant* (available on videotape), and expanded the story. Its antiwar elements detail Arlo's experiences at his draft physical. Convicted of littering, he was rejected as unfit for military service, one of the more hilarious accounts of how not to get drafted. With the resumption of draft registration, Arlo Guthrie has again made the song a staple of his concerts.

Pete Seeger wrote many antiwar songs, but his most famous act of anti-Vietnam War songwriting and singing occurred on 28 February 1968. The Smothers Brothers, a comic folk duo who made the politics of folk music apparent to middle America, had been hired in the summer of 1965 as a summer replacement for CBS's *Glen Campbell Good Time Hour*. They proved popular and earned respectable ratings. CBS was engaged in a war with NBC, which "owned" Sunday nights with *Bonanza,* its number-one rated show. The Smothers Brothers were rehired as CBS's not-so-secret weapon in midseason 1966 to get the drop on the legendary Cartwrights. Happily for CBS, their show drew viewers away from NBC, and the ratings climbed (Spector, 1983).

Not known then for its liberalism, CBS engaged the Smothers Brothers in a constant censorship battle over program content. The Smothers Brothers, like the Not Ready For Prime Time Players, the inheritors of their tradition a decade later on NBC's *Saturday Night Live,* preferred to do topical humor and include popular acts. Allusions to the Vietnam War, drugs, and sex were common on the show—when they could be concealed from, or rendered less controversial in, the eyes of the CBS censors.

Pete Seeger had been blacklisted from performing on television since 1955. The Smothers Brothers broke the ban by having him appear early in their first season, but CBS restricted him to singing traditional folk songs. He appeared again on 28 February 1968 and sang "Waist Deep in the Big Muddy," a song cut from his earlier appearance (Spector, 1983). One of his own compositions, the song was the story of a platoon on maneuvers in Louisiana in 1942. While fording the Mississippi, the platoon kept on losing men, and the closing line of each stanza referred to their platoon leader, "the big fool," who commanded them to "push on." Anyone who heard the song had no doubt that it was really about Vietnam and "the big fool" was Lyndon Johnson.

As antiwar activism escalated on college campuses, two songs by the Jefferson Airplane, "We Can Be Together" and "Volunteers," became popular with protesters as anthems of youth in rebellion, unity songs in the tradition of "Solidarity Forever." "We Can Be Together" epitomized the youth movement and the adjectives so often applied by parents and the establishment: obscene, dangerous, dirty, violent, and young. The song asserted a sense of pride in being a force for anarchy. Most of all, "We Can Be Together" was a call for unity among the members of the younger generation, followed by a call to join the revolution of a generation that had "soul" against a generation that had grown "old" in "Volunteers."

Protest music of the sixties, opposing war and social injustice, was unique in that it was mass marketed, thus enabling millions of young people to forge a musical identity as a generation in pursuit of a conscience. Overt message music and musical concern with society's ills gradually gave way to folk-rock. With the end of U.S. involvement in Vietnam, war was less frequently the subject of lyrics. However, the memory of Vietnam continued to haunt the music of the eighties.

In 1981, the Charlie Daniels Band recorded "Still in Saigon," a song about the veteran who did not go to college and did not go to Canada because he was "brought up differently," and "couldn't break the rules." Years later, he is back in the world (the United States), but in his mind he is "still in Saigon." A second Vietnam-remembered song was recorded by Billy Joel in 1982. "Goodnight Saigon" chronicled boot camp, the brotherhood of those who fought and died in Vietnam, and the futility of a war in which "we ruled the day," but "they ruled the night."

Rock and Roll

Rock and roll was born in the fifties and in many ways was always part of sixties protest music. Emerging in the late fifties and early sixties from the blues, country-western, and gospel music, and popularized by Elvis Presley, Chuck Berry, Buddy Holly, and Jerry Lee Lewis, rock and roll was a symbol of adolescent rebellion. Rock and roll had the power to speak to and for some people and to antagonize others in ways that traditional folk message music never had. Beatles records were regularly smuggled into Soviet bloc countries in the sixties; no one had ever smuggled Woody Guthrie records into any country (Gleason, 1969).

Until the confrontations and campus rebellions of the late sixties, rock and roll was one of the few avenues of public expression and rebellion for youth.

> Significant to that generation was the acute sense of standing alone and powerless. This was expressed by the antagonism toward the values established by the older generation. For many, and not only among youth, a person had become one of a nameless mass to be manipulated by an uncaring bureaucracy. (PERRIS, 1985, p. 182)

Because the recording industry and the media made rock and roll nationally accessible, every teenager could become a rebel, a surfer, a protester, a hippie, or whatever their taste in music identified them with. For thirty years, the music has been a voice for each new generation coming of age—and it still influences their frame of reference for viewing the world.

One of the momentous changes in rock and roll occurred in the mid-sixties, when the Beatles revived rock, made it fun again, and a part of the general youth culture. Their songs, life-styles, and appearances on *The Ed Sullivan Show*, were listened to, watched, and discussed by most American teenagers. What impact did they have?

> If the "dream" the Beatles helped create could not sustain itself in the real world, that speaks more to our false hopes than to their promises. They wrote and sang songs. We turned it into politics and philosophy and a road map to another way of life. (GREENFIELD, 1987, p. 43-44)

Rock changed message music. "Concept albums," which used all cuts to develop a mood or theme, became as important as individual songs. The work of two British groups that were especially popular with the counterculture, the Moody Blues and Jethro Tull, typify the concept album. The Moody Blues' *Days of Future Passed* was considered innovative and experimental, combining as it did elements of classical music with electronic rock. Taking the listener through a mystical day, the album articulated the idealism of the sixties. It continues to be a popular album, selling well on compact disc.

Before rock, some songs were intended to send a message whereas others were intended as entertainment. Rock was more expansive containing as it did elements of many kinds of music. It exercised the kind of persuasive power over an entire generation that previously had only been exercised by the leaders of military units, small groups of protesters, religious leaders, and labor unions over their members.

In a holistic sense, rock came to have political power and message potential beyond that of the individual message songs of the past.

> Rock often succeeds in doing what nothing else manages to do: give a divided people a sense that they have something in common. When both candidates in the 1984 presidential elections invoked rock star Bruce Springsteen in their speeches, they tacitly acknowledged that he was capable of symbolizing certain ideals and hopes for the public in a way that they could not. When rock bands appear among separatist religious groups like the Hasidim, rock can be said to have proved itself adaptable to the needs of virtually every segment of American society. When Paul Simon, a rock star from a "folk rock" background, can persuade his record company to underwrite a collaboration with South African and South American musicians, the cross-fertilization of cultures appears to be reaching global proportions. (PODELL, 1987, p. 5)

Rock musicians and folk-rock performers continue to use their music for political purposes. Arlo Guthrie's songwriting has included a "Watergate" song and several songs about the problems of Latin America. He constantly reinter-prets old message songs in light of new exigences. John Cougar Mellencamp's album, *Scarecrow,* chronicled the problems in American agriculture. Madonna and other artists have begun to record songs about AIDS. Tracy Chapman continues the tradition of the older folk message songs, writing about the home-less and disenfranchised.

In addition to individual songs and albums, concerts are used to raise funds for causes. Artists United Against Apartheid, forty-nine performers, joined to sing "Sun City" and provide information about apartheid to viewers of MTV. Concerts have been held to raise funds to fight famine in Africa. Cognizant of the problems at home, country-western singer Willy Nelson hosted a fourteen and one-half hour event, "Farm Aid," to raise money for American farmers. John Fogerty told the audience: "The next time you sit down to a very nice meal, remember, it didn't come from a cellophane bag from Safeway. Some guy gave his whole life to that meal you're eating" (Cocks, 1987, p. 96). On 4 July 1987, a group of musicians and television personalities, some former sixties antiwar activists, staged a "Wel-come Home" concert for Vietnam veterans. Part of the purpose was to raise money to help veterans and their families.

These fund-raising concerts follow the format of the old labor rallies—a little talking, lots of singing, and a message to unite for a cause—with one important difference: These concerts are normally broadcast to reach the widest possible audience. Viewers at home are told how they too can become involved. Their paid pledge usually results in receiving some tangible symbol of their concern and participation such as a T-shirt.

Doing Rhetorical Criticism of Music

As with other forms of rhetorical activity, the message of a song results from a combination of the rhetor's work and its reception by the audience. A careful investigation of the details of performance, the nature of the audience, and the musician's background will provide information for your criticism. When possi-ble, listen to or view the musical work yourself so that you have a sense of its production values. In some cases, this may not be possible, or even necessary if your goal is to examine the lyrics alone.

You may choose to study a single song or a category of songs. For instance, one category of country-western music includes songs about long-haul truckers. You might study several representative songs from that category to determine what messages it communicates to or about truckers. You might also choose to examine an entire album as a concept or the works of a particular singer or songwriter across several albums and singles.

In many cases, it may not be important to distinguish between the person who sang the song and the person who wrote it. For the purposes of rhetorical criticism, you are frequently concerned with the relationship between the song and its listeners. Joan Baez wrote very few songs, choosing instead to sing older folk songs and other songs she found appealing or well suited to her political purpose. Decide whether or not it is important to distinguish singer from writer according to what you are trying to accomplish critically. If you want to criticize the story-song as it was developed by Woody Guthrie, then restrict yourself to those songs he wrote. If you want to consider how the local teacher's union used music to protest an unfair labor practice, knowing who wrote the songs they sang may not be important.

The traditional approach to rhetorical criticism can be applied in terms of the nature of the singer or songwriter, the nature of the message, and the nature of the audience. When using the traditional approach, consider the singer/songwriter's ethos. How did her personality come across in the song? Did she create a persona other than that commonly associated with her? What was her relationship to the cause discussed or the image projected in the song? In other words, consider all of the techniques available to the rhetor to establish her credibility in your analysis.

You may want to examine message songs that contain an obvious argument in their lyrics, such as some of those mentioned in this chapter, as arguments in terms of logos. How is the argument developed, what proof is included? What circumstances or events are described in the lyric? How is the argument developed in terms of reasoning? Are cause-effect relationships established, are consequences of inaction identified, or is a better future prophesied as a result of undertaking some course of action? Even if a song does not immediately suggest an argumentative structure, consider how its lyrics develop the subject matter in terms of what the traditional approach says about logic and structure in rhetoric.

You also might want to consider the style of a song in terms of both its words and music, if possible. What does the music itself add to the lyrics' verbal elements? How is sound used to establish a mood, build to a climax, or create contrasts? The lyric itself also has emotive properties that appeal to the listener. Are the lyrics inflammatory? What emotions did the singer want the listener to experience through the lyric? How are the listener's interests, fears, and hopes engaged by the song?

Most protest songs and many rock songs reject some aspect of existing hierarchies, detailing a list of grievances with such agents as family, school, government, business, law enforcement, or the military. The dramatistic approach is particularly useful in analyzing any song whose purpose it is to oppose some established hierarchy.

The concept of identification can be used to discover how the song's message worked to unify listeners or join them with the singer in pursuit of some end. Many groups that specifically relied on songs to raise morale and create group unity used magnetic songs, as discussed in this chapter, as vehicles of identification. Some songs named the identity that those outside the group hold for its members. Many songs that portrayed the generation gap described older people's attitudes toward youth. "We are all outlaws" in the establishment's and our parents' eyes.

The pentad can also be used to analyze the song's structure and its treatment of subject matter. Find the important ratios as communicated by the song lyrics before making judgments about its ability to persuade its listeners.

Because songs can create rhetorical visions of how the singer/songwriter wants the listener to see this world, or a better world, fantasy theme analysis may also be an appropriate method of criticism. The message songs of the labor movement created worker-heroes and boss-villains. Utopian views of the benefits to the worker-as-union-member were typically featured in the messages of union music. Consider this rhetorical vision and the elements of its scenario. Was the sanctioning agent the singer or the listener? How was the listener to be brought into the singer's vision? How were heroes and villains portrayed? Fantasies view the world in particular dramatic ways. Did the song offer a conspiracy drama, a soap opera, or a comedy of life? Examine lyrics to identify possible instances of dramatic typologies.

Concepts from cultural models may be appropriate to doing criticism of songs popularized by a particular social movement. Songs may have been used at various stages in the movement's development to reflect what was happening to its members or to characterize the social ills the movement was formed to combat. Magnetic songs may have been used as in-gathering devices. Also look for evidence of the movement's use of the rhetorical song as described earlier in this chapter.

Any song reflects the value standards of its age, by either reinforcing a particular value or rejecting it in favor of another. Message songs frequently involve forced choices among values: "Which side are you on?" Many of the songs of the Civil War typified this sort of forced choice. Songs have also been used to reflect human value systems. Examining the themes or content categories of a song in terms of their relationship to the social-value structure of the group and the society at large may be useful in making your analysis.

Singing can be ritual behavior. Singing together has often been used to transform singer and audience, to move them closer together, and closer to some new state. Examine the possibility that a song may have functioned in such a transformational sense. If it was used in this way, ask yourself: What old symbols were rejected or revised? What new symbols were created? How was a change from one state to another accomplished by the lyrics and music? Asking and answering questions such as these enabled previous critics to explain the almost hypnotic power that Nazi rallies had on those who participated in them.

Historians and anthropologists tell us that one of the earliest uses of song was the oral transmission of a group's history in the form of stories. Many message songs retain this story format. The narrative approach is an extremely useful method of criticism when you are analyzing a song that tells a story, such as Arlo Guthrie's "Alice's Restaurant Massacree." When applying the narrative approach to a song, consider how the tale and its telling were developed through the lyrics, but do not ignore the song's musical properties. Remember how recurrent musical themes were used in "Peter and the Wolf" to literally tell the story.

Regardless of whether or not you elect to criticize music, we hope that this chapter has expanded your understanding of the role that music can play, and has played, in our nation's history. It is not true of every song that has been sung, but some music has been used in rhetorical ways and is legitimately an object of rhetorical criticism. If you choose to study music, you have at your disposal a full complement of methodologies from which to select.

Suggested Readings

Examples of Criticism

BLOODWORTH, J.D. (1975).   Communication in the youth counter culture: Music as expression. *Central States Speech Journal, 26,* 304–309.

> The rhetorical situation is used to discuss the music of the sixties. Folk-rock and rock lyrics are examined as the fitting response from the perspective of youth to their perceived alienation from society. Bloodworth focuses on themes and poetic qualities found in lyrics of the era. This is a good example of how a critic must develop arguments for his point of view. Bloodworth's premise is that for sixties youth, music was a primary communication form. You will see how a critic uses a variety of rhetorical concepts in this article.

CARTER, D.A. (1980).   The industrial workers of the world and the rhetoric of song. *Quarterly Journal of Speech, 66,* 365–374.

> This article examines how songs functioned rhetorically in the union activities of the IWW. Carter analyzes union songs in terms of two themes, separation and oppression, common to songs of the IWW's *The Little Red Song Book* and explains the role of these songs in IWW rhetoric. Although there is a limited organic approach to methodology in this article, it is a good example of analysis of the use of songs by social movements.

GONZALEZ, A., AND MAKAY, J.J. (1983).   Rhetorical ascription and the gospel according to Dylan. *Quarterly Journal of Speech, 69,* 1–14.

> "Ascription" is a communication concept that combines sound and lyric. The entire body of Bob Dylan's work is analyzed for how the music and lyrics combine for persuasive effect. This is a good example of organic criticism. The authors combine rhetorical principles from several works to develop their concept of ascription and apply it to Dylan's work. This is also a good example of how a critic's uses of a concept expand rhetorical theory.

MAKAY, J.J., AND GONZALEZ, A. (1987).   Dylan's biographical rhetoric and the myth of the outlaw hero. *Southern Speech Communication Journal, 52,* 165–180.

> This example of rhetorical criticism of music focuses on Bob Dylan's songs about people and mythical figures. The authors examine how Dylan's personal ethos derived from these songs that tell the stories of cultural outcasts. This is a good example of organic criticism that combines ideas about the rhetorical function of myth, social values, and the concept of ethos. Pay special attention to the authors' discussion of the outlaw as a cultural hero.

McGUIRE, M. (1984).   "Darkness on the edge of town": Bruce Springsteen's rhetoric of optimism and despair. In M.J. Medhurst and T.W. Benson (Eds.), *Rhetorical dimensions in media* (pp 233–253). Dubuque, IA: Kendall/Hunt.

> This critical study uses thematic analysis to study the meaning of Springsteen's lyrics. Concepts from the narrative paradigm are used to discover three common themes:

despair, optimism, and responsibility. McGuire views this artist as someone whose music is a rhetorical act in that it invites the audience to forge an identity with the musician. This is a good example of careful analysis of lyric and the interrelatedness of thematic elements in a particular song.

PERRIS, A. (1985). Music as propaganda. Westport, CN: Greenwood Press.
The author's approach is more a general consideration than an analysis of the persuasive properties and uses of music, but you will find evidence of concepts of the traditional, social-psychological, and narrative approaches in his work. The value of this book is in its depth of consideration of music as a rhetorical act. Perris gives special emphasis to the role of music in totalitarian states but also considers religious music, opera, Broadway musicals, and popular music of the sixties.

WEISMAN, E.R. (1985). The good man singing well: Stevie Wonder as noble lover. *Critical Studies in Mass Communication, 2,* 136–151.
The author's approach to analysis of Stevie Wonder's music combines ideas from classical Greek and Roman rhetorical theory and contemporary concepts of media. The focus is on Wonder's ethos as derived from his lyrics and linguistic style. This is a particularly good example of traditional concepts of ethos applied to popular music. Weisman also does an excellent analysis of style to support his ethical criterion evaluation of Wonder's appeal to a wide audience. This is an especially good example of rhetorical analysis and criticism that will serve as a model of how the critic functions as an arguer in his own right.

Resources for Doing Criticism

DENISOFF, R.S. (1971). *Great day coming.* Urbana, IL: University of Illinois Press.
The focus of this book is folk music and the American left, both old (1930s and 1940s) and new (1960s). This is a history of American folk music with an emphasis on labor songs, protest songs, and the work of the Almanac Singers. This is an excellent source for background information on message songs in the twentieth century. It is also an example of a sociological approach to analyzing message songs.

DENISOFF, R.S. (1972). *Sing a song of social significance.* Bowling Green, OH: Bowling Green State University Press.
This book provides the best discussion of Denisoff's view of magnetic and rhetorical songs. The focus is on folk and folk-rock. Of special interest is the discussion of teenage death songs as reflections of teen rebellion. Denisoff provides a sociological approach to popular music.

DENISOFF, R.S., AND PETERSON, R.A. (EDS.) (1972). *The sounds of social change.* Chicago: Rand McNally & Co.
This is an anthology of articles on music and its role in society as a form of communication. Included are pieces on country music, soul and black protest, Nazi use of music for social control, and rock. The authors include both liberal and conservative views. These articles do not provide rhetorical analysis of music but serve as a resource for the cultural view of music as a part of social history. The value of this anthology is the great variety of views offered.

EWEN, D. (1977). *All the years of American popular music.* Englewood Cliffs, NJ: Prentice-Hall.
As the title suggests, this is a history of popular music in America beginning with the Pilgrims and ending with contemporary rock and soul music. This exceptionally

thorough survey of American music will serve as a resource on music in American history. Patriotic songs, ballads, show business and Broadway, ragtime, blues, jazz, folk, rock, soul, hillbilly and country, and novelty songs are covered. This is the most comprehensive history of the scope of American music.

GREENWAY, J. (1970). *American folksongs of protest.* New York: Octagon Books.
This is a history of protest music in American history. It is particularly useful for studying the use of music in the labor movement. Historical background and lyrics are provided for songs of textile workers, miners, migratory workers, and industrial workers. Profiles of several songwriters are included. This book provides information on the rhetorical situations that produced protest songs but is not rhetorical criticism of music.

HOOD, P. (Ed.) (1986). *Artists of American folk music.* New York: William Morrow.
This collection of background pieces on important folksingers includes biographies, interviews, and commentary on their beliefs and music. Included are Woody Guthrie; Pete Seeger; the New Lost City Ramblers; Joan Baez; Peter, Paul, and Mary; Bob Dylan; Gordon Lightfoot; and Tom Paxton.

LAWRENCE, V.B. (1975). *Music for patriots, politicians, and presidents.* New York: Macmillan.
This is a history of the political uses of music. The first one-hundred years of American history are covered as the author surveys propaganda, war songs, campaign songs, and narratives of the place of each song in American history. Lyrics, facsimiles of sheet music, and the archaic spellings of history give a sense of music in our history. This is a resource that provides a wealth of historical detail.

RODNITZKY, J.L. (1976). *Minstrels of the dawn.* Chicago: Nelson-Hall.
This is one of the most comprehensive views of the folk-protest music of the sixties. Although the author takes a sociological rather than a rhetorical perspective, his analysis of folk-protest music has much in common with rhetorical analysis and criticism. Of particular interest are his profiles of Woodie Guthrie, Phil Ochs, Joan Baez, and Bob Dylan. Each profile addresses the relationship among singer, song, and audience, providing insights into how the singer functions as a persuader in a particular sociopolitical environment. Rodnitzky has a particularly strong sense of music as message.

WARD, E., STOKES, G., AND TUCKER, K. (1986). *Rock of ages.* New York: Rolling Stone Press/Summit Books.
This is the most comprehensive history of rock and roll available. The authors provide encyclopedic detail on trends, people, social history, and the interweaving of relationships in the rock music industry. This is a valuable source for background information on popular music from the fifties to the present. Every nuance and development are addressed.

12

The

Rhetoric of

Humor

Americans have used humor to cope with difficult situations and to probe social customs. Benjamin Franklin used quips and humorous drawings to urge colonists to form a national identity. Artemus Ward and Mark Twain, personas created by Charles Farrar Browne and Samuel Langhorn Clemens, poked fun at social customs. Thomas Nast's political cartoons made Americans aware of the dangers of Tammany Hall, and Bill Mauldin's cartoons chronicled the wit and wisdom of Willy and Joe, two World War II infantrymen. Humor has exposed social problems and forced us to confront taboo subjects. African-American comedians of the 1950s and 1960s—Moms Mabley, Flip Wilson, Godfrey Cambridge, and Dick Gregory—commented on the status of blacks in America, reflecting their own experiences and helping white audiences to understand (Martineau, 1972). Today, Robin Williams warns us of the danger of drugs when he takes on the role of a Peruvian chief and reminds us, "Cocaine is our little gift to the white man for what you did to us."

Humor is a part of being human. In his 1885 lectures on comedy, English essayist and literary critic William Hazlitt described humans as the only creatures who laugh and weep because only the human animal is able to recognize the difference between the real and the ideal. Hazlitt echoed the thoughts of classical thinkers: Tragedy and comedy are opposing poles of the human condition. He recognized the importance of humor as an emotional response.

> If everything that went wrong, if every vanity or weakness
> in another gave us a sensible pang, it would be hard
> indeed: but as long as the disagreeableness of the
> consequences of a sudden disaster is kept out of sight by
> the immediate oddity of the circumstances, and the
> absurdity or unaccountableness of a foolish action is the
> most striking thing in it, the ludicrous prevails over the
> pathetic, and we receive pleasure instead of pain from the
> farce of life which is played before us, and which
> discomposes our gravity as often as it fails to move our
> anger or our pity! (QUOTED IN MORREALL, 1987, p. 66)

Hazlitt found the essence of humor in the contradiction between what is expected and what actually occurs. The work of the comedian or humorist is planned and, to make us laugh, it plays upon some contradiction in reason, custom, event, character, or expectation. In Hazlitt's mind, the source of humor lies in misunderstandings, in which one person means one thing and a second means another. The rhetor who uses humor as a means of persuasion deliberately creates circumstances that reveal misunderstandings to forge new meanings out of contrived ambiguity and contrast, contradiction and resolution, or the absurdity of the rhetorical act. When the cartoon characters in Walt Kelly's strip *Pogo* opined "We have met the enemy and he is us," they not only altered the famous words of John Paul Jones; they also drew their audience's attention to the greatest source of danger in America in the 1950s.

Humor is a genre that provides rhetors with a means to communicate information and opinion.

> Humor is conceived generically to be any communicative
> instance which is perceived as humorous by any of the
> interacting parties. The humorous communicative instance
> becomes a vehicle or social mechanism employed for
> interaction. Humor may assume different forms and has
> different functions in various structural settings.
> (MARTINEAU, 1972, p. 114)

This suggests that something is properly labeled as humorous either if it was the rhetor's intent for it to be taken that way or if, in decoding the message, the audience found it humorous. Rhetor and audience need not agree.

> "What's fifty meters long and eats potatoes?"
> "A queue waiting to buy meat." (LUKES AND GALNOOR,
> 1987, p. 153).

Did you "get" the joke? Did you think it was funny? Probably not, because Americans do not usually have to wait in line to buy meat and seldom find it in short supply.

There are hundreds of variations on this joke in Eastern European countries where audiences find it hilarious because standing in line to try to buy something that is in short supply is an everyday experience. As a result, "queue" jokes, like other types of humor, serve the communication needs of rhetors and the audiences who understand them.

> Humor is a complex arrangement, involving cultural and psychological processes, which moves in external and internal ways: as a means of social control, as an internal fulcrum, as a retaliatory device and as a form of communalism. Humor is clearly ubiquitous. All humans possess a latent sense of humor, meaning a structured way of laughing, and all groups utilize and often institutionalize humor within their social structures. (BOSKIN, 1987, p. 253)

Queue jokes, and the fact that you probably did not find this one particularly funny, also illustrate the culture-bound nature of humor. Of all the genres of communication discussed in this book, humor may be the one most closely tied to the particulars of the rhetor's culture and its success most dependent on the audience's knowledge of that culture.

> The culture code is perhaps the elemental aspect in the structure of social humor. To be understood and possess meaning, humor must in some fashion relate to the experience and awareness of the majority. This does not mean that humor is constantly appreciated or comprehended but that it must relate, in an intimate way, to the scope and direction of society. A primary consequence of this process is the creation of culture and/ or sub-culture and a connection to a specific time and place. (BOSKIN, 1987, p. 254)

If you did not find anything amusing about "a queue waiting to buy meat," it is because you are culturally unprepared to identify with, let alone understand, queues and shortages.

Not all humor is rhetorical. What is rhetorical humor? The answer lies in the structure of the message and the use of humor to communicate ideas intended to influence belief or behavior. Contradiction or absurdity, which is the basis for humor, violates our typical conceptual patterns. Some humor is entirely verbal and some exclusively nonverbal, but it is the contradiction of verbal and visual elements in many rhetorical acts that makes them humorous.

Laughter is more than a reaction to some surprising change in the course of events. It is a consequence of a cognitive process that draws on both the human sense of order and systems and our appreciation for the clever violation of that order and those systems (Morreall, 1987). Our sense of order and systems reflect our fundamental social and political processes, and it is these processes that constitute the exigence that calls for a fitting, albeit humorous, response. In this chapter, we discuss the basic structure of humor, comic devices, the role of the audience, and the subgenres of American humor.

The Structure of Humor

Philosopher John Morreall believes that humor is an important part of the creative process; we frequently label it invention in communication. As such, humor is a rational process.

> Humor today goes hand in hand with our rationality, too, and not just rationality in the sense of cognitive sophistication, but also in the sense of a rational attitude toward the world. Part of this attitude is viewing things critically, and people with a well-developed sense of humor naturally look at things critically, because they are looking for incongruity. To be able to create humor, too, they need to cultivate imagination so as to be able to view things from unusual perspectives and create incongruous fictions. This imagination combined with a critical view of the world gives those with a rich sense of humor a flexible, versatile perspective and helps them overcome narrowness in their thinking. One of the most obvious traits of unimaginative, doctrinaire people is their lack of humor. (MORREALL, 1987, p. 203)

The rhetor who uses humor is putting forward an argument about some aspect of his or her world in which incongruity is proof of the rhetor's premise, and a laugh from the audience affirms it.

We can approach the structure of humor in terms of its most fundamental element: the joke as an argument. Whether it is a quip or a lengthy humorous essay, a joke has two parts: the setup and the punch line. The *setup* identifies the conditions in the rhetorical situation that lead to contradiction or absurdity. The *punch line* unravels the contradiction or renders the absurdity meaningful. When the audience gets the punch line, they understand the argument. If they never get it, they fail even to recognize that any argument has been offered. This structure and the need for the audience to get it make humor a cognitive process.

> [T]he recipient encounters an incongruity—the punch line. In the second stage, the perceiver engages in a form of problem solving to find a cognitive rule which makes the punch line follow from the main part of the joke and reconciles the incongruous parts. A cognitive rule is defined as a logical proposition, a definition, or a fact of experience. The retrieval of such information makes it

> possible to reconcile the incongruous parts of the joke. (SULS, 1972, p. 82)

What makes a joke rhetorical is its subject matter and the participation it elicits from the audience.

Audience recognition of subject matter and participation in logically getting the punch line are the key rhetorical elements in humor.

> Jokes involve some kind of unmasking. . . . Their effects, when successful, always seem to include some flash of recognition and illumination, understanding and perhaps self-understanding caused by an abrupt switch of train of thought to a different track. Perhaps, like intuition, a joke achieves this result through a kind of short-cut that avoids reflection and reasoning, though it may well stimulate both. Its essence is a sudden jolt or twist that deflates our expectations and both expresses and releases our anxieties. (LUKES AND GALNOOR, 1987, p. x)

If this seems like the enthymeme discussed in Chapter 3, it is because the structure of a joke is enthymematic.

Much humor is *topical,* meaning that at the time a joke is first told, it deals with a subject of social or political importance. This corresponds to the concept of *topoi* in classical rhetoric, which are the possible subjects for arguments. For a given topic, the rhetor-humorist supplies part of the material, the setup and the punch line, and the audience fills in the rest based on their knowledge of the topic. Consider the following enthymeme:

> After the Six-Day War, two Arabs were gloomily discussing the disastrous showing of the Arab armies:
> "Why do you think we did so badly? Was it because the Russian weapons were no good?"
> "The weapons were fine. It was the Russian military textbooks that let us down."
> "What did they say?"
> "First retreat and draw the enemy into your own territory. Then wait for the winter snows . . ." (LUKES AND GALNOOR, 1987, pp. 42–43)

The setup is based on the topic of Middle East conflict, specifically the Soviet Union's provision of arms and military advisers to Egypt, and Egypt's confrontation with Israel in 1967. The humor operates on two levels. First, the contradiction of a smaller force beating a larger one is obvious if not hilarious. Egypt and her allies outnumbered the Israelis and had more tanks and planes, yet the Israelis won. All of this is information the audience supplies, cued by the reference to the Six-Day War. The incongruity in the setup is resolved by the absurdity of the punch line, which is the second, and funnier level for audience members who get it. Once again the audience is cued to recall information, specifically the strategy used by the Russians to defeat the invading forces of Napoleon and Hitler. The absurdity of using military strategy developed for a northern climate to fight a war in the desert is obvious. The reputed inflexibility of Soviet military doctrine not only adds a modicum of plausibility to an implausible explanation but also is confirmed by the explanation.

Did you get the joke? Did you find it funny? If you did not, it may be because the topic concerns events that happened over twenty years ago, and the punch line requires a knowledge of history. This joke is an argument about incompetency produced by rigidity, and its basic structure might fit a number of topics. Like other forms of rhetorical activity, humor with a message is situationally derived. The setup comes from the rhetorical situation, in which the rhetor sees a contradiction or absurdity. The rhetorical situation also defines the knowledge the audience must possess to get the joke.

Political humor is the term often used to identify humor tied to a particular rhetorical situation. It is a reaction to the concentration of power in society and provides a safe outlet for frustrations and fears, a safety valve to reduce social tensions as they build up. As such, political humor is a stabilizing force that renders government and those who govern tolerable by making us laugh at them (Schutz, 1977). However, a change in the situation can render the joke destabilizing and its telling intolerable.

During the Kennedy administration, many stand-up comics developed routines about the Kennedy family. Vaughn Meader recorded two comedy albums entitled *The First Family,* volume one in 1962 and volume two in 1963. Meader mimicked the president's speech patterns, and he even resembled him a bit. The albums featured absurd sketches about life at the White House, but they so humanized the president that they could almost be termed pro-Kennedy propaganda. They certainly helped create the cult of personality that surrounded the Kennedy family (Hendra, 1987). The two albums were very popular, and a third was planned for release in 1964. The assassination of President Kennedy immediately ended Meader's career.

Humor is very much a time-bound communication genre. It evaluates, critiques, and interprets contemporary events. Although some humor is more durable because it pokes fun at human foibles that do not change significantly with time, audiences forget the details of past events that might be suitable topics for humor very quickly. A rhetor who chooses material too far removed from the audience's perception of the rhetorical situation may be unsuccessful.

The rhetor who uses humor is constrained by the availability of topics relevant to the rhetorical situation, by personal style, and by the talent to construct a humorous message. In addition to the constraints on rhetorical uses of humor imposed by the situation and what the audience must supply to get the joke, the structure of humor is constrained by the limited number of humorous devices that shape its content. Structurally, the basic pattern of setup and punch line is refined by any one of five comic devices: wordplay, invective, irony, parody, and satire. The use of a particular comic device is frequently the trademark of the rhetor-humorist. George Carlin is known for wordplay, Don Rickles for invective, Roseanne Barr for irony, and *Mad* magazine for parody.

Comic Devices

Wordplay

Cicero and Quintilian recognized humor as an important part of the process of invention in creating emotional proof and that some of the best humor is derived from language use. *Wordplay* is a game of language played between rhetor and audience. Verbal games, including riddles, double entendres, and puns, are learned early in life. Wordplay is enjoyable for both rhetor and audience, either because they feel a sense of superiority in the mastery of language demonstrated through wordplay or because they see powerful persons humbled by their ineptitude at the game of language. The key to audience participation in getting the joke is its knowledge of the structure of language and its vocabulary.

In the early 1960s "Tom Swift" jokes were a popular form of wordplay; they involved the use of modifiers ending in *ly*. In a Tom Swift joke, Tom always "said" something, and his act of saying it was colorfully described by an adverbial punch line. Passage of liquor-by-the-drink legislation in Iowa was marked by a Tom Swift joke: "I'll have a martini," said Tom, dryly.

Word twists and meaning shifts, either created by the rhetor or discovered in the words of others, are favorite forms of wordplay. Political humorist and journalist Russell Baker is known for his wordplay and he has frequently pointed out absurdities and exaggerations in American politics. In a 1961 column he took the Kennedy administration to task, unveiling the condemned words list of the National Society for the Preservation of the English Language to Say What You Mean.

> *Task force,* n.: any group appointed by the President to devise a program for Congress to ignore.
> *Responsible,* adj.: used to describe a speech, decision, action, etc. conforming to your personal prejudices about what is good for the country.
> *Irresponsible,* adj.: describing any course of conduct likely to cost you votes in the next election. (LEWIN, 1964, pp. 220–221)

Although these particular terms and their definitions might be meaningful today, other examples from Baker's lexicon demonstrate the time-bound nature of humor, having meaning only in the context of the Kennedy administration:

> *We will make a judgment* (Kennedyism): roughly, "Sorensen thinks we ought to keep quiet on this one until the next Gallup poll is in." (LEWIN, 1964, p. 221)

Habits of language use can become an unintentional form of wordplay. *Malapropisms,* a term derived from the character Mrs. Malaprop in Richard Brinsley Sheridan's play *The Rivals,* involve the misuse of terms, particularly those that sound somewhat alike. Humorists create malapropisms and delight in finding them in the speech of others. Presidential nominees for ambassadorial positions are frequently criticized for their lack of qualifications. Former Nevada Senator Chick Hect, President George Bush's designee for the post of ambassador to the Bahamas, was known for his malapropisms in the Senate, and the media was only too happy to remind the public that during a Senate debate he had opposed putting a "nuclear waste suppository" in Nevada.

A *spoonerism* results from the transposition of phonemes so that "gold card" comes out as "cold guard" or "spoiled brats" as "boiled sprats." Spoonerisms take their name from Reverend Spooner (1844–1930) of Oxford College, who is said to have made such mistakes in speaking. Spoonerisms can be used for comic effect to caricature an individual, or a humorist may search for the spoonerisms of others to expose them to ridicule. When this is done, the rhetorical effect is similar to that produced by invective.

Invective

Invective is the humorous use of an *ad hominem* argument. *Invective* is abuse, ridicule, or insult in humorous guise (Schutz, 1977). Comic invective is different from its direct, more personal form. Comic invective challenges the character of a person without real hostility or intent to destroy them. In political humor, comic invective becomes a form of mock warfare in which the rhetor and the target of invective may both enjoy the insult (Schutz, 1977). Norms regarding civil behavior set the bounds for public discourse. So long as these bounds are not crossed, invective is humorous. Once they are crossed, invective is just plain nasty.

Comic invective is the most frequently used device in political humor in America because our political humor tends to be antipolitics. A quip, stand-up routine, cartoon, or narrative seldom treats government or politicians positively (Schutz, 1977). Mark Russell is well known for his invective in quips and songs. He attacks Republicans and Democrats, liberals and conservatives, with equal vigor and humorous intent. After the 1988 conventions, his song "He Fought the War in Indiana" mocked Republican vice-presidential nominee Dan Quayle's military service in the National Guard during the Vietnam War. In his "Michael Row Your Tank Ashore," he ridiculed a photo opportunity designed to show that Democratic presidential nominee Michael Dukakis was strong on defense, during which he rode around with his head sticking out of a tank.

Because the point of a biting remark may be lost if circumstances change or are obscure, comic invective often draws on stock jokes. Hundreds of invective contrasts can be used to cast aspersion on the target's mental competence: He's one taco shy of a combination plate. She's one brick shy of a load. The pseudo-personal attack in comic invective must be personalized or at least appear so.

> Almost as soon as president Ford had been named to replace Nixon, commentators were quoting Lyndon Johnson's observation that Gerald Ford was the only man he knew who couldn't walk and chew gum at the same time, or that Ford had played football too long without a helmet. (CHARNEY, 1978, p. 37)

The key factor concerning audience participation in filling in the missing parts of the argument is that the audience, like the target, must accept the invective as a good-natured challenge, or they will be offended by it and refuse to play along. The audience takes its lead, in part, from the target in deciding what is within the bounds of good-natured comic invective.

Professional humorists are given wide latitude with public figures. Patrick Oliphant characterized President Ronald Reagan as a horse wearing blinders being ridden by Israeli Prime Minister Yitzhak Shamir; and Robin Williams ridiculed Reagan's Star Wars defense plan by referring to him as Obi-Ron-Kanobi. "In America it is also necessary to 'take a joke,' and dignifying an insult is a dangerous ploy" (Berger, 1988, p. 41). If a public figure, particularly a politician, dignifies comic invective by responding to it, the response can have an effect opposite to that desired. President George Bush was so sensitive to jokes about Vice-President Dan Quayle that after the inauguration he asked his staff to stop repeating them. The news media picked up the story and made it their purpose to report the latest Quayle joke making the rounds in Washington D.C. and his every public misstatement.

Irony

Irony is a factual or embellished statement in which the opposite of what is stated is really meant. Irony capitalizes on the possibility for double meaning in words or deeds. It functions by pointing out the absurdity or contradiction in these double meanings, such as the irony of the indictment and conviction of a number of top officials of an administration publicly committed to law and order.

Mad's Al Jaffee has used irony to expose the contradictions in some of the changes we make for our own good. In his series "Don't You Feel Like a Schmuck?!" he showed a man eating fish, with the caption "Don't you feel like a schmuck eating fish to cut down on cholesterol," followed by a picture of the same man in a physician's office, with the caption "and accumulating enough mercury in your system to kill a whale!" (Jaffee, 1989, p. 44).

This illustrates an important aspect of irony: It often derives from relating the facts of a situation to cue the audience. Some of the most successful political humor has emerged from factual accounts of ridiculous situations (Lewin, 1964) or accounts that embellish these situations. Irony that exists in actual events, rather than in something contrived or embellished by the rhetor, is termed *unintentional irony*.

Russell Baker's newspaper columns frequently feature accounts of things that really happen. During the Eisenhower administration, the following events were highlighted in one of his columns.

> The State Department decided against a showing of *South Pacific* at the Brussels Fair on the ground that its subplot, an interracial romance between a white man and an Asian girl, would annoy Southern senators. After several other Broadway successes, including works by Tennessee Williams and Arthur Miller, were rejected on the ground that they would irritate this or that pressure group, one diplomat suggested *Waiting for Godot*. Since no one could understand it, he argued, no one could possibly be offended. (LEWIN, 1964, p. 33)

Seeing the irony in the situation requires audience familiarity with the plays and playwrights mentioned.

Another example from the same Baker column demanded less audience knowledge.

> A two-hundred-pound panda residing in Peiping was denied admission to the United States by the State Department. State, disappointing domestic zoo men, invoked its taboo against trade with Communist China, ruling that the panda's admission would imperil national security. (LEWIN, 1964, p. 34)

Using irony as a comic device requires the rhetor to see the possibility of multiple, often opposing, meanings in language or action. The key to audience participation is their familiarity with both meanings and their ability to decode the contradiction.

Parody

A *parody* is an imitation, often ludicrous, of a nonhumorous work. Parodies are generally irreverent, and exaggerate or otherwise distort the original work while preserving its essential or identifiable elements. The part of the original that is preserved may be its basic idea, form, or style, verbal or visual elements selected by the parodist to cue audience recall.

Dwight Eisenhower was not a particularly good speaker, and humorists frequently attacked this inability. "The Gettysburg Address as done by Eisenhower" parodied his lack of speaking style by envisioning him, instead of Abraham Lincoln, giving this famous speech. The parodist claimed that President Eisenhower would have begun by saying:

> I haven't checked these figures but eighty-seven years ago,
> I think it was, a number of individuals organized a

> governmental setup here in this country, I believe it
> covered certain eastern areas, with this idea they were
> following up based on a sort of national-independence
> arrangement and the program that every individual is just
> as good as every other individual. (LEWIN, 1964, p. 242)

A parody succeeds in part by cueing recall which enables the audience to
identify elements of the original in the parody. Compare the parody to the
original and you will see that the parodist preserved the basic structure of
Lincoln's ideas but rendered them in the rambling Eisenhower style.

> Four score and seven years ago our fathers brought forth
> upon this continent, a new nation, conceived in Liberty
> and dedicated to the proposition that all men are created
> equal. (REID, 1988, p. 463)

The Harvard Lampoon, a student organization of Harvard University, has
existed for over a century. In 1956 the group did a parody of *Newsweek* that began
a series of magazine parodies, and their 1961 parody of *Mademoiselle* sold over a
million copies. Their 1989 target was *Time*. If you did not examine its content
closely, you might think it was the real *Time* because its visual elements replicate
Time's look; the table of contents suggests familiar *Time* features such as "The
American Scene," and the parody even contains real advertising. These magazine
parodies differ from the Eisenhower parody in that the look of the magazine is
preserved but the content is mostly absurd.

Others humorists parody both style and content in their work. Weird Al
Yankovic specializes in parodies of rock songs and music videos. Weird Al's "Eat
It" preserves the style of Michael Jackson's "Beat It," with similar costuming and
choreography. "Beat It" concerns a surrealistic confrontation between rival gangs.
The content of "Eat It" focuses on the confrontation between parents and children
over finishing dinner, but the lyrics of the parody parallel the pattern of the
original. In "Like a Surgeon," style and some content elements of Madonna's "Like
a Virgin" are parodied, with the materialism of American medicine providing an
interesting counterpoint to Madonna's "material girl" image. Once again the style,
particularly costuming and choreography, and the content of the original reso-
nate in the parody.

The *impression,* impersonation of a well-known person, is a form of parody.
Rich Little is one of the best contemporary impressionists, known for his ability to
mimic the verbal and nonverbal mannerisms of his subject to cue the audience.
The cartoon *caricature* is also a parody of sorts, in which the cartoonist exaggerates or distorts physical features of well-known persons to cue audience recognition. When the cartoonist portrays the subject as having animal-like features,
characteristics associated with the creature (dumb as an ox, sly as a fox) may be
cued as well.

The parodist, impressionist, and caricaturist deconstructs the original and
reconstructs it with a twist. Weird Al Yankovic's parody "Hooked on Polkas" is a

medley of popular rock songs with the lyrics unchanged but sung to the music of a polka band. What is deconstructed in this case is the musical style; in the Gettysburg Address parody, the words of the original were deconstructed and replaced with what could have been Eisenhower's words had he given the speech.

The key to audience participation in rhetorical acts that parody someone or something is their knowledge of the original and their ability to find humor in its parody. An audience unfamiliar with either the Gettysburg Address or President Dwight Eisenhower's style of speaking finds little meaning in a parody that juxtaposes the two. An audience too close to, or too familiar with, the original can also fail to appreciate its being parodied, finding the parody profane rather than humorously irreverent. J.R.R. Tolkien's *Lord of the Rings* was a cult classic in the 1960s, and the Harvard Lampoon published *Bored of the Rings* in 1969. It delighted some Tolkien fans and disgusted others who were possibly so enamored with the significance of the original as a literary work that they were unable to see humor in poking fun at it.

Satire

Satire is the broadest category of comic devices, and the term is often used as a synonym for humor and comedy. *Satire* finds humor in the human condition and holds up the vices, practices, and customs of a culture to comic scrutiny. Satire is found in cartoons, songs, quips, narratives, and other forms of humorous discourse. Satire and parody are easily confused. What distinguishes one from the other is a very fine categorical line: the existence of some original text to deconstruct in a parody and the absence of such a text in satire. Mel Brooks' *Young Frankenstein* is a parody based on the deconstruction of Frankenstein films of the 1930s and 1940s, whereas his *Blazing Saddles* is a satire of the generic Hollywood western.

As a comic device, satire has strong rhetorical properties. By poking fun at a practice or belief, the satirist can function as a conservator of culture, defending it against people and institutions that threaten its existence.

> First, the author is the initial aggressor against a political personage or social institution. By his comic genius he has translated his anger or resentment into a satirical attack in which his target is made the butt of humor for an audience. The target becomes a victim and the aggressor's anger is expended peacefully, and, possibly, constructively. He has revealed his victim's vices or failings for public correction, and he may have educated some of the public to his standards. (SCHUTZ, 1977, pp. 77–78)

When *All in the Family* first aired on CBS, viewers were variously astonished, horrified, or delighted to see a character talk openly about his racial and religious prejudices. Archie Bunker, a stereotypical bigot, was portrayed satirically, as were his stereotypical wife, daughter, and leftist-liberal son-in-law. Each week viewers had the opportunity to witness the impoverishment of intolerance and closed-mindedness.

The audience participates, not only by helping complete the satirical message but also by accepting, if they choose, the invitation to join in conserving the social order:

> Second, the audience has participated vicariously in the satirist's subliminated aggression. They too have been purged of the need for more direct action in expression of their aggressions. And the satirist's use of sexual allusions, comic blasphemy, and ridicule of authority allows the audience in its imaginative participation and laughter to express forbidden emotions and thoughts in a socially permissible and cathartic manner. The social and political system gains added stability at the same time that it views itself critically. The people become prepared for reform and are relieved of the need for rebellion. (SCHUTZ, 1977, p. 78)

All in the Family produced different responses from various viewers. Some, who did not get the joke, thought Archie was right, and the program confirmed their prejudices. Others were relieved to see bigotry acknowledged in a medium previously preoccupied with the world of Ward and June Cleaver. For them, public acknowledgment of the problem was the first step toward solving it. Others were challenged and disturbed by the program and forced to think about the continuing problem of racial and religious prejudice.

What makes social satire a conservative act is found in how it portrays values:

> Third, there always lurks in the dim background of satire a vision or standard of rightness. Ridicule, parody, irony proceed from a sensed wrongness of social reality to some apprehension of the rightness of what could be. But comedy is not moral censure, otherwise it would become diatribe or preachment. The satire humorously prods or tickles its audience into an awareness of absurdity or abnormality. They have then become more rational, but they aren't aware of their education, and their subsequent political action is their own. Satire is negative on its first level, and the positive remedy of the satirized must be inferred. (SCHUTZ, 1977, p. 78)

The sense of right and wrong was frequently the anchor for the characters' dialogue and the motive for their behavior. Although the characters on *All in the Family* were stereotypical, they were not unidimensional and unchanging. Over the course of several seasons, viewers saw a tenderness in Archie, a strength in Edith, a sentimentality in Mike, and a seriousness in Gloria that suggested these people were learning and growing from their experiences.

In considering other communication genres in this book, we have suggested that your criticism must be concerned with how the audience appreciates and uses the genre. In rhetorical acts that are humorous, the role of the audience is crucial because the unappreciated joke, the one the audience did not get, probably failed as a rhetorical act. In the next section, we explore how the audience responds to and makes sense of humor and what determines whether or not a humorous rhetorical act has "gone too far."

Audience Use of Humor

When the setup of a joke is resolved in its punch line, members of the audience who get the joke either feel superior, realize they understand the incongruity, or experience a sense of relief. One or more of these audience uses of humor explains how members of the audience decode the joke and use it to create meaning.

Superiority

The classical Greek view of humor, articulated in the works of Aristotle, Plato, and Aristophanes, was that laughter expresses a person's feeling of superiority over others. Derision, using humor to downgrade others, is a product of class structure in European societies. In Shakespeare's plays, humor often comes at the expense of characters who portray the lower class. In the eighteenth and nineteenth centuries, wealthy Europeans went to insane asylums to laugh at inmates. The central idea behind decoding humor according to the superiority theory is that an audience laughs when it is made to feel superior to whomever or whatever is made the butt of the joke.

Derogatory humor—invective that denigrates an individual or group because of their racial, ethnic, regional, or occupational status—is a staple in many cultures, and each culture seems to have its favorite targets. Derogatory jokes often follow the standard form of a stock question to which the punch line response cites some real or imagined characteristic to downgrade the group that is the butt of the joke.

> How many Southern Californians does it take to screw in a light bulb?
> Eight. One to screw in the bulb and seven to share the experience.

Humor may make the audience feel superior by giving them the opportunity to laugh at their leaders, neighbors, or even themselves. Consider the possibilities for feeling superior provided by the following joke.

> There are six people on an aircraft: the pilot, Brezhnev, Carter, Giscard, a priest, and a young man. When something goes wrong with the plane, the pilot announces

that he is taking one of the five parachutes, and that they must decide between themselves who will take the remaining four.

Brezhnev declares that since he is the only hope for the spread of Communism he must jump and taking a parachute jumps out of the plane.

Carter declares that he is the only hope for defence of the Free World against the spread of Communism, and he too takes a parachute and jumps.

Then Giscard gets up: "I am the leader of the French nation and the most intelligent of world leaders. I must jump," and he too jumps out of the plane.

Then the priest rises and says to the young man—"My son, I am old and have lived my time, take the last parachute and jump."

But the young man protests: "Father, hurry up—there are two parachutes left, one for each of us. Put on one of them and jump.

"But how is that?" asks the priest.

"That guy who said he is the most intelligent world leader—he took my sleeping bag." (LUKES AND GALNOOR, 1987, p. 74)

This joke operates on two levels: deflating the real or imagined pomposity of the French people on one level and the self-importance of world leaders on the other. Decoded either way, it could make audience members feel superior, though their nationality might influence the extent to which this joke elicits such feelings. Those who are French or consider themselves to be of French extraction might feel superior if they disapproved of former Prime Minister Valerie Giscard d'Estaing, but they might be insulted if they felt they were being made the butt of the joke along with the former French leader.

An audience may feel superior, not from seeing someone else put down but from satisfying their need for inclusion. As individuals, we want to feel, not just part of a group, but part of the right group. In the 1950s and 1960s, people went to see Lenny Bruce, Dick Gregory, and others because it was the "hip" thing to do. Going to see Lenny Bruce was hip because he used four-letter words and was frequently arrested for doing his act. He talked about racism, politics, and sex and seemed to spend as much time in court defending himself against obscenity charges as he spent performing. If you thought of yourself as a liberal, being hip meant being included in the right group, one that had special knowledge and was culturally superior to others, one that could "dig" Lenny Bruce. In such circumstances, it can be difficult to assess audience response, whether they feel superior because they get the joke or because they want others to include them and perceive them to be hip.

Incongruity

People also use humor to try to understand things that do not appear to make sense. We like to think of our world as an orderly place where things happen for good reasons. When our sense of this order is disturbed or purposely violated, we are troubled but we can also laugh. People who laugh for this reason are not merely registering their reaction to being suprised. Decoding humor in this way helps us understand and cope with life's incongruities cognitively, enabling us to appreciate these violations of our sense of order and thereby strengthening it. To laugh at such an event is to label it extraordinary and thus to affirm the underlying order of the ordinary. Because few events in our lives provoke such laughter, we are reassured that our belief in the inherent orderliness of human affairs is well founded.

It is part of human nature to seek novel experiences and sensory stimulation; people are curious. For the sake of our sense of security, however, we avoid novel experiences that place us in danger. Humorous incongruity provides nonthreatening cognitive stimulation that exercises the mind without risking the body (Morreall, 1987).

The incongruity of the setup may be resolved by the punch line, or the absurdity may remain for the audience to ponder. One of Charles Addams' most popular cartoons was a single cell showing ski tracks passing around a tree—one to the right of the trunk, the other to the left—with the skier moving off the left side of the cell while a bemused spectator in the right foreground looks on. The Addams skier cartoon may not be rhetorical (indeed, some humor is intended only to amuse rather than to enlighten or persuade), yet you might interpret this cartoon in a broader context: our inability to resolve conflicts between what we observe and what we believe, what our senses and our sensibility tell us.

The irony of a cartoonist such as Al Jaffee or a columnist such as Russell Baker rests on exposing the inherent incongruities in everything from personal life-style choices that affect our health to government policy on plays and pandas. Even though the audience may be unable to undo these incongruities, they can understand them and use this information to make decisions about their daily lives. Incongruity theory suggests that humor is both an audience-cueing mechanism that helps them recall information they already possess and a vehicle that affords them the opportunity to consider other possible meanings for that information. In this sense, the audience's use of humor is creative and affords them insights that might not have been gained through other, more serious, genres of communication.

Relief

The relief theory is based on Sigmund Freud's view that we laugh as a way of releasing the energy that builds up from forbidden thoughts and feelings. Incorporated in his notion of humor as a release mechanism is the belief that people laugh at things they fear. Political humor is often tied to our fears and anxieties and derives from trying to decide who we can trust or what we can rely on.

> Popular political jokes reflect a certain level of collective anxiety about public matters. But joking, that is the circulation of political jokes in a society, is a form of coping. Even when the situation is bad, and the jokes become destructive and vicious, they still represent a collective *intimacy,* a sign that people *belong,* that they *care* and consequently that they entertain *hope.* (LUKES AND GALNOOR, 1987, p. xi)

One role of humor must be to serve as a means of relieving our fears, otherwise there would be no jokes about death, terrorism, or nuclear war. Dave Barry, Pulitzer Prize winning humorist of the *Miami Herald,* was asked by a *Time* interviewer to explain his personal theory of humor. His answer expanded on Freud's view that people use humor to relieve fear.

> [I]t's fear that the world is not very sane or reliable or organized and that it's not controlled by responsible people. Anything can happen to you, and you have no say in it, and it could be bad. What a humorist does is sort of poke through that. . . . People laugh because it's easier to laugh than to really admit they're afraid. (BIRNBAUM, 1989, p. 69)

"Sick" jokes afford us relief from our fears. A sick joke goes beyond the bounds of good taste, but in realizing its sickness the audience reaffirms the existence of good taste. When an event is so overwhelming or tragic that people need an outlet for their anger and hostility, a joke is one way to cope. Viewed in this light, sick jokes can be seen as healthy ways to deal with failure and tragedy (Morrow, 1987).

The initial shock of the *Challenger* space shuttle disaster, and the experience of seeing it replayed again and again on television, gave rise to a series of grim jokes.

> *Question:* Do you know what NASA stands for?
> *Answer:* Needs Another Seven Astronauts.
> *Question:* Did you hear that Tang is no longer the official drink of the space program?
> *Answer:* Yes, now it's Ocean Spray.
> *Question:* Do you know what color Christa McAuliffe's eyes were?
> *Answer:* They were blue. One blew over this way and one blew over that way. (MORROW, 1987, p. 179)

The sick *Challenger* jokes, which tended to group the other astronauts but recognized Christa McAuliffe as an individual, served as a cloaking device for our outrage over their deaths. Christa McAuliffe was singled out because she had become a sort of "everyperson" through prelaunch publicity, a nonexpert like ourselves with whom we identified. When she and six others died, sick jokes were one way to express our outrage over the failure of NASA's management and technology (Morrow, 1987).

We close our discussion of how the audience decodes and uses humor by examining what happens when an audience rejects a joke because the rhetor has "gone too far." You may have felt we went too far by including some of the sick humor that followed the *Challenger* tragedy. You may have been more upset with us for bringing back painful memories than you were with the NASA bureaucracy that caused the tragedy. Whether or not you were upset, this reaction illustrates what happens when the audience feels the rhetor has gone too far. They refuse to participate in decoding and using the humorous message.

The degree to which audience members participate is determined by their ability to use a joke to feel superior, solve or cope with the incongruities of life, or find relief from what is troubling them. When an audience does not get the joke, it may be because they find no use for the argument it contains, or because they may be unable to draw on the topic because they lack key information the rhetor assumed they had. There is one other reason for the failure of an audience to get a joke: their perception that the rhetor has *gone too far* and their consequent rejection of the possibility of finding humor in the situation.

Rejection of a joke for going too far may result from an audience's involvement with the exigence in the rhetorical situation. No one at NASA found the *Challenger* jokes useful, even when they were current. Works of art, literature, or philosophy prized for their wisdom, quality, or insight may so involve their audience that a parody of them cannot be appreciated. Such jokes as quips and one-liners that question the wisdom of government policies may be unintelligible to an audience that is convinced of the truth or justice of these policies.

Frequently, our emotional involvement, or the combination of our emotional and intellectual attachment to something in the rhetorical situation, causes us to feel that a joke has gone too far. We may have strong feelings of fear, disgust, love, or reverence that preclude our ability to see anything humorous in a particular situation, and no comic device can draw us away from these feelings. A rhetor's humor may also be rejected because of its language. Many people find Eddie Murphy's concert performances insightful, and others refuse even to listen because he uses foul language.

An audience's sense of aesthetics and ethical standards of discourse are particularly important to their willingness to decode and use humorous rhetorical acts. These standards change over time and vary across generations. This is important to keep in mind if your criticism is focused on humor from an earlier era. Because the audience for humor, as for other genres of communication, is largely self-selected, societal and individual tastes influence who is and is not likely to be exposed to the rhetorical act.

However, lack of direct exposure does not remove an individual from the rhetorical situation or the audience in the larger sense of the term. Lenny Bruce appealed to the tastes of many Americans even though his material flew in the face of societal standards. Those who never saw Lenny Bruce were part of the rhetorical situation and the larger audience because media coverage of his running battle with the law over his act insured that practically everyone in America had some sense of what Lenny Bruce was doing and had some feelings about it.

Forms of Humorous Discourse

Stand-up comedy is one of several forms used to convey the humorous rhetorical act. Because structural differences among forms have implications for how humor functions and how you as a critic interpret and evaluate the rhetorical act, we discuss four broad subgenres of humor: stand-up comedy, cartooning, electronic and print humor, and public sloganeering.

Stand-up Comedy

The opening monolog by the host of late-night talk-variety shows incorporates stand-up comedy into the program format. The practice of opening with a comedy performance to entice the audience to stay tuned is a carry-over from the chautauqua tradition of weaving entertainment into the serious elements of the program to keep the audience involved.

Stand-up comedy generally means that the humorist does a comedy routine in front of a live audience; it closely resembles public speaking. A comedian has face-to-face contact with an audience and is able to draw them into the act. This degree of intimacy influences the subject matter of stand-up comedy, and routines frequently discuss subjects not usually associated with public discourse. The topical nature of stand-up comedy encourages the audience to examine

> cultural patterns, associations, meanings and values in their observations of human life. They consider the status of marriage, new life styles, received notions of male and female nature, qualities attributed to adolescents and older Americans, lines of authority existing between parent and child, wealth and status recognition, restrictions imposed on the expression of hostile impulses within and without the home, privacy definitions and rights, the ordering of physical space, the measurement and confirmation of status, as well as self-image, through clothing and other material goods, property distribution, ownership rules and the social implications of family. (KOZISKI, 1984, p. 68)

The stand-up comedian is a social anthropologist who studies living cultures to reveal aspects of habit, belief, and how institutions function.

> The comedian publicly witnesses or reads about socially enacted behavior. However, he exaggerates or distorts his

> observations as a participant observer talking to people in
> his own society about the familiar cultural rules and
> behavior patterns. . . . The audience may hear their own
> behavior described as if it is an alien culture in the sense
> that they knew that information all along but no one ever
> said it like that to them before. (KOZISKI, 1984, p. 61)

Stand-up comedy routines, like nonhumorous rhetorical acts, inform and
shape audience beliefs. The stand-up comedian frequently intends to make the
audience better informed about social problems and more receptive to change as
a result of the insights experienced through the act of decoding humor. By
participating in comedy, the audience experiences a combination of enhanced
understanding and of the aesthetic pleasure derived from an appreciation of the
stand-up comic's style. Taken together, these factors may explain the comedian's
ability to influence an audience in ways that other rhetors are unable to achieve.
One other factor must also be taken into account: Stand-up comedians address
their audience in ways other rhetors do not.

> Many standup comedians jar their audience's sensibilities
> by making individuals experience a shock of recognition.
> This occurs as deeply held popular beliefs about
> themselves—even the hidden underpinnings of their
> culture—are brought to an audience's level of conscious
> awareness. The standup comedian can elevate his
> audience to a new cultural focus. (KOZISKI, 1984, p. 57)

The stand-up comedian's style places him or her in one of two categories—
divine fool or comic sage—which have emerged from America's rich comic
tradition of older forms and unique creations. A stand-up comedy routine, like a
public speech, does not exist apart from the person who delivered it. Comic style
influences not only the rhetor-humorist's choice of topic but also how that topic
is developed and presented to the audience.

The *divine fool* or divine clown originated in the plays of Aristophanes. The
fool's behavior is outside the norm. Through humor, the fool opposes social
customs and institutions. Divine fools are childlike in their understanding of
society, rendering their criticism of it less threatening. Jerry Lewis, Steve Martin,
and the late Lucille Ball are contemporary comedians who portray divine fools in
their comedy. The style of the divine fool in stand-up comedy is also illustrated by
Don Novello.

Even though most stand-up comedians create personas or do impressions,
their identity apart from these creations is obvious. You would recognize Robin
Williams offstage, but not Don Novello without his costume, makeup, props, and
accent. You might recognize Father Guido Sarducci, a character created on
Saturday Night Live, a divine clown who also travels the comedy concert circuit.
Father Guido is the "gossip columnist" for the Vatican newspaper. Dressed in a
fashionably cut clerical suit, with a scarlet-lined cape and a broad-brimmed black
hat, he provides "inside information" about people and events in the Roman

Catholic church. Sarducci's topical material is drawn from events, real and imagined, in the church and attitudes about religion. The Sarducci persona satirizes, with a childlike sense of wonder, organized religion and the cult of personality of Pope John Paul II.

The *comic sage* is an American variation on the divine fool's role. The comic sage developed as the uneducated American folk comedian who was shrewd and had commonsense. What made the comic sage American was the element of class reversal. The comic sage reassured the audience of the superiority of common people and ridiculed conventional wisdom and authority (Schutz, 1977).

Benjamin Franklin, Artemus Ward, and Will Rogers all played roles in developing the tradition of the comic sage in American humor that lives on in the work of many of today's stand-up comedians. Benjamin Franklin (1706–1790) helped shape the persona of the comic sage in *Poor Richards Almanack,* published from 1732 to 1758. Poor Richard dispensed practical wisdom that was frequently irreverent and somewhat lewd. It reveals much about the values of colonial America.

> Let thy maid-servant be faithful, strong, and homely.
> After three days men grow weary of a wench, a guest, and rainy weather.
> He who marries for love without money has sorry days and happy nights. (QUOTED IN BLAIR AND HILL, 1978, p. 58)

We may not appreciate the sexism of Poor Richard's humor today, but these aphorisms were popular with Franklin's readers.

Artemus Ward was a Revolutionary War general, but the name is more frequently associated with the persona created by Charles Farrar Browne (1839–1867). The Ward persona was first created in a series of fictitious letters that Browne wrote as filler when he worked at the Cleveland *Plain Dealer.* Browne specialized in accounts of "the news" he thought people would enjoy reading, even if these accounts did not correspond to what actually happened. Circulation of the *Plain Dealer* increased after Browne's articles and the Artemus Ward letters began appearing (Blair and Hill, 1978).

As Artemus Ward, Browne moved on to write for *Vanity Fair* and other national magazines and became a success on the lecture circuit, attracting sell-out audiences. Abraham Lincoln was one of Ward's chief targets. He attacked Lincoln's appearance, policies, and style of speaking. The Ward persona established many of today's comic techniques, pioneering the stand-up comedy routine and the fake letters to newspapers and magazines that live on in *National Lampoon.* His comic invective aimed at Lincoln is echoed in barbs hurled at today's leaders and his wordplay, which made a hash of spelling, grammar, and vocabulary, resurfaced in the work of Will Rogers.

Will Rogers (1879–1935) brought the tradition of the comic sage into the twentieth century. The greatest American humorist of the Depression era, he dominated American comedy from 1915 until his death in 1935. Rogers, who was from Oklahoma, had been a cowboy and wild-west show performer before starring in vaudeville as a purveyor of frontier wisdom. He looked and talked the part:

> His outfit—battered broadbrim hat, bandana scarf, shirtsleeves and chaps—was that of a proletarian. "Grammar and I get along like a Russian and a bathtub," he boasted; and his store of words and frequently flawed spelling helped prove that he hadn't been besmirched by too much education. "Maybe ain't ain't so correct," he allowed, then he went on to state the time-hallowed American belief that book learning got you nowhere: "But I notice that lots of folks who ain't usin' ain't ain't eatin'." (BLAIR AND HILL, 1978, p. 522)

Will Rogers appeared on the lecture circuit, in live stage shows and films, and wrote books, magazine articles, and newspaper columns featuring his Wardian disregard for language. He used his weekly radio program, the best communication technology of its day, to reach a large audience with stand-up routines that emphasized his homespun sense of self-reliance and the work ethic. In his down-to-earth style, he said that Americans had lost their sense of purpose during the "Roaring Twenties" and that we were the first nation in the history of the world to go to the poorhouse in an automobile (Wertheim, 1976).

Will Rogers was immensely popular because he came across as a common man. His radio broadcasts featured rambling discussions of national events. He talked about everything from taxes to going fishing, but Franklin Roosevelt's plans for getting America out of the Depression were his favorite topic. Shortly before his death, he related how Congress had finally figured out the Depression.

> You couldn't guess this plan they've figured out what's the matter with the country, and they're going to spend a half a billion dollars on it. I'll bet you couldn't figure out what it is. Well, you know what it is? Well, it's that the people try to cross a railroad track without looking both ways. That's what it is. They're going to fix the grade crossings—that's what that is. Well, you'll say—well, the problem is to teach the people to look both ways. Drive up to the track and look up and down and then cross. Yes, well that's exactly what's the matter with, with us . . . even when, when it don't apply to railroad trains. . . . In 1928 and '29 around there. That's when the train hit all of us, remember? There wasn't a . . . there wasn't a soul in the United States that looked both ways then. (QUOTED IN GRAHAM, 1970, pp. 59–60)

Like many contemporary stand-up comedians, Will Rogers combined social commentary with a seemingly random discussion of everything under the sun, but he always made his point.

> Superficially he was a model of the poor speaker: he
> would get stuck, repeat himself, throw out irrelevancies,
> interrupt himself. His speeches were choked with voiced
> pauses and loaded with grammatical errors. His
> candidness could be labeled simple-minded tactlessness as
> he mocked America, prominent public figures, and
> himself. But while he slowly wound his way toward a
> point, his audience saw a man unable to conceal his
> thoughts, a man who honestly and tenaciously sought the
> human interpretation, the sensible solution to a problem.
> His art was the concealment of art. (GRAHAM, 1970, p. 55)

The memory of Will Rogers' humor was revived in the 1970s by James Whitmore's "Will Rogers' USA," available on videotape. His anti-intellectual, homespun style continues to be part of the tradition of the comic sage.

Roseanne Barr is among those who continue that tradition in her role as a "woman of the common people," whose speech is ungrammatical and whose style is "plain folks." Her persona, the lower-middle class working wife, struggles with the problems that confront today's woman. What makes her style unusual is contradiction. She speaks rapidly in a sing-song pattern that fluctuates between deadpan monotone and gross exaggeration. Her inflection, tone, and energy always seem to contradict her verbal content, as when she says she rejects the label, housewife, preferring instead to be called "a domestic goddess."

Roseanne Barr satirizes the lives of lower-middle class women. She talks about husband-wife relationships, being a mom and raising children, the differences between men and women, and, playing off her own body type, how society treats large women. Barr's humor is an excellent example of how satire functions rhetorically to conserve the culture. Even though the family receives the brunt of her humor, her message is strongly profamily and emphasizes the importance of respect among family members.

George Carlin carries on Lenny Bruce's tradition of using words as weapons. He is best known for his discussion of the seven words that cannot be said on television. Turning words and common usage upside down is his trademark: "Go into a *gift* shop and ask for your *gift*." He uses his voice, exaggerating sounds, changing pitch and tone, and increasing volume, to enhance the wordplay. Visually his style is characterized by informality.

Much of George Carlin's material is drawn from how others use words and name things. His stand-up routines work topical material into the war of words. He concludes that because members of the "right to life" movement also support capital punishment and the unrestricted sales of guns, what "right to life" really means is the right to determine who lives and who dies.

Although both Roseanne Barr and George Carlin are firmly anchored in the same comic tradition, no one would confuse one with the other because, in the act of reinventing themselves as comic sages, each has developed a distinctive style. The verbal and visual elements inherent in stand-up comedy are handled differently by each comedian, who thus establishes an individual comic signature. Language use and wordplay are as important to defining style as they are to creating messages. The comic's grammar and vocabulary, use of accent and dialect, creation of a persona, along with the development of catch phrases, combine to define verbal style. As a consequence of differences in verbal style, differences in the sense of timing emerge to suit the individual.

> Timing in comedy achieves remarkable effects of surprise and wonder that have nothing to do with the subject matter but are esentially aesthetic. It is not so much the joke that is funny, but the whole experience of listening to the joke, and, therefore, what we read on paper is only an echo of the joke. (CHARNEY, 1978, p. 45)

The visual element of stand-up comedy is also an essential part of the comedian's style. Sex, age, race, height, weight, dress, and the presence or absence of props are immediately obvious. Vocal variety, eye contact, posture, and body movement embellish the verbal message and emerge as the rhetorical act unfolds. Because getting the joke is sometimes a matter of deciding whether to believe the verbal or the visual message, the relationship between them is important both to the comic's task of establishing style and to the audience's task of decoding the rhetorical act.

The appeal and power of the stand-up comedians lie in their helping their audiences to encounter threatening circumstances in nonthreatening ways. By encouraging the audience to interpret reality humorously, the stand-up comedian gives the audience the ability to

> actively control circumstances, keep up courage and envision feelings of success and achievement. This allows one to cope with less than ideal life conditions. The inversion of reality can result in a healing catharsis. It is an important life-coping strategy. By breaking down the rules and behaviors ingredient in cultural situations, the comedian may increase the participant's awareness of the tacit cultural knowledge with which he operates. (KOZISKI, 1984, p. 70)

This may explain the popularity of comedy concerts and clubs. Examining social problems and technological complexity through the filter of humor reduces them to human scale.

Cartooning

The cartoon is a pervasive form of humor. Monarchs of old and dictators of today have feared the power of political cartoons to create unflattering caricatures, to cut to the point of complex issues, and to reach vast numbers of people, including the illiterate or politically naive. For this reason, cartoonists have often been imprisoned (Harrison, 1981).

Benjamin Franklin authored the first American political cartoon in 1754, "Join or Die." It featured a snake broken into eight parts, each labeled to represent the colonies of New England: New York, New Jersey, Rhode Island, Maryland, Virginia, and North and South Carolina. Political cartoons were regular features of American newspapers and magazines throughout the nineteenth century. Abraham Lincoln's public persona was as much a product of cartoons in the American and British press as it was of anything he did. His image as a tall, homely, awkward figure was imprinted on the American mind by cartoons that caricatured his physique, and the Lincoln image contributed to the Uncle Sam caricature (Morrison, 1969).

Cartoons are used to call attention to programs and products, to provide instructions, to prohibt acts, to amuse and celebrate, and to politicize. The cartoon amplifies and exaggerates to achieve "quick" communication. A cartoon mixes visual and verbal elements, often in unexpected ways, to create incongruous and unexpected relationships. The humor may be savage or cruel rather than merely amusing. A cartoon is a representational or symbolic drawing that makes a point through wit (Harrison, 1981).

A cartoon serves as a frame of reference for complex issues and events through the use of metaphor, or *metonymy,* the rhetorical figure that uses a part to stand for the whole. In a cartoon, the Russian Bear, Uncle Sam, or John Bull or the caricature of a person such as the president of the United States represents an entire nation. To use metonymy, "the cartoonist must concoct imagery that is at once compelling and powerful, drawing frequently from potent symbols within the political and cultural mythology" (DeSousa, 1984, p. 205).

"The political cartoonist as a caricaturist and polemicist aims at a purposeful condensation of sometimes complex meanings into a single striking image" (Morrison, 1969, p. 253). A political cartoon on the editorial page may have greater impact than an editorial on the same subject. The cartoon and its symbols offer an immediate message to the reader whereas the editorial takes more decoding to get its message across (Morrison, 1969).

Political cartoons are time-bound because they are usually linked to events that rapidly fade from the public's consciousness. In 1986, the Reagan administration's covert aid to the Contra rebels in Nicaragua was exposed when a plane carrying arms to the Contras was shot down and its pilot captured. Skeptical of U.S. government denials of any knowledge or involvement in Eugene Hasenfus' mission, Pat Oliphant put the episode into cartoon perspective (Figure 12.1).

Recognizing that the two people in the cow suit are CIA Director William Casey (in the rear) and President Reagan, recalling who Eugene Hasenfus was and interpreting the "we are not in Nicaragua" banner may be difficult from the vantage point of the 1990s. On 20 October 1986, when the cartoon first appeared, Oliphant's argument was quick and clear, the Reagan administration was in for a rude awakening if it thought the Hasenfus fuss would go quietly away.

Political, or editorial, cartoons usually contain a single cell or panel that deals with complex issues and events enthymematically. The cell distills the essence of

October 20, 1986

Mr. Hasenfus, a hapless gunrunner's assistant whom nobody
ever heard of, including his employers, is captured when his plane
crashes in Nicaragua.

Figure 12.1

Oliphant Copyright 1986 Universal Press Syndicate. Reprinted with permission.
All rights reserved.

the rhetorical situation into an image that may be captioned or contain dialogue.
The president of the United States and the director of the CIA in a cow suit may
not be an enduring image, but some images have greater staying power.

During the Iran hostage crisis, 4 November 1979 to 20 January 1981, images
of the Ayatollah Khomeini as a madman, religious fraud, and manipulator framed
political commentary by editorial cartoonists (DeSousa, 1984). After the return of
the hostages, Khomeini's cartoon image continued to be used to represent our
poor relations with Iran. A cartoon published during the period in 1987 when the
stock market was in precipitous decline showed the Ayatollah attacking "the
Great Satan" by selling stock to drive the market even lower.

The visual dimension of cartooning helps it achieve brevity while functioning
as an enthymeme.

> First and foremost, the cartoonist simplifies. The
> cartoonist radically "levels" what we usually see in our

> perceptual field. The cartoon is 2-dimensional rather than
> 3-dimensional. It is often black and white rather than full
> color, retaining the outline of a figure, but with perhaps
> only a suggestion of the form's texture, shade and shape.
> Even the outline is usually simplified, with the cartoonist
> dropping needless objects and details. If possible, the
> cartoonist does not use two lines where one line will
> do. (HARRISON, 1981, p. 57)

Cartoonists have a range of graphic techniques available to them to develop a style. Line and form create tone and mood. Objects and characters can be sized differently, caricature exaggerates certain features, and captions or dialogue can be manipulated against these visual elements (Medhurst and DeSousa, 1981). Taken together, the visual and verbal elements create a mise-en-scène for the cartoon.

Within the framework of cartooning, each cartoonist creates a unique style. Charles Addams created a somber world, Gahan Wilson's cartoons are grotesque (Harrison, 1981), and Pat Oliphant's cartoons feature a small bird who comments on what is depicted in the cell, acting as a Greek chorus of one. Jules Feiffer's political cartoons violate tradition by being done in a multicell comic strip style.

Feiffer said that he liked Lyndon Johnson until the Vietnam War escalated but that he was a challenge to draw.

> He was so odd he was lousy to draw. An overabundance
> of oversized features made caricature difficult, made
> friendly caricature damned near impossible. It was beyond
> ordinary talent to do a drawing of Johnson that looked
> like Johnson and, at the same time, made him look
> honest. However well disposed one was to the president,
> his eyes were cold and nasty and the set of his mouth
> bore an unfortunate resemblance to that of the man at the
> bank who turns down your loan. (HELLER, 1982, p. 79)

The Feiffer caricature of Johnson in Figure 12.2 demonstrates the cartoonist at work and the opportunities afforded by a multicell format.

The dialogue suggests how President Johnson might have wished to be portrayed and illustrates the relationship between visual and verbal elements in a cartoon. Without the images, the dialogue would not mean much and without the dialogue we would see Johnson's caricature emerge and then vanish for no reason. Because Feiffer's cartoons develop their message across several cells, his work bridges the single-cell cartoon and strip cartooning.

A comic strip is "an open-ended dramatic narrative about a recurring set of characters told in a series of drawings, often including dialogue in balloons and a narrative text, and published serially in newspapers" (Inge, 1979, p. 631). Comic strips began in 1895 with the appearance of *The Yellow Kid,* inaugurated by Joseph Pulitzer's *New York World* to steal readers from its rival, William Randolph Hearst's *New York Morning Journal.* Hearst retaliated with his own comic strip, and the American tradition of the newspaper comic page was born.

Figure 12.2

From *Feiffer: Jules Feiffer's America From Eisenhower To Reagan*, edited by Steven Heller. Copyright © 1982 by Jules Feiffer. Reprinted by permission of Alfred A. Knopf, Inc.

The potential of the comic strips to function as rhetorical acts lies in their vast readership, the largest of any form of popular culture (Turner, 1977). A majority of American newspaper readers consider the "funny page" or comic strips to be "must" reading. Garry Trudeau explains what the cartoonist does for the audience: "When he's doing his job, he provides us with the means to look back into ourselves; he's the benign conduit between our self-serious facades and those pockets of vulnerability buried deep within" (Harrison, 1981, p. 67).

Comics such as *Doonesbury, Bloom County, The Wizard of Id,* and *Shoe* are frequently political. *Garfield, Peanuts, Broom Hilda, The Born Loser, Calvin and Hobbes, B.C., Cathy,* and *Hagar the Horrible* offer social commentary. *Archie, Blondie, The Family Circus, Hi & Lois, Snuffy Smith, The Lockhorns,* and *Andy Capp* view family life satirically.

Comic strips resemble film in form and content, in their use of characters, plot lines, dialogue, props, and the suggestion of movement. The *panel* is the basic unit of the strip which, like a single frame of film, freezes the action at a particular moment. Comic strips also resemble series television in their continuing casts of characters and their stories that are continued over several episodes. Like the political cartoon, words and pictures are interdependent, though comic strips depend more heavily on their verbal component (Harvey,

1979), possibly because their continuing casts of characters are so familar to the audience that what they say carries more information.

Comic strips also have a fantasy quality to them because they are constrained by limited space, the relatively coarse graphic potential of newsprint and the daily publication schedule. The dialogue balloon and captioning add to this fantasy quality.

> [T]he medium's extreme brevity allows neither the time nor the space to develop elaborate fictional structures of plot or character. Each strip must have an individual integrity on a day to day basis, even in the storyline comic, to aid the recall of readers who have engaged in twenty-four hours of other activity since they last read the funnies. (TURNER, 1977, p. 27)

As with all humor, the message of a comic strip is jointly created by cartoonist and reader, that is, rhetor and audience. Because readers must supply information and use their own values in interpreting the message, comic strips rely on current events for their material. Although nominally set in the past, *B.C., Hagar the Horrible,* and *Wizard of Id* discuss contemporary issues. This juxtaposition of past and present, such as the "prehistoric women's liberation movement" that frequently surfaces in *B.C.,* provides a humorous twist to the rhetorical act (Turner, 1977).

> [T]he comic strip asks for ideas already possessed by the audience on topics known to them, requiring their participation in order to be completed. To successfully accomplish this, comics must choose topical subject matter of interest to the broad range of comic strip readers—a criterion which forces reality into the funnies. (TURNER, 1977, p. 28)

Because strips appear daily, they give their readers many opportunities to participate and identify with the themes and characters developed by the cartoonist.

A sense of knowing the characters and participating in their lives explains the hold the comic page has on millions of readers.

> Why do most of us devote a part of our day to these cartoon fantasies? Because they are a source of diversion and escape, and for many they supply the heroes and heroines that are all too rare in life. They also give us a chance to become morally involved. When Mary Worth dispenses folksy common sense to ease the troubled lives of her fellow characters, thousands write to agree or disagree with her advice. (WHETMORE, 1989, p. 76)

Comic strips can provide the advice of a comic sage, show new ways of thinking about complex social issues, and explain politics, fads, and trends.

Milton Caniff, creator of *Terry and the Pirates* and *Steve Canyon*, was one of America's leading cartoonists. *Terry and the Pirates* emerged in 1934 as an adventure story grounded in the politics and international tensions of the 1930s. Although the strip was set in the Orient and took its story from the war in China, Caniff avoided any mention of the Japanese, so the strip could be printed in Tokyo newspapers, which it was until the bombing of Pearl Harbor (Mintz, 1979).

In 1947, another cartoonist took over *Terry,* and Caniff created *Steve Canyon,* a military adventure strip that used real events in the Korean War in its story. Over the years *Steve Canyon* kept pace with society. The exclusive focus on the Cold War gave way to social issues including marriage, drug and alcohol abuse, the student movement, and women's rights, blending social satire with Caniff's conservative political views.

The story in *Steve Canyon* frequently focused on events at Maumee University where his niece Poteet and her classmates explored life as college students, the town-gown relationship, and the foibles of their professors. During the late 1960s and early 1970s, Caniff declared war on student radicals and the counterculture.

> Not only are these character-types portrayed as dirty, foolish, and lazy, they are shown in several strips to be insincere, adopting their positions to cover various psychological needs and questionable motives. Revered Paul, the leader of Maumee's radical group, really covets power and the sexual success it brings for him. When he is faced with *true* radicals, the school's Black Power contingent, he reveals himself to be weak, cowardly, and uncommitted. (MINTZ, 1979, p. 678)

Milton Caniff's comic strips had broad appeal because his characters embodied American values and behaved in ways his readers could admire.

> [Readers] can recognize qualities in Pat Ryan, Terry Lee, Flip Corkin, and Steve Canyon that are championed and regarded as realizable in our society; these heroes are not above the law nor do they transcend natural limits, rather they rely upon hard work, honesty, logical intelligence, honor, courage, diligence, and all of the other virtues for which our society aims and strives. Success, for such a hero, is neither easy nor guaranteed . . . but the reader knows that virtues pay off, not because of devine intervention and reward but because of a cause and effect relationship—if you do the right thing it will have the right effect. (MINTZ, 1979, p. 667)

Walt Kelly's *Pogo* was the most unusual political comic strip. Through the words and deeds of a group of cute animal characters living in a Georgia swamp, Kelly offered cautionary tales about society and life's problems, large and small.

Pogo was a multilayered strip that often packed an unexpected punch. Kelly called himself a "watchdog humorist" who called attention to political flaws rather than protesting them (Mishkin, 1979). For example, Kelly satirized McCarthyism by using a lynx named Simple J. Malarkey, who mounted an antibird campaign to protect the swamp from undesirables, asking the other creatures, "Is you a bird?" or "What kind of bird is you?" The strip ended when Walt Kelly died, but his work has been collected and reprinted.

The most political "new" comic strip is probably *Doonesbury*, begun in the *Yale Daily News* in 1968 by Garry Trudeau when he was an undergraduate at Yale. Some newspapers treat it as editorial material and run it on the editorial page rather than the comic page, and some papers occasionally do not print the strip at all when they think the material is too controversial.

The story originally revolved around a group of Yale University students, each of whom represented a different student group and its activities. The strip showed that the students' alternative life-styles were as constrained by rules and norms as those of the establishment. Although it satirized both the establishment and the counterculture, *Doonesbury* was considered anti-establishment by many, but it attracted an audience made up of members of both groups because of Trudeau's style and wit.

The strip's original cast of characters were student archetypes: B.D., the captain of the football team; Mike Doonesbury, the campus make-out king who mostly failed with women; Bernie, the nerdy science major; and Megaphone Mike, the campus radical. Over the years, new characters have been added and the old ones have "grown up," left college, become yuppies, and aged. In addition to the regular characters, Dan Rather, Frank Sinatra, Presidents Nixon, Ford, Carter, Reagan, and Bush, and other world figures have "appeared" in the strip.

Whether a comic strip is overtly political or whether its characters merely comment on life, it functions rhetorically.

> At this level we look at the strips for stereotypes they may contain, for the way women are presented (and the roles they are given), for allusions to social and political matters, and for the way they reflect fundamental values and beliefs. That is, we can examine the comics as "historical documents" that reflect many different things about our society. (BERGER, 1988, p. 31)

Comic strips expanded into comic books, which by the 1950s had gained many readers. Responding to charges that comic books were too violent and potentially harmful to children, the comic book industry imposed a code of ethics that led to the underground comics, which reached their zenith in the late 1960s. Uncensored, these underground comics covered political issues, drugs, and sex with varying levels of intellectual and aesthetic quality.

Print cartoons were also adapted to other new communication genres, and then animated film appeared early in the history of the movies. Popular comic strips were adapted to film in the silent era. In 1928, Walt Disney produced

Steamboat Willie starring Mickey Mouse, the first cartoon "talky," and his *Snow White and the Seven Dwarfs* (1937) was the first feature-length animated film.

> Disney created a powerful world of make-believe, a fabric of classic archetypes in an enveloping milieu. . . . On the one hand, the Disney world is saccharin sweet, with cutesy, cuddly little animals, virginal maidens, noble princes. But the Disney vision is also populated with classic stereotypes of wicked witches, scheming stepmothers, and villainous monsters. (HARRISON, 1981, p. 99)

Animated cartoons operate on the level of pure fantasy and are consequently freed of physical restraints. Disney blended the traditions of silent comedy with fantastic elements in his cartoon world: speedy physical comedy, surrealistic settings, and the transformation of objects before the viewer's eyes. Sound was a source of creativity in the *Silly Symphony* series and was carried to the ultimate, fantasy through sound, in *Fantasia* (1940). The addition of sound helped make Walt Disney America's premier animated cartoonist (Mast, 1981); and, in turn, Disney set the standards for cartoons on film.

The work of Walt Disney is rhetorical because it functions as a morality play. This is particularly true of the feature-length animated films. While the audience is amused by the antics of the Seven Dwarfs they are also exposed to a social-psychological exercise in getting along with others and respecting their individuality. Disney's animated films portray behaviors and relationships that support certain cultural norms; the image of clean-cut, virtuous heroes and heroines and the benefits of honesty and cooperation are the signatures of Disney films.

The signature is the same for the shorter Disney films that star cultural icons such as Mickey Mouse because these characters blend the fantasy of talking animals with decidedly human traits.

> Disney's talking animals, like Aesop's were caricatured human beings. . . . Not only did the animals behave like humans, distinct personalities were developed for each. Mickey, jaunty and optimistic, afflicted with less able companions for whom he assumed responsibility, performed heroic feats through a combination of pragmatism and ingenuity. Minnie was naive and coy, trusting and appreciative with some resourcefulness and more than a little spunk of her own. Pluto, plagued by conscience, almost suffocating in his canine loyalty and affection, remained rambunctiously good humored as he committed one blunder after another. Goofy, the country bumpkin protected by his own innocence, was given to hiccups and half-witted ruminations. Donald, the irascible Duck, sputtered a steady stream of nearly unintelligible expletives. (ELLIS, 1985, p. 196)

American animated films have either been a product of or a reaction to the work of Disney Studios (Ellis, 1985). Cartoonists who learned their craft at Disney left and created rival cartoon characters. At Warner Brothers, Chuck Jones created Bugs Bunny, Daffy Duck, Tweetie Pie, Sylvester, and the Road Runner and Wile E. Coyote in the 1940s. United Productions of America, begun by Disney alumni, created Mr. Magoo. More recently, Disney-trained Don Bluth produced the feature length *The Secret of NIMH* (1980). Others have also moved beyond the Disney style. Ralph Bakshi's *Fritz the Cat* (1972), *Heavy Traffic* (1973), and *American Pop* (1980) are X- and R-rated attempts to handle adult themes in animated films.

Animated cartoons have been explicitly and intentionally rhetorical. During World War II, cartoons played an important part in Hollywood's war effort. Warner Brothers made a series of patriotic cartoons that were shown to movie audiences at home and troops overseas. The Warner Brothers characters became mascots during the war, and likenesses of Daffy Duck and Bugs Bunny were painted on airplanes, used to sell war bonds, and appeared on informational posters.

The *Weakly Reporter* (1944) parodied newsreels that showed how Americans were participating in the war effort. In *Super Rabbit* (1943), Bugs Bunny capers about in a Superman costume for most of the film; but at the end, he claims he has "some real work to do" and emerges in a Marine uniform. *Fifth Column Mouse* (1943) is a parable about a group of mice, enslaved by a cat, who decide to work together and fight back.

The World War II cartoons portray Hitler and other Nazi leaders as buffoons and Axis soldiers as inept. In *Daffy—the Commando* (1943), German soldiers salute a skunk, mistaking it for Hitler. In *Plane Daffy* (1944), a slinky Nazi spy, Hatta Mari, tries to steal a secret message from Daffy Duck. When she discovers the message is "Hitler is a stinker," she responds "that's no military secret, everybody knows that." In *Herr Meets Hare* (1944), Bugs Bunny impersonates Adolph Hitler and leads Hermann Göring on a chase through the Black Forest. When Bugs pops up wearing a mask that makes him look like Joseph Stalin, Hitler and Göring run off terrified.

On television, cartoons have become an important part of programming, mostly during daytime and especially on Saturday mornings. In the 1960s, the cartoon became a regular part of prime-time programming. Many began as children's programming and were adapted for adult audiences, whereas others were created with an eye toward social satire that would appeal to adults.

The Bullwinkle Show (1961–1962) featured the adventures of Rocket J. Squirrel, Bullwinkle the Moose, and their friends. Rocky and Bullwinkle were often pitted against two inept, vaguely Eastern European spies, Boris Badanov and Natasha Fatale. The cliff-hanger endings for each episode of their adventures parodied the style of serial films of the 1940s and 1950s. Good, honest, and trusting Rocky and Bullwinkle would always triumph over bad, dishonest, and paranoid Boris and Natasha in this wickedly funny satire of the Cold War.

The Flintstones (1960–1966) was a parody set in prehistoric times of the television show *The Honeymooners*. *The Jetsons* (1962–1963) satirized suburban life, family situation comedies of the 1950s, and how little technology really changed our lives.

Electronic and Print Humor

Prime-time and late-night television has included shows other than animated cartoons and situation comedies that offer social commentary and political humor.

The first effort to bring political invective and satire to prime-time television in America was *That Was The Week That Was* (1964–1965), a show that interpreted the news humorously. Because much of the news in 1964 concerned the presidential elections, TW3 (as it was known) heaped invective on the candidates, especially Republican Barry Goldwater. Although the show was very popular, it fell victim to the NBC executives' fears that it went too far. The show was preempted so many times that it lost its audience and wound up last in the ratings in 1965.

Rowan and Martin's Laugh-In (1968–1973) indulged in as much invective as TW3 but escaped ham-fisted treatment by the same network. Fast-paced and contemporary, *Laugh-In* employed several recurring settings and features to frame its topical humor. At the "Cocktail Party," guests made wry comments on current events and social trends. "The Flying Fickle Finger of Fate Award" afforded Dan Rowan and Dick Martin the opportunity to acknowledge dubious accomplishments. "Laugh-In Looks at the News" reprised TW3's idea of a satirical look at the week in review, though at times that week would be fifty years in the future or the past. *Laugh-In* was very popular, and millions of Americans adopted its catch phrases: "Look that up in your Funk and Wagnalls," "You bet your bippy," and "Sock it to me."

Saturday Night Live, aired for the first time in 1975, was NBC's third major humor program. Its late-night time slot gave it a degree of freedom in selecting and presenting material it would not have had in prime time. *Saturday Night Live* (SNL) stretched the limits of going too far on television with its overt references to sex and drugs. Politics and presidents were also frequent targets of the show's writers.

> Probably the most notorious episode in SNL's history was during the 1976 campaign. Chase had been developing a parody of President Ford during the first part of the season. Ford, in Chevy's version, was an idiotic stumblebum who fell down stairs, stapled himself to things, and generally behaved in an unpresidential manner in everyday situations. Chase's technique here was characteristically and disarmingly crude. Looking nothing

> like Ford, and attempting nothing in the way of an
> impression, he simply announced himself in various ways
> as the President and proceeded to fall around. So total
> was the dislike and mistrust of Ford in the country that
> this met with tremendous reaction. The joke character
> quickly became one of Chevy's trademarks. (HENDRA,
> 1987, p. 437)

Constant repetition of the premise that President Gerald Ford was a bumbling fool may have influenced some voters.

Besides invective, one of the comic devices that *Saturday Night Live* used effectively was parody. Over the years, parodies of popular game shows, situation comedies, and films have appeared, but one of *SNL*'s most biting parodies actually caused CBS to change the format of *60 Minutes*. A recurring program segment was a weekend news program that included a parody of the *60 Minutes*' signature closing, the debate between liberal Shana Alexander and conservative James Kilpatrick on the policy implications of some item in the news. In *SNL*'s parody, Jane Curtin played one role and Dan Aykroyd the other, always opening his comments with the phrase, "Jane you ignorant slut." The parody caught on, and CBS dropped the Alexander-Kilpatrick segment, replacing it with their own contribution to humor, "A few minutes with Andy Rooney."

Radio was a major source of entertainment and information for Americans during the Great Depression, an era of great radio comedy. Comedians not only helped their listeners find a way to escape their personal and economic problems but also helped them understand these problems. Radio comedies of the Depression reaffirmed American values of work, success, morality, and family (Wertheim, 1976). Radio comedy was series comedy, the precursor of television's sit-com and comedy-variety formats, and topical humor was central to its success.

Radio comedies were usually broadcast in the early evening and became a central part of America's experience with the media. Radio gave people the opportunity to share something never before possible.

> Radio extended the listener's environment away from an
> emphasis on self to involvement in the outside world.
> During the depression loneliness was widespread and
> radio tended to mitigate the feelings of solitude. People
> shared with their friends last night's comedy jokes and
> often adopted the new language of radio comedy
> (malapropisms and catch phrases) in their everyday
> conversation. (WERTHEIM, 1976, p. 513)

Jack Benny, Fred Allen, Edgar Bergen and Charlie McCarthy, The Great Gildersleeve, George Burns and Gracie Allen, Amos and Andy, Bob Hope, and Fibber McGee and Molly were not only big celebrities, they were part of the family. Jack Benny joked about the Depression, as did the popular comedy team, George

Burns and Gracie Allen. Benny told his listeners that even the birds couldn't afford to fly south for the winter this year. Gracie Allen suggested that unemployment could be solved if all the men in the world were dispatched to an island in the middle of the ocean. They'd all find jobs making boats (Wertheim, 1976).

Amos 'n' Andy premiered shortly before the stock market crash in 1929 and became one of the most popular comedy series on radio. Its characters were blacks (although they were played by white actors) who, like most people were hit hard by the economic collapse. The program featured a series of running gags and various schemes as Amos and Andy tried to make a living.

> The serial's daily plots frequently concerned the pair's endeavors to make ends meet. Risky investments in a lunch room, garage, hotel, and furniture store lead to constant harassment by creditors. Andy, a sucker for a fast buck, is victimized by phony salesmen and hucksters. . . . How to earn money and how to keep it out of the hands of confidence men dominated the early plots. Consequently, listeners facing similar problems in the 1930s readily identified with Amos's and Andy's predicaments. The characters' hopes for monetary success and subsequent business failures mirrored the lives of many American people at this time. (WERTHEIM, 1976, p. 507)

Like many popular radio series, *Amos 'n' Andy* was later adapted for television with black actors. The series came under fire from the NAACP and civil-rights leaders for perpetuating negative racial stereotypes. The series was dropped, but in 1961 a prime-time cartoon, *Calvin and the Colonel,* with animals as characters to avoid criticism, reprised the old Amos and Andy story lines.

Radio comedy has staged a comeback, primarily on public radio. Garrison Keillor's *A Prairie Home Companion* has been the biggest reason for the revival. Public radio carried the series for thirteen years until it ended in 1987. Keillor's monologs created the midwestern town of Lake Wobegon, Minnesota, a place where "all the women are strong, all the men are good-looking, and all the children are above average." Also contributing to the revival of radio humor is the Duck's Breath Mystery Theatre, a comedy group whose *Ask Dr. Science,* ninety seconds of off-the-wall explanations of science and technology by someone "with a Master's degree in science," and *Duck's Breath Homemade Radio,* social satire, are heard on public broadcasting stations.

Humor magazines are also a forum for extensive rhetorical activity here and abroad. There are many humor magazines, each with its own style and content. The humor magazine differs from the comic book in that it is not governed by any code other than sanctions against pornography. It may use cartoons, but plain text, photography, and other means of communication are used as well. *Mad* and *National Lampoon* are the two largest, most influential, contemporary humor magazines in America.

Mad magazine began publication in 1952 and influenced many contemporary humorists as they were growing up. Television satire, including *That Was The Week That Was* and *Saturday Night Live,* also bear the mark of *Mad's* influence (Norris, 1984).

Mad originally attracted a younger audience and addressed their fears. It acknowledged that there might be something wrong with a society that had to build bomb shelters because it insisted in engaging in nuclear brinksmanship, and it reminded its readers about the phoniness of television advertising (Norris, 1984). Over the years, the magazine continued this topical approach while serving as a chronicler of popular culture.

Mad specializes in parody and satire. Television programs and films are regular targets for parody. Regular features such as "Spy vs. Spy" and the famous fold in (rather than fold out) back cover often satirize national security and defense issues. *Mad's* style combines visual and verbal elements with the visual elements rendered in cartoon form.

National Lampoon was created in 1970 by a group of ex-Harvard Lampoon writers. In its early issues, they carried forward the idea of each issue having a theme, such as politics, sex, religion, or education, with most of the material in the issue devoted to that topic. The tradition of the Harvard Lampoon parody was also adopted for special publications, such as *1964 Kaleidoscope,* the marvelous 1974 parody of high-school yearbooks.

Material in *National Lampoon* is topical, drawn from all aspects of society: politics, music, personalities, sports, relationships, childhood, and sex. *National Lampoon* combines a variety of forms, including fictitious letters to the editor, cartoons, comic strips, essays, "true facts" contributed by readers, columns, and articles; and every comic device is employed one place or another.

Historically, prose essays and short stories have been popular vehicles for humor. Mark Twain exemplified the work of the comic sage as writer in the nineteenth century. More recently, Patrick McManus has written humorously about our attempts to commune with nature, and Jean Shepard has satirized childhood, college life on the G.I. bill, and suburbia. Almost every newspaper features a humor columnist, as do many magazines. Several new forms of electronic and print humor are becoming popular, including telephone dial-a-joke services, newsletters, computer games, and bulletin boards, but they have not yet attracted much attention from rhetorical critics.

Public Sloganeering

The slogan is a brief, humorous message, that is distinct from the cartoon in that the message is primarily verbal. Although typeface, color, and the material on which the slogan is printed are factors in the humor of the message, words are its main ingredient.

A primary rhetorical use of slogans is on campaign buttons, which first appeared in the McKinley-Bryan election of 1896. There were over a thousand different campaign buttons that year, many of them satirical. They played on the personalities and politics of the candidates. William Jennings Bryan's reputation as an active campaigner was lampooned on buttons that "pictured corpses or skeletons in coffins with the slogans 'TOO MUCH POLITICS' or 'TALKED TO DEATH' " (Fischer, 1980, p. 645). In 1908, William Howard Taft's supporters mocked Bryan's nomination as Democratic candidate with a button that read "VOTE FOR TAFT THIS TIME, YOU CAN VOTE FOR BRYAN ANYTIME" (Fischer, 1980, p. 646). Campaign buttons have contributed to political satire as "a vehicle for partisans to impugn the character, intelligence, even paternity of opposition candidates through cartoons and caricatures, puns and poetry, and many other ways of conveying imaginative insults" (Fischer, 1980, p. 645).

Invective is the comic device most commonly used on campaign buttons, but wordplay may also be used to attack the opposition. The 1964 race between Lyndon Johnson and Barry Goldwater provided sloganeers with great opportunities. Democrats used wordplay on the film *Dr. Strangelove* and Goldwater's position on the use of nuclear weapons with buttons reading "NO GENERAL STRANGEWATER FOR AMERICA and one featuring a skull superimposed on an atom captioned DR. STRANGEWATER" (Fischer, 1980, p. 649). Goldwater's own campaign slogan and his name provided opportunities for anti-Goldwater buttons:

> The two finest anti-Goldwater items both parodied familiar Goldwater campaign gimmicks, his slogan "In Your Heart, You Know He's Right" and the chemical formula AuH_2O (gold-water). One pictured Goldwater with the slogan IN YOUR GUTS, YOU KNOW HE'S NUTS. The other read "$C_5H_4N_4O_3$ on AuH_2O," quite literally "uric acid on Goldwater." (FISCHER, 1980, p. 649)

Slogans satirizing candidates and their stands on issues, or their seeming inability to take a stand also find their way onto buttons. In the 1976 Carter-Ford contest, Jimmy Carter was the favorite target. His pro-abortion stand was met by a button popular with anti-abortion groups: SUPPORT HUMAN LIFE, ABORT CARTER. His failure to take a clear stand on other issues was lampooned by a plaid button which read: JIMMY CARTER'S FAVORITE COLOR. Carter and his running mate, Walter "Fritz" Mondale had been nicknamed "Gritz & Fritz" by the Democrats, and Republican buttons played up these names: LET'S BLITZ GRITS & FRITZ and GRITZ & FRITZ GIVE ME THE SHITZ (Fischer, 1980).

Caricatures are also used to attack the opposition candidates. In the 1976 and 1980 elections, Carter's much caricatured smile and previous occupation as a Georgia peanut farmer were used on buttons with slogans such as JIMMY CARTER IS THE TOOTH FAIRY, CARTER HASN'T SHOWN ME ANYTHING BUT HIS TEETH, YOUR CHANCE TO PUT ANOTHER NUT IN THE WHITE HOUSE, and NOW WE CAN PUT A *REAL* NUT IN THE WHITE HOUSE (Fischer, 1980).

In addition to their use in political campaigns, buttons have become a popular medium for expressing beliefs about issues of public policy in a humorous way.

> The button craze dredged up all kinds of immediate social commentary and social protest, such as: "Make Love, Not War," "Draft Beer, Not Students," "Save Water, Shower with a Friend," "When This Button Begins to Melt You Know You Are in the Midst of an Atomic Attack.". . . The The wearing of topical buttons replaced the commonplace book as a source of epigrammatic and very temporary wit, and many of the buttons gave advice on lifestyle and ultimate values: "Jesus Saves, Moses Invests," "Dress British, Think Yiddish . . ." and the enigmatic "Thimk." (CHARNEY, 1978, p. 37)

These same slogans, sometimes combined with graphic elements, also appear on posters, bumper stickers, and T-shirts.

Doing Rhetorical Criticism of Humor

Humorous rhetorical acts can be found in nearly every form of communication. In addition to the generic forms we have described in this chapter, you could also consider humor in speeches, television situation comedy, films, and songs. Should you decide to explore the rhetoric of humor, an abundance of opportunities exist.

Since comedy clubs and concerts have become popular, you have the opportunity to be a participant-observer by attending a live performance. Stand-up comedians typically include material from their live performances in their records and videos, so if you are unable to see a live act, you may be able to recapture it from an album or videotape. Many videos and performances aired on premium cable channels feature the comedian performing before an audience, so you can make judgments about their response.

The collected works of political and comic strip cartoonists are also available, including some of the earliest work. Anthologies of columns by humorous writers are available, as well as mixed collections of jokes, essays, and newspaper columns on themes such as politics. Many old radio programs are now available on audiocassette, and Warner Brothers has released many of the World War II cartoons on videotape, making it possible to study the use of humor during the Depression and World War II. Recordings of the more contemporary radio programs, Duck's Breath Mystery Theatre and National Lampoon programs, are also available.

Because the role of the audience in getting the joke is so important to evaluating a humorous rhetorical act, you need to discover as much as you can about the audience. For historical examples of rhetorical humor, newspaper and magazine reviews, biographies of humorists and literary reviews may be useful. The Journal of Popular Culture is also a useful reference on historical and contemporary humor, and the Bowling Green State University Press publishes works on many aspects of popular culture, including humor.

The traditional approach to rhetorical criticism offers many options for doing humor criticism. Because stand-up comedy has parallels with public speaking, all elements of traditional criticism can be applied. In this type of humor, the rhetor is easily identified and often a celebrity. Traditional concepts about the rhetor and how he or she develops and manages ethos may be examined. The enthymeme can be used to study the argumentative structure of any humorous message, and traditional concepts of style and delivery are useful in studying cartoons, particularly how style and delivery relate to aesthetic appeals.

The traditional approach to criticism judges rhetorical acts in terms of results and whether or not they are perceived as probable truth. Because the audience participates in humor by getting the joke, a results-oriented traditional approach can help you determine how and why they decoded and used the joke as they did. Not getting the joke or perceiving that the rhetor has gone too far suggests the audience may have doubted the truth of what the rhetor-humorist was saying.

The audience's use of humor to feel superior or to experience inclusion may be a consequence of their identification with the rhetor. If you find Roseanne Barr funny and on target about male-female and family relationships, it might be because you identify with her. Concepts from dramatism might help you explain how a rhetor achieves identification through humor. Invective can be understood in terms of the process of guilt, purification, and redemption because its attack is often designed to make the target either a victim or a scapegoat. The pentad and the concept of examining a message in terms of how it manipulates the ratios between elements of the pentad provide an alternative to the enthymeme as a basis for interpreting the structure of humor.

Humor stretches, exaggerates, and generally looks at the rhetorical situation in an unusual way. The joint participation of rhetor and audience in finding the humor in contradictions and absurdities can be viewed as the creation of a shared fantasy. Satire often characterizes people as heroes and villians and norms and institutional practices as complex plots. Applying concepts from the fantasy theme approach is an excellent way to discover how an audience came to share the sense of social reality created by a rhetor-humorist. The setup and punch line, especially in single-cell cartoons and the one-line jokes of public sloganeering, represent a fantasy theme in shorthand form; so concepts from this approach are particularly well suited to explaining these more abbreviated forms of humor.

Many subgenres of humor, even those that make their arguments briefly, tell stories that contain the elements of narrative structure. Comic strips, animated cartoons, and skits on television humor programs are particularly suited to narrative analysis. The concepts of narrative structure and narrative fidelity can be used to evaluate how an audience develops an affinity for a humorous work, and what uses they make of it.

Because humor often depends on the cultural knowledge of the audience, concepts from the cultural approaches to rhetorical criticism are also useful to humor critics. Understanding of satire is based on cultural knowledge because satire is used to critique a culture. Applying an existing social-values model or creating your own would be an effective way to do rhetorical criticism of satire; it would enable you, for example, to explore how the style of a particular stand-up comedian involves the audience in a dialogue on the need for social change.

Concepts from the Jungian model of cultural criticism can be applied to any form of cartoon. The Jungian model is particularly suited to examining surreal images and the cultural icons depicted in graphic art. A Marxist critique of various subgenres of humor might explore how humor created a sense of class superiority or how it perpetuated the hegemony of a particular class in American society. The feminist model could be used to examine how humor from earlier eras helped create stereotypes of women's roles or how contemporary humor attacks these stereotypes. As more women become professional humorists, feminist criticism can be used to judge how their work influences the way society views and values women.

Steve Martin once joked that humor is serious business. You may be concerned that doing rhetorical critcism of humor might be taking it a little too seriously or, if you are a fan of a particular humorist or form of humor, that subjecting your favorite to rhetorical criticism will take all the enjoyment out of it. Let us assure you that neither fear is well founded. As a rhetorical critic of humor, you will gain insight into a highly complex communication genre and a greater appreciation of those who practice it well.

Suggested Readings

Examples of Criticism

BOSTDORFF, D.M. (1987). Making light of James Watt: A Burkean approach to the form and attitude of political cartoons. *Quarterly Journal of Speech, 73,* 43–59.
>The author examined eighty-three cartoons about James Watt, Ronald Reagan's first secretary of the interior. Concepts of rhetorical strategy from dramatism and Kenneth Burke's ideas on the stylistic devices of metaphor, synedoche, irony, and metonymy were used to determine how the cartoons created a series of arguments about Watt's inadequacies as a public official. This is an excellent example of criticism of cartoons that functioned to explain the incongruity of Watt's anticonservationist public image and his public office as conservator of the nation's environmental resources.

BROWN, W.R. (1972). Will Rogers: Ironist as persuader. *Speech Monographs, 39,* 183–192.
>This essay explores how Will Rogers helped Depression-era audiences achieve a sense of superiority in the face of economic hardship. Using ideas from the traditional concept of audience and classical Greek theories of irony, Brown explains Rogers' success in creating irony that was used and appreciated by many Americans. There is an especially good discussion of how a humorist creates a comic persona.

CARLSON, A.C. (1988). Limitations on the comic frame: Some witty American women of the nineteenth century. *Quarterly Journal of Speech, 74,* 310–322.
>This criticism of the work of women humorists, primarily novelists from 1820 to 1880, applies concepts of identification and the dramatistic process of guilt, purification, and redemption. Carlson explains why these humorists were at first successful and then lost their audience. Initially women humorists wrote for other women, using irony and focusing on the absurdity of norms about a woman's place,

her alleged inferiority, and the reality of what she had to do. These humorists' work paralleled the growing feminist movement; but when their humor shifted to satire and tried to appeal to male audiences, it failed. This is an excellent historical view of humor and analysis of why a comic device works or does not work to achieve social change.

MEDHURST, M.J., AND DeSOUSA, M.A, (1981).   Political cartoons as rhetorical form: A taxonomy of graphic discourse. *Communication Monographs, 48,* 197–236.
>   The authors used the traditional approach to criticism, organized around the five canons of classical rhetoric, to evaluate contemporary political cartooning. How the cartoonist approaches the subject through the process of invention, the resources of style and organization in graphic art, and a superior discussion of how a cartoon is an enthymeme make this an outstanding example of a formulary approach to humor criticism. This is an excellent model of how traditional concepts can be used.

MORRIS, B.A. (1987).   The communal constraints on parody: The symbolic death of Joe Bob Briggs. *Quarterly Journal of Speech, 73,* 460–473.
>   Joe Bob Briggs is the persona created by John Bloom. The Joe Bob character began life at the *Dallas Times Herald* as a parody of movie review columnists, and "his" column was eventually syndicated in fifty-five newspapers. This essay examines the nature of parody from the perspectives of social values and identification and applies these concepts to explain the time that Joe Bob went too far, concluding with a discussion of Joe Bob as sacrificial victim on the public altar. Although Joe Bob's style was to offend almost every group in America on a regular basis, the column remained popular until Joe Bob did a parody of "We Are the World." The public responded negatively to "We Are the Weird," and the reaction was serious enough that Joe Bob's newspaper career ended. This analysis expands the discussion of parody to develop four bases on which a parody may be rejected for going too far: content, context, propriety, and detrimental effects.

TURNER, K.J. (1977).   Comic strips: A rhetorical perspective. *Central States Speech Journal, 28,* 24–35.
>   This essay discusses comic strips as rhetorical acts through a combination of concepts from fantasy theme, traditional, and feminist critical approaches. This is a clear, well-written example of organic criticism. Turner focuses on how comic strips have portrayed women, with an emphasis on more contemporary strips. She provides a good explanation of how a comic strip's message is created through enthymemes.

Resources for Doing Criticism

BERGER, A.A. (1973).   *The comic-stripped American.* New York: Walker.
>   This is a social history of the comic strip in America, beginning with the earliest strips and concluding with *Peanuts.* Not every comic strip is covered, but Berger provides insightful commentary on selected strips, including *Little Orphan Annie* as American capitalism; *Buck Rogers, Batman, Dick Tracy, Flash Gordon,* and *Superman* as heroic archetypes; and *Pogo* as the irony of American democracy. There is also a brief discussion of underground comics.

BERGER, A.A. (1988).   *Media USA: Process and effect.* New York: Longman.
>   This is a history of American media, including reviews of newspapers, magazines, books, radio, television, film, recording, and media-related issues. This is a good

general reference on mass media. In the context of humor, chapter 3, "Politics in the Comics," updates some of the ideas in Berger's 1973 book and provides an extensive discussion of *Superman*. Berger views *Superman* as symbolizing our national experience. Like the pilgrims, *Superman* came to a new land, had a mission, and represented clear-cut ideals.

BLAIR, W., AND HILL, H. (1978). *America's humor from Poor Richard to Doonesbury*. New York: Oxford University Press.

This an excellent history of humor in America. The authors provide examples of humor, biographical information on humorists, and discuss the impact of humor on American culture. This is an especially good source for information about how audiences received and used the work of prominent humorists.

HARRISON, R.P. (1981). *The cartoon: Communication to the quick*. Beverly Hills, CA: Sage.

The many applications of cartoons and their special communication properties are discussed in this comprehensive book on cartooning. A major section is devoted to the verbal and visual codes of cartooning, and the history of cartoons and comic strips is also covered in some depth. There are some excellent suggestions for future cartoon research in the final section.

HELLER, S. (ED.) (1982). *Jules Feiffer's America from Eisenhower to Reagan*. New York: Alfred A. Knopf.

This collection of Feiffer's political cartoons is organized by presidential administrations. Each section begins with Feiffer's thoughts about how he viewed the rhetorical situations faced by each administration, what he thought of each man, and how he created caricatures of each. This collection allows the reader to get inside the mind of a cartoonist as Feiffer explains his intent and how he hoped readers would interpret his cartoons and the events they reflected.

LUKES, S., AND GALNOOR, I. (1987). *No laughing matter: A collection of political jokes*. London: Penguin.

This is a collection of political jokes from around the world, organized by themes: identity, debunking and unmasking, power and resistance, and the facts of life. Variations on topics and joke types, such as the derogatory ethnic joke, are included under each theme. This is an excellent source for finding jokes from Eastern European countries, Western Europe, Israel, Latin and South America, the Middle East, as well as the United States.

MORREALL, J. (1987). *The philosophy of laughter and humor*. Albany, NY: State University of New York Press.

In the first half of this book, Morreall surveys theories of humor from Plato, Aristotle, and Cicero through the nineteenth century, ending with Freud. The explanation of these works is clear and builds a theory of humor as a cognitive process leading to rational thought. The second half of the book contains articles on contemporary theories of humor as rational thought, including several by Morreall. This is a good source on humor theory, and humor as a form of argument.

References

ANDREWS, J.R. (1983). *The practice of rhetorical criticism*. New York: Macmillan.

ANDREWS, J.R., and ZAREFSKY, D. (1989). *American voices: Significant speeches in American history, 1640–1945*. New York: Longman.

ANG, I. (1982). *Watching Dallas*. London: Metheun.

ARNOLD, C.C. (1974). *Criticism of oral rhetoric*. Columbus, OH: Charles E. Merrill.

AUFDERHEIDE, P. (1986). Music videos: The look of sound. *Journal of Communication, 36,* 57–78.

BANTZ, C.R. (1975). Television news: Reality and research. *Western Speech Communication, 39,* 123–130.

BARKAN, E.R. (1966). *Diplomatic history of the United States*. New York: Monarch Press.

BECKER, S.L. (1984). Marxist approaches to media studies: The British experience. *Critical Studies in Mass Communication, 1,* 66–80.

BEHL, W.A. (1947). Theodore Roosevelt's principles of invention. *Speech Monographs, 14,* 93–110.

BEHLMER, R. (1982). *America's favorite movies*. New York: Frederick Ungar.

BELTZ, L. (1969). Theodore Roosevelt's "man with the muckrake." *Central States Speech Journal, 20,* 97–103.

BENNETT, W.L., and EDELMAN, M. (1985). Toward a new political narrative. *Journal of Communication, 35,* 156–171.

BERGER, A.A. (1981). Semiotics and tv. In R.P. Adler (Ed.), *Understanding television: Essays on television as a social and cultural force* (pp. 91–114). New York: Praeger.

BERGER, A.A. (1988). *Media U.S.A.: Process and effect.* New York: Longman.

BERGMAN, A. (1971). *We're in the money.* New York: New York University Press.

BIRNBAUM, J. (1989, July 3). Madcap airs all. *Time,* 68–69.

BITZER, L.F. (1968). The rhetorical situation. *Philosophy and rhetoric, 1,* 1–15.

BLACK, E. (1965). *Rhetorical criticism.* New York: Macmillan.

BLAIR, W., and HILL, H. (1978). *America's humor, from Poor Richard to Doonesbury.* New York: Oxford University Press.

BLOOMFIELD, L.P. (1974). *In search of American foreign policy.* New York: Oxford University Press.

BLUEM, A.W. (1965). *Documentary in American television.* New York: Hastings House.

BOHMAN, G.V. (1943). The colonial period. In W.N. Brigance (Ed.), *A history and criticism of American public address,* Vol. I (pp. 3–54). New York: McGraw-Hill.

BORMANN, E.G. (1972). Fantasy and rhetorical vision: The rhetorical criticism of social reality. *Quarterly Journal of Speech, 58,* 396–407.

BORMANN, E.G. (1980). *Communication theory.* New York: Holt, Rinehart, & Winston.

BORMANN, E.G. (1982a). A fantasy theme analysis of the television coverage of the hostage release and the Reagan inaugural. *Quarterly Journal of Speech, 68,* 133–145.

BORMANN, E.G. (1982b). Fantasy and rhetorical vision: Ten years later. *Quarterly Journal of Speech, 68,* 288–305.

BORMANN, E.G. (1983). Fantasy theme analysis and rhetorical theory. In J.L. Golden, G.F. Berquist, and W.E. Coleman, *The rhetoric of western thought* (3rd ed.) (pp. 432–449). Dubuque, IA: Kendall/Hunt.

BORMANN, E.G. (1985). Symbolic convergence theory: A communication formulation. *Journal of Communication, 35,* 128–138.

BORMANN, E.G., KOESTLER, J., and BENNETT J. (1978). Political cartoons and salient rhetorical fantasies: An empirical analysis of the '76 presidential campaign. *Communication Monographs, 45,* 317–329.

BOSKIN, J. (1987). The complicity of humor: The life and death of Sambo. In J. Morreall (Ed.), *The philosophy of laughter and humor* (pp. 250–263). Albany, NY: State University of New York Press.

BOSLEY. H.A. (1969). The role of preaching in American history. In D. Holland (Ed.), *Preaching in American history* (pp. 17–35). Nashville, TN: Abingdon Press.

BOWERS, C.G. (1932). *Beveridge and the progressive era.* Boston: Houghton Mifflin.

BOWERS, J.W., and OCHS, D.J. (1971). *The rhetoric of agitation and control.* Reading, MA: Addison-Wesley.

BRADEN, W.W. (1987). Theodore Roosevelt. In B.K. Duffy and H.R. Ryan (Eds.), *American orators of the twentieth century,* (pp. 353–360). New York: Greenwood Press.

BRANDT, C.G., and SHAFTER, E.M. (1960). *Selected American speeches on basic issues (1850–1950).* Boston: Houghton Mifflin.

BRAZIER, R. (1968). The industrial workers of the world's little red song book. In R.S. Denisoff and R.A. Peterson (Eds.), *The sounds of social change* (pp. 60–71). Chicago: Rand McNally.

BREEN, M., and CORCORAN, F. (1982). Myth in the television discourse. *Communication Monographs, 49,* 127–136.

BROCKRIEDE, W. (1974). Rhetorical criticism as argument. *Quarterly Journal of Speech, 60,* 165–174.

BRYANT, D.C. (1973). *Rhetorical dimensions in criticism.* Baton Rouge, LA: Louisiana State University Press.

BRYANT, M.D. (1982). Cinema, religion, and popular culture. In J.R. May and M. Bird (Eds.), *Religion in film* (pp. 101–114). Knoxville, TN: University of Tennessee Press.

BURKE, K. (1961). *Attitudes toward history.* Boston: Beacon Press.

BURKE, K. (1965). *Permanence and change.* Los Angeles: University of California Press.

BURKE, K. (1966). *Language as symbolic action.* Los Angeles: University of California Press.

BURKE, K. (1969a). *A rhetoric of motives.* Los Angeles: University of California Press.

BURKE, K. (1969b). *A grammar of motives.* Los Angeles: University of California Press.

BYWATER, T., and SOBCHACK, T. (1989). *Introduction to film criticism.* New York: Longman.

CAGIN, S., and DRAY, P. (1984). *Hollywood films of the seventies.* New York: Harper & Row.

CAMPBELL, K.K. (1972). *Critiques of contemporary rhetoric.* Belmont, CA: Wadsworth.

CAMPBELL, K.K. (1982). *The rhetorical act.* Belmont, CA: Wadsworth.

CAPRA, F. (1971). *The name above the title: An autobiography.* New York: Macmillan.

CARTER, D.A. (1980). The industrial workers of the world and the rhetoric of song. *Quarterly Journal of Speech, 66,* 365–374.

CARTER, E. (1983). Cultural history written with lightning: The significance of *The Birth of a Nation* (1915). In P.C. Rollins (Ed.), *Hollywood as historian* (pp. 9–19). Lexington, KY: University of Kentucky Press.

CASTLEMAN, H.H., and PODRAZIK, W.J. (1982). *Watching tv: Four decades of American television.* New York: McGraw-Hill.

CATHCART, R.S. (1966). *Post communication criticism and evaluation.* Indianapolis: Bobbs-Merrill.

CATHCART, R.S. (1980). Defining social movements by the rhetorical form. *Central States Speech Journal, 31,* 267–273.

CHARNEY, M. (1978). *Comedy high and low: An introduction to the experience of comedy.* New York: Peter Lang Publishing.

CHATMAN, S. (1978). *Story and discourse, narrative structure in fiction and film.* Ithaca, NY: Cornell University Press.

CHESEBRO, J.W. (1986). Communication, value, and popular television series—an eleven-year assessment. In G. Gumpert and R. Cathcart (Eds.), *Intermedia: Interpersonal communication in a media world* (3rd ed.) (pp. 477–512). New York: Oxford University Press.

COCKS, J. (1987). Songs from the high ground. In J. Podell (Ed.), *Rock music in America* (pp. 96–99). New York: H.W. Wilson.

COMBS, J.E., and MANSFIELD, M.W. (Eds.) (1976). *Drama in life.* New York: Hastings House.

CORN, I.G., Jr. (1981). The changing role of corporations in political affairs. *Vital Speeches of the Day, 47,* 463–468.

CRAGEN, J.F. (1981). The origins and nature of the cold war rhetorical vision 1946–1972: A partial history. In J.F. Cragan and D.C. Shields (Eds.), *Applied communication research: A dramatistic approach* (pp. 47–66). Prospect Heights, IL: Waveland Press.

CRAGEN, J.F., and SHIELDS, D.C. (1981). *Applied communication research: A dramatistic approach* (pp. 47–66). Prospect Heights, IL: Waveland Press.

CRIPPS, T., and CULBERT, D. (1983). *The Negro Soldier* (1944): Film propaganda in black and white. In P.C. Rollins (Ed.). *Hollywood as historian* (pp. 109–133). Lexington, KY: University of Kentucky Press.

CROCKETT, J. (1986). Joan Baez. In P. Hood (Ed.), *Artists of American folk music* (pp. 71–73). New York: William Morrow.

CROSS, D.W. (1983). *Media-speak: How television makes up your mind.* New York: The New American Library.

CULBERT, D. (1983). Television's Nixon: The politician and his image. In J.E. O'Connor (Ed.), *American history/American television* (pp. 184–207). New York: Frederick Ungar.

DAVIES, R.A., FARRELL, J.M., and MATTHEWS, S.S. (1982). The dream world of film: A Jungian perspective on cinematic communication. *Western Journal of Speech Communication, 46,* 326–343.

DEMING, C.J. (1985). *Hill Street Blues* as narrative. *Critical Studies in Mass Communication, 2,* 1–22.

DENISOFF, R.S. (1969). Folk rock: Folk music, protest, or commercialism? *Journal of Popular Culture, 3,* 214–230.

DENISOFF, R.S. (1971). *Great day coming.* Urbana, IL: University of Illinois Press.

DENISOFF, R.S. (1972a). *Sing a song of social significance.* Bowling Green, OH: Bowling Green State University Popular Press.

DENISOFF, R.S. (1972b). The evolution of the American protest song. In R.S. Denisoff and R.A. Peterson (Eds.), *The sounds of social change* (pp. 15–25). Chicago: Rand McNally.

DeSOUSA, M.A. (1984). Symbolic action and pretended insight: The Ayatollah Khomeini in U.S. editorial cartoons. In M.J. Medhurst and T.W. Benson (Eds.), *Rhetorical dimensions in media* (pp. 204–230). Dubuque, IA: Kendall/Hunt.

DeVITO, J.A. (1987). *The elements of public speaking* (3rd ed.). New York: Harper & Row.

DIONISOPOULOS, G.N. (1988). A case study in print media and heroic myth: Lee Iacocca 1978–1985. *Southern Speech Communication Journal, 53,* 227–243.

DOWNIE, L., Jr. (1976). *The new muckrakers.* New York: Mentor Books.

DOYLE, M.V. (1985). The rhetoric of romance: A fantasy theme analysis of Barbara Cartland novels. *Southern Speech Communication Journal, 51,* 24–48.

DUNCAN, H. (1968). Axiomatic propositions. In J.E. Combs and M.W. Mansfield (Eds.), *Drama in life* (pp. 30–39). New York: Hastings House.

EBENSTEIN, W. (1964). *Today's isms* (4th ed.). Englewood Cliffs, NJ: Prentice-Hall.

EHNINGER, D.H. (1968). On systems of rhetoric. *Philosophy and Rhetoric, 1,* 131–144.

EISNER, M.O. (1987). The business people and television. *Vital Speeches of the Day, 53,* 665–667.

ELIOT, M. (1981). *American television: The official art of the artifact.* Garden City, NY: Anchor Press/Doubleday.

ELLIS, J.C. (1985). *A short history of film.* Englewood Cliffs, NJ: Prentice-Hall.

EVANS, W. (1982). Monster movies: A sexual theory. In M.T. Marsden, J.G. Nachbar, and S.L. Grogg, Jr. (Eds.), *Movies as artifacts* (pp. 129–136). Chicago: Nelson-Hall.

EWEN, D. (1977). *All the years of American popular music.* Englewood Cliffs, NJ: Prentice-Hall.

FARRELL, T.B. (1980). Critical models in the analysis of discourse. *Western Journal of Speech Communication, 44,* 300–314.

FISCHER, R.A. (1980). Pinback put-downs: The campaign button as political satire. *Journal of Popular Culture, 13,* 645–653.

FISHER, W.R. (1973). Reaffirmation and subversion of the American dream. *Quarterly Journal of Speech, 59,* 160–167.

FISHER, W.R. (1978). Toward a logic of good reasons. *Quarterly Journal of Speech, 64,* 376–384.

FISHER, W.R. (1980). Rationality and the logic of good reasons. *Philosophy and Rhetoric, 13,* 121–130.

FISHER, W.R. (1984). Narration as a human communication paradigm: The case of public moral argument. *Communication Monographs, 51,* 1–22.

FISHER, W.R. (1985a). The narrative paradigm: An elaboration. *Communication Monographs, 52,* 347–367.

FISHER, W.R. (1985b). The narrative paradigm: In the beginning. *Journal of Communication, 35,* 74–89.

FISHER, W.R. (1987a). *Human communication as narration: Toward a philosophy of reason, value, and action.* Columbia, SC: University of South Carolina Press.

FISHER, W.R. (1987b). Technical logic, rhetorical logic, and narrative rationality. *Argumentation, 1,* 3–22.

FISHER, W.R. (1989). Clarifying the narrative paradigm. *Communication Monographs, 56,* 55–58.

FISKE, J. (1987a). British cultural studies and television. In R.C. Allen (Ed.), *Channels of discourse* (pp. 254–290). Chapel Hill, NC: University of North Carolina Press.

FISKE, J. (1987b). *Television culture.* New York: Methuen.

FISKE, J., and HARTLEY, J. (1978). *Reading television.* London: Methuen.

FONER, P.S. (1975). *American labor songs of the nineteenth century.* Urbana, IL: University of Illinois Press.

FOSS, S.K. (1989). *Rhetorical criticism: Exploration and practice.* Prospect Heights, IL: Waveland Press.

FRENTZ, T.S., and RUSHING, J.H. (1978). The rhetoric of "Rocky": Part two. *Western Journal of Speech Communication, 42,* 231–240.

GALLANTER, M. (1986). Interview with Pete Seeger. In P. Hood (Ed.), *Artists of American folk music* (pp. 29–35). New York: William Morrow.

GASHBOW, A. (1989). State of the band, January 14, 1989. *Vital Speeches of the Day, 55,* 409–413.

GERBNER, G., GROSS, L., SIGNORIELLI, N., MORGAN, M., and JACKSON-BEECK, M. (1979). The demonstration of power: Violence profile No. 10. *Journal of Communication, 29,* 177–196.

GINGER, R. (1967). *William Jennings Bryan: Selections.* Indianapolis: Bobbs-Merrill.

GLEASON, R.J. (1969). A cultural revolution. In R.S. Denisoff and R.A. Peterson (Eds.), *The sounds of social change* (pp. 137–146). Chicago: Rand McNally.

GOLD, E.R. (1978). Political apologia: The ritual of self defense. *Communication Monographs, 45,* 306–316.

GOLDEN, J.L., BERQUIST, G.F., and COLEMAN, W.E. (1989). *The rhetoric of western thought* (4th ed.). Dubuque, IA: Kendall/Hunt.

GOLDZWIG, S. (1987). A rhetoric of public theology: The religious rhetor and public policy. *Southern Speech Communication Journal, 52* 128–150.

GOULD, C., STERN, D.C., and ADAMS, T.D. (1981). TV's distorted vision of poverty. *Communication Quarterly, 29,* 309-314.

GOULD, J.E. (1961). *The chautauqua movement.* Albany, NY: State University of New York Press.

GRAHAM, J. (1970). *Great American speeches 1898–1963.* New York: Appleton-Century-Crofts.

GREENFIELD, J. (1987). They changed rock, which changed the culture, which changed us. In J. Podell (Ed.), *Rock music in America* (pp. 42–51). New York: H.W. Wilson.

GREENWAY, J. (1970). *American folk songs of protest.* New York: Octagon Books.

GREGG, R.B. (1977). The rhetoric of political newscasting. *Central States Speech Journal, 28,* 221–237.

GRONBECK, B.E. (1973). The rhetoric of social-institutional change: Black action at Michigan. In C.J. Stewart, D.J. Ochs, and G.P. Mohrmann (Eds.), *Explorations in rhetorical criticism* (pp. 98–123). University Park, PA: Pennsylvania State University Press.

GRONBECK, B.E. (1980). Dramaturgical theory and criticism: The state of the art (or science?). *Western Journal of Speech Communication, 44,* 315–330.

GRONBECK, B.E. (1983). The "scholar's anthology": An introduction. *Central States Speech Journal, 34,* viii.

GRONBECK, B.E. (1984). Audience engagement in "Family." In M.J. Medhurst and T.W. Benson (Eds.), *Rhetorical dimensions in media: A critical casebook* (pp. 4–32). Dubuque, IA: Kendall/Hunt.

HANCE, K.G. (1944). The American lecture platform before 1930. *Quarterly Journal of Speech, 30,* 273–279.

HARPER, N.L. (1979). *Human communication theory: The history of a paradigm.* Rochelle Park, NJ: Hayden Book Co.

HARRINGTON, J. (1973). *The rhetoric of film.* New York: Holt, Rinehart, & Winston.

HARRISON, R.P. (1981). *The cartoon: Communication to the quick.* Beverly Hills, CA: Sage.

HARVEY, R.C. (1979). The aesthetics of the comic strip. *Journal of Popular Culture, 12,* 640–652.

HELLER, S. (Ed.) (1982). *Jules Feiffer's America from Eisenhower to Reagan.* New York: Alfred A. Knopf.

HENDRA, T. (1987). *Going too far.* New York: Doubleday.

HENRY, D. (1988). The rhetorical dynamics of Mario Cuomo's 1984 keynote address: Situation, speaker, metaphor. *Southern Speech Communication Journal, 53,* 105–120.

HILLBRUNER, A. (1966). *Critical dimensions: The art of public address criticism.* New York: Random House.

HIMMELSTEIN, H. (1984). *Television myth and the American mind.* New York: Praeger.

HOFFER, T.W., and NELSON, R.A. (1980). Evolution of docudrama on American television networks: A content analysis, 1966–1978. *Southern Speech Communication Journal, 45,* 149–163.

HOLLAND, D. (1973). *American in controversy: History of American public address.* Dubuque, IA: William C. Brown.

HOLLAND, V.L. (1955). Kenneth Burke's dramatistic approach to criticism. *Quarterly Journal of Speech, 41,* 352–358.

HOLLIHAN, T.A., and RILEY, P. (1987). The rhetorical power of a compelling story: A critique of a "toughlove" parental support group. *Communication Quarterly, 35,* 13–25.

HOOVER, J.D. (1989). Big boys don't cry: The values constraint in apologia. *Southern Communication Journal, 54,* 235–272.

HUMM, M. (1986). *Feminist criticism.* Brighton, Sussex, Great Britain: Harvester Press.

IACOCCA, L.A. (1987). In order to: Compromise and competency. *Vital Speeches of the Day, 53,* 745–748.

INGE, M.T. (1979). The comics as culture: Introduction. *Journal of Popular Culture, 12,* 630–639.

IVIE, R.L. (1980). Images of savagery in American justifications for war. *Communication Monographs, 47,* 279–294.

JAFFEE, A. (1989, Winter). Misfortune kookie department, don't you feel like a schmuck?! *Mad Mania 2,* 44–47.

JAMIESON, K.H., and CAMPBELL, K.K. (1982). Rhetorical hybrids: Fusions of generic elements. *Quarterly Journal of Speech, 68,* 146–57.

Japanese-American and Aleutian Wartime Relocation (June 20, 21, 27 and September 12, 1984). Serial No. 90. Washington, D.C.: Committee on the Judiciary House of Representatives.

JARVIE, I.C. (1978). *Movies as social criticism.* Metuchen, N.J.: Scarecrow Press.

JEWETT, R., and LAWRENCE, J.S. (1977). *The American monomyth.* Garden City, NY: Anchor Press/Doubleday.

JOHANNESEN, R.L. (1985). The jeremiad and Jenkin Lloyd Jones. *Communication Monographs, 52,* 156–172.

KEAN, T.H. (1989). Keynote address. *Vital Speeches of the Day, 55,* 7–10.

KENNEDY, J.F. (1960). Acceptance address. *Vital Speeches of the Day, 26,* 610–612.

KERR, H.P. (1960). Politics and religion in colonial fast and thanksgiving sermons, 1763–1783. *Quarterly Journal of Speech, 46,* 372–386.

KERR, H.P. (1962). The election sermon: Primer for revolutionaries. *Speech Monographs, 29,* 13–22.

KLUMPP, J.F., and HOLLIHAN, T.A. (1979). Debunking the resignation of Earl Butz: Sacrificing an official racist. *Quarterly Journal of Speech, 65,* 1–11.

KLUMPP, J.F., and HOLLIHAN T.A. (1989). Rhetorical criticism as moral action. *Quarterly Journal of Speech, 75,* 84–96.

KNOCK, T.J. (1983). History with lightning: The forgotten film *Wilson* (1944). In P.C. Rollins (Ed.). *Hollywood as historian* (pp. 88–108). Lexington, KY: University of Kentucky Press.

KOPPES, C.R., and BLACK, G.D. (1987). *Hollywood goes to war.* New York: The Free Press.

KOZISKI, S. (1984). The standup comedian as anthropologist: Intentional culture critic. *Journal of Popular Culture, 18,* 57–76.

KRUSE, N.W. (1981). The scope of apologetic discourse: Establishing generic parameters. *Southern Speech Communication Journal, 46,* 278–291.

LARSON, C. (1940). Patriotism in carmine: 162 years of July 4th oratory. *Quarterly Journal of Speech, 26,* 12–25.

LAWRENCE, V.B. (1975). *Music for patriots, politicians, and presidents.* New York: Macmillan.

LEFF, M. (1983). Topical invention and metaphoric interaction. *Southern Speech Communication Journal, 48,* 214–228.

LESSL, T.M. (1989). The priestly voice. *Quarterly Journal of Speech, 75,* 183–197.

LEVENTHAL, H., and GUTHRIE, M. (1976). *The Woody Guthrie songbook.* New York: Woody Guthrie Publications.

LEVY, S. (1987). Ad nauseam: How MTV sells out rock and roll. In J. Podell (Ed.), *Rock music in America* (pp. 120–143). New York: H.W. Wilson.

LEWIN, L.C. (1964). *A treasury of American political humor.* New York: Delacorte Press.

LEWIS, W.F. (1987). Telling America's story: Narrative form and the Reagan presidency. *Quarterly Journal of Speech, 73,* 280–302.

LOMAS, C.W. (1968). *The agitator in American society.* Englewood Cliffs, NJ: Prentice-Hall.

LOTT, D.N. (1961). *The inaugural addresses of the American presidents from Washington to Kennedy.* New York: Holt, Rinehart & Winston.

LUCAITES, J.L., and CONDIT, C.M. (1985). Re-constructing narrative theory: A functional perspective. *Journal of Communication, 35,* 90–108.

LUCAS, S.E. (1988). The renaissance of American public address: Text and context in rhetorical criticism. *Quarterly Journal of Speech, 74,* 241–260.

LUKE, C. (1985). Television discourse processing: A schema theoretic. *Communication education, 34,* 91–105.

LUKES, S., and GALNOOR, I. (1987). *No laughing matter: A collection of political jokes.* London: Routledge and Kegan Paul Ltd.

LYNCH, J.D. (1984). Music videos: From performance to dada-surrealism. *Journal of Popular Culture, 18,* 53–57.

LYNES, R. (1985). *The lively audience.* New York: Harper & Row.

MAKAY, J.J., and GONZALEZ, A. (1987). Dylan's biographical rhetoric and the myth of the outlaw-hero. *Southern Speech Communication Journal, 52,* 165–180.

MALAND, C. (1983). *Dr. Strangelove* (1964): Nightmare comedy and the ideology of liberal consensus. In P.C. Rollins (Ed.). *Hollywood as historian* (pp. 190–210). Lexington, KY: University of Kentucky Press.

MALTBY, R. (1983). *Harmless entertainment: Hollywood and the ideology of consensus.* Metuchen, NJ: Scarecrow Press.

MARSDEN, M.T. (1982). Western films: America's secularized religion. In M.T. Marsden, J.G. Nachbar, and S.L. Grogg, Jr. (Eds.), *Movies as artifacts* (pp. 105–113). Chicago: Nelson-Hall.

MARTIN, H.H. (1958). The Fourth of July oration. *Quarterly Journal of Speech, 44,* 393–401.

MARTIN, W. (1986). *Recent theories of narrative.* Ithaca, NY: Cornell University Press.

MARTINEAU, W.H. (1972). A model of the social functions of humor. In J.H. Goldstein and P.E. McGhee (Eds.), *The psychology of humor* (pp. 101–128). New York: Academic Press.

MAST, G. (1981). *A short history of the movies* (3rd ed.). Indianapolis: Bobbs-Merrill.

MATSON, F.W. (1967). *Voices of crisis.* New York: Odyssey Press.

MAYNARD, R.A. (1975). *Propaganda on film: A nation at war.* Rochelle Park, NJ: Hayden Book.

McGEE, M.C., and NELSON, J.S. (1985). Narrative reason in public argument. *Journal of Communication, 35,* 139–155.

MEDHURST, M.J., and DeSOUSA, M.A. (1981). Political cartoons as rhetorical form: A taxonomy of graphic. *Communication Monographs, 48,* 197–236.

MILES, E.A. (1960). The keynote speech at national nominating convention. *Quarterly Journal of Speech, 46,* 26–31.

MINTZ, L.E. (1979). Fantasy, formula, realism, and propaganda in Milton Caniff's comic strips. *Journal of Popular Culture, 12,* 653–680.

MISHKIN, D. (1979). Pogo = Walt Kelly's American dream. *Journal of Popular Culture, 12,* 681–690.

MISTER, S.M. (1986). Reagan's Challenger tribute: Combining generic constraints and situational demands. *Central States Speech Journal, 37,* 158–165.

MOHRMANN, G.P. (1982). An essay on fantasy theme criticism. *Quarterly Journal of Speech, 68,* 109–132.

MOHRMANN, G.P., and LEFF, M.C. (1974).   Lincoln at Cooper Union: A rationale for neo-classical criticism. *Quarterly Journal of Speech, 60,* 459–467.

MORREALL, J. (1987).   *The philosophy of laughter and humor.* Albany, NY: State University of New York Press.

MORRIS, B.S., and NYDAHL, J. (1983).   Toward analysis of live television broadcasts. *Central States Speech Journal, 34,* 195–202.

MORRISON, M.C. (1969).   The role of the political cartoonist in image making. *Central States Speech Journal, 20,* 252–260.

MORROW, P.D. (1987).   Those sick Challenger jokes. *Journal of Popular Culture, 20,* 174–184.

MURA, S. (1983).   Linguistic sexism: A rhetorical perspective. In J.L. Golden, G.F. Berquist, and W.E. Coleman, *The rhetoric of western thought* (3rd ed.) (pp. 251–260). Dubuque, IA: Kendall/Hunt.

MURPHY, R. (1955).   Theodore Roosevelt. In M.K. Hocmuth (Ed.), *A history and criticism of American public address,* Vol. 3 (pp. 313–364). New York: Longman, Green.

NORDVOLD, R.O. (1968).   Rhetoric as ritual: Hubert H. Humphrey's acceptance address at the 1968 democratic national convention. *Today's Speech, 18,* 34–38.

NORRIS, V.P. (1984).   Mad economics: An analysis of an adless magazine. *Journal of Communication, 34,* 44–61.

OLIVER, R.T. (1965).   *History of public speaking in America.* Boston: Allyn & Bacon.

ORLIK, P.B. (1988).   *Critiquing radio and television content.* Boston: Allyn & Bacon.

PALMER, W.J. (1987).   *The films of the seventies, a social history.* Metuchen, NJ: Scarecrow Press.

PERRIS, A. (1985).   *Music as propaganda.* New York: Greenwood Press.

PETERSON, M.D. (1987).   *The great triumvirate: Webster, Clay, and Calhoun.* New York: Oxford University Press.

PETERSON, O. (1981).   *Representative American speeches 1980–1981.* New York: H.W. Wilson.

PETERSON, O. (1982).   *Representative American speeches 1981–1982.* New York: H.W. Wilson.

PETERSON, O. (1984).   *Representative American speeches 1983–1984.* New York: H.W. Wilson.

PETERSON, O. (1985).   *Representative American speeches 1984–1985.* New York: H.W. Wilson.

PETERSON, O. (1986).   *Representative American speeches 1985–1986.* New York: H.W. Wilson.

PHILLIPS, D.E. (1985).   *Student protest, 1960–1970: An analysis of the issues and speeches.* Lanham, MD: University Press of America.

PHILLIPS, W.H. (1985).   *Analyzing films.* New York: Holt, Rinehart, & Winston.

PODELL, J. (Ed.) (1987).   *Rock music in America.* New York: H.W. Wilson.

POSTMAN, N. (1985).   *Amusing ourselves to death: Public discourse in the age of show business.* New York: Viking-Penguin.

POTTER, D., and THOMAS, G.L. (1970).   *The colonial idiom.* Carbondale, IL: Southern Illinois University Press.

POWERS, J. (1985).   Bringing the war home: War is hell and here are ten tapes to prove it. *American Film, 10,* 63–66.

RASMUSSEN, K. (1973).   An interaction analysis of justificatory rhetoric. *Western Speech, 37,* 111–117.

REAGAN, R. (1980).   Acceptance address. *Vital Speeches of the Day, 46,* 642–646.

REID, R.F. (1988).   *Three centuries of American rhetorical discourse: An anthology and a review.* Prospect Heights, IL: Waveland Press.

REIN, I.J. (1981).   *The public speaking book.* Glenview, IL: Scott, Foresman.

RICHARDS, A. (1988).   Keynote address. *Vital Speeches of the Day, 54,* 647–649.

RIEKE, R.D., and SILLARS, M.O. (1984).   *Argumentation and the decision-making process.* Glenview, IL: Scott, Foresman.

RITTER, K.W. (1980).   American political rhetoric and the jeremiad tradition: Presidential nomination acceptance addresses, 1960–1976. *Central States Speech Journal, 31,* 153–171.

RODNITZKY, J.L. (1969).   The evolution of the American protest song. *Journal of Popular Culture, 3,* 35–45.

RODNITZKY, J.L. (1976).   *Minstrels of the dawn.* Chicago: Nelson-Hall.

ROOSEVELT, F.D. (1940).   A call to duty: I had not planned to run again. *Vital Speeches of the Day, 6,* 610–613.

ROOSEVELT, T. (1926).   American problems. In Vol. 16 of H. Hagedorn (Ed.), *The works of Theodore Roosevelt* (Vols. 1–20). New York: Charles Scribner's Sons.

ROSENTHAL, A. (1980).   *The documentary conscience.* Berkeley, CA: University of California Press.

ROSENFIELD, L.W. (1972).   The anatomy of critical discourse. In R.L. Scott and B.L. Brock (Eds.), *Methods of rhetorical criticism* (pp. 131–156). New York: Harper & Row.

ROWLAND, R.C. (1987).   Narrative: Mode of discourse or paradigm? *Communication Monographs, 54,* 264–275.

ROWLAND, R.C. (1989).   On limiting the narrative paradigm: Three case studies. *Communication Monographs, 56,* 39–54.

RUECKERT, W.H. (1963). *Kenneth Burke and the drama of human relations*. Minneapolis: University of Minnesota Press.

RUSHING, J.H., and FRENTZ, T.S. (1978). The rhetoric of "Rocky": A social value model of criticism. *Western Journal of Speech Communication, 41*, 63–72.

RUSHING, J.H., and FRENTZ, T.S. (1980). "The Deer Hunter": Rhetoric of the warrior. *Quarterly Journal of Speech, 66*, 392–406.

RUSHING, J.H. (1983). The rhetoric of the American western myth. *Communication Monographs, 50*, 14–32.

RYAN, H.R. (1983). *American rhetoric from Roosevelt to Reagan: A collection of speeches and critical essays*. Prospect Heights, IL: Waveland Press.

RYBACKI, K.C., and RYBACKI, D.J. (1989). Should we laugh or cry: *ALF* as mediated American. Paper presented at the annual meeting of the Speech Communication Association, San Francisco, CA.

SCHUTZ, C.E. (1977). *Political humor from Aristophanes to Sam Ervin*. Cranbury, NJ: Associated University Presses.

SCOTT, R.L., and BROCK, B.L. (1972). *Methods of rhetorical criticism*. New York: Harper & Row.

SEEGER, M.W. (1986). C.E.O. performances: Lee Iacocca and the case of Chrysler. *Southern Speech Communication Journal, 52*, 52–68.

SHARF, B.F. (1986). Send in the clowns: The image of psychiatry during the Hinckley trial. *Journal of Communication, 36*, 80–93.

SHINDLER, C. (1979). *Hollywood goes to war, films and American society 1939–1952*. London: Routledge and Kegan Paul.

SILVERSTONE, R. (1988). Television myth and culture. In J.W. Carey (Ed.), *Media myths and narratives: Television and the press* (pp. 20–47). Newbury Park, CA: Sage.

SMITH, C.R. (1976). *Orientations to speech criticism*. Chicago: Science Research Associates.

SMITH, M.J. (1988). *Contemporary communication research methods*. Belmont, CA: Wadsworth.

SOLOMON, S.J. (1976). *Beyond formula*. New York: Harcourt, Brace, Jovanovich.

SPECTOR, B. (1983). A clash of cultures: The Smothers Brothers vs. CBS television. In J.E. O'Conner (Ed.), *American history/American television* (pp. 159–183). New York: Frederick Ungar.

STEEVES, H.L. (1987). Feminist theories and media studies. *Critical Studies in Mass Communication, 4*, 95–135.

STEWART, C.J. (1980). A functional approach to the rhetoric of social movements. *Central States Speech Journal, 31*, 298–305.

SUID, L.H. (1978). *Guts & glory*. Reading, MA: Addison-Wesley.

SULS, J.M. (1972). A two-stage model for the appreciation of jokes and cartoons: An information-processing analysis. In J.H. Goldstein and P.E. McGhee (Eds.), *The psychology of humor* (pp. 81–100). New York: Academic Press.

TARVER, J. (1987). *The corporate speech writer's handbook*. New York: Quorum Books.

THOMPSON, W.N. (1979). Barbara Jordan's keynote address: The juxtaposition of contradictory values. *Southern Speech Communication Journal, 44,* 223–32.

THONSSEN, L., BAIRD, A.C., and BRADEN, W.W. (1970). *Speech criticism* (2nd ed.). New York: Ronald Press.

TOMPKINS, P.K. (1988). An act of will. *Journal of Communication, 38,* 138–144.

TOULMIN, S. (1958). *The uses of argument*. London: Cambridge University Press.

TOULMIN, S., RIEKE, R., and JANIK, A. (1984). *An introduction to reasoning* (2nd ed.). New York: Macmillan.

TRUJILLO, N., and EKDOM, L.R. (1985). Sportswriting and American cultural values: The 1984 Chicago Cubs. *Critical Studies in Mass Communication, 2,* 262–281.

TURNER, K.J. (1977). Comic strips: A rhetorical perspective. *Central States Speech Journal, 28,* 24–35.

WANDER, P. (1981). Cultural criticism. In D.D. Nimmo and K.R. Sanders (Eds.), *Handbook of political communication* (pp. 497–528). Beverly Hills, CA: Sage.

WANDER, P. (1983). The ideological turn in modern criticism. *Central States Speech Journal, 34,* 1–8.

WANDER, P. (1984). The third persona: An ideological turn in rhetorical theory. *Central States Speech Journal, 35,* 197–216.

WARD, E., STOKES, G., and TUCKER, K. (1986). *Rock of ages*. New York: Summit Books/ Rolling Stone Press.

WARE, B.L., and LINKUGEL, W.A. (1973). They spoke in defense of themselves: On the generic criticism of apologia. *Quarterly Journal of Speech, 59,* 273–283.

WARNICK, B. (1987). The narrative paradigm: Another story. *Quarterly Journal of Speech, 73,* 172–182.

WEAD, G., and LELLIS, G. (1981). *Film: Form and function*. Boston: Houghton Mifflin.

WEISMAN, E.R. (1985). The good man singing well: Stevie Wonder as noble lover. *Critical Studies in Mass Communication, 2,* 136–151.

WERTHEIM, A.F. (1976). Relieving social tensions: Radio comedy and the great depression. *Journal of Popular Culture, 10,* 501–519.

WHETMORE, E.J. (1989). *Mediamerica* (4th ed.). Belmont, CA: Wadsworth.

WHITE, M. (1987). Ideological analysis and television. In R.C. Allen (Ed.), *Channels of discourse* (pp. 113–133). Chapel Hill, NC: University of North Carolina Press.

WHITMAN, W.W. (1969). *Songs that changed the world.* New York: Crown Publishers.

WICHELNS, H.A. (1925). The literary criticism of oratory. In *Studies in rhetoric and public speaking in honor of James Albert Winans* (rpt. 1962, pp. 181–216). New York: Russell and Russell.

WRAGE, E.J., and BASKERVILLE, B. (1960). *American forum: Speeches on historic issues, 1788–1900.* Seattle: University of Washington Press.

ZETTL, H. (1981). Television aesthetics. In R.P. Adler (Ed.), *Understanding television: Essays on television as a social and cultural force.* New York: Praeger.

Acknowledgments

Chapter 3

Harper, N.L. (1979). *Human communication theory: The history of a paradigm*. Rochelle Park, NJ: Hayden Book Co.

Toulmin, S.; Rieke, R.; & Janik, A. (1984). *An introduction to reasoning* (2nd. ed.). New York: Macmillan.

Chapter 5

Bormann, E.G. (1972). Fantasy and rhetorical vision: The rhetorical criticism of social reality. *Quarterly journal of speech, 58*, 396–407. Reprinted with permission of the Speech Communication Association and the author.

Borman, E.G. (1985). Communication criticism. *Journal of communication, 35*(3), 128–138. Copyright © The *Journal of communication*. Reprinted with permission.

Chapter 6

Fisher, W.A. (1987a). *Human communication as narration: Toward a philosophy of reason, value, and action.* Columbia, SC: University of South Carolina Press. Reprinted with permission.

Palmer, W.J. (1987). *The films of the seventies: A social history*. Metuchen, NJ: The Scarecrow Press. Reprinted with permission.

Chapter 7

Farrell, T.B. (1980). Critical models in the analysis of discourse. *Western journal of speech communication, 44*, 300–314. Reprinted with permission of Western Speech Communication Association.

Rieke, R.D. & Sillars, M.O. (1984). *Argumentation and the decision making process.* Glenview, IL: Scott, Foresman. Reprinted with permission.

Rushing, J.H. & Frentz, T.S. (1978). The rhetoric of "Rocky": A social value model of criticism. *Western journal of speech communication, 41*, 63–72. Reprinted with permission of Western Speech Communication Association.

Davies, R.A.; Farrell, J.M.; & Matthews, S.S. (1982). The dream world of film: A Jungian perspective on cinematic communication. *Western journal of speech communication, 46*, 326–343. Reprinted with permission of Western Speech Communication Association.

Gronbeck, B.E. (1973). The rhetoric of social-institutional change: Black action at Michigan. In C.J. Stewart, D.J. Ochs, & G.P. Mohrmann (Eds.), *Explorations in rhetorical criticism* (pp. 96–123). University Park, PA: Pennsylvania State University Press. Reprinted with permission.

Bowers, J.W. & Ochs, D.J. (1971). *The rhetoric of agitation and control.* Reading, MA: Addison-Wesley. Reprinted with permission of the authors.

Chapter 8

Ritter, K.W. (1980). American political rhetoric and the jeremiad tradition: Presidential nomination acceptance addresses, 1960–1976. *Central states speech journal, 31*, 153–171. Reprinted with permission of Central States Speech Association.

Ware, B.L. & Linkugel, W.A. (1973). They spoke in defense of themselves: On the generic criticism of apologia. *Quarterly journal of speech, 59*, 273–283. Reprinted with permission of the Speech Communication Association, B.L. Ware, and W.A. Linkugel.

Goldzwig, S. (1987). A rhetoric of public theology: The religious rhetor and public policy. *Southern speech communication journal, 52*, 128–150. Reprinted with permission of Southern States Communication Association.

Chapter 9

Phillips, W.H. (1985). *Analyzing films: A practical guide.* New York: Holt, Rinehart & Winston. Copyright © 1985 by Holt, Rinehart and Winston, Inc. Reprinted by permission of the publisher.

Capra, F. (1971). *The name above the title: An autobiography.* New York: Macmillan.

Ellis, J.C. (1985). *A short history of film.* Englewood Cliffs, NJ: Prentice-Hall. Reprinted with permission.

Suid, L.H. (1978). *Guts & glory: Great American war movies.* Reading, MA: Addison-Wesley.

Black, G.D. & Koppes, C.R. (1987). Politics, profits, and propaganda. *Hollywood goes to war.* New York: The Free Press, a division of Macmillan, Inc. Copyright © 1987 by the Free Press. Reprinted with permission.

Chapter 10

Fiske, J. (1987b). *Television culture*. New York: Methuen & Co. Reprinted with permission.

Orlick, P.B. (1988). *Critiquing radio and television content*. Boston: Allyn & Bacon.

Gregg, R.B. (1977). The rhetoric of political newscasting. *Central states speech journal, 28*, 221–237. Reprinted with permission of Central States Speech Association.

Chesebro, J.W. (1986). Communication, value, and popular television series—an eleven year assessment. In G. Gumpert & R. Cathcart (Eds.), *Intermedia: Interpersonal communication in a media world* (3rd. ed.), (477–512). New York: Oxford University Press. Reprinted with permission of the author.

Himmelstein, H. (1984). *Television myth and the American mind*. New York: Praeger Publishers. Copyright © 1984 by Praeger Publishers. Reprinted with permission.

Aufderheide, P. (1986). *Watching television*. T. Gitlin (Ed.). New York: Pantheon Books, a division of Random House, Inc. Copyright © 1986 by Pat Aufderheide. Reprinted with permission.

Chapter 11

Perris, A. (1985). *Music as propaganda*. New York: Greenwood Press. Reprinted with permission.

Ewen. D. (1977). *All the years of American popular music*. Englewood Cliffs, NJ: Prentice-Hall, Inc. Copyright © 1977 by Prentice-Hall, Inc. Reprinted with permission.

Guthrie, W. (1961). "The 1913 Massacre." New York: Fall River Music Inc. Copyright © 1961 by Fall River Music Inc. Reprinted with permission.

Chapter 12

Morreall, J. (1987). *The philosophy of laughter and humor*. Albany, NY: State University of New York Press. Reprinted with permission.

Lukes, S. & Galnoor, I. (1987). *No laughing matter: A collection of political jokes*. London: Routledge and Kegan Paul Ltd. Reprinted with permission.

Charney, M. (1978). *Comedy high and low: An introduction to the experience of comedy*. New York: Peter Lang Publishing.

Schutz, C.E. (1977). *Political humor from Aristophanes to Sam Ervin*. Cranbury, NJ: Associated University Presses. Reprinted with permission.

Koziski, S. (1984). The standup comedian as anthropologist: Intentional culture critic. *Journal of popular culture, 18*, 57–76.

Wertheim, A.F. (1976). Relieving social tensions: Radio comedy and the great depression. *Journal of popular culture, 10*, 501–519. Reprinted with permission.

Fischer, R.A. (1980). Pinback put-downs: The campaign button as political satire. *Journal of popular culture, 13*, 645–653. Reprinted with permission.

Name Index

Adams, John, 80
Adams, John Quincy, 188
Adams, Samuel, 80, 162–163, 193, 279
Adams, Timothy D., 261–262
Addams, Charles, 323, 334
Addams, Jane, 218
Ainsworth, Henry, 278
Alexander, Shana, 342
Allen, Fred, 342
Allen, Gracie, 342–343
Allen, Woody, 217, 225
Altman, Robert, 217, 231
Anderson, Lonnie, 266
Andrews, James R., 9, 25, 32, 47, 49, 64, 161, 169–170, 193–194
Ang, Ien, 242
Anthony, Susan B., 168
Aristophanes, 108, 321, 327
Aristotle, 39, 50, 113, 248, 275, 321
Arnold, Carroll C., 15, 27
Arnold, Hap, 228
Astor, John Jacob, 169
Aufderheide, Pat, 265
Aykroyd, Dan, 342

Baez, Joan, 278, 294, 298, 302
Baird, A. Craig, 11
Baird, John, 236
Baker, Ray Standard, 43
Baker, Russell, 314, 317, 323
Bakshi, Ralph, 340
Bales, Robert Freed, 87
Ball, Lucille, 327
Bantz, Charles R., 247
Barkan, Elliot R., 93
Barlow, Joel, 278
Barr, Roseanne, 314, 330, 347
Barry, Dave, 324
Baskerville, Barnet, 195
Becker, Samuel L., 148
Beecher, Henry Ward, 168

Beethoven, Ludwig van, 276
Behl, William A., 43–44
Behlmer, Rudy, 209–215
Belin, Edward, 236
Beltz, Lynda, 43–44, 49, 55
Bennett, Janet, 93
Bennett, W. Lance, 124
Benny, Jack, 342–343
Bergen, Edgar, 342
Berger, Arthur A., 245, 316, 338
Bergman, Andrew, 207–208, 223, 225
Bernardin, Cardinal Joseph, 197
Bernstein, Joan Z., 191
Berquist, Goodwin F., 7, 32, 42, 68
Berry, Chuck, 300
Beveridge, Albert J., 90, 92, 101
Birnbaum, John, 324
Bitzer, Lloyd F., 23
Black, Edwin, 64, 160
Black, Gregory D., 227–228, 230
Blair, Walter, 328–329
Bloomfield, Lincoln P., 93
Bluem, A. William, 252–253
Bluth, Don, 340
Bogart, Humphrey, 217, 223–224, 228, 230
Bohman, George V., 187
Bono, Sonny, 67
Bormann, Ernest G., 86–90, 93, 96–97, 102–103, 110, 126
Boskin, J., 310
Bosley, Harold A., 160–161
Bowers, Claude G., 93
Bowers, John W., 152–153
Braden, Waldo W., 11, 43
Brandt, Carl G., 7, 94, 186, 188–190
Brazier, Richard, 287
Breathed, Berke, 140
Breen, Myles, 241–242
Brock, Bernard L., 73, 75
Brockreide, Wayne, 30
Brooks, Mel, 225, 319

Brown, John, 285
Browne, Charles Farrar (Artemus Ward), 308, 328
Bruce, Lenny, 322, 325–326, 330
Bryan, William Jennings, 5, 7, 111, 166, 170, 178, 344, 345
Bryant, Donald C., 34
Bryant, M. Darrol, 206–209
Burke, Kenneth, 68–70, 72–74, 76–79, 82, 102–103, 110, 126
Burns, George, 342–343
Bush, George, 136, 315–316, 338
Butz, Earl, 67
Bywater, Tim, 209, 211, 217

Cagin, Seth, 206, 231
Cagney, James, 223
Calhoun, John C., 187–190
Cambridge, Godfrey, 308
Campbell, Karlyn K., 9, 20, 22, 27, 30, 32, 54, 76, 79–80, 160, 176–177
Caniff, Milton, 337
Capra, Frank, 123, 206, 208, 213–214, 217, 226
Carlin, George, 314, 330
Carter, David A., 287
Carter, Everett, 218
Carter, Jimmy, 45, 137, 181, 338, 345
Cartland, Barbara, 85–86, 88, 96, 102, 123
Cary, Jennie, 281
Casey, William, 332
Castleman, Harry H., 236–237, 250, 252–253, 261
Cathcart, Robert S., 32, 35, 151
Chaplin, Charlie, 208
Chaplin, Ralph, 287
Charney, Maurice, 316, 331, 346
Chatman, Seymour, 110–114, 116–117, 123–124, 126
Chesebro, James W., 256–262
Chopin, Frederic F., 276

Churchill, Winston, 214, 226
Cicero, 39, 314
Clark, Champ, 226
Clay, Henry, 187–190
Clemens, Samuel Langhorne, 308. *See also* Mark Twain
Cleveland, Grover, 180
Cocks, Jay, 302
Coleman, William E., 7, 32, 42, 68
Combs, James E., 69
Condit, Celeste M., 108, 125
Conwell, Russell, 123, 168, 169
Copernicus, Nicolaus, 33
Coppola, Francis Ford, 112, 217, 223
Corcoran, Farrel, 241–242
Corn, Ira G., Jr., 171
Cosell, Howard, 252
Craft, Christine, 249
Cragan, John F., 87, 100
Cripps, Thomas, 206
Crockett, Jim, 294
Crosby, David, 295
Cross, Donna W., 247–250
Crowe, Jim, 220
Culbert, David, 3, 206
Cuomo, Mario, 38–39, 78–80
Curtin, Jane, 342

Daley, Richard J., 295
Danforth, Samuel, 162
Darrow, Clarence, 111, 166
Davies, Joseph E., 229
Davies, Robert A., 139–140
Davis, Peter, 206
Dean, John, 67
Debs, Eugene V., 166, 291
Deming, Caren J., 111, 124
Denisoff, R. Serge, 276–277, 290, 295–296
DeSousa, Michael A., 332–334
DeVito, Joseph A., 61
Dickens, Charles, 79, 168
Dickinson, Anna, 168
Diller, Phyllis, 292
Dionisopoulos, George N., 171
Disney, Walt, 338–339
Dixon, Thomas, 218
Donovan (Donovan Leitch), 298
Douglass, Frederick, 194
Downie, Leonard, Jr., 44, 49
Doyle, Marsha, 85–86
Dray, Philip, 206, 231
Dukakis, Michael, 136, 315
Dula, Tom, 292
Duncan, Howard, 70–73
Dylan, Bob, 293–295, 297

Ebenstein, William, 145
Edelman, Murray, 124
Edwards, Jonathan, 161
Ehninger, Douglas H., 39
Eisenhower, Dwight, 3, 5, 178, 317–319
Eisner, Michael, 172
Ekdom, Leah, 130–131, 133

Eliot, Marc, 238
Ellis, Jack C., 217–219, 223, 239–240
Emerson, Ralph Waldo, 168
Evans, Walter, 226
Everett, Edward, 29
Ewen, David, 277–278, 281–282, 284, 291

Fall, George L., 168
Falwell, Reverend Jerry, 198
Farrell, James M., 139–140
Farrell, Thomas B., 133–134
Feiffer, Jules, 5, 334–335
Fillmore, Millard, 190
Firestone, Cinda, 212
Fischer, Roger A., 345
Fisher, Walter R., 108–110, 115–116, 119, 122–124, 126, 164
Fiske, John, 131, 146, 238–243, 245–249, 265–266
Fletcher, Andrew, 275
Fogerty, John, 298, 302
Foner, Philip S., 75
Ford, Gerald, 5, 67, 316, 338, 342, 345
Ford, John, 214–215, 217, 222
Foreman, Carl, 208
Foss, Sonja K., 9
Franklin, Benjamin, 80, 308, 328, 332
Frentz, Thomas S., 135, 137, 139, 142, 268
Freud, Sigmund, 87, 323–324

Gable, Clark, 205
Gallanter, Marty, 291
Galnoor, Itzhak, 309, 312, 322, 324
Garfunkel, Art, 294–295
Garrison, William Lloyd, 168, 195
Gashbow, Arthur, 173–174
Gerbner, George, 262
Gifford, Frank, 252
Gilbert, William S., 276
Ginger, Ray, 170
Giscard, Valerie, 322
Gleason, Ralph J., 300
Gold, Ellen R., 165
Golden, James L., 7, 32, 42, 68
Goldwater, Barry, 341, 345
Goldzwig, Steven, 196–197
Gompers, Samuel, 166
Gonzalez, Alberto, 293
Gorbachev, Mikhail, 100
Gordon, William, 174
Göring, Hermann, 340
Gough, John B., 168
Gould, Christopher, 261–262
Gould, Joseph E., 168
Graham, John, 166–167, 177, 329–330
Greenfield, Jeff, 301
Greenway, John, 288–289
Gregg, Richard B., 247–248
Gregory, Dick, 308, 322
Griffith, D. W. (David Wark), 217–219

Gronbeck, Bruce E., 87, 102, 131, 150–153, 257
Gross, Larry, 262
Guthrie, Arlo, 297–299, 301
Guthrie, Marjorie, 290
Guthrie, Woody, 275, 289–291, 293, 295, 300, 303

Hammerstein, Oscar, 276
Hance, Kenneth G., 168
Hancock, John, 175
Harper, Nancy L., 39
Harrington, John, 211
Harrison, Randall P., 332, 334–335, 339
Hartley, John, 249
Harvey, Robert C., 335
Hasenfus, Eugene, 332
Hawks, Howard, 217, 229
Hayden, Tom, 195
Hayes, Ira, 220
Haywood, William, 166
Hazlitt, William, 308–309
Hearst, William Randolph, 44, 50, 334
Hect, Chick, 315
Heller, Steven, 334
Hemings, Sally, 280
Hendra, Tony, 313, 342
Henry, David, 38
Henry, Patrick, 80, 117
Herbert, Frank, 99
Hill, Hamlin, 328–329
Hill, Joe, 287
Hillbruner, Anthony, 26, 28
Himmelstein, Hal, 237–238, 249, 255, 260
Hitchcock, Alfred, 123, 217
Hitler, Adolph, 340
Hoffer, Thomas W., 254
Holbrook, Josian, 168
Holland, Dewitte, 94
Holland, Virginia L., 68, 74
Hollihan, Thomas A., 9, 67, 106–107
Holly, Buddy, 300
Hoover, Judith D., 165
Hope, Bob, 342
Howe, Julia W., 285
Humm, Maggie, 142
Humphrey, Hubert, 176

Iacocca, Lee, 164, 171–172
Inge, M. Thomas, 334
Isocrates, 39
Ivie, Robert L., 185

Jackson, Andrew, 188
Jackson, Michael, 318
Jackson-Beeck, Marilyn, 262
Jaffee, Al, 316, 323
Jamieson, Kathleen H., 160, 176–177
Janik, Allan, 52
Jarvie, Ian C., 232
Jefferson, Thomas, 80, 184, 280
Jenkins, Charles F., 236

Jewett, Robert, 114
Joel, Billy, 300
Johannesen, Richard L., 164
Johnson, Lyndon, 5, 177, 186, 220, 299, 316, 334, 345
Johnson, Nunnally, 215
Jones, Chuck, 340
Jones, John Paul, 309
Jordan, Barbara, 179–180
Jung, Carl, 139–140

Kean, Thomas, 179
Kefauver, Estes, 252
Keillor, Garrison, 343
Kelly, Walt, 309, 337–338
Kennedy, Edward, 164
Kennedy, John, 5, 174, 176–177, 180–181, 206, 254, 292, 313
Kennedy, Robert, 176
Kerr, Harry P., 162–163
Key, Francis Scott, 281
Khomeini, Ayatollah Ruhollah, 333
Kilpatrick, James, 342
King, Dr. Martin Luther, Jr., 20, 33, 292
King, Stephen, 90, 123, 125, 140
Kirkland, Lane, 56
Kissinger, Henry, 5
Klein, James, 212
Klumpp, James F., 9, 67
Knock, Thomas J., 218–220
Koestler, Jerome, 93
Koppes, Clayton R., 227–228, 230
Kopple, Barbara, 212
Korda, Alexander, 226
Koziski, Stephanie, 326–327, 331
Kramer, Stanley, 208
Kruse, Noreen W., 165, 167
Kubrick, Stanley, 140, 207, 217

Lansen, Snooky, 264
Larson, Cedric, 174–175
Lautenberg, Frank R., 182–183
Lawrence, John S., 114
Lawrence, Vera B., 280–286
Lear, Norman, 52–53, 257, 267
Leff, Michael, 56, 64
Lellis, George, 207, 212–214, 221, 224, 226
Leopold, Nathan, 166
Lessl, Thomas M., 160
Leventhal, Harold, 290
Levy, Steven, 265
Lewin, Leonard C., 314, 316–318
Lewis, Jerry, 327
Lewis, Jerry Lee, 300
Lewis, William F., 124
Lincoln, Abraham, 29, 184–185, 190, 200, 284, 317–318, 328, 332
Linkugel, Wil A., 165–166
Little, Rich, 318
Locke, John, 162
Loeb, Richard, 166
Lomas, Charles W., 192–195
Lott, David N., 184–185

Lucaites, John L., 108, 125
Lucas, George, 96, 217
Lucas, Stephen E., 64
Lukes, Steven, 309, 312, 322, 324
Lynch, John D., 264
Lynes, Russell, 217–218

Mabley, Moms, 308
Macarthy, Harry, 283
Madonna (Madonna L. Ciccone), 266, 318
Makay, John J., 293
Maland, Charles, 207
Maltby, Richard, 208
Mansfield, Michael W., 69
Manson, Charles, 10
Marsden, Michael T., 221–222
Marshall, George C., 22, 213–214
Martin, Dick, 341
Martin, Howard H., 174–175
Martin, Steve, 327, 348
Martin, Wallace, 114–117
Martineau, W. H., 308–309
Marx, Chico, 225
Marx, Groucho, 225
Marx, Harpo, 225
Marx, Karl, 145, 278
Marx, Zeppo, 225
Mason, James, 188
Mast, Gerald, 218, 339
Matson, Floyd W., 4, 186
Matthews, Steven S., 139–140
Mauldin, Bill, 308
Mayhew, Jonathan, 162, 198
Maynard, Richard A., 213–214
McAuliffe, Christa, 324–325
McCarthy, Joseph, 117–118, 208, 252–253
McCurdy, Ed, 297
McGee, Michael C., 125
McKinley, William, 344
McLuhan, Marshall, 131
McManus, Patrick, 344
Meader, Vaughn, 313
Medhurst, Martin J., 334
Mellencamp, John Cougar, 302
Meredith, Don, 252
Miles, Edwin A., 178
Miller, Arthur, 117, 317
Miller, Lewis, 168
Mineta, Norman, 191
Minow, Newton, 4
Mintz, Lawrence E., 337
Mishkin, Daniel, 338
Mister, Steven M., 176
Mohrmann, Gerald P., 64, 102
Mondale, Walter, 345
Monroe, Marilyn, 266
Moore, Robin, 220
Morgan, Michael, 262
Morreall, John, 309–311, 323
Morris, Barbara S., 251
Morrison, Matthew C., 332
Morrow, Patrick D., 324–325
Mura, Susan, 142–143
Murphy, Eddie, 325

Murphy, Dr. Joseph S., 59–60
Murphy, Richard, 43
Murrow, Edward R., 253

Nash, Graham, 295
Nast, Thomas, 308
Nelson, John S., 125
Nelson, Richard A., 254
Nelson, Willie, 302
Nicholson, Jack, 224
Nixon, Richard, 3–5, 45, 72, 117, 154, 167, 254, 316, 338
Nordvold, Robert O., 180
Norris, Vincent P., 344
Novello, Don, 327. See also Father Guido Sarducci
Nydahl, Joel, 251
Nye, Gerald, 226

Ochs, Donovan, 152–153
Ochs, Phil, 132, 294, 296
Oliphant, Patrick, 316, 332–334
Oliver, Robert T., 168, 170–171, 190, 193
Orlik, Peter B., 239, 243–244, 246, 255–256
Otis, James, 279

Paine, Thomas, 80
Palmer, William J., 110, 112, 115, 206, 208, 224
Parker, Theodore, 190
Parks, Rosa, 292
Perris, Arnold, 275–276, 299–300
Peterson, Merrill D., 187–188, 190
Peterson, Owen, 17, 53, 56, 60, 79, 182–184, 197–198
Phillips, David Graham, 44, 47
Phillips, Donald E., 150, 196
Phillips, Wendell, 168
Phillips, William H., 209–210
Plato, 39, 275, 280, 321
Podell, Janet, 301
Podrazik, Walter J. 236–237, 250, 252–253, 261
Polanski, Roman, 224
Postman, Neil, 248–250
Potter, David, 163
Powers, John, 231
Presley, Elvis, 99, 300
Pulitzer, Joseph, 334

Quayle, Dan, 315–316
Quintilian, 28, 32, 39, 108, 314

Randall, Ryder, 281
Randolph, Innes, 285
Rasmussen, Karen, 185
Rather, Dan, 338
Reagan, Ronald, 38–39, 56, 79, 96, 100, 136–138, 178, 181, 197, 230, 250, 316, 332, 338

Redpath, James C., 168
Reichert, Julia, 212
Reid, Ronald F., 22, 44—45, 47, 92, 175, 318
Rein, Irving J., 4
Richards, Ann, 178—179
Rickles, Don, 314
Riefenstahl, Leni, 214
Rieke, Richard D., 52, 135
Riley, Patricia, 106—107
Rimsky-Korsakov, Nikolai, 276
Ritter, Kurt W., 163, 181
Robinson, Edward G., 223
Rodgers, Richard, 253, 276
Rodnitzky, Jerome L., 277, 289, 292—296
Rogers, Will, 328—330
Roosevelt, Franklin D., 73, 118, 178, 180, 182, 225, 227, 229, 297, 329
Roosevelt, Theodore, 43—49, 54—56, 61
Root, George F., 284
Rosenfield, Lawrence W., 133
Rosenthal, Alan, 212
Rowan, Dan, 341
Rowland, Robert C., 124—125
Ruby, Jack, 254
Rueckert, William H., 73
Rushing, Janice H., 134—135, 138—139, 142, 268
Russell, Mark, 315
Ryan, Halford R., 167, 198
Rybacki, Donald J., 257
Rybacki, Karyn C., 257

Sainte-Marie, Buffie, 298
Saldich, Anne Rawley, 16, 18
Salomon, Henry, 253
Sarducci, Father Guido (character), 327—328
Schneider, Bert, 206
Schutz, Charles E., 313, 315, 319—20, 328
Scopes, John, 111, 166
Scorsese, Martin, 217
Scott, Robert L., 73, 75
Scott, Willard, 270
Seeger, Matthew W., 171
Seeger, Pete, 275, 289—293, 295, 299
Shafter, Edward M., 7, 94, 186, 188—190
Shakespeare, William, 68, 321
Shamir, Yitzhak, 316
Sharf, Barbara F., 89
Sheen, Bishop Fulton J., 264

Shepard, Jean, 344
Sheridan, Ann, 230
Sheridan, Richard Brinsley, 315
Shields, Donald J., 87
Shindler, Colin, 227—228, 231
Shoup, David, 220
Signorielli, Nancy, 262
Silkwood, Karen, 212
Sillars, Malcolm O., 135
Silverstone, Roger, 238, 242, 252
Simon, Paul, 294—295
Sinatra, Frank, 338
Sinclair, Upton, 43, 49, 55
Smith, Craig R., 32
Smith, Mary J., 107, 261
Sobchack, Thomas, 209, 211, 217
Solomon, Stanley J., 221—223, 225—226
Sommers, Suzanne, 266
Spector, Bert, 291, 299
Spielberg, Steven, 217
Spock, Benjamin, 106
Spooner, Reverend W. A., 315
Stalin, Joseph, 229, 340
Stanton, Elizabeth Cady, 168
Steeves, H. Leslie, 142—143
Steffens, Lincoln, 43, 49
Steinbeck, John, 214, 289
Stern, Dagmar C., 261—262
Stevenson, Adlai E., 176—177
Stewart, Charles J., 151
Stills, Stephen, 295
Sting (Gordon Summer), 277
Stockman, David, 56
Stokes, Geoffrey, 264, 292—293, 295
Stone, Oliver, 217
Stowe, Harriet Beecher, 73
Suid, Lawrence H., 207, 220, 229
Sullivan, Sir Arthur S., 276
Suls, J. M., 312
Summer, Charles, 168

Taft, William Howard, 345
Talbot, Jerry, 297
Talbot, John, 297
Tarbell, Ida, 43, 49
Tarver, Jerry, 171
Taylor, Zachary, 190
Thomas, Gordon L., 163
Thompson, Wayne N., 179—180
Thonssen, Lester, 11
Tolkein, J. R. R., 319
Tompkins, Phillip K., 125
Toulmin, Stephen, 52
Travolta, John, 137—138
Trudeau, Garry, 335, 338
Trujillo, Nick, 130—131, 133

Tucker, Ken, 264, 292—293, 295
Turner, Kathleen J., 335—336
Twain, Mark (pseudonym), 308, 344

Vidor, King, 208
Vincent, John H., 168

Wagner, Richard, 276
Wallace, Karl, 7
Wander, Philip, 132, 141—142, 148
Ward, Artemus (pseudonym), 308, 328
Ward, Ed, 264, 292—293, 295
Ware, B. L., 165—166
Warner, Jack, 228, 229
Warnick, Barbara, 125
Washington, George, 173, 182, 184
Wayne, John, 217, 220, 222
Wead, George, 207, 212—214, 221, 224, 226
Webster, Daniel, 187, 189, 190
Weisman, Eric R., 7
Wertheim, Arthur F., 329, 342—343
Wesley, John, 278
Westmoreland, William, 206
Wheeler, Burton K., 73
Whetmore, Edward J., 336
White, James, 118, 122
White, Mimi, 146
Whitman, Wanda W., 279
Whitmore, James, 330
Whittier, John Greenleaf, 168
Wichelns, Herbert, 159
Williams, Robin, 308, 316
Williams, Roger, 192
Williams, Tennessee, 317
Williams, Vanessa, 72—73
Wilson, Flip, 308
Wilson, Gahan, 334
Wilson, Woodrow, 185, 218—219
Winner, Septimus, 282
Wiseman, Frederick, 212—213
Wonder, Stevie, 7
Wrage, Ernest J., 195
Wyler, William, 227

Yankovic, Al, 318
Young, Neil, 295

Zanuck, Darryl F., 219
Zarefsky, David, 161, 169—170, 193—194
Zettl, Herbert, 245
Zimmerman, Robert, 293

Subject Index

Acceptance speech
  jeremiad in, 181
  in political campaign speaking, 180,
    182
Accretion of televised messages
  persuasiveness as a result of, 256
Act
  in the dramatistic pentad, 76
  forms of, 69
  verbal strategies in, 70
Action
  the aesthetic standard and, 81
  defined, 68
  dichotomy between motion and, 69
  dramatism and, 68, 72, 78
  language and, 69
  motive and, 70
  rhetorical situation and, 70
  rituals in public theology, 197
  social change and, 70
Adornment
  aesthetics and the evaluation of, 63
  devices of, 21
  language choice and, 20
  style and, 61
Aesthetic properties of film, 209–210
Aesthetics
  audience use of humor and, 325
  discourse in narrative and, 111
  dramatic elements in a fantasy and,
    101
  identification and, 81
  rhetorical strategies and, 81
  as a standard of evaluation, 34, 35
  story in narrative and, 122
  symbolic action and, 81
Aesthetics evaluation
  in the dramatistic approach, 81
  in the fantasy theme approach, 101
  in feminist criticism, 145
  in ideological criticism, 149
  in Jungian criticism, 141
  in the narrative approach, 121–122

of social movements, 156
  in social-values criticism, 139
  in the traditional approach, 63
Agency
  in the dramatistic pentad, 76–77
Agent
  in the dramatistic pentad, 76
Agitation
  dissent and, 192
  outcomes sought from, 194, 195
  public speaking in social movements
    and, 201
  types of, 195
Allegory
  as a device of adornment, 21
  use of, 55
Alliteration
  as a device of adornment, 21
Allusion
  as a device of adornment, 21
Analogy
  as evidence, 19
  reasoning in the form of, 59
Antithesis
  as a device of adornment, 21
Apologia
  absolution and, 165
  denial and, 165
  differentiation and, 165
  exigence prompting, 167
  explanation and, 166
  justification and, 165
  outcomes of, 165–166
  strategies of, 165
  traditional approach and, 199
  transcendence and, 165
  vindication and, 165–166
Appropriateness
  action and, 78
  delivery and, 62
  oral style and, 61
  purification and, 73
  validity of enthymeme and, 55

Appropriate response
  audience perception of, 45
  exigence and an, 25, 51
Argument
  analysis of, 58
  claims in, 19
  criticism as, 13, 15, 30
  describing unit of, 19–20, 50
  determining validity of, 52–53, 55
  documentary television as, 271
  ethos and, 50
  evaluating truth in, 63
  evidence in, 19
  fantasy and, 89
  humor as, 311, 313
  invention and, 51
  message song as, 303
  metaphor as a form of, 55–57
  models of, 52, 54–57
  narrative as, 124
  narrative rationality and, 125
  political cartoons as, 332
  reasoning in, 19, 58
  reconstruction of, 52
  traditional approach to speeches
    and, 199
Arrangement
  in classical rhetoric, 40
  in contemporary usage, 41
  grammar of film and, 232
Attitude
  enthymeme and, 54
  fantasy and the formation of, 88
  motives and, 70
  symbol usage and, 69
Audience
  actual, 22, 25–27
  adaptation to, 43, 48–49, 51
  agents-of-change, 23, 123
  characterizing in the rhetorical
    situation, 25–27, 43
  constraint imposed by the, 45, 50
  created, 23

describing rhetor's concept of,
22–23
empirical, 23, 123
enthymeme and the role of the, 55
humor and uses by the, 321–325
ideal, 22–23
metaphor and the role of the, 56
multiple, 26, 45, 47, 183
narrative rationality and, 120–122
social-values model and the, 136
traditional approach and the,
45–50
variables describing the, 47–49
Audience knowledge
irony and, 317
metaphor and, 57
topical humor and, 313
Auteur criticism
film criticism focused on, 217–221
film director and, 218, 219
film stars and, 220
organic criticism and, 221
Auteur theory
defined, 217
rhetor in the, 232

Campaign buttons
rhetoric and, 344–346
Cartoons
animated, 339–340
and comic strips, 334–338
political, 5, 332–334
and underground comics, 338
Characterization
implied rhetor and, 124
in narrative, 126
narrative rationality and, 116, 120
Chautauqua
enterprise speaking and, 169–170
history of, 168
purpose of, 171
Claim
in argument, 19
definition of, 19, 52
example of, 54
Classical rhetoric
canons of, 39–41, 50
enthymeme in, 54
ethos in, 42
genres of rhetorical acts in, 76
humor and, 312
narrative and, 108
persuasion in, 39
Climax
as a device of adornment, 21
Comedy
narrative plot type and, 113
Comedy film
escapism and screwball, 208
film genres and the, 224
screwball defined, 207
types of, 225
Comic sage
comic strips and the, 336
stand-up comedy and the, 328–330

Comic strips
audience involvement with, 336
development of, 334
political themes in, 337–338
rhetorical properties of, 335
underground, 338
Commemorative speaking
ceremonial speaking and, 22
purpose of, 174
social values and, 178
symbol in, 175
tone of, 177
Communication
medium of, 10
purpose of, 2
rhetorical act as instrumental, 2–3
rhetorical defined, 2
Communication systems and symbolic
convergence
consciousness-creating, 88, 90
consciousness-raising, 88–90
consciousness-sustaining, 89–90
Communication systems and television
defined, 256
ironic fiction, 257–258
leader-centered fiction, 259–260
mimetic fiction, 258–259
mythical fiction, 260–261
rhetorical vision of, 262–263
romantic fiction, 260
Conflict
in drama, 71
symbolic, 136–137
Consistency
evaluation of evidence for, 58
narrative rationality and questions
of, 119
Constraints
analysis of, 199
audience-imposed, 45, 50
and choice of language, 29
definition of, 27
eulogy and, 177
fantasy type and, 96
on film, 232
on humor, 313
media of communication and, 101,
122
motive and the identification of, 70
occasion imposes, 45–46
organization and adaptation to, 61
on rhetor in the traditional
approach, 42–43
rhetorical act affected by, 29
rhetorical situation and, 46, 51, 74
rhetorical strategies and, 75
substance and, 74
on television news, 247–249
types of, 28–29
and use of symbols, 29
values impose, 165
Credibility
elements of, 32, 42
ethos and, 42
mass media and, 28
message and, 50

results standard and, 62
variation in, 45
Crime drama
film genre and the, 222–224
film noir and, 223
types of, 223
Critical approaches
definition of, 30
impact on standard of
evaluation, 35
impulse to do criticism and, 11
need for, 31–32
rhetorical theory and, 11
selection of, 31, 32
standards of evaluation in, 32, 35
See also Cultural approaches;
Dramatistic approach; Fantasy
theme approach; Narrative
approach; Traditional approach
Critical process model
evaluation in the, 30–35
rhetorical act in the, 16–23
rhetorical situation in the, 23–30
Criticism
analysis in, 8
as argument, 13, 15, 30
expansion of knowledge and, 12
formulary, 31
ideological, 141, 148
impulse to do, 9–12
models of, 133–134
organic, 31
responsibilities of critics doing, 12
rhetorical, 8
as a rhetorical act, 12–13
stance in, 12
subjectivity of, 12, 13, 15, 132
Cultural approaches
critical process in the, 131–134
difference from other approaches,
134
feminist criticism and, 142–145
ideological criticism and, 141–149
Jungian model in, 139–141
Marxist criticism and, 145–148
models in, 133
social movements and, 149–156
social-values model in, 134–139
Culture
defined, 131
film as social history of, 206
forces that shape, 150–151
humor and, 310
mass media, 132
message song and, 281
nature of, 134
rhetoric and, 131
social movement criticism and, 149
values in American, 135

Delivery
in classical rhetoric, 40
in contemporary usage, 41
criteria for analyzing, 62
ethics and evaluation of, 63
medium of communication and, 62

Demographic variables
  group identification and, 49
  types of, 26–27
Dissent
  American history and, 193
  outcomes sought through, 194–195
  social forces speaking and, 192, 196
Divine fool
  in stand-up comedy, 327–328
Docudrama
  types of television, 254
Documentary film
  definition of, 211
  evaluating results of a, 232
  evaluating truth in a, 232
  propaganda and, 213
  propaganda in World War II, 214
  slice-of-life, 212
  television and, 252–254, 271
Drama
  chaining out, 89
  conflict in, 71
  definition of, 70
  fantasy theme analysis and, 88
  hierarchy and, 72
  life as social, 86
  rhetorical situation and, 74
  types of, 72
Dramatism
  fantasy theme approach and, 86
  motion and action in, 68
  rhetorical act in, 126
  social movement criticism and, 156
Dramatistic approach
  acceptance and rejection, 71–72
  aesthetic standard, 81
  difference from other drama-based
    approaches, 108, 110, 126–127
  dramatistic process, 69–74
  ethical standard, 79–80
  ethics and the, 68
  film criticism using, 233
  hierarchy, 71
  humor criticism using, 347
  identification, 69, 74–75
  limitations, 81
  motive, 69–70
  pentad, 76–77
  pentadic ratios, 77–79
  public speaking criticism using, 200
  redemptive process, 72–74
  results standard, 81
  rhetorical strategies, 75–76
  song criticism using, 303
  television criticism using, 268
  truth standard, 80–81

Emotions
  actual audience and, 27
  arousing the, 50
  pathos and, 59
Enterprise speaking
  chautauqua and, 169–170
  contemporary, 171–172
  history of, 168
  lecture bureaus and, 171

Enthymeme
  argument in the form of, 52
  audience role in completing, 55
  classical rhetoric and the, 54
  defined, 54
  humor structure and, 312
  inference in, 58
  political cartoons as, 333
  psychological properties of, 57
  reconstruction of, 55
  validity of, 55
Ethics
  audience use of humor and, 325
  definition of, 28
  dramatism and, 126
  identification and the evaluation of,
    79–80
  rhetorical strategies and the
    evaluation of, 80
  as a standard of evaluation, 32
Ethics evaluation
  in the dramatistic approach, 68,
    79–80
  in the fantasy theme approach,
    101–102
  in feminist criticism, 145
  in ideological criticism, 148–149
  in Jungian criticism, 141
  in the narrative approach, 123–124
  of social movements, 156
  in social-values criticism, 138
  in the traditional approach, 63
Ethos
  argument and, 50
  in classical rhetoric, 42
  criticism and, 32
  delivery and, 62
  evaluation of, 63
  invention and the use of, 42
  message adaptation and, 51
  rhetor's management of, 44, 45
  traditional approach to speeches
    and, 199
  as a type of proof in the
    message, 50
  See also Credibility
Eulogy
  constraints on, 177
  as point-in-time speaking, 175
  purpose of, 176
  social values and, 178
  song as, 287
  tone of, 177
Evaluation
  impact of critical approach on, 8, 35
  in the critical process model, 16
  cultural approaches and, 138–139,
    141, 145, 148, 155–156
  dramatistic approach and, 79–81
  fantasy theme approach and,
    99–102
  narrative approach and, 121–125
  ratios in dramatism and, 79
  in rhetorical criticism, 8
  standards of, 32–35
  traditional approach and, 62, 63

Evidence
  in argument, 19
  criteria for evaluating, 58
  external consistency and, 58
  narrative and tests of, 125
  properties of, 57
  rhetor's use of, 19
  types of, 19, 57–58
Exigence
  audience perception of, 25
  audience response to competing, 27
  audience response to film and the,
    227
  controlling, 24
  fantasy type and the, 96
  forces which shape the, 25–26
  impact on management of ethos on
    the, 45
  occasion and, 46
  rhetorical act as fitting response
    to, 59
  in rhetorical situation, 24–25, 43
  salience of, 49

Fantasy
  attitude formation and, 88
  audience role in, 127
  comic strips and, 336
  defined, 86
  life cycle of a, 88–90
  motivation for, 87–88
  rhetorical act and, 89
  salience of a, 89
  social reality and, 88
  truth and, 87
Fantasy theme approach
  aesthetic standard, 101
  as alternative form of dramatism, 86,
    102–103
  differences from other drama-based
    approaches, 108, 110, 126–127
  ethical standard, 101–102
  fantasy chains, 88–89, 98
  fantasy themes, 90–92, 126
  fantasy types, 89, 92–96, 101
  film criticism using, 232
  humor criticism using, 347
  limitations, 102
  mass media and the, 89, 102
  public speaking criticism using, 200
  results standard, 100–101
  rhetorical vision, 88, 96–98
  salience in the, 87
  song criticism using, 304
  symbolic convergence theory and,
    86–87, 103
  television criticism using, 270
  traditional approach and, 87
  truth standard, 99–100
Feminist criticism
  critical evaluation and, 145
  goals of, 143
  humor and, 348
  ideological assumptions of, 142–143
  public speaking criticism using, 201

questions asked by, 144
television criticism using, 269
Film
  antiwar, 231
  aesthetic properties of, 209–210
  auteur theory of, 217
  comedy in, 224–225
  constraints on, 232
  crime dramas in, 222–224
  differentiated from television, 239–241
  documentary, 211
  fictional differentiated from realistic, 211–213
  fitting response in, 227–228
  genres of, 221–231
  grammar of, 215–216
  propaganda, 213
  realism and truth in, 211–212
  realist depiction and economic imperatives, 215
  as rhetorical activity, 205
  rhetorical functions of, 206–209
  science fiction and horror in, 225–226
  slice-of-life documentary in, 212
  as symbolic action, 69
  on television, 240
  war, 226–231
  Western, 221–222
Film criticism
  using the dramatistic approach, 233
  using fantasy theme analysis, 232
  using ideological criticism, 233
  using the Jungian model, 233
  using the narrative approach, 232
  using the social-values model, 233
  using the traditional approach, 232
Folk music
  civil-rights movement and, 292
  domestic communism and, 291
  folk-rock and, 293, 295–296
  labor lore in, 290
  protest and, 292–295
  television and, 293
Formulary criticism, 31

Gender inequality in feminist ideology
  language and, 142
Grammar of film, 215–216
Group identification
  audience description based on, 47–49
  demographics and, 49
Guilt
  dramatistic process and, 70
  ethical standard of evaluation and, 80
  purification of, 72
  rejection of hierarchy and, 72
  rhetor's attitude toward, 76
  rhetorical strategies and, 75
  truth standard of evaluation and, 80

Hegemony
  Marxist criticism and, 147
  Marxist ideology and, 146

Hero
  fantasy theme approach and, 88–90
  film noir and, 224
  transformation into a villain of a, 100
  in Western films, 221–222
Hierarchy
  acceptance or rejection of, 71–72
  defined, 71
  drama and, 72
  dramatistic process and, 70
  flaws in the, 73
  rejection of the, 74
  rhetor's attitude toward, 76
  rhetorical strategies and, 75
  symbols in, 71
  types of, 71
Humor
  animated cartooning and, 339, 340
  audience uses of, 321–325
  cartooning and, 332–338
  classical rhetoric and, 312
  constraints on, 313
  culture and, 310
  devices of, 314–320
  feeling of superiority and, 321–322
  as a fitting response, 311
  forms of discourse in, 326–346
  incongruity and, 323
  invective in, 315–316
  irony in, 316–317
  magazines devoted to, 343–344
  parody in, 317–319
  political, 313
  public sloganeering and, 344–346
  radio and, 342–343
  rhetorical nature of, 309–310
  satire in, 319–320
  sense of relief and, 323–325
  setup and punch line in, 311
  sick jokes and, 324–325
  stand-up comedy and, 326–331
  structure of, 311–313
  television and, 341–342
  that goes too far, 325
  topical, 312
  word play in, 314–315
Humor criticism
  using cultural approaches, 347–348
  using the dramatistic approach, 347
  using fantasy theme analysis, 347
  using feminist ideology, 348
  using the Jungian model, 348
  using Marxist ideology, 348
  using the narrative approach, 347
  using the social-values model, 347–348
  using the traditional approach, 347
Hyperbole
  as a device of adornment, 21

Identification
  consequences of, 75
  defined, 69
  nalization and, 75, 80

identity and, 74
language and, 126
magnetic song and, 303
message meaning and, 76
motive and, 74
persuasion and, 74
public speaking and, 200
rhetorical situation and, 75
unification and, 74
Ideological criticism
  evaluation and, 148–149
  feminism and, 142–145
  film and, 233
  Marxism and, 145–148
  social movements differ from, 150
  stance in, 141
Ideology
  as act, 69
  feminist, 142
  Marxist, 145–146
  social movement criticism and, 149
  television and, 255
Initiation speaking
  inaugural speech in, 184–185
  maiden speech in, 182–183
Intertextuality
  theory of, 266
Introduction
  audience and, 46
  occasion and, 46
  purpose statement in the, 60
  rhetor's purpose and, 51
Invective
  campaign buttons and, 345
  comic sage and, 328
  feeling of superiority and, 321
  as a humorous device, 315–316
  television humor and, 341–342
Invention
  argument and the use of, 51–60
  in classical rhetoric, 40
  in contemporary usage, 41
  ethos used in, 41
  grammar of film and, 232
  humor and, 311
  rhetor's purpose and, 51
  rhetor's use of, 50
Irony
  audience knowledge and, 317
  as a device of humor, 316
  unintentional, 316
Issues
  control of and social change, 9
  critical impulse and, 9
  flag, 154
  interpretation of, 51

Jeremiad
  in acceptance speeches, 181
  American dream and, 164
  elements of, 163

Jungian model
  critical evaluation using the, 141
  elements in the, 139
  film criticism using, 233
  function of the, 140
  humor criticism using, 348
  television criticism using, 268–269
Justificatory speaking
  as a social forces speech, 185, 186,
    187

Keynote speaking, 38, 79
  in political campaign speaking,
    178–180

Language
  action and, 69
  as adornment, 20
  aesthetic standard and, 81
  as symbol, 20, 68, 74–75
  choice of, 29
  connotative meaning of, 20, 61
  creation of virtual experience
    using, 20
  critical focus on in dramatism, 69
  denotative meaning of, 61
  feminist criticism and, 142
  gender inequality and, 143
  identification and, 126
  motive and, 70
  psychological climate and use of, 61
  rhetorical act and, 4
  rhetorical strategies and, 75
  style and, 61
  substance and, 74
Legislative speaking
  Congressional testimony and,
    190–191
  as a social forces speech, 187–190,
    192
Logos
  message adaptation and, 51
  reasoning and, 50
  as a type of proof in the
    message, 50
Lyceum
  history of, 168
  lecture bureaus and, 171
  purpose of, 171

Magnetic song
  during the Civil War, 281
  identification and, 303
  as propaganda, 277–278
Maiden speech
  in initiation speaking, 182–183
Malapropism
  in humor, 315
Marxist criticism
  crime dramas and, 222
  critical evaluation and, 148
  cultural approach and, 145
  hegemony in, 146

humor criticism using, 348
  ideology in, 145
  mass media and, 146, 147, 148
  public speaking criticism using, 201
  question asked in, 147
  television criticism using, 269
Marxist feminism, 143
Mass media
  cultural approaches and, 131
  culture and, 132
  fantasy theme approach and
    analysis of, 89, 102
  Marxist criticism of, 146–148
  narrative and, 107
  political campaign speaking and,
    178
  rhetor credibility and, 28
Medium of communication
  constraints imposed by, 51
  constraints on narrative, 122, 125
  delivery and, 62
  story in narrative and, 111
Message
  adaptation to audience, 48–49
  in cultural approaches, 132
  as element in rhetorical situation, 50
  in social movements, 152
  in traditional approach, 50–62
  in war films, 226–227
Message-movie criticism
  film criticism focused on, 211–216
  truth and, 213
Message song
  as argument, 303
  cultural factors and, 281
  development of, 285
  economic hardship and, 286
  Great Depression and, 289
  organized labor and, 288
  as propaganda, 277
  religious hymns as, 278
  rhetorical situation and the, 276
  rock and roll as, 301
Metaphor
  analysis of, 56
  as a device of adornment, 21
  as a form of argument, 52, 55–57
  audience role in completing the, 56
  clusters of, 57
  enthymeme compared to, 55
  examples of, 20–22, 79
  film as, 208
  frame of reference and, 56
  in political cartoons, 332
  in song, 279
  inference in, 58
  psychological properties of, 57
  vehicle and tenor in, 56–57
Methodology
  See Critical approaches
Monomyth
  aesthetic evaluation of, 122
  defined, 114
Motion
  dichotomy between action and, 69

dramatism and, 68
  rhetorical situation and, 70
Motive
  action and, 70
  attitude and, 70
  dramatistic pentad and, 77
  identification and, 74
  language-symbol use and, 69–70
  substance and, 74
Multiple audiences, 26, 45, 47, 183
Music television (MTV)
  intertextual reading of, 266
  narrative structure and, 265
  narrow-casting and, 264
  as a rhetorical act, 265
  symbol and myth in, 266
Myth
  materialistic and moralistic, 164
  music videos and, 266
  public speeches and the creation of,
    201

Narrative
  defined, 108
  group use of, 106
  levels of, 110–111
  locus of, 107
  medium of communication and, 125
  as a pattern of organization, 18
  rhetor's role in, 127
  rhetorical act in, 126
  rhetorical situation and, 110
  structure, 111–118, 125–126
  symbols and, 108
  as a thematic model, 133
  tradition of, 107
  traditional approach and, 125
  truth and, 126
  uses of, 108, 109
Narrative approach
  aesthetic standard, 122
  characterization, 115–116
  difference from other approaches,
    108, 110, 126–127
  discourse level, 111–113
  ethical standard, 124
  fidelity, 121–122, 125, 200–201
  film criticism using, 232
  humor criticism using, 347
  kernels, 115, 120
  limitations, 124–125
  monomyth, 114
  plot, 114–115
  process statements, 112
  public speaking criticism using,
    200–201
  rationality, 110, 113, 116, 118–121,
    125–126
  results standard, 123
  satellites, 115, 120
  setting, 116–118
  song criticism using, 304
  stasis statements, 112–113
  story elements, 113–118
  television criticism using, 268
  truth standard, 121–122

Narrative paradigm
  concept of, 124, 126
  criticism of, 125
  premises underlying the, 108–109
Neo-Aristotelian approach, 39
  See also Traditional approach
Nonverbal communication
  aesthetics and evaluation of, 63
  delivery and, 62
  nonverbal symbols, 4

Occasion
  audience and the, 45
  constraints imposed by, 45–46
  exigence and, 46
  management of ethos affected by
    the, 45
Oral style
  elements of, 61
Organic criticism
  aesthetic standards and, 101
  auteur criticism and, 221
  cultural approaches and, 132
  defined, 31
Organization
  complex, 17
  describing the rhetor's, 17–19
  pattern of, 5, 60–61
  See also Arrangement
Oxymoron
  as a device of adornment, 21

Parody
  animated cartoons and, 340
  audience role in, 318
  deconstruction and reconstruction of,
    318–319
  as a device of humor, 317
  in humorous magazines, 344
  in television humor, 342
Pathos
  message adaptation and, 51
  style and, 50
  as a type of proof in the
    message, 50
  use of, 59–60
Pentad
  criticism and the, 78
  dramatistic, 74
  elements of the, 76–77
  motive and the, 77
  ratios in the, 77–78
Persona
  Jungian criticism and the, 139
  rhetor's creation of a, 62
Persuasion
  in classical rhetoric, 39, 69
  identification and, 74
  ironic television fiction and, 258
  leader-centered television fiction
    and, 259–260
  mimetic television fiction and,
    258–259
  music and, 10
  music videos and, 265

mythical television fiction and,
    260–261
  rhetorical act and, 9, 12, 24
  rock and roll as, 301
  romantic television fiction and, 260
  songs as, 277
  television accretion and revelation
    and, 256–257
  television's rhetorical vision and,
    262–263
Phenomenology
  rhetorical act and genres and, 10
Plot
  aesthetic evaluation of, 122
  elements of, 115
  in a fantasy theme, 91
  monomyth and, 114
  in narrative, 113, 126
  types, 113
  in Western films, 222
Point of view
  implication for film criticism, 213
  in message-movie criticism, 211
Point-in-time speaking
  acceptance speech as, 180–182
  commemorative speech as, 174–175
  eulogy as, 175–177
  inaugural speech as, 184–185
  initiation speeches and, 182–185
  keynote speech as, 178–180
  maiden speech as, 182–183
  political campaigns and, 178–182
  types of, 173
Political campaigns
  acceptance speech in, 180–182
  keynote speech in, 178–180
  mass media and, 178
  public sloganeering in, 344–345
Political cartoons
  enduring images in, 333
  fantasy types and, 93–95
  purpose of, 332
  style in, 5, 334
Political humor
  anxiety and, 324
  audience role in, 316
  comic invective in, 315
  purpose of, 313
Prior reputation
  credibility and, 42, 45
  ethics and the evaluation of, 63
Probable truth
  evaluating the, 63
  fantasy and, 87
  nature of, 33–34
  rhetorical situation and, 87
Proof
  fantasy and, 89
  rhetorical act and, 40, 50–51
  types of, 50
Propaganda
  film and, 206, 213
  message song and, 277, 281
  World War II documentaries and,
    214
Psychological appeals
  pathos and, 59

rhetorical situation and, 60
Psychological climate
  style and the creation of, 61
Psychological properties
  of evidence, 57
Public persona speaking
  apologia as, 165–167
  enterprise speaking as, 168–172
Public sloganeering
  humor and, 344–346
Public speaking
  acceptance speech in, 180–182
  apologia in, 165–167
  commemorative speech in, 174–175
  difficulties in categorizing, 160
  dissent in, 192–196
  enterprise speaking in, 168–172
  eulogy in, 175–177
  inaugural speech in, 184–185
  initiation speeches in, 182–185
  jeremiad in, 164
  justificatory speeches in, 185–187
  keynote speech in, 178–180
  legislative speeches in, 187–192
  maiden speech in, 182–183
  point-in-time, 173–185
  political campaigns and, 178–182
  public persona in, 165–172
  public theology in, 196–198
  sermons in, 161–163
  social forces in, 185–198
Public speaking criticism
  using the dramatistic approach, 200
  using fantasy theme analysis, 200
  using feminist ideology, 201
  using Marxist ideology, 201
  using the narrative approach, 200,
    201
  using social movement analysis, 201
  using the social-values model, 201
  using the traditional approach, 61,
    64, 199, 200
Public theology
  as social forces speaking, 198
  elements of, 196–197
Punch line
  in derogatory humor, 321
  in humor, 311
  incongruity and the, 323
  in topical humor, 312
Purification
  appropriateness and, 73
  dramatistic process and, 70
  the ethical standard of evaluation
    and, 80
  film as a vehicle of, 233
  guilt and, 72
  redemptive process of, 74
  rhetorical strategies and, 75
  rhetor's attitude toward, 76
  the truth standard of evaluation
    and, 80
  types of, 72, 73
  use of narrative to achieve, 109
Purpose
  audience receptivity to the rhetor's,
    26, 47, 49

Purpose (*continued*)
    describing the, 16–17
    implicit, 17
    in the dramatistic pentad, 77
    invention and, 51
    multiple, 17
    the results standard and evaluation
        of, 32–33, 63
    rhetorical, 9, 11–12
    speech introduction and the, 51, 60

Radical feminism, 143
Radio
    humor on, 342, 343
Real audience
    narrative and, 123
Realism in film
    definition of, 211
    evaluating results of, 232
    evaluating truth in, 232
    propaganda and, 213
    truth and, 212
Reality
    fantasy and, 88
    rhetoric and the sense of, 12
    rhetorical vision and, 88, 97
    television and the impression of, 246
Reasoning
    argument and the use of, 19, 57–58
    evaluating truth and the use of, 63
    logos and, 50
    narrative and types of, 125
    rhetor's use of, 19, 40
    techniques of, 54
    types of, 59
Reconstruction of arguments
    defined, 52
    enthymeme and the, 55
    metaphor and, 57
Redemption
    dramatistic process and, 70, 73
    the ethical standard of evaluation
        and, 80
    film as a vehicle of, 233
    rhetor's attitude toward, 76
    rhetorical strategies and, 75
    the truth standard of evaluation
        and, 80
Reform movement
    change advocated by, 151
Rejection
    definition of, 71
    dramatistic process and, 70, 73
    guilt and, 72
    hierarchy and, 71, 72
Reliability
    evaluation of evidence on the basis
        of, 58
Religious hymns
    as message song, 278
Religious speaking
    in colonial America, 160–162, 164
    contemporary, 196–198
    jeremiad in, 163
Repetition
    as a device of adornment, 21

Reputation
    ethics and evaluation of, 63
    impact on credibility, 45
Resistance movement
    change advocated by, 151
Resistance, nonviolent, 154
Results
    documentary film and evaluation of,
        232
    identification and evaluation of, 81
    qualitative and quantitative measures
        of, 123
    realism in film and the evaluation of,
        232
    in speech criticism, 200
    as a standard of evaluation, 32–33
Results evaluation
    in the dramatistic approach, 81
    in the fantasy theme approach,
        100–101
    in feminist criticism, 145
    in ideological criticism, 149
    in Jungian criticism, 141
    in the narrative approach, 123
    of social movements, 155
    in social-values criticism, 138
    in the traditional approach, 62–63
Revelation from televised message
    persuasiveness of, 256
Revival movement
    change advocated by, 151
Revolutionary agitation, 195
Rhetor
    audience adaptation by the, 43
    auteur criticism and focus on the,
        217, 232
    constraint on the, 27–29
    ethos management by the, 42,
        44–45
    exigence's impact on perception
        of, 43
    intent in humor, 309
    the narrative approach and the, 111,
        123–124, 127
    phenomenology and the, 10
    responsibilities of the, 51
    sportscaster as, 251
    the traditional approach and the,
        40–45
Rhetoric
    culture and, 131–132
    meaning of, 1–2
    pejorative sense of, 11
    sense of reality and, 12
    symbolic action and, 68–69
    traditional concept of persuasion
        and, 69
    types of, 159–160
Rhetorical act
    argument in the, 50–51
    artistic aspects of, 5–7
    characteristics of, 2–8
    comic strip as, 335
    in the critical process model, 16–23
    criticism as a, 12–13
    describing argument in the, 19–20

    describing concept of audience in,
        22–23
    describing purpose of the, 16–17
    describing structure of the, 17–19
    describing symbols in the, 20–22
    empowerment and the, 24
    ethical implications of, 7–8
    impact of constraints on the, 29
    as instrumental communication, 2–3
    live sports coverage as, 251
    message song as, 276
    music television as, 265
    scientific filmmaking as a, 215
    selection of critical approach and, 31
    as social activity, 3–4
    stance and evaluating truth for a, 34
    stand-up comedy as, 327
    symbols in the, 4, 122
    See also Message
Rhetorical communication
    defined, 2
Rhetorical community
    fantasy chain and formation of, 98
    identifying the boundaries of, 99
    rhetorical vision and creation of, 97
    shared sense of truth in, 99
Rhetorical criticism
    analysis in, 8
    evaluation in, 8
    of film, 232–233
    of humor, 346–348
    of public speeches, 198–201
    of song, 302–304
    stance in, 12
    subjectivity of, 12–13
    of television, 268–271
Rhetorical properties
    of fictional television, 255–256
    of film, 205–209
    of humor, 310–312
    of ironic television, 257–258
    of leader-centered television,
        259–260
    of mimetic television, 258–259
    of music videos, 265–266
    of mythical television, 260–261
    of news on television, 247–248
    of romantic television, 260
    of satire, 319
    of song, 276
    of sports on television, 250–252
Rhetorical question
    as a device of adornment, 21
Rhetorical situation
    action in the, 70
    apologia and the, 165
    audience in the, 43
    characterizing the, 23–30
    constraints imposed by the, 24, 27,
        46, 51, 70, 74
    in the critical process model, 16,
        23–30
    exigence in the, 24–25, 43, 122
    fantasy type used to describe, 96
    impact on perception of rhetor,
        42–43

message as an element in the, 50
occasion and, 46
phenomenology and the, 10
rhetor's management of the, 49
role of characterizing in criticism, 35
social forces and the, 185
style and management of the, 61
uniqueness of the, 160
Rhetorical song
as propaganda, 277–278
Rhetorical strategies
the aesthetic standard and, 81
defined, 75
drama and the use of, 75
dramatism and, 126
dramatistic pentad and, 77
the ethical standard and, 80
genres of, 76
the truth standard and, 81
Rhetorical tactics
of social movements, 153–154
Rhetorical vision
analyzing a, 98
convergence on a, 100
evaluating a, 97, 200
fantasy and, 88
fantasy theme and type in, 96–97
going public with a, 89
reality and, 88, 97
rhetorical community and a, 97
salience of, 89, 97
television fiction and, 261–263
time binding and shifts in, 100
truth and, 99
Rock and roll
persuasive power of, 300–301
political activism in, 302
Romance
narrative plot types and, 113

Salience
exigence, 49
fantasy theme approach and,
87, 89
rhetorical vision and, 89, 97
time binding and the loss of, 99
Satire
audience role in, 320
campaign buttons and, 345
comic sage and, 330
as a device of humor, 319
in film, 225
in humorous magazines, 344
in television humor, 341
Scene
in the dramatistic pentad, 76
fictional in narrative, 117–118
grammar of film and, 216
identifying in a fantasy theme, 91
in narrative, 116, 126
Screwball comedy
defined, 207
escapism and, 208
in film, 225
Serial television
program format in, 241–242

Series television
program format in, 241–242
Sermons
in colonial America, 160–161, 164
election day, 162
of fast and thanksgiving, 163
Setup
in derogatory humor, 321
in humor, 311
in topical humor, 312
incongruity and the, 323
Sick humor
purpose of, 324
that goes too far, 325
Slapstick comedy
in film, 225
Social forces speeches
dissent and, 192–196
justificatory speaking and, 185–187
legislative speaking and, 187–192
public theology and, 196–198
Socialist feminism, 143
Social movements
agitative speaking and, 201
critical evaluation of, 155–156
cultural approach to, 149
life cycle of, 152–153
nature of, 150–151
rhetorical activity in, 152
rhetorical tactics of, 153–154
television criticism using, 269–270
types of, 151
Social-values model
critical evaluation and, 138–139
cultural approach and, 134
dialectical opposition in, 135
dialectical synthesis in, 136–137
dialectical transformation in,
136–137
elements in the, 135–137
film criticism using, 233
humor criticism using, 347–348
public speaking criticism using, 201
song criticism using, 304
television criticism using, 268
Song
antiwar, 296–300
audience involvement through, 289
during the Civil War, 281–286
eulogy in, 287
folk music and, 290–292
folk-protest music and, 293–295
folk-rock music and, 296
metaphor used in, 279
organized labor and, 287–288
persuasion and, 10, 277
as a political instrument, 279–280
rhetorical properties of, 276
rock and roll, 300–302
as symbolic action, 69
types of message, 277
use of labor lore in, 289
Song criticism
using cultural approaches, 304
using the dramatistic approach, 303
using fantasy theme analysis, 304
using the narrative approach, 304

using the social-values model, 304
using the traditional approach, 303
Spoonerism
in humor, 315
Stance
critic's, 12
evaluating ethics and the critic's, 149
evaluating truth and the critic's, 34
ideological criticism and, 141
Stand-up comedy
categories of, 327–329
differences in style in, 330–331
nature of, 326
rhetorical properties of, 327
Story
narrative and, 110–111, 125
television news elements of, 248
Structure
in rhetorical act, 5
television programming and, 238,
240–241
See also Organization
Style
appropriateness of in public
speaking, 199
choice of language and, 61
in classical rhetoric, 40
in contemporary usage, 41
devices of adornment and, 22
elements of comic, 331
ethics and the evaluation of, 63
grammar of film and, 232
managing the rhetorical situation
with, 61
pathos and, 50
political cartooning and, 334
psychological climate created by, 61
stand-up comedy and, 330
Subjectivity
of criticism, 12–13, 15
Symbolic convergence theory, 86–87,
103
See also Fantasy theme approach
Symbols
the aesthetic standard and, 81, 101
choice of, 29
in commemorative speaking,
174–175
describing rhetor's use of, 20–22
fantasy and, 87
fantasy theme approach and
evaluation of, 98
film and, 210, 233
hierarchy and, 71
humans as users of, 68
interpretation of in criticism, 8
Jungian model and, 140
language and the use of, 74–75
meaning of in dramatism, 70
motive and the use of, 69
music videos and, 266
narrative and, 110
purification of guilt and, 72
in rhetorical act, 4
types of, 71
verbal, 10, 68
visual, 10, 22

Symptomatic model
  in cultural approaches to criticism,
    134
Synecdoche
  as a device of adornment, 21

Television
  audience interpretation of, 241, 243
  audience levels of experiencing,
    246
  camera work on, 244–245
  communication of ideology on, 255
  differentiated from film, 239–241
  docudrama on, 254
  documentary on, 252–253
  editing on, 245–246
  Federal Communications
    Commission and, 237–238
  fictional entertainment on, 255–261
  flow of programming on, 242–243
  folk music on, 293
  humor on, 341–342
  impression of reality on, 246
  lighting on, 244
  narrow-casting on, 263–266
  news on, 247–250
  rhetorical vision of, 261–263
  sports on, 250–252
  structure of programming, 238,
    240–241
  technical properties of, 244–246
  types of program format, 241–242
Television criticism
  using cultural approaches, 268
  using the dramatistic approach, 268
  using fantasy theme analysis, 270
  using feminist ideology, 269
  using the Jungian model, 268–269
  using Marxist ideology, 269
  using the narrative approach, 268
  and social movements, 269–270
  using the social-values model, 268
  using the traditional approach,
    270–271
Television fiction
  audience use of, 255–256
  persuasiveness of, 256–261
  rhetorical properties of, 255–256
Television narrow-casting
  defined, 263
  music (MTV) and, 264–266
Television news
  audience uses of, 250
  concept of story, 248
  constraints on, 247–249
  editing of, 249
  problems with, 249
  rhetorical properties of, 247–248
Television sports
  rhetorical properties of, 250–252
Tenor in metaphor, 56–57
Terministic screen
  vehicle in metaphor as a, 56–57
Text
  of a film, 232
  of a rhetorical act, 132

Thematic documentary
  television and the, 252–253
Thematic model
  and cultural approaches to criticism,
    133
Theory
  definition of, 39
  rhetorical, 11, 39
Toulmin model of argument
  inference in the, 58
  logical properties of, 57
  parts in the, 52–54
Traditional approach
  aesthetic standard, 63
  apologia and, 199
  audience, 45–50
  audience group identification,
    48–49
  audience knowledge, 48
  audience receptivity, 49
  auteur criticism and, 221
  classical rhetoric and the, 39–40
  credibility in, 42–43, 45
  enthymeme, 54–55
  evidence tests, 58
  evidence types, 57–58
  fantasy theme approach and, 87
  film criticism using, 270–271
  humor criticism using, 347
  invention, 50–60
  limitations, 64
  message elements, 50–62
  metaphor as argument, 55–57
  narrative approach and, 125
  occasion as situational constraint,
    46–47
  organization, 60–61
  psychological appeals, 59–60
  public speaking criticism using, 40,
    61, 199–200
  reasoning patterns, 59
  results standard, 62–63
  rhetor in the, 40, 42–45
  rhetor's background, 42–43
  rhetor's purpose, 51
  rhetor's use of invention, 51
  salience, 49
  situational constraints on the
    rhetor, 43
  song criticism using, 303
  style, 61–62
  television criticism using, 270–271
  as a thematic model, 133
  truth standard, 63
Tragedy
  narrative plot type and, 113
Truth
  difficulties in applying in
    dramatism, 81
  documentary film and the evaluation
    of, 232
  fantasy and, 87
  identification and the evaluation
    of, 80
  intersubjectivity and, 99
  message-movie criticism and, 213

  narrative and, 108, 126
  narrative fidelity and, 121–122
  narrative rationality and, 110
  realism in film and, 212
  realism in film and the evaluation of,
    232
  rhetorical act as expression of, 9
  rhetorical strategies and the
    evaluation of, 81
  rhetorical vision as, 99
  role of critical stance in
    evaluating, 34
  in speech criticism, 200
  as a standard of evaluation, 33, 34
  time binding and the, 99
Truth evaluation
  in the dramatistic approach, 80–81
  in the fantasy theme approach,
    99–100
  in feminist criticism, 145
  in ideological criticism, 148
  in Jungian criticism, 141
  in the narrative approach, 121–122
  of social movements, 156
  in social-values criticism, 138
  in the traditional approach, 63

Unintentional irony
  humor and, 316
Unit of argument
  enthymeme as a, 54
  in the rhetorical act, 50
Universal archetype
  Jungian model and, 139

Validity
  of arguments, 52
  diagramming arguments to
    assess, 53
Value conflict
  in the social-values model, 136
Value systems, 135
Values
  actual audience and, 27
  commemorative speaking and, 178
  constraints imposed by, 165
  enthymeme and, 54
  eulogy and, 178
  in film, 207, 210
  ironic television fiction and, 258
  leader-centered television fiction
    and, 259–60
  mimetic television fiction and, 259
  mythical television fiction and, 261
  psychological appeals and, 60
  rhetorical vision of television and,
    262–263
  role in evaluating rhetor's ethics, 32
  romantic television fiction and, 260
  television and, 256
  typical American, 135
Vehicle in metaphor, 56–57
Verbal symbols, 4, 10, 68

Villain
    fantasy theme approach and the,
        88–90, 92
    transformation into a hero of a, 100
    in Western films, 221–222
Voice
    use of in delivery, 62

War
    film genre and, 226–231
Western
    film genre and the, 221–222
Wordplay
    comic sage and, 328
    comic style and, 331
    as a device of humor, 314
    malapropism in, 315
    spoonerism in, 315
Written style
    oral style compared to, 61

Zapping, 240